Lecture Notes in Computer Science   6391

Commenced Publication in 1973
Founding and Former Series Editors:
Gerhard Goos, Juris Hartmanis, and Jan van Leeuwen

Fabio Martinelli   Bart Preneel (Eds.)

Public Key Infrastructures, Services and Applications

6th European Workshop, EuroPKI 2009
Pisa, Italy, September 10-11, 2009
Revised Selected Papers

 Springer

Volume Editors

Fabio Martinelli
National Research Council (CNR)
Institute of Informatics and Telematics (IIT)
Pisa Research Area, Via G. Moruzzi 1, 56125 Pisa, Italy
E-mail: fabio.martinelli@iit.cnr.it

Bart Preneel
Katholieke Universiteit Leuven
Dept. Electrical Engineering-ESAT/COSIC
Kasteelpark Arenberg 10, Bus 2446, 3001 Leuven, Belgium
E-mail: bart.preneel@esat.kuleuven.be

Library of Congress Control Number: 2010936512

CR Subject Classification (1998): K.6.5, C.2, E.3, D.4.6, J.1, K.4.4

LNCS Sublibrary: SL 4 – Security and Cryptology

ISSN   0302-9743
ISBN-10   3-642-16440-4 Springer Berlin Heidelberg New York
ISBN-13   978-3-642-16440-8 Springer Berlin Heidelberg New York

springer.com

© Springer-Verlag Berlin Heidelberg 2010
Printed in Germany

Typesetting: Camera-ready by author, data conversion by Scientific Publishing Services, Chennai, India
Printed on acid-free paper   06/3180

Preface

This book contains the postproceedings of the 6th European Workshop on Public Key Services, Applications and Infrastructures, which was held at the CNR Research Area in Pisa, Italy, in September 2009.

The EuroPKI workshop series focuses on all research and practice aspects of public key infrastructures, services and applications, and welcomes original research papers and excellent survey contributions from academia, government, and industry. Previous events of the series were held in: Samos, Greece (2004); Kent, UK (2005); Turin, Italy, (2006); Palma de Mallorca, Spain, (2007); and Trondheim, Norway (2008).

From the original focus on public key infrastructures, EuroPKI interests expanded to include advanced cryptographic techniques, applications and (more generally) services. The Workshops brings together researchers from the cryptographic community as well as from the applied security community, as witnessed by the interesting program.

Indeed, this volume holds 18 refereed papers and the presentation paper by the invited speaker, Alexander Dent. In response to the EuroPKI 2009 call for papers, a total of 40 submissions were received. All submissions underwent a thorough blind review by at least three Program Committee members, resulting in careful selection and revision of the accepted papers. After the conference, the papers were revised and improved by the authors before inclusion in this volume.

We thank all the people who have contributed to the success of this workshop: the submitters, the authors, the invited speaker, the members of the Program Committee, the members of the Local Organization Committee, the staff at Springer, the sponsor IIT-CNR for its support, and finally all the workshop participants. It was our pleasure to serve the EuroPKI community as program chairs. We are confident that the EuroPKI workshop will remain a valuable forum for the exchange of experiences and ideas.

June 2010

Fabio Martinelli
Bart Preneel

EuroPKI 2009

The 6th European Workshop on Public Key Services, Applications and Infrastructures

CNR Research Area, Pisa, Italy

September 10–11, 2009

Organized by the *Institute of Informatics and Telematics* of the *National Council of Research (IIT-CNR)*

General Chair

Anna Vaccarelli, National Research Council, Italy

Program Chairs

Fabio Martinelli   National Research Council, Italy
Bart Preneel   Katholieke Universiteit Leuven, Belgium

Program Committee

C. Boyd   Queensland University of Technology, Australia
D. Chadwick   Kent University, UK
C. Cremers   ETH Zurich, Switzerland
G. Danezis   Microsoft Research, UK
G. Dini   University of Pisa, Italy
J. Domingo-Ferrer   Universitat Rovira i Virgili, Catalonia
S. Farrell   Trinity College Dublin, Ireland
D. Galindo   University of Luxembourg, Luxembourg
K. Gjøsteen   NTNU, Norway
S. Gritzalis   University of the Aegean, Greece
J.-H. Hoepman   TNO and Radboud University Nijmegen,
                              The Netherlands
A. Jøsang   University of Oslo, Norway
S. Katsikas   University of Piraeus, Greece
S. Kent   BBN Technologies, USA
K. Kursawe   Philips Research, The Netherlands

A. Lioy	Politecnico di Torino, Italy
J. Lopez	University of Malaga, Spain
D. M'Raihi	Verisign, USA
F. Martinelli	National Research Council, Italy
S. Mauw	University of Luxembourg, Luxembourg
C. Meadows	NRL, USA
C. Mitchell	Royal Holloway, University of London, UK
S. Mjølsnes	NTNU, Norway
D. Naccache	ENS Paris, France
E. Okamoto	Tsukuba University, Japan
R. Oppliger	eSECURITY Technologies, Switzerland
M. Pala	Dartmouth College, USA
T. Pedersen	Cryptomathic, Denmark
O. Pereira	Université Catholique de Louvain, Belgium
G. Pernul	University of Regensburg, Germany
R. Di Pietro	University of Rome III, Italy
B. Preneel	Katholieke Universiteit Leuven, Belgium
I. Agudo Ruiz	University of Malaga, Spain
A. Sadeghi	Ruhr-Universität Bochum, Germany
P. Samarati	University of Milan, Italy
R. Scandariato	Katholieke Universiteit Leuven, Belgium
S. Smith	Dartmouth College, USA
J. Zhou	Institute Infocomm Research, Singapore

External Reviewers

Baptiste Alcalde	Sebastian Gajek	Peter van Rossum
Claudio Ardagna	Dimitris Geneiatakis	Stefan Schiffner
Frederik Armknecht	John Iliadis	Koen Simoens
Christian Broser	Rieks Joosten	Angelo Spognardi
Lukasz Chmielewski	Elisavet Konstantinou	Douglas Stebila
Claudio Cicconetti	Benoit Libert	Klara Stokes
Alessandro Colantonio	Jun Pang	Patrick Tsang
Ton van Deursen	Bo Qin	Marcel Winandy
Gianluca Dini	Scott A. Rea	Qianhong Wu
Markulf Kohlweiss	Evangelos Rekleitis	Michele Zanda
Stefan Dürbeck	Alfredo Rial Duran	Lei Zhang
Christoph Fritsch	Moritz Riesner	

Table of Contents

Encryption and Auctions

Reputation and User Aspects

Digital Signatures

A Brief Introduction to Certificateless Encryption Schemes and Their Infrastructures

Alexander W. Dent

Information Security Group,
Royal Holloway, University of London, U.K.
a.dent@rhul.ac.uk

Abstract. Certificateless encryption is a form of public-key encryption that is designed to eliminate the disadvantages of both traditional PKI-based public-key encryption scheme and identity-based encryption. Unlike public-key encryption, there is no requirement for digital certificates or a public-key infrastructure. Unlike identity-based encryption, the trusted third party need not be given the ability to decrypt ciphertexts intended for users. In this invited paper we will review the concept of certificateless encryption from an infrastructure point of view and show that many of the different formulations for "certificateless" encryption can be instantiated using public-key infrastructures after all.

1 Introduction

Certificateless encryption is a type of public-key encryption which combines the advantages of traditional PKI-based public-key encryption and identity-based encryption [1,2]. All three types of cryptosystem aim to transmit a message confidentially between a sender and receiver without the aid of shared secret keys. We approach the different types of primitive by considering the infrastructures needed to support them:

- In a public-key encryption scheme, a sender encrypts a message based on a public key which has been certified by a PKI [11]. The certificate binds the receiver's digital identifier with their public key. As well as performing the encryption operation, the sender must verify (at least) one digital signature on a certificate in order to verify the authenticity of the public key. This places a computational burden on the sender.
- In an identity-based encryption scheme, a sender encrypts a message based only on the digital identifier of the receiver [17]. This eliminates the (primary) need for a digital certificate. Unfortunately, identity-based encryption schemes have a systematic weakness. In order to obtain a valid decryption key for their digital identifier, the receiver must contact a key generation centre. This key generation centre can compute decryption keys for all the users in the system; the receiver has to trust that this third party will not abuse this ability to read confidential messages.

F. Martinelli and B. Preneel (Eds.): EuroPKI 2009, LNCS 6391, pp. 1–16, 2010.
© Springer-Verlag Berlin Heidelberg 2010

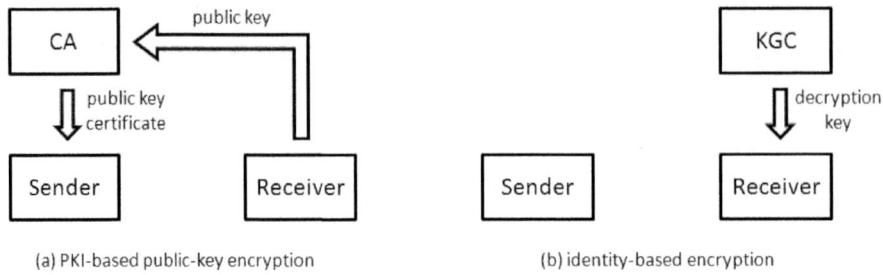

(a) PKI-based public-key encryption   (b) identity-based encryption

Fig. 1. The infrastructures for PKI-based public-key encryption (left) and identity-based encryption (right). In both cases it is assumed that every entity knows the other entities' digital identities.

The two architectures are shown in Figure 1.

Certificateless encryption schemes are characterised by two properties: (a) the scheme provides security without the need for a public key to be verified via a digital certificate, and (b) the scheme remains secure against attacks made by any third party (including a key generation centre or a certificate authority). This is achieved by having two public/private key pairs:

- A traditional public/private key pair generated by the receiver. The private key value is called a *secret value* to avoid confusion with the full private key of the scheme. The public key value is widely publicised but crucially is not authenticated with a digital certificate.
- An identity-based key pair consisting of the receiver's digital identifier and the associated identity-based private key supplied by a key generation centre. This private key is called a *partial private key.*

To encrypt a message, the sender uses the receiver's digital identifier and the receiver's public key. The receiver decrypts the ciphertext using the secret value generated by the receiver and the partial private key supplied by the key generation centre.

The intuition is that the sender does not require a digital certificate as the creation of a false public key for an identity will not help an attacker break the confidentiality of a transmitted message because the attacker does not know the partial private key for that identity. (This logic is similar to that of an identity-based encryption scheme.) The key generation centre cannot break the confidentiality of a transmitted message as it does not know the secret value corresponding to the receiver's public key. Of course, this makes the assumption that key generation centre will not publish a false public key for a receiver, but this attack seems unavoidable (and comparable to a CA publishing a false certificate for an identity).

The situation is complicated by a number of different infrastructures that can be put in place to support the distribution of the receiver's public key:

- **AP Formulation:** In the original Al-Riyami and Paterson (AP) formulation [1,2], the receiver can generate their public key at any time. This means that the receiver can publish their public key before receiving their partial private key from the key generation centre.
- **BSS Formulation:** In the Baek, Safavi-Naini and Susilo (BSS) formulation [4], the receiver can only generate their public key after receiving the partial private key. The partial private key is obtained via a single secure message from the key generation centre.
- **LK Formulation:** In the Lai and Kou (LK) formulation [13], the receiver can only generate their public key after completing a protocol with the key generation centre.

These three architectures are shown in Figure 2. The situation is further complicated by a series of complex and contradictory provable security models.

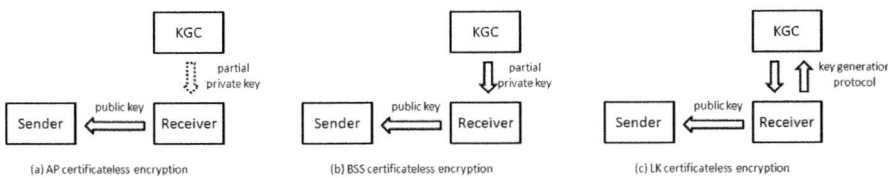

Fig. 2. The three certificateless encryption scheme architectures: (a) the AP formulation; (b) the BSS formulation; and (c) the LK formulation. The dotted arrow (in the AP formulation) denotes the fact that the public key can be published before the partial private key is obtained. In all cases, public keys are provided without a certificate. All entities are assumed to know the other entities' digital identities.

In this invited paper, we examine the relationship between certificateless encryption and other forms of public-key encryption. We show that in most cases, certificateless encryption infrastructures can be implemented using the very public-key infrastructure that they claim to eliminate. We will also briefly discuss security models.

2   Syntax and Infrastructure

The architecture for a certificateless encryption scheme involves three entities: a sender, a receiver, and a key generation centre (KGC). The syntax for a certificateless encryption scheme differs depending on the formulation. In all cases, the scheme is described by five probabilistic, polynomial-time (PPT) algorithms. We use to $\leftarrow$ to denote the assignment of the output of a deterministic algorithm (or fixed value) to a variable and $\overset{\$}{\leftarrow}$ to denote the assignment of the output of a probabilistic algorithm to a variable.

2.1   The AP Formulation

Al-Riyami and Paterson [1,2] first defined a certificateless encryption scheme as a tuple of seven algorithms; however, a conceptually simpler five algorithm version has become widely accepted. In this version of the AP formulation, the schemes are defined by the following tuple of algorithms (Setup, Extract, KeyGen, Encrypt, Decrypt). These form an infrastructure as follows:

- Setup(1^k): The setup algorithm is run by the KGC; it takes the security parameter as input and outputs a master public/private key pair $(mpk, msk) \xleftarrow{\$}$ Setup(1^k). The master public key mpk is widely distributed; the master private key msk is kept secret by the KGC and used by the KGC to create partial private key values.
- Extract(msk, ID): The partial private key extraction algorithm is run by the KGC to create a partial private key for an identity ID. It takes as input the master private key msk and the identity ID, and outputs a partial private key $d \xleftarrow{\$}$ Extract(msk, ID). This partial private key value is then sent (in a confidential manner) to the receiver.
- KeyGen(mpk, ID): The key generation algorithm is run by the receiver to create a key pair for that user. It takes as input the master public parameters for the scheme and the identity of the receiver, and outputs the key pair $(pk, sk) \xleftarrow{\$}$ KeyGen(mpk, ID). The receiver widely publicises the public key pk, but keeps the secret value sk secret. We stress that the public key is not authenticated with a digital certificate.
- Encrypt(mpk, pk, ID, m): The encryption algorithm is used by the sender to send a message to the receiver. It takes as input the master public key of the system mpk, the receiver's public key pk, the receiver's digital identifier ID, and a message m drawn from some message space $\mathcal{M}$. It outputs either a ciphertext C in some ciphertext space $\mathcal{C}$ or an error symbol $\perp$ indicating that the public key was not valid for that identity.
- Decrypt(mpk, sk, d, C): The decryption algorithm is used by the receiver to decrypt a ciphertext. It takes as input the master public key of the system mpk, the receiver's secret value sk, the receiver's partial private key d, and a ciphertext $C \in \mathcal{C}$. It outputs either a message $m \in \mathcal{M}$ or the error symbol $\perp$ indicating that the ciphertext is invalid.

As you can see, since the receiver runs the KeyGen algorithm with public information as input, the receiver doesn't have to interact with the KGC before publishing their public key. Indeed, there is nothing to stop any user publishing a valid public key for any other user (see Section 3.3).

One interesting aspect of the AP formulation is that it implies the existence of both traditional PKI-based public-key encryption and identity-based encryption. To derive an identity-based encryption scheme from a certificateless encryption scheme, the receiver does not publish a public key. The sender instead generates a public/private key pair for the receiver by running the key generation algorithm KeyGen with a fixed random tape. The receiver can recover the associated secret value by running the key generation algorithm with the same random tape, but can only decrypt a message if it has received the partial private key value for that identity. Hence, we can immediately conclude that it is not possible to build a certificateless encryption scheme (within the AP formulation) from a trapdoor one-way permutation (in a black-box manner) [9]. The relationship between the AP formulation of certificateless encryption and public-key encryption was further investigated by Farshim and Warinschi [12].

2.2   The BSS Formulation

Unsurprisingly, due to its close relationship with identity-based cryptography, all of the certificateless encryption schemes which are designed in the AP formulation make use of elliptic curve pairings. Baek, Safavi-Naini and Susilo asked if it is possible to construct a certificateless encryption scheme without the use of elliptic curve pairings [4]. Their solution was to modify the architecture for a certificateless encryption scheme so that the receiver can not publish their public key until *after* they have obtained their partial private key value.

The BSS formulation is formally defined by five algorithms:

- Setup(1^k): This algorithm is identical to the Setup algorithm in the AP formulation. It is run by the KGC and produces a master key pair for the system $(mpk, msk) \xleftarrow{\$} \mathtt{Setup}(1^k)$.
- Extract(msk, ID): This algorithm is identical to the Extract algorithm in the AP formulation. It is run by the KGC to obtain a partial private key $d \xleftarrow{\$} \mathtt{Extract}(msk, ID)$ for an identity ID. This partial private key value is confidentially distributed the appropriate user.
- KeyGen(mpk, ID, d): The key generation algorithm differs from the AP formulation in that it now takes the partial private key as input. It still outputs a key pair $(pk, sk) \xleftarrow{\$} \mathtt{KeyGen}(mpk, ID, d)$ where the public key pk should be widely distributed and the private key sk should be kept secret. Notice that there is no concept of a secret value in this system; the output of the key generation algorithm is a full private key that can be used to decrypt ciphertexts. This is because the partial private key d can be included in the private key sk if necessary.
- Encrypt(mpk, pk, ID, m): The encryption algorithm is identical to the Encrypt algorithm in the AP formulation. It is run by the sender to create a ciphertext C which is then sent to the receiver.
- Decrypt(mpk, sk, C): The decryption algorithm differs from the AP formulation in that it does not take the partial private key as an explicit input. The algorithm takes as input the master private key mpk, the receiver's private key sk, and a ciphertext $C \in \mathcal{C}$. It outputs either a message $m \in \mathcal{M}$ or the error symbol $\perp$.

The existing BSS certificateless encryption schemes are complex and have challenging security proofs. However, we will show that for the first time that secure BSS certificateless encryption can be derived using a PKI-based system. We will postpone a formal description of our new certificateless encryption scheme until after we introduce the certificateless security models. The basic idea, however, is very easy to understand. It is based on the concept of a certificate chain, with the key generation centre acting as the parent CA and each user acting as a subordinate CA which can only issue certificates that correspond to its own digital identity. In other words, the complete key generation process runs as follows:

1. As part of the Setup algorithm, the KGC generates a signature key pair. We call this the primary signature key pair. The primary public verification key is widely disseminated as part of the master public key mpk. The primary private signing key is kept secret as part of the master private key msk.
2. If the KGC wishes to produce a partial private key for the identity ID, then the Extract algorithm generates a secondary signature key pair and a digital certificate (signed using the primary signing key) which links the identity ID to the secondary public verification key. The partial private key contains the complete secondary key pair and the digital certificate.
3. The receiver's KeyGen algorithm creates a receiver public key by generating a standard (PKI-based) encryption key pair. The receiver generates a digital certificate for the public encryption key using the secondary signing key provided by the KGC. The receiver's complete public key contains the secondary verification key, the digital certificate for that key provided by the KGC, the public encryption key, and the digital certificate for that key computed by the receiver.

Now, if a sender wishes to send a message to the receiver, then the sender checks the authenticity of the public key by checking both certificates provided with the public encryption key (and only sends the message if both certificates verify correctly). The whole process is illustrated in Figure 3 and a more formal description will be given in Section 4.

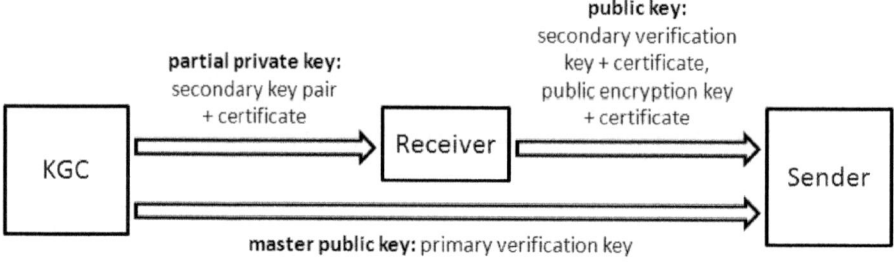

Fig. 3. Public key distribution in the certificate-chain certificateless encryption scheme

2.3   The LK Formulation

The Lai-Kou formulation [13] can be viewed as a generalisation of the BSS formulation. Instead of a single message (the partial private key) being passed between the receiver and the KGC prior to public key publication, the receiver and the KGC must undertake a protocol before the receiver can publish its public key. Formally, it is defined by the following algorithms:

- Setup(1^k): This algorithm is identical to the Setup algorithm in the AP and BSS formulation. It is run by the KGC and produces a master key pair for the system $(mpk, msk) \xleftarrow{\$} \text{Setup}(1^k)$.
- KGCKeyGen(msk, ID) and RecKeyGen(mpk, ID): These two interactive algorithms define the protocol between the KGC (KGCKeyGen) and the receiver (RecKeyGen). These replace the Extract and KeyGen algorithms in the AP and BSS formulation. The KGC runs KGCKeyGen algorithm using the master private key msk and the receiver's identity ID as input; the receiver runs the RecKeyGen algorithm using the master public key and the receiver's identity as input. If the protocol is successfully completed then the receiver's algorithm (RecKeyGen) will output a user key pair (pk, sk). The KGC's algorithm (KGCKeyGen) has no output. The receiver then widely publicises the public key pk and keeps the private key sk secret.
- Encrypt(mpk, pk, ID, m): The encryption algorithm is identical to the Encrypt algorithm in the AP and BSS formulation. It is run by the sender to create a ciphertext C which is then sent to the receiver.
- Decrypt(mpk, sk, C): The decryption algorithm is identical to the Decrypt algorithm in the BSS formulation. It is run by the receiver to recover the message $m \in \mathcal{M}$ or the error symbol $\perp$.

It is easy to see that the traditional notion of PKI-based encryption can instantiate the LK formulation of certificateless encryption. The protocol interaction between the receiver and the KGC runs as follows:

1. The KGC's Setup algorithm generates a signature key pair and publishes the public verification key as part of the master public key mpk. The private signing key is kept secret as part of the master private key msk.
2. To generate a user key pair, the receiver generates an encryption key pair and sends the KGC the public key. (This is the first part of the RecKeyGen algorithm.)
3. The KGC then creates a digital certificate (signed using the KGC's private signing key) which binds the receiver's encryption key to their identity. This certificate is returned to the receiver (as part of the KGCKeyGen algorithm).
4. The receiver's full public key contains the public encryption key and the digital certificate for that key. This is computed as the final part of the RecKeyGen algorithm.

If a sender wishes to encrypt a message, then the sender first checks whether the certificate correctly authenticates the encryption key for the receiver's identity. This observation was made by Dent [10] who cited a security proof given by Boldyreva et al. [7] in the context of public-key encryption schemes which incorporate the PKI into their security/efficiency models. Indeed, the LK formulation of a certificateless encryption scheme is so similar to Boldyreva et al. model of a public-key encryption scheme with PKI that they may effectively be considered one security model. As pointed out by Boldyreva et al., the advantage of considering this enhanced security model is that it allows for the construction of public-key encryption schemes which are more efficient as a whole process (i.e. when the time spent verifying the correctness of the certificate is taken into account).

3   Security Models

One of the major problems with the development of certificateless encryption schemes has been the development of correct security models. These models should be powerful enough to demonstrate that the scheme resists all practical attacks, but not so powerful that they require overly complex and inefficient schemes in order to meet the security notions. The original models by Al-Riyami and Paterson [1,2] made important conceptual decisions, but have been criticised for not reflecting the reality of a certificateless encryption scheme's usage scenario; the models are too strong in some aspects and too weak in others. Other security models have been suggested and a survey of these models was produced by Dent [10].

One important contribution by Al-Riyami and Paterson [1] was to split the security requirements into two separate models: the first concerns the security of the scheme against attacks made by an outsider and the second concerns the security of the scheme against attacks made by the KGC. These are traditionally called Type I and Type II attacks respectively, although efforts are being made to change the nomenclature to something more descriptive.

The reason for the dual security model is to account for a trivial attack that can be made by the KGC. The attacker is trying to break the confidentiality of a message that is sent by a sender to a receiver. Since there are no (explicit) digital certificates in the system, the sender has no guarantee that he has an authentic copy of the receiver's public key. In other words, our models have to cope with a situation in which the attacker convinces the sender to use a receiver public key generated by the attacker. Recall that the schemes should resist attacks of this form made by an outside attacker (as such an attacker would not know the partial private key for the receiver). However, a certificateless encryption scheme can never resist such an attack if it is made by the KGC. By definition, the KGC can compute all partial private keys; hence, it can always replace the public key with one for which it knows the underlying secret value and therefore decrypt all ciphertexts computed by the sender. This gives rise to two security modes:

1. The outsider (or Type I) security model. The attacker is allowed to replace the public key that the sender uses to encrypt messages.
2. The KGC (or Type II) security model. The attacker is not allowed to replace the public key that the sender uses to encrypt messages, but can compute the master public key value maliciously.

We give formal security models for the BSS formulation of a certificateless encryption scheme as these will be used to prove the security of the certificate chain scheme described in Section 2.2. We will mostly want to show that an attacker's "advantage" is negligible, where the term negligible means that the success probability falls away faster than the reciprocal of any polynomial (as a function of the security parameter). Technically, a function f is negligible if for all polynomials p there exists a constant $N(p)$ such that $f(k) \leq 1/|p(k)|$ for all $k \geq N(p)$.

3.1 Outsider Attacks

This security model is designed to show that an outside attacker cannot break the confidentiality of the scheme unless it somehow obtains a user's partial private key *and* replaces the public key with one which has been maliciously generated.

A security model is typically presented as a game played between an arbitrary (probabilistic polynomial-time) attacker and a challenger (who represents the system with which the attacker interacts). Crucially, the challenger keeps a list of users in the system, their real public/private key pairs, and the public key value that the sender associates with each user. The attacker interacts with the system via a series of oracles which force the challenger to perform certain operations and model the different ways that the attacker can interact with the system. The attacker is modelled as a pair of PPT algorithms $\mathcal{A} = (\mathcal{A}_1, \mathcal{A}_2)$ and the security game is as follows:

1. The challenger generates a master key pair $(mpk, msk) \xleftarrow{\$} \text{Setup}(1^k)$.
2. The attacker runs $\mathcal{A}_1$ on mpk. $\mathcal{A}_1$ may query the following oracles:
   - **Request Public Key**: This oracle takes an identity ID as input and generates a full public/private key (pk, sk) for the identity ID using the Extract and KeyGen algorithms. The oracle returns the public key pk. The oracle also records (pk, sk) as ID's real public/private key and pk as the public key that the sender associated with ID.
   - **Replace Public Key**: This oracle takes an identity ID and a public key pk' as input. The oracle changes the records so that the sender now associates the public key pk' with the identity ID.
   - **Extract Partial Private Key**: This oracle takes an identity ID as input and outputs ID's partial private key $d \xleftarrow{\$} \text{Extract}(msk, ID)$.
   - **Decrypt**: This oracle takes as input an identity ID and a ciphertext C. It outputs $m \leftarrow \text{Decrypt}(mpk, sk, C)$ where sk is the private key for ID computed during the "Request Public Key" query.
   $\mathcal{A}_1$ terminates with the output of an identity ID^*, two equal-length messages (m_0, m_1), and some state information ω.
3. The challenger randomly generates a bit $b \xleftarrow{\$} \{0, 1\}$ and computes the challenge ciphertext $C^* \xleftarrow{\$} \text{Encrypt}(mpk, pk', ID^*, m_b)$ where pk' is the public key that the sender associates with the identity ID^*.
4. The attacker runs $\mathcal{A}_2$ on the challenge ciphertext C^* and the state information ω. $\mathcal{A}_2$ may query the same oracles as in the first phase of its execution. It terminates with the output of a bit b'.

The attacker can trivially win this security game if:

- The attacker replaces the public key of ID^* in Step 2 *and* requests the partial private key of ID^* at any time (as the attacker can then compute a full decryption key for ID^*).
- The attacker does not replace the public key of ID^* in Step 2 *and* requests the decryption of the challenge ciphertext C^* by ID^* in Step 4 (as this trivially returns the message m_b).

The attacker wins the game if it outputs $b' = b$ without performing these trivial attacks. The attacker's advantage is defined to be $Adv_{\mathcal{A}}^{\text{out}}(k) = |\Pr[b = b'] - 1/2|$ and the scheme is said to be *outsider secure* if this advantage is negligible.

One interesting quirk of the original outsider (Type I) security model is that if the attacker replaced the public key of an identity and then queried the decryption oracle, then the decryption oracle would decrypt the ciphertext using the private key corresponding to the replaced public key rather than the original public key. This security model is widely believed not to reflect an attacker's real-life capabilities and we encourage the use of the simpler model.

3.2   KGC Attacks

The security model for KGC attacks is slightly simpler than the model for outsider attacks as the KGC is forbidden from replacing public keys. This means that the challenger does not have to keep track of the public keys that the sender believes are associated with each user. Originally, the security model for KGC attacks still used a "correctly generated" master public key mpk [1,2]; however, Au *et al.* noted that this does not reflect the reality of a malicious key generation centre and allowed the KGC to generate their master public key in an adversarial manner [3]. This model was later refined by Dent [10].

The formal model involves a PPT attacker $\mathcal{A} = (\mathcal{A}_0, \mathcal{A}_1, \mathcal{A}_2)$ and a hypothetical challenger. The security game runs as follows:

1. The attacker generates the master public key and some state information $(mpk, \omega) \xleftarrow{\$} \mathcal{A}_0(1^k)$.
2. The attacker runs $\mathcal{A}_1$ on the state information ω. $\mathcal{A}_1$ may query the following oracles:
   - **Request Public Key**: This oracle takes an identity ID and a partial private key d as input. It computes a public/private key pair $(pk, sk) \xleftarrow{\$}$ KeyGen(mpk, ID, d) and returns pk.
   - **Decrypt**: This oracle takes an identity ID and a ciphertext C as input, and returns $m \leftarrow$ Decrypt(mpk, sk, C) where sk is the private key for identity ID.

   The attacker terminates with the output of an identity ID^*, two equal-length messages (m_0, m_1), and some state information ω.
3. The challenger generates a bit $b \xleftarrow{\$} \{0, 1\}$ and computes the challenge ciphertext $C^* \xleftarrow{\$}$ Encrypt(mpk, pk, ID^*, m_b) where pk is the public key associated with identity ID^*.

4. The attacker runs $\mathcal{A}_2$ on the challenge ciphertext C^* and the state information ω. $\mathcal{A}_2$ may query the **Request Public Key** and **Decrypt** oracles as
   above. $\mathcal{A}_2$ terminates with the output of a bit b'.

The attacker may trivially break the scheme if $\mathcal{A}_2$ queries the Decrypt oracle
for ID^* with C^*. The attacker wins the game if it outputs $b' = b$ and does not
perform this trivial attack. The attacker's advantage is defined to be $Adv_{\mathcal{A}}^{\text{KGC}}(k) = $
$|\Pr[b = b'] - 1/2|$ and the scheme is said to be KGC secure if this advantage is
negligible.

3.3   Denial of Decryption Attacks

Another attractive feature that we may require from a certificateless encryption
is that it prevents denial of decryption attacks. Liu, Au and Susilo [14] were the
first to notice that a certificateless encryption scheme didn't prevent a sender
from encrypting a message using an "incorrect" public key — i.e. a public key
which does not correspond to the identity ID for which the message is intended.
This was termed a "denial of decryption" or "DoD" attack as an attacker that
convinces a sender to use an incorrect public key denies the receiver the opportunity to decrypt the message.

   At one end of the spectrum, a certificateless encryption scheme in the AP
formulation can never achieve this notion security. Since the KeyGen algorithm
does not depend on a secret information known only to the user with identity
ID, anybody can run the KeyGen algorithm to create a valid public key for ID.
On the other end of the spectrum, a traditional PKI-based public-key encryption scheme (which can be viewed as an example of the LK formulation of a
certificateless encryption scheme — see Section 2.3) resists these attacks. The
minimum requirement for a certificateless encryption scheme to achieve denial
of decryption security is that it is expressed in the BSS or LK formulations.

   The formal model of security for denial of decryption attacks is designed
to capture the notion that the attacker cannot convince a sender that a false
public key is correct unless it encrypts message in such a way that it can still
be decrypted correctly by the legitimate receiver with the original key pair. It is
formally described as a game played between a PPT attacker $\mathcal{A}$ and a challenger:

1. The challenger generates a master key pair $(mpk, msk) \xleftarrow{\$} \text{Setup}(1^k)$.
2. The attacker runs $\mathcal{A}$ on mpk. $\mathcal{A}$ may query **Request Public Key**, **Replace
   Public Key**, **Extract Partial Private Key** and **Decrypt** oracles as in
   the outsider security model (see Section 3.1). $\mathcal{A}$ terminates with the output
   of an identity ID^* and a message m^*.

The attacker wins if $C^* \xleftarrow{\$} \text{Encrypt}(mpk, pk', ID^*, m^*)$ satisfies $C^* \neq \bot$ and
$m^* \neq \text{Decrypt}(mpk, sk, C^*)$ where the encryption operation is performed with
the public key pk' that the sender associates with the identity ID^* and the
decryption operation is performed with the original private key sk that was
generated during the Request Public Key query. The scheme is said to be DoD
secure if the probability $Adv_{\mathcal{A}}^{\text{DoD}}(k)$ that an attacker wins is negligible.

4 BSS Certificateless Encryption Based on a PKI

In this section, we will describe the certificate-chain certificateless encryption scheme briefly discussed in Section 2.2. This scheme demonstrates that a PKI-based public-key encryption scheme can be used to instantiate a BSS certificateless encryption scheme. Since this construction combines a digital signature scheme and a traditional public-key encryption scheme, we begin by formally defining these primitives.

4.1 Digital Signature Schemes

A digital signature scheme is a triple of algorithms $(\mathcal{G}_s, \mathcal{S}, \mathcal{V})$. The key generation algorithm $\mathcal{G}_s$ takes the security parameter 1^k as input and outputs a key pair $(pk, sk) \xleftarrow{\$} \mathcal{G}_s(1^k)$. The signing algorithm $\mathcal{S}$ takes a message m and the private key sk as input, and outputs a signature $\sigma \xleftarrow{\$} \mathcal{S}(sk, m)$. The verification algorithm $\mathcal{V}$ takes a message m, a signature σ, and the public key pk as input. It outputs either a symbol $\top$ to indicate the signature is valid or a symbol $\bot$ to indicate the signature is invalid.

We require that the digital signature scheme is sUF-CMA secure. This means that it should be infeasible for an attacker to find a new signature on any message (even if the attacker has previously obtained a signature on that message). The security model considers a PPT attacker $\mathcal{A}$ playing the following game:

1. The challenger generates a key pair $(pk, sk) \xleftarrow{\$} \mathcal{G}_s(1^k)$.
2. The attacker runs $\mathcal{A}$ on the input pk. $\mathcal{A}$ may query a signing oracle with a message m and the oracle will return $\sigma \xleftarrow{\$} \mathcal{S}(sk, m)$. $\mathcal{A}$ terminates with the output of a message m^* and a signature σ^*.

The attacker wins if $\mathcal{V}(pk, m^*, \sigma^*) = \top$ and it did not query the signing oracle with the message m^* and receive the signature σ^* in response. The scheme is sUF-CMA secure if the probability $Adv_{\mathcal{A}}^{\text{sig}}(k)$ of the attacker winning the game is negligible.

4.2 Public-Key Encryption Schemes

A public-key encryption scheme is a triple of PPT algorithms $(\mathcal{G}_e, \mathcal{E}, \mathcal{D})$. The key generation algorithm $\mathcal{G}_e$ takes as input a security parameter 1^k and outputs a key pair $(pk, sk) \xleftarrow{\$} \mathcal{G}_e(1^k)$. The encryption algorithm $\mathcal{E}$ takes as input a message $m \in \mathcal{M}$ and the public key pk, and outputs a ciphertext $C \in \mathcal{C}$. The decryption algorithm $\mathcal{D}$ takes as input a ciphertext $C \in \mathcal{C}$ and the private key sk, and outputs either a message $m \in \mathcal{M}$ or the error symbol $\bot$.

We require the IND-CCA2 notion of security for the encryption scheme. This captures the notion that no attacker can determine any information about a message from a ciphertext even if they can obtain the decryptions of any other ciphertext. This is formalised via the following security game played between a PPT attacker $\mathcal{A} = (\mathcal{A}_1, \mathcal{A}_2)$ and a hypothetical challenger:

1. The challenger generates a key pair $(pk, sk) \xleftarrow{\$} \mathcal{G}_e(1^k)$.
2. The attacker runs $\mathcal{A}_1$ on the public key pk. $\mathcal{A}_1$ may query a decryption oracle with any ciphertext $C \in \mathcal{C}$. The oracle returns $\mathcal{D}(sk, C)$. $\mathcal{A}_1$ terminates with the output of two equal-length messages (m_0, m_1) and some state information ω.
3. The challenger generates $b \xleftarrow{\$} \{0, 1\}$ and computes the challenge ciphertext $C^* \xleftarrow{\$} \mathcal{E}(pk, m_b)$.
4. The attacker runs $\mathcal{A}_2$ on the challenge ciphertext C^* and the state information ω. $\mathcal{A}_2$ may query the decryption oracle as before with the exception that $\mathcal{A}_2$ may not query the decryption oracle on C^*. $\mathcal{A}_2$ terminates with the output of a bit b'.

The attacker wins the game if $b = b'$. The attacker's advantage is defined to be $Adv_{\mathcal{A}}^{enc}(k) = |\Pr[b = b'] - 1/2|$. The scheme is said to be IND-CCA2 secure if every PPT attacker has negligible advantage.

4.3 The Certificate-Chain BSS Certificateless Encryption Scheme

We now formally present the BSS certificateless encryption scheme based on certificate chains discussed in Section 2.2. The scheme makes use of a digital signature scheme $(\mathcal{G}_s, \mathcal{S}, \mathcal{V})$ and a public-key encryption scheme $(\mathcal{G}_e, \mathcal{E}, \mathcal{D})$. It is described in Figure 4.

Setup(1^k):
   $(mpk, msk) \xleftarrow{\$} \mathcal{G}_s(1^k)$
   Return (mpk, msk)

Extract(msk, ID):
   $(pk_s, sk_s) \xleftarrow{\$} \mathcal{G}_s(1^k)$
   $m_1 \leftarrow ID \| pk_s$
   $cert_1 \xleftarrow{\$} \mathcal{S}(msk, m_1)$
   $d \leftarrow (pk_s, sk_s, cert_1)$
   Return d

KeyGen(mpk, ID, d):
   Parse d as $(pk_s, sk_s, cert_1)$
   $(pk_e, sk_e) \xleftarrow{\$} \mathcal{G}_e(1^k)$
   $m_2 \leftarrow pk_e$
   $cert_2 \xleftarrow{\$} \mathcal{S}(sk_s, m_2)$
   $pk \leftarrow (pk_s, cert_1, pk_e, cert_2)$
   $sk \leftarrow sk_e$
   Return (pk, sk)

Encrypt(mpk, pk, ID, m):
   Parse pk as $(pk_s, cert_1, pk_e, cert_2)$
   $m_1 \leftarrow ID \| pk_s$
   If $\mathcal{V}(mpk, m_1, cert_1) = \perp$ then
      Return $\perp$
   $m_2 \leftarrow pk_e$
   If $\mathcal{V}(pk_s, m_2, cert_2) = \perp$ then
      Return $\perp$
   $C \xleftarrow{\$} \mathcal{E}(pk_e, m)$
   Return C

Decrypt(sk, C):
   $m \leftarrow \mathcal{D}(sk, C)$
   Return m

Fig. 4. The Certificate-Chain BSS Certificateless Encryption Scheme

The scheme provides outsider security (Section 3.1), KGC security (Section 3.2), and denial of decryption security (Section 3.3). This is summarised by the following three theorems:

Theorem 1. *Suppose there exists an attacker $\mathcal{A}$ against the certificateless encryption scheme in the outsider security model which makes at most q_{req} queries to the Request Public Key oracle. Then there exists an attacker $\mathcal{B}$ against the first instance of the signature scheme, an attacker $\mathcal{B}'$ against the second instance of the signature scheme, and an attacker $\mathcal{B}^*$ against the public-key encryption scheme such that*

$$Adv_{\mathcal{A}}^{out}(k) \leq Adv_{\mathcal{B}}^{sig}(k) + q_{req} Adv_{\mathcal{B}'}^{sig}(k) + q_{req} Adv_{\mathcal{B}^*}^{enc}(k). \tag{1}$$

Theorem 2. *Suppose there exists an attacker $\mathcal{A}$ against the certificateless encryption scheme in the KGC security model which makes at most q_{req} queries to the Request Public Key oracle. Then there exists an attacker $\mathcal{B}$ against the public-key encryption scheme such that*

$$Adv_{\mathcal{A}}^{KGC}(k) \leq q_{req} Adv_{\mathcal{B}}^{enc}(k). \tag{2}$$

Theorem 3. *Suppose there exists an attacker $\mathcal{A}$ against the denial of decryption security of the certificateless encryption scheme which makes at most q_{req} queries to the Request Public Key oracle. Then there exists an attacker $\mathcal{B}$ against the first instance of the digital signature scheme and an attacker $\mathcal{B}'$ against the second instance of the digital signature scheme such that*

$$Adv_{\mathcal{A}}^{DoD}(k) \leq Adv_{\mathcal{B}}^{sig}(k) + q_{req} Adv_{\mathcal{B}'}^{sig}(k). \tag{3}$$

The proofs of these theorems are given in the full version of the paper but all of the proofs essentially rely on two observations:

- If the attacker does not replace the public key of the identity ID^* then the attacker is essentially attacking the IND-CCA2 security of the public-key encryption scheme.
- In order to replace the public key of an identity then the attacker has to forge either $cert_1$ or $cert_2$. This is an attack against the sUF-CMA security of the digital signature scheme.

The proof of Theorem 1 can be adapted to show that the scheme is secure in the original outsider (Type I) security model of Al-Riyami and Paterson [1,2]. Nonetheless, we prove the theorem in the (weaker) outsider security model described in Section 3.1 as we believe that this is the appropriate security model for all practical applications.

Since it is possible to construct both public-key encryption schemes [6,16] and digital signature schemes [5] from trapdoor one-way permutations, this construction demonstrates that it is possible to construct BSS certificateless encryption schemes from trapdoor one-way permutations in a black-box manner. This is in contrast to AP certificateless encryption schemes which cannot be constructed from trapdoor one-way permutations in a black-box manner [9]. The state of the art in digital signature and public-key encryption schemes suggests that BSS certificateless encryption schemes can be efficiently constructed without elliptic curve pairings.

We also note that there is no requirement for the two "certificates" to be computed using the same signature scheme. Indeed, the security proof allows for the second signature scheme to be a one-time signature scheme. Furthermore, the schemes becomes more bandwidth efficient if an aggregate signature scheme [8] or sequential aggregate signature scheme [15] is used to compress $cert_1$ and $cert_2$ into a single signature. However, the use of such schemes will reduce the computational efficiency and so their use should be considered a trade-off between computational and bandwidth requirements.

Acknowledgements

I would like to thank the programme chairs (Fabio Martinelli and Bart Prenneel) for the opportunity to speak at this conference and Pooya Farshim for his comments on the paper. This is an invited paper and has not been refereed by external reviewers or the programme committee. Any mistakes should be solely attributed to me. This work has been supported by the European Commission through the IST Program under Contract ICT-2007-216646 ECRYPT II.

References

1. Al-Riyami, S.: Cryptographic schemes based on elliptic curve pairings. PhD thesis, Royal Holloway, University of London (2004),
   http://www.isg.rhul.ac.uk/~kp/sattthesis.pdf.
2. Al-Riyami, S.S., Paterson, K.G.: Certificateless public key cryptography. In: Laih, C.-S. (ed.) ASIACRYPT 2003. LNCS, vol. 2894, pp. 452–473. Springer, Heidelberg (2003)
3. Au, M.H., Chen, J., Liu, J.K., Mu, Y., Wong, D.S., Yang, G.: Malicious KGC attack in certificateless cryptography. In: Proc. ACM Symposium on Information, Computer and Communications Security. ACM Press, New York (2007)
4. Baek, J., Safavi-Naini, R., Susilo, W.: Certificateless public key encryption without pairing. In: Zhou, J., López, J., Deng, R.H., Bao, F. (eds.) ISC 2005. LNCS, vol. 3650, pp. 134–148. Springer, Heidelberg (2005)
5. Bellare, M., Micali, S.: How to sign given any trapdoor function. Journal of the ACM 39(1), 214–233 (1992)
6. Bellare, M., Yung, M.: Certifying permutations: Non-interactive zero-knowledge based on any trapdoor permutation. Journal of Cryptology 9(1), 149–166 (1996)
7. Boldyreva, A., Fischlin, M., Palacio, A., Warinschi, B.: A closer look at PKI: Security and efficiency. In: Okamoto, T., Wang, X. (eds.) PKC 2007. LNCS, vol. 4450, pp. 458–475. Springer, Heidelberg (2007)
8. Boneh, D., Gentry, C., Lynn, B., Shacham, H.: Aggregate and verifiably encrypted signatures from bilinear maps. In: Biham, E. (ed.) EUROCRYPT 2003. LNCS, vol. 2656, pp. 416–432. Springer, Heidelberg (2003)

9. Boneh, D., Papkonstantinou, P.A., Rackoff, C., Vahlis, Y., Waters, B.: On the impossibility of basing identity based encryption on trapdoor permutations. In: Proc. of the 49th Annual IEEE Symposium on Foundations of Computer Science – FOCS 2008, pp. 283–292 (2008)
10. Dent, A.W.: A survey of certificateless encryption schemes and security models. International Journal of Information Security 7(5), 349–377 (2008)
11. Diffie, W., Hellman, M.: New directions in cryptography. IEEE Transactions on Information Theory 22, 644–654 (1976)
12. Farshim, P., Warinschi, B.: Certified encryption revisited. In: Preneel, B. (ed.) AFRICACRYPT 2009. LNCS, vol. 5580, pp. 179–197. Springer, Heidelberg (2009)
13. Lai, J., Kou, K.: Self-generated-certificate public key encryption without pairing. In: Okamoto, T., Wang, X. (eds.) PKC 2007. LNCS, vol. 4450, pp. 476–489. Springer, Heidelberg (2007)
14. Liu, J.K., Au, M.H., Susilo, W.: Self-generated-certificate public key cryptography and certificateless signature/encryption scheme in the standard model. In: Proc. ACM Symposium on Information, Computer and Communications Security. ACM Press, New York (2007)
15. Lysyanskaya, A., Micali, S., Reyzin, L., Shacham, H.: Sequential aggregate signatures from trapdoor permutations. In: Cachin, C., Camenisch, J.L. (eds.) EUROCRYPT 2004. LNCS, vol. 3027, pp. 74–90. Springer, Heidelberg (2004)
16. Sahai, A.: Non-malleable non-interactive zero knowledge and adaptive chosen-ciphertext security. In: 40th Annual Symposium on Foundations of Computer Science, FOCS 1999, pp. 543–553. IEEE Computer Society, Los Alamitos (1999)
17. Shamir, A.: Identity-based cryptosystems and signature schemes. In: Blakely, G.R., Chaum, D. (eds.) CRYPTO 1984. LNCS, vol. 196, pp. 47–53. Springer, Heidelberg (1985)

A Computational Framework
for Certificate Policy Operations⋆

Gabriel A. Weaver, Scott Rea, and Sean W. Smith

Dartmouth College, Hanover, NH 03755, USA

Abstract. The trustworthiness of any Public Key Infrastructure (PKI)
rests upon the expectations for trust, and the degree to which those expectations are met. Policies, whether implicit as in PGP and SDSI/SPKI
or explicitly required as in X.509, document expectations for trust in a
PKI. The widespread use of X.509 in the context of global e-Science
infrastructures, financial institutions, and the U.S. Federal government
demands efficient, transparent, and reproducible policy decisions. Since
current *manual* processes fall short of these goals, we designed, built,
and tested *computational* tools to process the citation schemes of X.509
certificate policies defined in RFC 2527 and RFC 3647. Our *PKI Policy
Repository*, *PolicyBuilder*, and *PolicyReporter* improve the consistency
of certificate policy operations as actually practiced in compliance audits, grid accreditation, and policy mapping for bridging PKIs. Anecdotal
and experimental evaluation of our tools on real-world tasks establishes
their actual utility and suggests how machine-actionable policy might
empower individuals to make informed trust decisions in the future.

Keywords: PKI, Certificate Policy Formalization, XML.

1 Introduction

The fundamental purpose of PKI is to allow relying parties to trust users based
upon a set of credentials the user has proven they have control over. Confidence in
these user credentials requires the relying party to evaluate the trustworthiness of
an association between a public key and one or more attributes. These attributes
may serve to identify a person, machine, or organization, or they may simply
associate an arbitrary property with a public key.

Foundations for Trust in a X.509 PKI. In X.509, these associations are
expressed in a machine-actionable document called a *certificate* and a *certificate
authority (CA)* attests to the validity of these associations. The *certificate policy*

⋆ This work was supported in part by the NSF (under grant CNS-0448499), the
U.S. Department of Homeland Security (under Grant Award Number 2006-CS-001-
000001), and AT&T. The views and conclusions contained in this document are
those of the authors and should not be interpreted as necessarily representing the
official policies, either expressed or implied, of any of the sponsors.

F. Martinelli and B. Preneel (Eds.): EuroPKI 2009, LNCS 6391, pp. 17–33, 2010.

(CP) of an organization contains a set of expectations that define its notion of a trustworthy public key certificate and how it may be used. The *Certification Practices Statement (CPS)* states how a CA actually implements a CP. In principle, the trustworthiness of a certificate is a function of the similarity of stated policy to personal trust expectations (measured in the *Policy Comparison* process) and the similarity of stated policy to actual practice (*Compliance Audit*).

Evaluating the similarity of policies depends upon the comparison of CPs. Ideally users should evaluate trusted roots based on their personal expectations. In actual practice, the average user blindly adopts the trust expectations of their employers, application vendors, or of companies like Thawte and VeriSign. Until user-friendly policy becomes a reality, requirements for trust will continue to be expressed for organizations, by organizations.

Currently, people manually compare the two policies involved, reading both documents line by line. Bridge CAs relieve organizations of much of this burden, employing this same manual process to establish trust relationships between member organizations. Bridge CAs attest that the expectations of trust for all of its member organizations are logically consistent. If a member organization issues a certificate, that certificate is viewed as trustworthy among all members of the bridge at a predetermined level of assurance [20].

A policy is probably useless unless it is followed in practice. *Compliance audits* determine whether a CA issues certificates according to a CP in actual practice. Federations and bridges ensure that the requirements for trust are met through such audits, whether for accreditation or cross-certification respectively. For example, the current approach to accreditation at the *International Grid Trust Federation (IGTF)* defines a mostly manual process; one step involves *Policy Management Authority (PMA)* members reviewing a CP in detail, comparing its contents against requirements in an *authentication profile (AP)* [21]. Auditing PKIs within financial institutions also involves following a manual process described in ISO 21188 [22] [25]. Cross-certification, the operation necessary to establish a bridge, similarly requires comparing CPs.

We claim that informed trust decisions should be based on processes that consistently estimate actual organizational behavior. *Consistent processes* occur frequently in a manner transparent to the user; their results are both reproducible and auditable. Currently-practiced, manual CP operations are costly, time-consuming, lack end-user transparency, and are difficult to reproduce. We claim that computationally processing machine-actionable certificate policies would be more efficient and consistent.

Our Contributions to Certificate Policy Formalization. Our *PKI Policy Repository, PolicyBuilder*, and *PolicyReporter* codify certificate policy processes used in PKI compliance audits, grid accreditation, and bridging PKIs. We claim that these tools improve the efficiency and consistency of policy retrieval, creation, and comparison. This section presents our contributions in the context of previous work on the identification, representation, and manipulation of certificate policies.

Identification. Our tools identify certificate policies using a hierarchical, human-readable, machine-actionable reference string called a *Canonical Text Services Uniform Resource Name (CTS-URN)* [14]. CTS-URNs emerge from some of our previous work on the *Multitext of Homer Project* [15] to perform computations on Classical Greek texts [32]. One of this paper's contributions is to use CTS-URNs encoded as Object Identifiers (OID)s to identfy individual CPs, arbitrary sets of policy documents, or other versions or translations of that same document.

CTS-URNs also identify sets of policy requirements organized within a citation (or reference) scheme. RFC 3647, Section 6 [12] explicitly defines a citation scheme organized in terms of policy requirements to facilitate the comparison of CPs and CPSs. CTS-URNs enable the tools we built to compute with respect to a policy's reference structure, identifying individual security provisions[1] or the document in its entirety.

Our identification scheme increases the expressiveness of policy related certificate extensions by encoding CTS-URNs as OIDs. Accepting or rejecting CPs is currently a binary decision; policy documents must be "completely accepted or forbidden" [24]. CTS-URNs let people and machines reference arbitrary sections of a policy; rather than accepting or rejecting an entire policy document, users may whitelist or blacklist agreeable or offending provisions.

Representation. We encode certificate policies using *Text Encoding Initiative (TEI) P5 Lite*, an XML standard for representing texts in digital form [5]. Like previous efforts to encode policies using XML [8] [7], we model a security policy as a tree.[2] Given a policy's text, we only mark up its citation scheme, the outline of provisions defined in Section 6 of RFC 3647 or Section 5 of RFC 2527 [11]. This results in a *semi-formal* [7] policy representation that is both machine-actionable and human-readable. This approach simplifies the overhead of encoding a policy.

The *Federal PKI Policy Authority (FPKIPA)* Technical Specification recommends writing CPs and CPSs in a natural language [12]. Our representation honors that recommendation and leaves the natural language of the policy unchanged. Alternate representations of policies such as data-centric XML[3], matrices, or ASN.1 require a person to read the source text and fit their interpretation of that text to a data format. Such representations are unsuitable for relying parties to easily understand the meaning of a policy [7] [19] [12]. Our contribution is a policy representation that humans can use as a primary source for informed policy decisions and which computers can process.

Manipulation. Computing on certificate policies overcomes many of the drawbacks and limitations of manual processes. We claim that implementations of

---

[1] Trcek et al.'s DNS-like system organized the set of all possible security requirements hierarchically into domains that were referenced by human-readable, machine-actionable strings [34].

[2] Our approach is inspired by current approaches to digitizing Classical texts [15] [13].

[3] *Document-centric* XML is the type of documents "written by hand, by an author" like a letter or chapter. *Data-centric* XML is used to transport data between computers [30].

algorithms are efficient and *consistent* processes for explicitly imposing a model on policy content. Algorithms may be run frequently. Unlike deriving a model of policy content from text and encoding it by hand, algorithms can be run on demand any time as CPs change. Algorithms are unambiguous and when their implementations are open-source, the underlying process is transparent to the user. Finally, the output of algorithms may be reproduced by running the same input and interpreted to make informed trust decisions.

This Paper. This paper is organized as follows. Section 2 describes some real-world use cases for certificate policy and the reliability of current practices. Section 3 introduces the design and implementation of the tools we built for processing certificate policy and illustrates how they address real-world needs while improving actual practice. We evaluate these tools in Section 4, using anecdotal and experimental evidence. Section 5 reviews related work. Section 6 describes future research directions building upon this work, and Section 7 concludes.

2   Problems with Manual Certificate Policy Processes

Certificate policy defines the trustworthiness of a CA and therefore is fundamental to the trust one places in a PKI. This section discusses three real-world X.509 processes which directly use certificate policy: PKI compliance audits, IGTF accreditation, and policy mapping for bridging PKIs. In each case, we'll describe the process in principle and its importance to the trustworthiness of a PKI. Then we'll describe how the current implementation of this process limits trustworthiness and motivate the need for *consistent* operations on certificate policies.

PKI Compliance Audits. Like accreditation processes, PKI audits verify that the certificate policies and certification practice statements are consistent with a "framework of requirements." In the financial services industry, ISO 21188 specifies such a framework that evolved from WebTrust and ANSI X9.79 [25]. Audits for WebTrust compliance should occur at least every 6 months [18]. During these audits, PKIs are evaluated with respect to five objectives: *security, availability, processing integrity, confidentiality,* and *privacy.* Each of these objectives are defined using principles, "broad statements of objectives," and criteria, "benchmarks that should be objective, measurable, complete, and relevant" [35]. Through Assurance Services, a *Certified Public Accountant (CPA)* may express a WebTrust opinion on whether an objective is met. By keeping objective observations separate from opinion, WebTrust audits are an important and objective process for certifying that actual practice reflects written policy. Additionally, the *International Collaborative Identity Management Forum (ICIDM)* and *Four Bridges Forum (4BF)* [1] are working to define a standard PKI audit process. The IGTF also publishes a set of auditing guidelines [33].

Frequency. Compliance audits are expensive in time and money, and limited by the bottleneck of human observation. Although compliance audits like WebTrust are supposed to occur at least every 6 months, in actual practice they usually happen less often. Even when these audits occur on schedule, auditors' observations only sample a glimpse of much larger, continuous business processes. By necessity, PKI audits require human intervention; expressing an opinion based upon observed criteria requires human judgement. However, the criteria themselves, measureable and objective by definition, do not require human judgement to measure.

Transparency. Current auditing schemes lack transparency. Users cannot evaluate an organization's observed behavior in terms of their own trust requirements. Instead users implicitly delegate trust decisions to a CPA or other audit professional. Furthermore, because ISO 21188 and ANSI X9.79 are not freely available, the average user has no way of knowing the trust decisions being delegated.[4] These institutional and economic walls ensure that trust evaluation resides at the organizational level in spite of trust's personal nature. Through combining documentation with computational methods, measurements of trust criteria could be made accessible to users to individually decide the degree of trust they place in an organization.

Reproducibility. Compliance audits, as currently practiced, are difficult to reproduce because they are so dependant upon auditors' individual observations. Certainly audits attest to an organization's trustworthiness at the time of the last audit; however they say nothing about the current state of the organization. Were an auditor to try to reproduce an audit, the conditions under which the original audit occurred may be extremely difficult or impossible to reproduce because organizations are dynamic, changing entities. Audits rely upon the past as the sole indicator of current and future performance.

IGTF Accreditation. Researchers using computational grids employ many thousands of distributed nodes to solve complex computational problems by sharing resources. *Grids* often group users under very large *Virtual Organizations (VOs)* which usually reflect real-world collaborations between researchers and institutions. Computational power, data storage, and network bandwidth all must be shared between members of a VO. Since these resources are valuable, access is limited based on the requested resource and the user's identity. Each grid must enforce these limits by providing secure authentication of users and applications. Unauthorized access to resources is unacceptable, especially given the large size of a VO [29]. The IGTF uses X.509 PKI to ensure that grid authentication mechanisms meet a defined level of assurance.

A distributed architecture like the grid requires compatible, non-contradictory policies among member organizations. An IGTF-accredited member should issue policy consistent with all other members, and thereby satisfy the IGTF's standard for trust. The purpose of the IGTF is to "harmonize the work on authentication for e-Science production infrastructures."[21] It accomplishes this by establishing common policies and guidelines between PMAs as well as ensuring compliance to the resulting Federation Document amongst the participating PMAs. Currently, the IGTF maintains a set of authentication profiles (AP) which specify the policy and technical requirements. During accreditation the prospective member sends the Certificate Policy (CP) around to other members

---

[4] Anecdotally, we believe the costs of ISO 21188 and ANSI X9.79 may discourage organizations from following these standards in actual practice.

for comments and asks multiple PMA members to review it in detail. Eventually this CP, along with recommendations from the reviewers, is presented at the PMA meeting for immediate approval or deferral.

The IGTF defines accreditation in terms of manual procedures, institutionalizing bottlenecks that might be eliminated through technology. Accreditation should be defined in terms of functional requirements, not in terms of a particular implementation of those functions.

Frequency. The IGTF's requirement that any change in policy requires reaccreditation may penalize organizations that change policy to reflect actual practice. Since organizational practices change rapidly and policies should reflect practice, policies need to be able to change rapidly to mirror the actual organization. So as not to penalize organizations for reporting their actual practices, reaccreditation should be defined to accommodate frequent organizational changes. Furthermore, when the IGTF changes an AP, all members have just 6 months to re-certify that they are compliant with the new profile.

Transparency. Users authenticating to the grid are unable to see for themselves how well member institutions satisfy APs and are implicitly forced to trust IGTF accreditation. While users may not be able to learn every nuance of an accreditation process, the evidence leading to an accreditation should be readily available to grid users. All members are equally trusted under the current scheme. In reality some of them may satisfy the AP or portions of the AP better than others. Grid authentication will only be as strong as its weakest member.

Reproducibility. Since IGTF accreditation is defined in terms of a manual process, reproducing or auditing an accreditation decision is difficult. Members review a CP in private and then present their findings at an IGTF meeting. The process places much burden on volunteers who may not have much experience in the accreditation process. These reviewers then present their own opinions on the compatibility of the CP with the federation's AP. Since CPs are large documents, other IGTF members may trust the reviewers' opinion rather than reading the CP on their own. While reviewers' opinions determine much of the accreditation decision, the criteria used in forming that opinion may not be captured for future reference.

Policy Mapping for Bridging PKIs. Bridge CAs, though not themselves anchors of trust, establish relationships with different PKIs so that users from different PKIs can decide whether to trust one another. Bridges exist to mediate trust in several areas including the pharmaceutical industry, the U.S. Federal government (FPKIPA), the defense and aerospace industry, and higher education (HEBCA). Creation of these bridges requires mapping policies between member PKIs. When a new organization wishes to join a bridge, the bridge CA will compare the candidate organization's CP to its own. If suitable, the bridge CA will then sign the certificate of the candidate organization's trust root. Sometimes a bridge CA may even use the policy mapping certificate extension to establish an equivalence between a member organization's policy and one of its own CPs.

Frequency. Policy mapping occurs when an organization first requests to join a bridge and becomes invalid when actual practice changes. The timelines over which written policy, policy mapping, and actual practice change are not in sync. Policy mapping happens much more infrequently than actual practice changes. As such, diligent organizations keeping their policy statement up to date pose a challenge to bridge CAs who must manually map a member CP into their own. If the policy of the bridge CA changes, it may be important to know how well the CPs of member organizations satisfy the new policy.

Transparency. The actual evidence used to decide whether an organization belongs to a bridge is not readily available to its users. Without this evidence, users know whether or not an organization meets the bridge requirements but do not know the extent to which those requirements are met.

Reproducibility. Policy mapping in actual practice does not distinguish between expressed opinion and criterion; there is no way to easily reproduce or evaluate the mapping process for relying parties. Although the policy mapping claimed by the bridge CA may be documented in a certificate extension, these mappings only reference entire policy documents and as such are unsuitable for reconstructing the evidence for membership in a bridge. Mapping matrices are used to document CP compliance, but these are not typically available to the relying party.

3   Computational Tools: Design and Implementation

We designed and implemented the *PKI Policy Repository*, *PolicyBuilder*, and *PolicyReporter* to improve the *efficiency* and *consistency* of policy retrieval, creation, and comparison. Each of these tools rests upon our formalization of certificate policy: we identify and reference policy via CTS-URNs and represent policy in TEI-XML. Each tool fully or partially automates one or more of the policy operations and improves their frequency, transparency, and reproducibility. These tools will be released in an open source distribution following publication. Figure 1 illustrates the design and implementation of the tools we will now consider. For each tool, we briefly discuss its relevance to the previous use cases. We then present each of our solutions in the context of current actual practice and prior research on policy formalization.

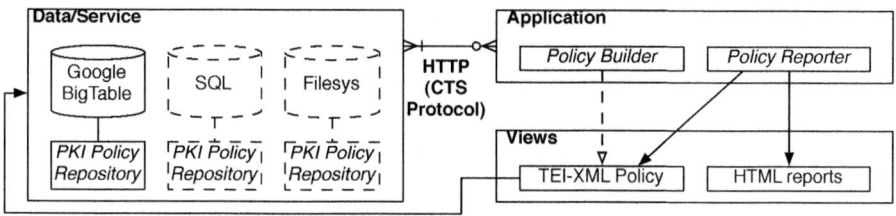

Fig. 1. System architecture for our certificate policy framework. (Dashed modules not yet implemented).

PKI Policy Repository. The *PKI Policy Repository* stores certificate policies for retrieval by their reference structure. PKI audits, accreditation, and policy mapping depend upon the reference, and retrieval of certificate policies and yet little work has been done to automate or partially automate these fundamental processes. The *PKI Policy Repository* fills this void, and sets the stage for individuals to access and evaluate certificate policy.

Reference. We extended OIDs to cover the entirety of a certificate policy's reference structure. Furthermore we implemented a bidirectional mapping from a machine-actionable OID to a human-readable and machine-actionable CTS-URN. Certificate policies are reference works by design. The ability to reference these policies motivated RFC 3647, its predecessor 2527, and a parallel reference structure (or citation scheme) in *Certification Practice Statements (CPSs)*. Policy comparison proceeds much more quickly between two policies sharing the same reference structure. Bridge CAs attest to the trustworthiness of PKIs by listing references to equivalent CPs in the policy mapping extension. Unfortunately the OIDs they use only reference the entire certificate policy, causing shallow, very coarse policy mappings. In actual practice, people are interested in referencing meaningful sets of security requirements. This is why policies have a reference structure in the first place! Trcek et al.'s DNS-like system used machine-actionable, human-readable references to security policy domains, allowing one to reference meaningful sets of security requirements [34]. RFC 3647 and 2527 define meaningful sets of security requirements through the reference structure.

Table 1 shows how we encoded CTS-URNs as OIDs for referencing arbitrary sets of certificate policies, as well as different editions and translations of the same Certificate Policy. Compliance audits, grid accreditation, and bridging PKIs all attest to the trustworthiness of a CP at a particular point in time. Since policies change over time, we claim such attestations should reference the version of the policy at the time of the audit. In prior work, Grimm proposed using multiple versions of the same policy, one expressed formally for machines to process and one expressed informally for administrators to understand its meaning [19]. Although our policy is *semi-formal*, it would be possible to treat other policies–such as Casola et al.'s highly-structured XML [8] [7] and perhaps even ASN.1 representations–as versions of a policy which can be referenced. Since code is text, we can even reference code claiming consistency with a certificate policy provision as if it were another version of that provision. Using OID-encoded CTS-URNs allow multiple versions of a policy, whether plain text, XML, or code to be uniformly

Table 1. Encoding CTS-URNs as OIDs

Semantics	CTS-URN	OID
All texts in the 'pkipolicy' namespace.	urn:cts:pki:pkipolicy	n/a
The ULAGrid CP (and CPS).	urn:cts:pki:pkipolicy.ulagrid	1.3.6.1.4.1.19286.2.2.2
A specific edition of the ULAGrid CP.	urn:cts:pki:pkipolicy.ulagrid.version1	1.3.6.1.4.1.19286.2.2.2.1.0.0
The ULAGrid CP's 'Technical Security Controls'	urn:cts:pki:pkipolicy.ulagrid.version1:6	1.3.6.1.4.1.19286.2.2.2.1.0.0.6
The ULAGrid's policy unit on Key pair generation	urn:cts:pki:pkipolicy.ulagrid.version1:6.1.1	1.3.6.1.4.1.19286.2.2.2.1.0.0.6.1.1

referenced through a parallel citation scheme. This accomplishes Grimm's idea of associating an implementable part of security policy with the "set of specified security measures" realized by the implemented security functions [19].

Retrieval. Retrieving referenced sections of security policy traditionally involves turning printed pages or scrolling through a PDF. Given a reference to a CP such as section 7.1, a CA typically browses his file system to the appropriate PDF, opens it and then scrolls through it until he gets to the appropriate section. Even when searching the PDF, results tend to be reported in page numbers. In actual practice, the mechanisms for policy retrieval are largely unrelated to the mechanisms for citing (referencing) policy. In prior research on policy formalization, little work has been done with policy retrieval. One exception is *PolicyMaker* which allows one to query policy actions using a database-like syntax [3].

For digital editions of reference works, we claim that page numbers are an unnecessary artifact of print. Digitization allows one to navigate texts by logical reference rather than by page number. The *PKI Policy Repository* is a *Canonical Text Services (CTS)* server[5], loaded with certificate policies. The CTS protocol [17] uses HTTP to provide a simple REST XML web service for retrieving canonical texts. Users or applications can retrieve sections of policy by supplying a CTS-URN and other HTTP request parameters. The *PKI Policy Repository* currently uses a Google AppEngine implementation of CTS, although a Groovy/Java implementation also exists.[6] Programs may process the XML policy fragments from a CTS service and transform it into PDF or HTML. This tool lets CAs query an entire database of policy in terms of how it is traditionally referenced, saving them from having to manage PDFs or other representations on their own. Furthermore, this tool opens the door for algorithms to process the content of certificate policy.

PolicyBuilder. The *PolicyBuilder* assists CAs in creating new policies from extant ones. In actual practice new certificate policies may be created when a CA wants to join a federation or bridge. Typically CAs copy and paste passages of extant policy into their new policy and selectively edit a few words and phrases as needed. The more similar the new, derivative certificate policy is to older, already accepted policies, the greater the chances for the new policy to be accepted. Under these circumstances, policy creation is quickly followed by policy review. While Klobucar et al. have stated the need for machine-assisted policy creation [24], no tools have been built to fill this need and none have emerged that consider policy creation as a means to streamline policy review.

The *PolicyBuilder* fills the need for machine-assisted policy creation while facilitating the review and evaluation of newly-created policies. Rather than copying and pasting policy statements from PDFs, *PolicyBuilder* imports policy content directly from CPs in one or more *PKI Policy Repositories*. More specifically, the PolicyBuilder initializes an empty reference tree as defined in

---

[5] Again, we helped to develop the CTS Protocol for serving Classical texts in the *Multitext of Homer Project* [15].

[6] A corpus of sample policies is publicly available in a *PKI Policy Repository* at http://pkipolicy.appspot.com/.

RFC 3647 and populates it with corresponding content from selected policies. Policy content currently includes assertions, or security requirements qualified by MUST, SHOULD, or other adjectives from RFC 2119. Rather than copying and pasting content, policy assertions are imported into the new document by simply clicking on them. Once a document tree is built to satisfaction, the CA may serialize policy to XML, PDF, or HTML. Since each assertion includes a CTS-URN to its source policy, CAs can see how many security requirments they imported from bridge or grid-approved CPs. Similarly, reviewers can process the XML and measure how much content is original and how much comes from already-approved policies.

PolicyReporter. The *PolicyReporter* helps users obtain more, higher-quality information useful for comparing certificate policies. Although policy comparison is a fundamental operation in bridging PKIs and grid accreditation, it remains a highly-manual, highly-subjective process, making it difficult to perform consistently. People compare two CPs at a time, line-by-line, evaluating their similarity. For a person with a lot of experience, this can take 80-120 hours depending upon the reference structure of the policies compared. The hardest comparisons include policies with non-standard reference schemes.

Prior work in machine-assisted policy comparison encompasses a variety of techniques ranging from using fuzzy theory on highly-formal policy representations [7] to imposing a partial or full order on specific values in policy content [24]. Still others organize sets of security requirements into a tree and compare policies by looking at where they sit within the tree [34]. However none of these approaches automatically process the texts as they were designed to be compared, by reference structure. Certainly not all policies follow RFC 3647 neatly or even at all [31]. However our work illustrates further benefit to following RFC 3647 or even 2527, for it allows a standard set of analyses for comparing CPs to develop.

The *PolicyReporter* aggregates information about a set of policy provisions (the criteria for comparison) into a report by walking the citation structure[7] of each text. Given a reference to a policy, it queries one or more *PKI Policy Repositories*, retrieves the referenced content, and processes it using some algorithm. The results of these algorithms are either human-readable HTML report or an XML document. Although *PolicyReporter* currently operates on *semi-formal* source texts, it could just as easily analyze other, more structured interpretations of the source like the markup proposed by Casola et al. Our immediate goal is to help CAs find large discrepancies between CPs such as the number of security requirements of a certain significance.

Currently three algorithms for extracting information from certificate policies are implemented for the *PolicyReporter*.

RFC 2119 Analysis. The *RFC2119Analyzer* counts the number of occurrences of words in one of three categories defined in RFC 2119 [4] to indicate the significance of a requirement. Policy statements with the highest importance contain the words MUST, REQUIRED, or SHALL, the next most important

---

[7] The FPKIPA recommends *all* members use 3647 format for *all* cross-certified CPs [2].

provisions contain SHOULD or RECOMMENDED, and the least significant requirements use MAY or OPTIONAL.

Since security provisions in CPs use RFC 2119-like language, counting the number of words in each category indicates how strictly a section of certificate policy needs to be followed. Interpreting the results of this analysis is simple. A large difference in these counts indicates discrepancies in the requirement levels of two sections of policy.

RFC 2527 Policy Mapper. The *RFC 2527 Policy Mapper* takes a section of text from an RFC 2527 certificate policy and automatically maps it into RFC 3647 TEI-XML. Every mapped provision contains a reference to its source policy. The generated RFC 3647 policy can then be loaded into the *PKI Policy Repository* and used like any other document.

Source Text Analysis. The *SourceTextAnalyzer* leaves the retrieved passage unchanged. This operation is useful for arbitrarily aggregating sections of the policy. This analyzer may be used to assist auditors. For example, WebTrust auditors must evaluate "the procedures to add new users, modify the access level of existing users, and remove users who no longer need access" [35]. Extracting the content from CP sections[8] pertaining to issuing new certificates (RFC 3647, Section 3.1), revocation requests (3.4), certificate issuance (4.3), and certificate modification (4.8) would quickly provide auditors with relevant policy information. Other reports could give an overview of PKI processes, or aggregate information on user enrollment [31].

4   Evaluation

This section demonstrates that our tools, in particular the *PolicyReporter*, actually address current limitations of compliance audits, IGTF accreditation, and policy mapping. Empirical results are combined with anecdotal evidence to argue improvements in the *efficiency* and *consistency* of certificate policy operations in actual practice.

Our experimental evaluations compare the duration of two common certificate policy operations when performed manually and when using our *PolicyReporter*. The first experiment measures the time needed to aggregate information used to compare two CPs while the second measures the time needed to map a policy from 2527 format into 3647 format. Our hypothesis is that the automated processes take less time and provide better-quality information than the non-automated processes.

Experiment 1: Aggregating Information for Policy Comparison. The first experiment assumes that the policies being compared are readily available on disk in PDF format for the manual case and are sitting in the *PKI Policy Repository* as TEI-XML in the automated case. Since comparing policies is subjective and varies widely across CAs, we decided to measure the time required to aggregate the information needed to perform a comparison. Additionally, we

---

[8] We are assuming the CP is structured according to RFC 3647 in this example.

Table 2. Timing results of experiment 1

Id	Trial Information Sections	#P-units	Manual View	Manual Count	Manual Total	Policy-Reporter	View Difference	Total Difference
1	3.1.2	1	01:03	01:41	02:44	00:38	00:25 (40%)	02:06 (76%)
2	6.1.1	1	00:46	00:59	01:45	00:44	00:02 (04%)	01:01 (58%)
3	5.4.5	1	01:02	00:31	01:33	00:39	00:23 (37%)	00:54 (58%)
4	7.1.2, 7.13	2	00:56	01:28	02:24	00:50	00:06 (11%)	01:34 (65%)
5	5.3.1, 5.1.2	2	01:18	03:51	05:09	00:51	00:27 (35%)	04:18 (83%)
6	4.5, 6.1.5	3	01:22	04:32	05:54	00:50	00:32 (39%)	05:04 (86%)
7	6.7, 6.2.6, 5.7.1	3	01:44	04:04	05:48	01:01	00:43 (41%)	04:47 (82%)
8	2.1, 1.5.4, 4.4.1, 9.1.4	4	02:18	03:28	05:46	01:01	01:17 (56%)	04:45 (82%)
9	8	5	01:15	03:28	04:43	00:46	00:29 (39%)	03:57 (84%)
10	5.3, 1.3.4, 3.1.4	10	01:56	14:52	16:48	01:01	00:55 (47%)	15:47 (94%)
	Total	**32**	**13:40**	**38:54**	**52:34**	**08:21**	**05:19 (39%)**	**44:13 (84%)**

Table 3. Discrepancies in manual and automated RFC 2119 keyword counts

Trial	4	7	8	9	10	10
2119 Category	SHALL	MAY	MUST	MUST	MUST	SHALL
Manual	0	0	2	9	30	9
PolicyReporter	1	1	0	10	22	10

used a highly-experienced certificate authority operator so that we could compare our approach to the fastest manual times possible. In the automated case, we timed the steps necessary to generate a report using the *SourceTextAnalysis* and *RFC2119Analysis* and to view each of the sections in that report. In the manual case, we timed the steps needed to load the two PDFs, position them, and view each of the sections in that report side by side. We also timed how long it took to manually count the words appearing in RFC 2119. Since the steps done to perform these tasks may vary from person to person, we explicitly defined each of the steps to be followed.

We performed ten time trials to control for variables which could affect the time necessary to collect the information specified by the evaluation *criteria*[9]. More *policy units (p-units)*, defined as passages of depth 3 within the policy's citation tree (such as Section 3.1.4), within the *criteria* will require more information to be collected and potentially require more time. The length of the *policy unit* passages will affect how long it takes to analyze the text. The proximity of passages within a policy will affect how much a person or machine must navigate through the text. Finally, since the time it takes to manually gather this information decreases with experience, we had a very experienced subject perform the manual and automated tasks. Tables 2 and 3 display the times for each trial and the accuracy of the RFC 2119 key word counts respectively.

The timing and counting results reveal a great deal about the efficiency of manual versus automated certificate policy operations. An initial glance at trials 8, 9, and 10 in the timing data reveals that the speed of consolidating information

---

[9] In this context, *criteria* consist of the policy sections to be compared and the algorithms to run on them.

for policy reviews depends less on the number of *unit policies* to compare and more upon the proximity of those passages to one another in the text. We suspect that the length of the policy unit passages will affect the time required to actually compare the passages, though that is out of the scope of this experiment. Additionally notice that the times to view each passage manually are significantly less than those required to view and count the RFC 2119 words. This indicates that machine-actionable policy comparison makes it possible to gather useful information, such as the significance of a policy requirement, for making policy decisions that are intractible using current methods. Overall the automated policy comparison saved our CP analyst 5 minutes (39%) of his time when he was just viewing passages, and 44 minutes (84%) of his time when working more closely with the material by counting keywords.

Efficiency is also a function of accuracy. In this experiment we measured the accuracy of manual versus automated comparison of policy using in terms of the RFC 2119 Analysis. Table 3 shows that manual and automatic methods disagreed with each other in 50% of the trials. In trials 4 and 7, our CP analyst missed 1 occurrence of a keyword. In trial 8, our CP analyst counted *requires* as belonging to the *required* category while our algorithm did not. This example highlights how encoding such textual analyses resolves subtle differences in evaluation that occur in manual policy comparison. Finally in trial 10, although our subject missed a MUST occurrence in section 5.3 of the ULAGrid policy, our analyzer missed a number of occurrences as Section 3.1.4 of the TACC policy refers to Sections 3.1.1 and 3.1.2. Future versions of *PolicyReporter* will have to resolve such references.

Overall however these results indicate that automated PKI operations are more efficient. Additional analyses such as the RFC 2119 Analysis that are manually costly but informative take 84% less time and provide better quality information when automated, allowing these operations to occur more frequently in a manner that can be reproduced. Since the *PolicyReporter* generates HTML reports, the information upon which policy decisions are based can be saved, leading to more transparency. We have experimentally demonstrated that the *PolicyReporter* does make CP comparison more efficient and *consistent*. We can only posit how much more efficient automated policy becomes when comparing dozens of security provisions rather than no more than ten at a time. Furthermore, the *PolicyReporter* makes it possible to easily compare more than two policies at a time whereas current manual operations make such comparisons impractical.

Experiment 2: Timing Automated Policy Mapping. The second experiment makes the same assumptions as the first; PDF policies are available on disk for the manual case and TEI-XML policies are available in the *PKI Policy Repository* in the automated case. The design of the second experiment was much simpler as we simply timed how long it took to automatically map the set of *policy units* in Section 1 of an RFC 2527 policy into the RFC 3647 citation scheme. We used the mapping defined in RFC 3647 and in three time trials the *PolicyReporter* enabled us to complete the mapping in 50, 39, and 35 seconds respectively.

These results highlight the speed of machine-actionable certificate policy. In under *one minute, policy units* from *one* section of a certificate policy were automatically mapped. It is estimated that mapping 2527 to 3647 requires 20% more effort than a direct mapping between 3647 CPs. Considering that the average mapping takes 80-120 hours, although the comparison is not exact, we claim that our results indicate a significant time savings in policy mapping.

In preparation for the experiment, automation of the mapping process immediately revealed an error in RFC 3647's mapping framework: RFC 3647 maps 2527, section 2.1 to 3647, section 2.6.4. A closer look at RFC 3647, Section 6 revealed that section 2.6.4 does not exist in the outline of provisions! Automatic mapping allows one to easily change a mapping and rerun the process as frequently as desired. Our approach also increases the transparency of the mapping process because generated RFC 3647 policies contain references to the source RFC 2527 provisions from which they are mapped. Finally, automatic policy mapping is easily reproduced; generated policies can be compared to other policies by loading them into the *PKI Policy Repository*. It takes roughly 1 minute to load a policy into the repository depending upon the size of the document.

5   Related Work

Chadwick developed various XML-based *Role-Based Access Control (RBAC)* authorization policies so that domain administrators and users can manage their own resources [9] [10]. SAML [6] and XACML [27] formalize authentication and authorization policies in XML.

Previous work in certificate policy formalization focuses less on human-readable, machine-actionable representation. Blaze [3], Mendes [26], and Grimm [19] all use ASN.1 to model properies inferred from the policy's source text. Others like Casola [8] [7], have developed data-centric XML representations, suitable for machines but not for readily understanding policy semantics [19]. Recent work by Jensen [23] encodes the reference scheme of a certificate policy using DocBook [36]. His work closely relates to our work in policy formalization and is compatible with our approach. Additionally, others have built systems to compute a trust index from XML-formatted CPS documents [16]. Such calculations demonstrate another type of analysis one could use when comparing certificate policies in our system.

We reference and compute upon the citation scheme of certificate policies to drive tools that we have empirically verified to increase the *efficiency* and *consistency* of certificate policy operations. Our work builds upon established standards and mature technologies. TEI P5 [5] represents 15 years of research in encoding texts with XML. The CTS Protocol [17] has been in development for 5 years and is based upon over 20 years of experience [13] in computing with a variety of digitized texts[10].

---

[10] We used this experience in designing the CTS Protocol, requiring compatibility with texts encoded in TEI, DocBook, or any other valid XML format encoding a citation scheme.

6   Future Work

In future work, we plan to package our tools for release in an open source distribution hosted at OpenCA Research Labs [28]. Most urgently we need to extend the automated policy mapping to include all security provisions, not just *policy units* in Section 1. Our first experiment also revealed the need to extend the tools to resolve references to other sections of text that occur within a policy statement.

In general this work sets the stage for two complimentary problems: *extracting* useful information from natural language policies and *designing* usable certificate policies for man and machine. For the former problem, we intend to design, build, and test additional algorithms for processing policy text. Just as we filtered for RFC 2119 key words, so could we filter phrases indicating the size of the CA key in Section 6.1.5 or extract SHA-2 hash requirements. We also may investigate more sophisticated *Natural Language Processing (NLP)* algorithms. Algorithmic analyses of a policy's source text may lay the foundation for usable security policy metrics with real-world utility.

Computing on certificate policies informs the design of security policies that can be processed by human and computer. Certificate policies encoded in XML formats like TEI and DocBook are currently compatible with the *PKI Policy Repository*. However, other texts such as configuration files or code intended to be consistent with a policy statement might be aligned through the common citation framework that CTS-URNs provide. Given that high-level policy statements can be mapped into software, we also plan to investigate how they might be explictly mapped into hardware. Finally, some of Chadwick and Sasse's research on controlled languages might prove helpful in making policies useable for humans and computers [10].

7   Conclusions

To conclude, our *PKI Policy Repository*, *PolicyBuilder*, and *PolicyReporter* make real-world CP operations more *efficient* and *consistent*. We have empirically demonstrated their utility in aggregating information for policy comparison and policy mapping, two common tasks performed in compliance audits, grid accreditation, and bridging PKIs. Our tools streamline these processes, making them more efficient and provide auditors with more, higher quality information. Our tools allow people to to specify a set of provisions that mimic how they actually make trust decisions. Instead of forcing people to accept or reject a policy in its entirety, CTS-URNs encoded as OIDs allow one to blacklist or whitelist arbitrary policy provisions. While we hope that our tools will reduce the costs associated with creating and maintaining a PKI, more importantly we hope to empower individuals to make their own trust decisions through a usable policy framework.

References

1. 4BF - Four Bridges Foru http://www.the4bf.com/ (retrieved May 29, 2009)
2. Alterman, P.: Reformatting Entity CP's into RFC 3647 Format (November 2006), http://www.cio.gov/fpkipa/documents/PolicyMemoRFC3647v1.pdf (retrieved May 30, 2009)
3. Blaze, M., Feigenbaum, J., Lacy, J.: Decentralized Trust Management. In: IEEE Symposium on Security and Privacy, pp. 164–173 (1996)
4. Bradner, S.: RFC 2119: Key words for use in RFCs to Indicate Requirement Levels (March 1997)
5. Burnard, L., Bauman, S.: TEI P5: Guidelines for Electronic Text Encoding and Interchange, 5th edn (2007)
6. Cantor, S., Kemp, J., Philpott, R., Maler, E.: Assertions and Protocols for the OASIS Security Assertion Markup Language (SAML V2.0) (2005)
7. Casola, V., Mazzeo, A., Mazzocca, N., Rak, M.: An Innovative Policy-Based Cross Certification Methodology for Public Key Infrastructures. In: Chadwick, D., Zhao, G. (eds.) EuroPKI 2005. LNCS, vol. 3545, pp. 100–117. Springer, Heidelberg (2005)
8. Casola, V., Mazzeo, A., Mazzocca, N., Vittorini, V.: Policy Formalization to Combine Separate Systems into Larger Connected Network of Trust. In: Net-Con, p. 425 (2002)
9. Chadwick, D.W., Otenko, A.: RBAC Policies in XML for X.509 Based Privilege Management. In: SEC, p. 39 (2002)
10. Chadwick, D.W., Sasse, A.: The Virtuous Circle of Expressing Authorization Policies. In: Semantic Web Policy Workshop (2006)
11. Chokhani, S., Ford, W.: RFC 2527: Internet X.509 Public Key Infrastructure Certificate Policy and Certification Practices Framework (March 1999)
12. Chokhani, S., Ford, W., Sabett, R., Merrill, C., Wu, S.: RFC 3657: Internet X.509 Public Key Infrastructure Certificate Policy and Certification Practices Framework (November 2003)
13. Crane, G.: The Perseus Digital Library from http://www.perseus.tufts.edu/hopper/ (retrieved May 29, 2009)
14. Smith, D.: CTS-URNs: Overview (December 2008), http://chs75.harvard.edu/projects/diginc/techpub/cts-urn-overview (retrieved May 29, 2009)
15. Dué,C., Ebbott,M., Blackwell,C., Smith,D.: The Homer Multitext Project (2007), http://chs.harvard.edu/chs/homer_multitext (retrieved May 29, 2009)
16. Ball, E., Chadwick, D.W., Basden, A.: The Implementation of a System for Evaluating Trust in a PKI Environment. Paper presented at the Trust in the Network Economy, Evolaris (2003)
17. Anonymized for Submission. Canonical Text Services CTS, http://cts3.sourceforge.net/ (retrieved May 29, 2009)
18. Gold, R.: WEBTrust / client FAQ (1997-2004), http://www.webtrust.net/faq-client.shtml (retrieved May 29, 2009)
19. Grimm, R., Hetschold, T.: Security Policies in OSI-Management Experiences from the DeTeBerkom Project BMSec. Computer Networks and ISDN Systems 28, 499 (1996)
20. Housley, R., Polk, T.: Planning for PKI: Best Practices Guide for Deploying Public Key Infrastructure. Wiley Computer Publishing, Chichester (2001)
21. International Grid Trust Federation Charter, http://www.igtf.net/new-doc/IGTF-Federation-20051005-1-igtf.html/ (retrieved May 29, 2009)

22. ISO 21188: Public Key Infrastructure for Financial Services—Practices and Policy Framework (2006)
23. Jensen, J.: Presentation for the CAOPS-IGTF session at OGF25 (March 2009)
24. Klobucar, T., Blazic, B.J.: A Formalisation and Evaluation of Certificate Policies. Computer Communications 22, 1104 (1999)
25. Koorn, R., van Walsem, P., Lundin, M.: Auditing and Certification of a Public Key Infrastructure. Information Systems Control Journal 5 (2002)
26. Mendes, S., Huitema, C.: A New Approach to the X.509 Framework: Allowing a Global Authentication Infrastructure without a Global Trust Model. In: Network and Distributed System Security, pp. 172–189 (1995)
27. Moses, T.: eXtensible Access Control Markup Language XACML Version 2.0 (2005)
28. OpenCA Research Labs, http://www.openca.org/ (retrieved May 29, 2009)
29. Pala, M., Cholia, S., Rea, S., Smith, S.: Extending PKI Interoperability in Computational Grids. In: IEEE International Symposium on Cluster Computing and the Grid, pp. 645–650 (2008)
30. Powell, G.: Beginning XML Databases, p. 260. Wiley Publishing, Chichester (2007)
31. Schmeh, K.: A Critical View on RFC 3647. In: López, J., Samarati, P., Ferrer, J.L. (eds.) EuroPKI 2007. LNCS, vol. 4582, p. 369. Springer, Heidelberg (2007)
32. Anonymized For Submission. Applying Domain Knowledge from Structured Citation Formats to Text and Data Mining: Examples Using the CITE Architecture. In: Text Mining Services, p. 129 (2009)
33. Tanaka, Y., Viljoen, M., Rea S.: Guidelines for Auditing Grid CAs version 1.0 (February 2009), http://www.ggf.org/Public_Comment_Docs/Documents/2009-02/AuditGuidelines-Feb26_2009.pdf (retrieved May 30, 2009)
34. Trcek, D., Jerman-Blazic, B., Pavesic, N.: Security Policy Space Definition and Structuring. Computer Standards & Interfaces 18(2), 191–195 (1996)
35. Trust Services Principles, Criteria and Illustrations for Security, Availability, Processing Integrity, Confidentiality, and Privacy (2006), http://infotech.aicpa.org/NR/rdonlyres/05A9970C-A574-406D-BE82-5BE60D17F90F/0/Trust_Services_PC_10_2006.pdf (retrieved May 29, 2009)
36. Walsh, N., Muellner, L.: DocBook: The Definitive Guide (July 1999)

Resource Management with X.509 Inter-domain Authorization Certificates (InterAC)

Vishwas Patil[1], Paolo Gasti[2], Luigi Mancini[3], and Giovanni Chiola[2]

[1] Cryptography and Security Department
Institute for Infocomm Research, Singapore
vtpatil@i2r.a-star.edu.sg
[2] Dipartimento di Informatica e Scienze dell'Informazione
Università di Genova, Italy
{gasti,chiola}@disi.unige.it
[3] Dipartimento di Informatica
Università di Roma – La Sapienza, Italy
mancini@di.uniroma1.it

Abstract. Collaboration among independent administrative domains would require: i) confidentiality, integrity, non-repudiation of communication between the domains; ii) minimum and reversible modifications to the intra-domain pre-collaboration setup; iii) maintain functional autonomy while collaborating; and, iv) ability to quickly transform from post-collaboration to pre-collaboration stage. In this paper, we put forward our mechanism that satisfies above requirements while staying within industry standards so that the mechanism becomes practical and deployable. Our approach is based on X.509 certificate extension. We have designed a non-critical extension capturing users' rights in such a unique way that the need for collaboration or the post-collaboration stage does not require update of the certificate. Thus, greatly reducing the revocation costs and size of CRLs. Furthermore, rights amplification and degradation of users from collaborating domains into host domain can be easily performed. Thus, providing functional autonomy to collaborators. Initiation of collaboration among two domains require issuance of one certificate from each domain and revocation of these certificates ends the collaboration – ease of manageability.

Keywords: inter-domain authorization, collaboration, access control, PKI, manageability.

1 Introduction

In the age of globalization, organizations have to collaborate to stay competitive so that they can concentrate on their core competencies. A collaboration happens in several forms like; outsourcing, workflow integration. Collaboration is an agreement between two or more organizations to achieve a common goal. It can be short-term or long-term. To initiate a collaboration, the organizations share their users and resources. An organization allowing users from collaborator's domain to perform actions on its resources is called host domain. And, a domain is an independent administrative domain when the state of its users, resources, and their relations, is readily available within

F. Martinelli and B. Preneel (Eds.): EuroPKI 2009, LNCS 6391, pp. 34–50, 2010.
© Springer-Verlag Berlin Heidelberg 2010

the domain. Change in state of an administrative domain happens when the need for change in access control arises. The internal change in state, at times, may be needed to communicate across collaborating domains. A mechanism that facilitates collaboration should ensure that the internal state changes of a domain should not always necessitate the change to be communicated to peer collaborating domains. That is, the mechanism should allow internal state changes in a host domain while keeping the cost of inter-domain communication for such state changes to a minimum. Let us list out the other requirements from a collaboration mechanism and the rationale behind our mechanism.

As collaborators open up their resources for users from collaborating domains, off-line authentication of the users, and confidentiality, integrity, non-repudiation of communication between the domains becomes important. These properties can be easily achieved through a public-key infrastructure (PKI) like X.509; which is a widely deployed ITU (International Telecommunication Union) standard across organizations. Building a collaboration facilitating mechanism around X.509 keeps the mechanism practical and widely acceptable. Several other collaboration facilitating mechanisms exist that rely on X.509 for authentication and communication security but perform actual authorization decisions through other means. We are interested in finding a solution within X.509 specifications because this is the bare minimum common thing two diverse organizations would have.

The collaboration facilitating mechanism should also keep the modifications needed in intra-domain setup to a minimum in order to quickly gear up for collaboration. Also, such modifications should be reversible so that in case of unsuccessful collaboration, due to unforeseen reasons, the domain quickly reverts back to its pre-collaboration status. This property is very important for successful but ephemeral collaborations.

It is paramount to maintain the functional autonomy of collaborating domains during the collaboration period. That is, the fact of being in collaboration state should not hinder a collaborating domain from performing a task that could be performed in its pre-collaboration state. Depending upon the type of collaboration facilitating mechanism, there is a cost associated with functional autonomy of a domain. The cost can be quantized in terms of the number of revocation of assertions (therefore, size of CRL and associated overheads) performed and communicated across domains. The functional autonomy should also allow the domain, from which users are accessing resources of collaborating domain, to degrade or amplify rights over collaborator's resources apart from resource owner doing the same.

Post collaboration, it is equally important to see how quickly a domain can fall-back to its pre-collaboration state. If the modifications to the pre-collaboration setup are kept to a minimum and non-intrusive, it is evident that post collaboration a domain can quickly fall back to its pre-collaboration state.

Having listed the expectations from a collaboration facilitating mechanism we should also note the fact about digital certificate around which we are building our mechanism. Digital certificates are static, off-line verifiable, cryptographic data structures. The static nature of certificates limits the later rights (authorizations/permissions) amplification or reduction and collaborators sharing resources may not always know the complete authorization requirements *a priori*. Off-line verifiability of certificate does guarantee the freshness of assertions made via that certificate. Despite these facts, digital certificates provide tangible assertions which can be relied upon with varying degree of trust and context under which they are used. Revocation or suspension of a single permission/right over a collaborating resource requires appropriate changes in permissions previously conferred on users participating from peer domain. Therefore, we started this work to investigate to find whether it is possible to re-arrange permissible rights on a shared resource so that the number of certificate revocations/issuance are minimized when rights are withdrawn/added. We could address this quandary by introducing two things in our mechanism: segregation of permissions/rights and hierarchy in flow of permission. This our approach brought huge advantage, in terms of number of certificate revocations, autonomy, manageability. These benefits under our approach come with a slight computational cost which is justifiable.

Organization of the paper: In the next section, we take a stock of current relevant works on the lines of cross-domain authorization mechanisms based on digital certificates and policy languages. In Sect. 3 we give the rationale behind our approach and present our mechanism in Sect. 4. In Sect. 5 we show how our mechanism brings functional autonomy and manageability to collaborators while in collaboration. Section 6 gives the algorithm for certificate chain composition and rights computation. In Sect. 7 we compare our approach with existing certificate based approach in terms of computational cost and functionality. We conclude in Sect. 8.

2 Background and Related Work

Several proposals exist in literature to address collaboration in distributed environment. Most of these proposal are policy based approaches in which certificates are used as assertions and actual authorizations of a user are computed based on policy-based language. In authentication-cum-authorization approach [1] certificates play a role of identity authentication and in policy based approach they play a role of conveying assertions. In a dynamic distributed setup, policy based authorization mechanism provide a better solution over authentication-cum-authorization mechanism. Policy based authorization mechanisms [2, 3, 4, 5, 6, 7, 8, 9] overcome the shortcomings like, for example, context-sensitive authorizations, dynamic rights amplification, suspension or degradation of rights. Certificates are prone to revocation in a dynamic setup if one does not carefully choose the "security assertion values" (permissions) to be embedded into the certificates. It is a common practice to insert only the information that is not going to change for a relatively longer time period, and dynamic information is captured and interpreted separately, using a policy language [2, 3, 4, 5, 8]. The problem overlooked by existing approaches is to make a systematic distinction between dynamic and static information (permissions), which we feel is almost impossible or cannot be precisely captured *a priori* while issuing the certificates [10]. Through our approach, we put forward a mechanism that shields the authorization certificates from the need of revocation/reissuance in synchronization with the dynamic state changes in a domain.

X.509 was originally conceived to authenticate the entries in X.500 directory structure. Later on, it was exploited to perform authentication-cum-authorization decisions over resources scattered across independent administrative domains. Efforts to embed authorizations of a subject into the certificate itself were made through certificate extensions [11]. The obvious challenge in such an approach of embedding is to maintain the certificate's validity due to change in subject's authorization status. This challenge led to the need for separating authentication and authorization of a subject, and attribute certificates [12] were conceived. Attribute certificates provide the foundation upon which the Privilege Management Infrastructure (PMI) can be built. They don't contain any public key, but attributes that may specify group membership, role, security clearance or other authorization information corresponding to the attribute certificate holder. A subject may have multiple attribute certificates associated with each of its PKCs. There is no requirement that the same authority create both the public key certificate and attribute certificate(s) for a user. This also brought along the need for attribute authority (AA, similar to Certificate Authority – CA) and attribute revocation lists (ARLs). PERMIS [13], Akenti [14], Argos [15], Shibboleth [16], CAS/Globus [17], WS-Security [6], SALSA [18], etc., are some of the existing inter-domain authorization mechanisms or frameworks that mainly rely on X.509 type of PKI. There also exist policy based approaches like PolicyMaker/KeyNote [2, 3] that use cryptographic security assertions to derive to an authorization decision. RBAC (Role-Based Access Control [19]) is a *de facto* standard in industry to perform authorizations over an organization's resources by its users. In [20, 1, 21], the authors propose a X.509 based approach to extend the framework of RBAC across domains. There also exist standards like SAML [4], XACML [5], RT/RTML [8, 9] meant for designing interoperation interfaces for organizations that need to collaborate. Specification languages [4, 5] and frameworks [6] have gathered much relevance in work-flow and grid computing fields.

A deep analysis of these practices made us conclude that in most of the existing approaches for collaboration, cryptographic primitives are mainly used to perform authentication. The authorization related attributes are specified in XML-like language with a plausible integration of cryptographic primitives over such attributes to provide authenticity and non-repudiation properties for the credentials flowing across domains. Policy-based approaches may not be able to quickly gear up for collaborations as the participating domains may have different policy languages used in their setups. Domains' transition from post-collaboration to pre-collaboration state may not be smooth and quick. Therefore, it was interesting for us to investigate if we could design a mechanism purely within X.509 framework. We would like to quickly highlight that though policy based inter-domain access control mechanisms (SAML, XACML, RT/RTML, *et.al.*) are more expressive than our approach, it would be unfair to compare them with our mechanism as they fall in different categories. We postpone the comparative analysis to Sect. 7.1.

3   Need for Hierarchy and Segregation of Rights

Before we introduce you to our proposal, we would like to underline the need for hierarchy in authorization flow and segregation of rights. In a collaboration realized solely using digital certificates, a collaborator sharing its resource will issue a certificate, to user from peer domain, containing appropriate permissible rights on the resource. Assume two collaborating domains D_1 and D_2, where D_2 is offering its resource R_2 for collaboration for user *Alice* from peer domain D_1. Domain administrator of D_2 issues a digital certificate containing permissions $\{a, b, c, d\}$ to *Alice*. When *Alice* needs to

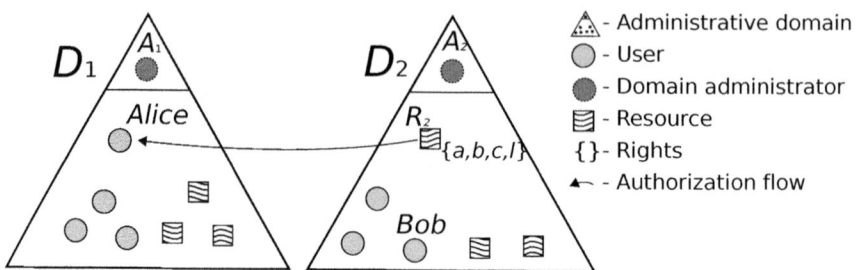

Fig. 1. Flow of authorization using direct authorization certificate

access resource R_2, she simply makes an access request along with the authorization certificate. The flow of authorization from R_2 to *Alice* due to the authorization certificate is shown in Figure 1. Domain D_2 starts incurring collaboration cost (affecting functional autonomy) when there is a state change in its domain. For example, D_2 needs to withdraw permission d over its resource R_2. This change requires revocation and re-issuance of certificate to *Alice*. The cost is directly proportional to the number of collaborating users having access to resource R_2. Imagine D_2 sharing several other of its resources with D_1 and most of these resources having some permissions that are frequently enabled/suspended. Introduction of a new permission will either require re-issuance of certificates or issuance of separate certificates containing new permission.

To reduce the collaboration costs to participating domains and to retain their functional autonomy we propose a novel approach in which we segregate the permissions on collaborating resource into static and dynamic sets. Static permission are those permission that are less likely to be withdrawn by resource administrator for a relatively longer period as compared to dynamic permissions that may be suspended (temporarily or permanently) frequently. We also introduce a level of indirection in the flow of authorization flowing from resource to its collaborating users. In next section, we give the details of our approach with the help of a running example.

4   *InterAC*: Dynamic Inter-domain Authorization via X.509

In this section, we explain our collaboration facilitating mechanism *InterAC*. *InterAC* is purely within X.509 specifications. Under *InterAC* we have designed a *non-critical* extension to X.509 digital certificate [Appendix A]. Through this extension we allow segregation of permissions on a collaborating resource. *InterAC* uses its type of certificates for the following three purposes:

- for subject binding,
- to define an ACL over resource, and
- as a collaboration agreement.

Using such certificates, *InterAC* allows a domain administrator to initiate collaboration and define the flow of authorization over its resource from collaborating users from

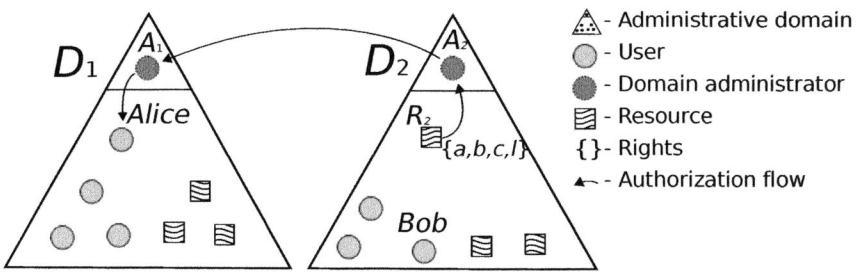

Fig. 2. Flow of authorization using indirect authorization certificate

peer domain. In Fig. 2 one such flow of authorization from resource R_2 to user *Alice* is shown. In short, to access a resource from a collaborating domain, a user need to compose a chain of certificates that proves a valid flow of authorization from the resource to the user. The chain composition and evaluation algorithm is explained in Sect. 6. Let us explain the syntax of *InterAC* certificate and semantics behind it.

Let us denote the *InterAC* digital certificate as CERTIFICATE. Let D_1 and D_2 be two independent administrative domains willing to collaborate. That is, for example, D_2 agreeing to share its resources with the users from domain D_1 as shown in Fig. 2. To share resource R_2, A_2 – domain administrator of D_2 – issues a special type of certificate to R_2 that R_2 will use as an ACL for requests coming from collaborating users. The short hand notation of this CERTIFICATE is: $R_2 \longrightarrow R_2 \boxed{\{a,b,c\}, \{l,m,n\}}$. Where, $\{a,b,c\}$ are the set of static permissions and $\{l,m,n\}$ are the set of dynamic permissions. As a next step, A_2 takes ownership of this resource: $R_2 \longrightarrow A_2 \boxed{\{a,b,c\}, \{l,m,n\}}$.

To initiate a collaboration with domain D_1, A_2 confers rights on R_2 to A_1 – the domain administrator for D_1. Therefore, $A_2 \longrightarrow A_1 \boxed{\{a,b,c\}, \{l\}}$. In turn, A_1 issues a CERTIFICATE to *Alice* so that *Alice* contributes to collaboration: $A_1 \longrightarrow Alice \boxed{\{*\}, \{*\}}$. The wild character in permission set has a special meaning under *InterAC*. It signifies that the decision to grant permissions to the subject of the certificate has been deferred or, in other words, the subject of the certificate can perform all possible actions provided that the subject comes up with a valid proof (certificate chain showing flow of authorization from resource to the requester). Intuitively, Alice can perform $\{a,b,c,l\}$ rights on resource R_2 with the above set of certificates. The computation of effective rights of a requester are done by taking a positional intersection[1] over permissions present in the certificates used for composition of proof. This indirect flow of authorization (hierarchy) from the resource to *Alice* allows each intermediate principal to decide the actual set of permissions *Alice* will have over resource R_2, at any given time. In the following

---

[1] Though the permissions in static and dynamic sets is treated similarly, i.e., a simple intersection across respective sets in the CERTIFICATE chain, it is important that across all the participating collaborative domains the CERTIFICATES should be issued with a consistent position of permission set – static permission set followed by dynamic permission set.

section we shall see how this introduction of hierarchy and segregation of permissions into static and dynamic set contributes to autonomy and manageability of collaboration.

It is interesting to note that as there is no mention of exact rights *Alice* has been given, the same certificate can be used by *Alice* to participate in collaborations with other domains. Since the extension is *non-critical*, the certificate can be used as an identification certificate by *Alice* for purposes other than collaboration. As no rights are specified inside *Alice*'s certificate, privacy violations do not happen when this authorization certificate is used for just authentication purpose.

5   Bringing Autonomy and Manageability to Collaborators

Continuing with the setup shown in Fig. 2 we will introduce more scenarios to explain utility of *InterAC* towards autonomy and manageability. Let us begin with an example of effective rights computation for user *Alice* with a sample scenario.

In the following D_2's domain administrator A_2 is preparing R_2 for collaboration with $\{a,b,c\}$ permissions.

$$R_2 \longrightarrow A_2 \boxed{\{a,b,c\},\{\ \}} \tag{1}$$

where, $\boxed{\{a,b,c\},\ \{\ \}}$ is the authorization string in the CERTIFICATE used as an ACL on resource R_2. Note that D_2 has abstained from conferring permission c over resource R_2 to its collaborator. Let the following be the CERTIFICATE denoting the collaboration agreement between domain D_1 and D_2, where domain D_2 is offering its resource to the users from domain D_1;

$$A_2 \longrightarrow A_1 \boxed{\{a,b\},\{*\}} \tag{2}$$

In a slight modification to the setup in domain D_1, we introduce two roles G_1 and G_2 and let *Alice* be part of G_1, for time being. Therefore;

$$A_1 \longrightarrow G_1 \boxed{\{a\},\ \{*\}} \tag{3}$$

$$A_1 \longrightarrow G_2 \boxed{\{b\},\ \{*\}} \tag{4}$$

$$G_1 \longrightarrow Alice \boxed{\{*\},\ \{*\}} \tag{5}$$

Therefore, *Alice* constructs the following CERTIFICATE chain to access R_2

$$R_2 \longrightarrow A_2 \boxed{\{a,b,c\},\ \{\ \}}$$
$$A_2 \longrightarrow A_1 \boxed{\{a,b\},\ \{*\}}$$
$$A_1 \longrightarrow G_1 \boxed{\{a\},\ \{*\}}$$
$$G_1 \longrightarrow Alice \boxed{\{*\},\ \{*\}}$$

And the effective permissions at the disposal of user *Alice* are $\{a\}$, upon positional intersection of permissions present in the CERTIFICATE chain;

$$\text{static } permissions = \{a,b,c\} \cap \{a,b\} \cap \{a\} \cap \{*\} = \{a\}$$
$$and, \text{ dynamic } permissions = \{\ \} \cap \{*\} \cap \{*\} \cap \{*\} = \{\ \}$$

Should A_1 decide *Alice* to avail permission b, G_2 issues the following to *Alice*

$$G_2 \longrightarrow Alice \boxed{\{b\}, \{*\}} \tag{6}$$

Having shown the CERTIFICATE chain construction and evaluation of effective permissions due to the chain, we would like to show you how each principal in the authorization hierarchy can amplify or degrade effective rights of *Alice*.

5.1 Rights Amplification

Rights (alternatively referred as permissions or authorizations) can be amplified, that is, extra permissions can be added to the existing permission-set, by either resource controller or collaboration administrators (on either side of the collaboration). The only condition for rights amplification is the entity performing amplification operation itself should have the permission to be amplified. Following are the three instances of rights amplification that amplify the rights of *Alice*.

By resource controller. Resource controller is the fundamental authority to decide the actual set of permissions possible over the resource. Let m be a new permission that resource controller wants to make available to its collaborators. To do so, the resource controller updates its ACL (CERTIFICATE) with the following.

$$R_2 \longrightarrow A_2 \boxed{\{a,b,c\}, \{m\}} \tag{7}$$

Therefore, the authorization proof (CERTIFICATE chain) by *Alice* for accessing R_2 in domain D_2 becomes;

$$R_2 \longrightarrow A_2 \boxed{\{a,b,c\}, \{m\}}$$
$$A_2 \longrightarrow A_1 \boxed{\{a,b\}, \{*\}}$$
$$A_1 \longrightarrow G_1 \boxed{\{a\}, \{*\}}$$
$$G_1 \longrightarrow Alice \boxed{\{*\}, \{*\}}$$

And the effective permissions at the disposal of *Alice* are $\{a,m\}$, because;

$$static\ permissions = \{a,b,c\} \cap \{a,b\} \cap \{a\} \cap \{*\} = \{a\}$$
$$and,\ dynamic\ permissions = \{m\} \cap \{*\} \cap \{*\} \cap \{*\} = \{m\}$$

By host domain administrator. A_1 can perform rights amplification for *Alice* by issuing the following CERTIFICATE.

$$A_1 \longrightarrow G_1 \boxed{\{a,b\}, \{*\}} \tag{8}$$

Therefore, the authorization proof (CERTIFICATE chain) by *Alice* for accessing R_2 becomes;

$$R_2 \longrightarrow A_2 \boxed{\{a,b,c\}, \{\ \}}$$

$$A_2 \longrightarrow A_1 \boxed{\{a,b\}, \{*\}}$$

$$A_1 \longrightarrow G_1 \boxed{\{a,b\}, \{*\}}$$

$$G_1 \longrightarrow Alice \boxed{\{*\}, \{*\}}$$

And the effective permissions at the disposal of *Alice* are $\{a,b\}$, because;

$$\text{static } permissions = \{a,b,c\} \cap \{a,b\} \cap \{a,b\} \cap \{*\} = \{a,b\}$$
$$and, \text{ dynamic } permissions = \{\} \cap \{*\} \cap \{*\} \cap \{*\} = \{\}$$

By peer domain administrator. A_2 can perform rights amplification for the users from its collaborating domain by issuing the following CERTIFICATE

$$A_2 \longrightarrow A_1 \boxed{\{a,b,c\}, \{*\}} \tag{9}$$

Of course, this amplification will not be reflected in domain D_1 until D_1 does further rights amplification.

5.2   Rights Degradation

In this sub-section we show rights degradation, which is similar to rights amplification but the permissions will be removed from the existing set of permissions available to the principal that is performing rights degradation. Before proceeding to the examples of rights degradation let us bring back the CERTIFICATE states to the pre-amplification steps performed in previous sub-section.

By resource controller. As mentioned before, resource controller is the fundamental authority to decide the actual set of permissions possible over the resource. Let a be the permission that resource controller wants to make unavailable to its collaborators. To do so, the resource controller updates its ACL (CERTIFICATE) with the following.

$$R_2 \longrightarrow A_2 \boxed{\{b,c\}, \{\}} \tag{10}$$

Therefore, the authorization proof (CERTIFICATE chain) by *Alice* for accessing the resource R_2 becomes;

$$R_2 \longrightarrow A_2 \boxed{\{b,c\}, \{\}}$$

$$A_2 \longrightarrow A_1 \boxed{\{a,b\}, \{*\}}$$

$$A_1 \longrightarrow G_1 \boxed{\{a\}, \{*\}}$$

$$G_1 \longrightarrow Alice \boxed{\{*\}, \{*\}}$$

And the effective permissions at the disposal of *Alice* are $\{\}$, because;

$$\text{static } permissions = \{b,c\} \cap \{a,b\} \cap \{a\} \cap \{*\} = \{\}$$
$$and, \text{ dynamic } permissions = \{\} \cap \{*\} \cap \{*\} \cap \{*\} = \{\}$$

By host domain administrator. A_1 can perform rights degradation for *Alice* by issuing the following CERTIFICATE

$$A_1 \longrightarrow G_1 \boxed{\{\,\}, \{*\}} \tag{11}$$

Therefore, the authorization proof (CERTIFICATE chain) by *Alice* for accessing R_2 becomes;

$$R_2 \longrightarrow A_2 \boxed{\{a,b,c\}, \{\,\}}$$
$$A_2 \longrightarrow A_1 \boxed{\{a,b\}, \{*\}}$$
$$A_1 \longrightarrow G_1 \boxed{\{\,\}, \{*\}}$$
$$G_1 \longrightarrow Alice \boxed{\{*\}, \{*\}}$$

And the effective permissions at the disposal of *Alice* are { }, because;

$$\text{static } permissions = \{a,b,c\} \cap \{a,b\} \cap \{\,\} \cap \{*\} = \{\,\}$$
$$and, \text{ dynamic } permissions = \{\,\} \cap \{*\} \cap \{*\} \cap \{*\} = \{\,\}$$

By peer domain administrator. A_2 can make use of rights degradation facility to achieve an important aspect required in collaboration – temporary suspension of collaboration. To do so, A_2 issues the following CERTIFICATE

$$A_2 \longrightarrow A_1 \boxed{\{b\}, \{\,\}} \tag{12}$$

Therefore, the authorization proof (CERTIFICATE chain) by *Alice* for accessing R_2 is;

$$R_2 \longrightarrow A_2 \boxed{\{a,b,c\}, \{*\}}$$
$$A_2 \longrightarrow A_1 \boxed{\{b\}, \{\,\}}$$
$$A_1 \longrightarrow G_1 \boxed{\{a\}, \{*\}}$$
$$G_1 \longrightarrow Alice \boxed{\{*\}, \{*\}} \tag{13}$$

And the effective permissions at the disposal of *Alice* are { }, because;

$$\text{static } permissions = \{a,b,c\} \cap \{b\} \cap \{a\} \cap \{*\} = \{\,\}$$
$$and, \text{ dynamic } permissions = \{*\} \cap \{\,\} \cap \{*\} \cap \{*\} = \{\,\}$$

Several combinations of rights amplification and degradation can be engineered by resource controller and corresponding domain administrator, independently or collectively to achieve desired effects in the availability of permissions to the users from collaborating domain.

5.3   Rights Suspension

This operation is a special instance of rights degradation. The resource controller can take down the resource temporarily for various reasons by issuing the following CER-TIFICATE.

$$R_2 \longrightarrow A_2 \boxed{\{\ \}, \{\ \}} \tag{14}$$

Based on the internal dynamics (state changes) of the domain sharing resources, domain administrators can roughly estimate life expectancy (certificate validity period) of CERTIFICATES at different hierarchy levels. We assume that domain administrators issue/revoke *InterAC* certificates to users and resources. The domain administrators are also responsible to initiate the collaboration (by issuing authorization certificate to peer domain administrator). We also assume that the semantics of permissions embedded inside the *InterAC* certificate issued for collaboration initiation is agreed upon. PKI Resource Query Protocol (PRPQ) [22] is a promising utility for seamless, dynamic integration of resources across independent administrative domains.

6   Chain Composition and Evaluation

In this section we provide an algorithm to compute a valid CERTIFICATE chain. We assume that the users of a collaborative domain have been made available with the set of CERTIFICATES that affect the permission-set of the user. The onus of authorization proof generation is on the requester of the resource. We continue referring to principals (R_2, A_1, *Alice*, etc.) from the scenarios presented in previous sections.

Composition of CERTIFICATE chain: Authorization proof construction (performed by requester)

> **CERTIFICATE validation** – Discard CERTIFICATES whose validity has expired or stand revoked.

> **Filter CERTIFICATES** – Include CERTIFICATES containing the permission for which request is being made in its authorization string. Discard CERTIFICATES with $\{\ \}, \{\ \}$ in its authorization string (i.e., empty static and dynamic permission-sets).

> **Construct directed graph** – For each principal (issuer or subject of a certificate) add a vertex to the graph. For each CERTIFICATE put a directed edge originating in the "issuer" vertex and ending in "subject" vertex.

> **Find path** – Find all possible paths starting in the vertex denoted by the principal "resource controller" (i.e., R_2) and terminating in the vertex denoted by the principal "requester" (i.e., *Alice*)

> **Purge paths** – Discard paths in which the positional intersection of the permission under consideration leads to an empty set
> If no paths are left after **Purge paths** step, a valid authorization proof is not available.

Evaluation of CERTIFICATE chain: Authorization proof verification (performed by verifier)

> **CERTIFICATE validation** – Check CERTIFICATES in authorization proofs for their validity and revocation status.

Intersection – Take positional intersection over the authorization strings present in the CERTIFICATES of the authorization proofs.

Access will be granted with effective permissions evaluated upon positional intersection.

7   Comparative Analysis

In this section we would like to compare our mechanism with a mechanism that does not treat permissions as we do. The closest contender of such an approach is the X.509 attribute certificate framework defined in [11] that provides the foundation upon which the Privilege Management Infrastructure (PMI) can be built. This framework has been the most commonly used approach to realize inter-domain authorizations.

The PMI approach for inter-domain authorization has following shortcomings: i) size of ARL (attribute revocation list) keeps on growing as the number of collaborating domains of a host domain go on increasing when the state of collaborating domain changes. ii) each collaborating domain of a host domain necessitates issuance of attribute certificates to the users of host domain – collaboration-specific certificates that expire upon completion of collaboration and may be added to ARL. iii) such an approach of embedding exact set of permission-set into user's certificate leaves no scope for later rights amplification or degradation. iv) and, lack of functional autonomy and manageability.

Intuitively, under *InterAC* the number of users in peer domain do not *proportionally* influence the cost of any operation performed towards collaboration. That is, the cost to establish/break a collaboration or to do rights amplification/degradation/suspension is constant.

Table 1 compares our approach with the traditional PMI approach using the example discussed in Sect. 4, as a test-bed; where n is the number of collaborating users and h is the length of CERTIFICATE chain or depth of authorization flow hierarchy. We assume that A_1 already issued the appropriate certificates to its users and that there has been no previous interaction between domains D_1 and D_2. The comparison also assumes that the "push" model is adopted for the PMI [12]. The computational cost introduced by *InterAC* on resource R_2 is greater than the computational cost in traditional PMI. This is because, in PMI the authorizations are asserted in one or few attribute certificates, while in our approach the authorizations must be calculated by positional intersection of the authorizations contained in the CERTIFICATE chain. The actual computational overhead is given in Appendix A. We feel the cost overhead is justifiable given the numerous advantages our mechanism brings in for collaboration.

7.1   *InterAC* in Perspective of Policy-Based Mechanisms

To facilitate collaboration among independent administrative domains, two other distinct research tracks exist: i) policy-based languages (e.g., [3, 4, 5, 6]) that allow to capture collaboration requirements, and ii) extensions to RBAC model (e.g., [23, 24, 1, 7, 8, 9]). These approaches have more expressive power as compared to *InterAC*. We

Table 1. *InterAC* vs. PMI-based mechanisms *w.r.t.* certificate issuance/verification/revocation cost to a collaborating domain

	InterAC	**PMI-based mechanisms**
Cost of collaboration initiation	$O(1)$ Issuance of certificate by a domain administrator to peer domain's administrator. It is assumed that collaboration-independent *InterAC* certificates have been already issued in participating domains.	$O(n)$ [a] Since the authorization certificates are specific to a collaboration, new certificates need to be issued each time a new collaboration is initiated.
Cost of incoming authorization request verification	$O(h)$ [b]	$O(1)$
Cost of rights amplification or degradation	$O(1)$	$O(n)$
Cost of rights suspension	$O(1)$	$O(n)$ - by revoking all user certs $O(1)$ - by updating the resource ACL, which also disables the access to the resource for users in host domain
Cost to revert to pre-collaboration state	$O(1)$	$O(n)$

[a] n – number of participating users from a collaborating domain.
[b] h – authorization hierarchy or length of the CERTIFICATE chain.

say so because *InterAC* does not provide a language to capture context-aware decisions, neither it provides fancy constructs like separation-of-duty as under RBAC family. We refrained from devising an accompanying language in our proposal because all the above mentioned policy/model-based proposals face interoperability issues. We observe that the minimum common that the administrative domains willing to collaborate have is a PKI (digital certificates). *InterAC* provides the basic requirements of collaboration purely through non-intrusive certificate extension. The policy/model-based mechanisms for collaboration use digital certificates as assertions and take access control decisions based on such set of assertions and plausibly other contexts. The *InterAC* certificates can also be used as assertions thus enriching the higher level policy/model-based approaches.

8   Conclusion

In this paper, we have argued that it is possible to realize flexible inter-domain authorizations within the X.509 specifications, which is the most widely deployed type of PKI across the industry. We have shown how our X.509 extension helps collaborators maintain their functional autonomy. The use of $\{*\}, \{*\}$ as an authorization string in leaf certificates allow users to participate in any collaboration initiated by its domain, thus reducing the number of certificates a user need to maintain, obviously reducing the size of CRL. The feature of rights amplification and degradation was not possible under any other X.509-compatible approach. The ability to quickly initiate/break collaborations while maintaining domain's functional autonomy is specially very useful for ephemeral collaborations. The performance analysis of our implementation showed that the additional cost introduced by our proposal is usually negligible compared to the benefits *InterAC* offers.

In RBAC framework, a role is a set of permissions. Therefore, the treatment we provide to permissions in our approach can be easily extended to roles when the collaborating domains have RBAC as their underlying access control framework. The static and dynamic permission sets can be further supplemented with an additional set whose members may carry semantics for context-aware, exception-tolerating authorization.

Acknowledgements. The authors would like to thank the anonymous reviewers of EuroPKI 2009 workshop and the shepherd Massimiliano Pala for providing useful comments, observations, and suggestions that helped us in improving the paper.

References

1. Linn, J., Nyström, M.: Attribute certification: an enabling technology for delegation and role-based controls in distributed environments. In: RBAC 1999: Proc. of the 4th ACM workshop on Role-based access control, pp. 121–130 (1999)
2. Blaze, M., Feigenbaum, J., Strauss, M.: Compliance Checking in the PolicyMaker Trust Management System. In: Hirschfeld, R. (ed.) FC 1998. LNCS, vol. 1465, pp. 254–274. Springer, Heidelberg (1998)
3. Blaze, M., Feigenbaum, J., Ioannidis, J., Keromytis, A.: The KeyNote Trust-Management System Version 2. RFC 2704, IETF (1999)
4. Security Assertion Markup Language. OASIS Std (2005),
   http://www.oasis-open.org/committees/security
5. eXtensible Access Control Markup Language. OASIS Std (2005),
   http://www.oasis-open.org/committees/xacml
6. Web Services Security v1.1: (OASIS standards)
   http://www.oasis-open.org/specs/index.php#wssv1.1
7. Joshi, J.B.D., Bhatti, R., Bertino, E., Ghafoor, A.: Access-control language for multidomain environments. IEEE Internet Computing 8(6), 40–50 (2004)
8. Li, N., Mitchell, J.C., Winsborough, W.H.: Design of a role-based trust-management framework. In: Proceedings of the 2002 IEEE Symposium on Security and Privacy, pp. 114–130. IEEE Computer Society Press, Los Alamitos (2002)
9. Li, N., Mitchell, J.C., Winsborough, W., Seamons, K., Halcrow, M., Jacobson, J.: RTML: A Role-based Trust-management Markup Language. Technical report (Purdue University)
10. Patil, V., Shyamasundar, R.K.: Towards a Flexible Access Control Mechanism for E-Transactions. In: EGCDMAS 2004: International Workshop on Electronic Government, and Commerce: Design, Modeling, Analysis and Security, INSTICC, pp. 66–81 (2004)
11. ITU X.509 Recommendations: Information technology - Open Systems Interconnection - The Directory: Public-key and attribute certificate frameworks (2005),
   http://www.itu.int/rec/T-REC-X.509/en

12. Farrell, S., Housley, R.: An Internet Attribute Certificate Profile for Authorization. RFC 3281, IETF (2002)
13. Chadwick, D.W., Otenko, A.: The PERMIS X.509 Role Based Privilege Management Infrastructure. In: SACMAT 2002: Proc. of ACM Symp. on Access Control Models & Tech., pp. 135–140 (2002)
14. Thompson, M., Johnston, W., Mudumbai, S., Hoo, G., Jackson, K., Essiari, A.: Certificate-based Access Control for Widely Distributed Resources. In: 8th USENIX Security Symp., pp. 215–228 (1999)
15. Jonscher, D., Dittrich, K.R.: Argos – Configurable Access Control System for Interoperable Environments. In: Proc. of the 9th annual IFIP TC11 WG11.3 working conf. on Database security IX: status and prospects, pp. 43–60. Chapman & Hall Ltd, Boca Raton (1996)
16. Shibboleth (2005), http://shibboleth.internet2.edu/
17. CAS - Community Authorization Service. The Globus Alliance, http://www.globus.org/grid_software/security/cas.php
18. Kang, M.H., Park, J.S., Froscher, J.N.: Access Control Mechanisms for Inter-organizational Workflow. In: SACMAT 2001: Proc. of ACM Symp. on Access Control Models & Tech., pp. 66–74 (2001)
19. Ferraiolo, D.F., Sandhu, R.S., Gavrila, S.I., Kuhn, D.R., Chandramouli, R.: Proposed NIST Standard for Role-based Access Control. ACM Trans. on Info. and Sys. Sec. 4(3), 224–274 (2001)
20. Herzberg, A., Mass, Y., Michaeli, J., Ravid, Y., Naor, D.: Access Control Meets Public Key Infrastructure, Or: Assigning Roles to Strangers. In: SP 2000: Proc. of the IEEE Symp. on Security and Privacy, pp. 2–14 (2000)
21. Shands, D., Yee, R., Jacobs, J., Sebes, E.J.: Secure Virtual Enclaves: Supporting Coalition use of Distributed Application Technologies. ACM Trans. Inf. Syst. Secur. 4(2), 103–133 (2001)
22. PRPQ: (OpenCA PKI Project)
23. Cohen, E., Thomas, R.K., Winsborough, W., Shands, D.: Models for coalition-based access control (CBAC). In: SACMAT 2002: Proc. of ACM Symp. on Access Control Models & Tech., pp. 97–106 (2002)
24. Chadwick, D., Dimitrakos, T., Dam, K.K.V., Randal, D.M., Matthews, B., Otenko, A.: Multi-layer privilege management for dynamic collaborative scientific communities. In: Workshop on Grid Security Practice and Experience, Oxford, pp. II: 7–14 (2004)
25. Pearlman, L., Welch, V., Foster, I., Kesselman, C., Tuecke, S.: A Community Authorization Service for Group Collaboration. In: POLICY 2002: Proc. of the 3rd International Workshop on Policies for Distributed Systems and Networks, pp. 50–59 (2002)
26. Housley, R., Polk, T., Ford, W., Solo, D.: Internet X.509 Public Key Infrastructure Certificate and Certificate Revocation List (CRL) Profile. RFC 3280, IETF (2002)
27. Clarke, D., Elien, J.E., Ellison, C., Fredette, M., Morcos, A., Rivest, R.: Certificate Chain Discovery in SPKI/SDSI. Journal of Computer Security 9(4), 285–322 (2001)
28. Denker, G., Millen, J., Miyake, Y.: Cross-Domain Access Control via PKI. In: POLICY 2002: Proc. of the 3rd International Workshop on Policies for Distributed Systems and Networks, pp. 202–205 (2002)
29. Fisher, J.L.: Side-Effects of Cross-Certification. In: 4th PKI R&D Workshop (2005), http://middleware.internet2.edu/pki05/proceedings/fisher-cross_cert.pdf
30. Ford, W., Baum, M.S.: Secure Electronic Commerce: Building the Infrastructure for Digital Signatures and Encryption, 2nd edn. Prentice Hall, Englewood Cliffs (2002)

31. Gasti, P., Patil, V.: Interdomain Access Control (2006),
    http://www.disi.unige.it/person/GastiP/publications/interac/
32. Harrington, A., Jensen, C.: Cryptographic Access Control in a Distributed File System. In:
    SACMAT 2003: Proceedings of the eighth ACM symposium on Access control models and
    technologies, pp. 158–165. ACM Press, New York (2003)

Appendix

A   Implementation and Performance Analysis

A.1   Extension's Structure

The ASN.1 notation for our X.509v3 certificate extension is depicted in Fig. 3. Static and Dynamic are two strings which hold the permissions that are less prone (non-volatile) and more prone (volatile) to frequent modifications, respectively. Effective permissions of a certificate's subject are captured in two distinct sets. Depending upon the requirements, authorization delegation authority may include either a "$*$" or a " " (null) or a comma-separated list of permissions in any of the set. For example, static $= a, b, c$ means that the set of non-volatile permissions for the certificate's subject are $\{a, b, c\}$, where a, b and c represent three different permissions.

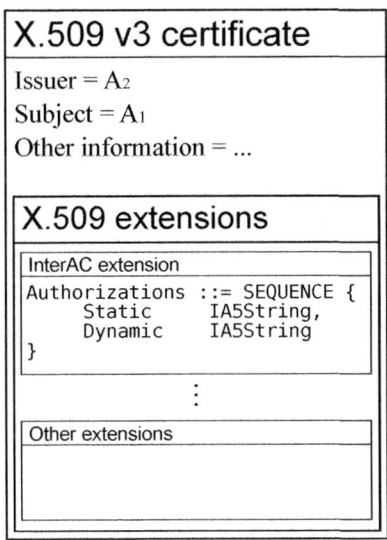

Fig. 3. Sample X.509v3 certificate with the *InterAC* extension

A.2 Performance Analysis

Our prototype implementation [31] is done in C (gcc 4.1.2) on a Pentium III (933MHz processor with 512MB RAM) hardware running GNU/Linux (kernel 2.6). The cryptographic primitives are supported by OpenSSL library (0.9.8e). The certificates used for measuring performance results are generated with 1024-bit RSA public keys. An inter-domain authorization request consists of a well-formed sequence of digital certificates as a proof of credentials. The resource controller verifies such certificate chains before granting access. The algorithm to perform verification is given in Sect. 6. The performance results of our approach against PMI-based approach is summarized in the graph shown in Fig. 4.

The graph is plotted for two different authorization proof chains consisting certificates with different extension types: i) typical authorization extension (i.e., without segregated permission-sets), and ii) our extension. The slight increase in the computational cost for our approach is justifiable by the benefits it provides. Taking a closer look at the difference between the two values we observe that it is around 1% on an average. For chains with realistic length (i.e., composed of 15 certificates or less), the actual computational cost overhead is around 0.5 ms in our operating environment.

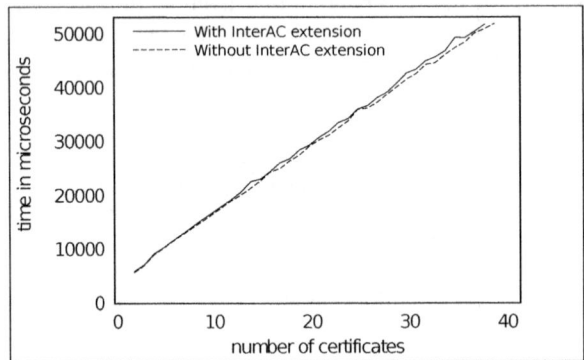

Fig. 4. Time to evaluate certificates with different types (*InterAC* and non-*InterAC*) of authorization extensions

Reducing the Cost of Certificate Revocation: A Case Study

Mona H. Ofigsbø[1], Stig Frode Mjølsnes[1], Poul Heegaard[1], and Leif Nilsen[2]

[1] Department of Telematics, NTNU, Trondheim, Norway
{monaof,sfm,poul}@item.ntnu.no
[2] Department of Informatics, UiO/Unik, Oslo, Norway
l_nilsen@unik.no

Abstract. We investigate how to reduce the cost of certificate revocation in the PKI system of UNINETT (The Internet of Norwegian Universities and Colleges), by analyzing and characterizing existing users' needs and behavior. The focus is on how to reduce the number of revoked certificates and bandwidth consumption in order to achieve better scalability. We distinguish between three main types of revocation mechanisms: list pull, list push, and short validity period. We try to find the optimal parameter values with respect to revocation method, the number of groups, group size, validity period duration, application type access, and certificate security policy. The current user categories are permanent employees, temporary employees and students. This paper analyzes the collected empirical data for how long the users actually stay in the system, and the reasons and frequency of user terminations that require certificate revocations, and then models the consequences for certificate revocation.

Keywords: Revocation schemes, scalability, architecture, policies, network aspects.

1 Introduction

The traditional public key infrastructure (PKI) is an information processing system which issues and revokes digital certificates. A typical PKI contains the components: Registration Authority (RA), Validation Authority (VA), Certificate Authority (CA) and end entity. The process is that the end user requests a certificate from RA which verifies and registers the user information before the certificate's request is sent to CA. CA issues, revokes and signs the digital certificate which binds the end user's public key and ID. VA replaces parts of CA by validating the certificates. The certificates are valid until the lifetime expires or the certificates are revoked. This means that the certificate revocation is necessary when the private key is compromised, CA is compromised, job resignation, or names/IDs change. Revocation scheme is important in a PKI system and must prevent bottlenecks in the network. Additionally, the revocation schemes have challenges as availability, correctness and freshness of the certificate revocation information.

F. Martinelli and B. Preneel (Eds.): EuroPKI 2009, LNCS 6391, pp. 51–66, 2010.
© Springer-Verlag Berlin Heidelberg 2010

Many revocation schemes have been proposed since the Mitre report was published in 1994 [1]. The most common method is Certificate Revocation List (CRL), other variants of CRL has been proposed such as Segmented CRL, Delta CRL, Redirect CRL, CRL Distribution Points, Indirect CRL, End-entity Public-key Certificate Revocation Lists (EPRLs) or Certification Authority Revocation Lists (CARLs) [2]. These mechanisms are often called push: in which the relying parties or end entities periodic retrieve lists of revocation information from CA. The drawbacks with these mechanisms are the scalability and the high costs [2,3,4,5]. Various periodic publication schemes have been proposed to be more scalable than CRL like Distribution point (Partitioned CRL) [2,4]. Pull mechanisms which are online based, require online access to a trusted third party. It is hard to reach in a large scale system which makes often use of the certificates. Examples of pull schemes are NOVOMODO, OCSP, CRT [2,6]. In addition to pull and push schemes, we have short validity period which are a validation scheme based only on the certificate's lifetime. These certificates are good until expiry date [2]. The drawback is when the private key becomes compromised. The certificate will not be revoked before the lifetime is expired. However, the choice of revocation mechanism; pull, push or short validity period depends on the PKI applications and environments. There are no revocation schemes which have met the freshness and performance requirements for all applications and environments [5].

Previous researches have analyzed and derived the probability function of certificate revocation request based both on theoretical and empirical data. Cooper [3] presented models for distributing of revocation information using CRLs, Segmented CRL and Over-issued CRL for any particular environment. The focus was to minimize the peak loads on the repository. Both Segmented CRLs and Over-issued CRLs reduced the peak loads on CA and improved the response time better than the traditional CRLs.

Cvrcek [7] criticized that CRLs became very large and mentioned four reasons for that; 1) the number of issued certificates, 2) the environments, 3) the period of certificate's lifetime and 4) the certificate owners' activity.

Årnes [4] analyzed and compared existing schemes for certificate revocation in some scenarios. The analysis was based on criteria such as timeliness, performance, scalability, security, standard compliance, expressiveness, scheme management and on-line vs. off-line. None of the revocation schemes fulfilled all the criteria. The conclusion was that none universal revocation scheme can be expected to exist. Zheng [8] did an overlap analysis with Årnes and the differences were: Zheng focus on bandwidth and operational costs and classified the revocation schemes to help engineers to understand the schemes more clearly. Others previous research of revocation mechanisms are Wohlmacher [9] and Jain [10].

Both Cooper [3] and Årnes [4] assumed a negative exponential probability of certificate revocation request. Ma and Li [12] investigated how often a CA should release the CRLs, based on empirical data from Verisign. The goal was to balance the trade off between cost and risk to find the optimal release for CRL.

Rivest [11] proposed to eliminate the revocation lists and move the evidence from CA to the certificate's owner and acceptor. His proposition was: 1) it is the acceptor who takes the risk if something goes wrong. Therefore, the requirements have to be set by acceptor and not CA. 2) The signer has to supply the evidence the acceptor wants. 3) The best evidence to convince the acceptor is to re-issue a new certificate. 4) In many cases it will be enough to have reasonably short validity period of the certificates. McDaniel and Rubin [5] responded on the paper from Rivest and analyzed three distinct PKI environments based on theirs requirements. The three classes of applications were electronic commerce, intranet services and Internet mail and conclusion was that CRLs do not apply to all environments. The design of revocation mechanisms must be driven by the applications in the specific PKI environment.

With this background, we will investigate the amounts revoked certificates in the PKI environment of Uninett, the educational system in Norway. Our contribution is to reduce the volume of revoked certificates and bandwidth consumption to make more efficient distribution of revocation information. Therefore, we propose optimal revocation models based on different user groups such as students, temporary employees and permanent employees. For each user groups we reduce the amount of revocation by adjusting certificate lifetime, propose policies for issuing of certificates and architecture. We define the optimal revocation model when it is scalable, secure and has low cost.

The rest of the paper is organized as follows. Section 2 describes the Norwegian educational system and the reference model where the requirements for the revocation investigations are collected. Section 3 the collection of empirical data is described, followed by the analysis in section 4. The analysis is separated into three parts; students, temporary employees and permanent employees where a revocation model is proposed for each group. In section 5 is the conclusion.

2   Feide

The Norwegian colleges and universities are connected in a common network called Uninett. This network is connected to a similar network, NORDUnet (the Nordic infrastructure for research and education). NORDUnet is a partner in GEANT2 which has currently 30 European national research and education networks (NRENs) across 34 countries.

Feide is a project in Uninett which started in 2001 [13]. The members are currently six universities, fifty-two colleges, eighty-two research establishments and seven high schools. It is an identity management system on a national level for the educational system in Norway. It offers digital services to people in the educational system, currently by username and password. Uninett consider digital certificates for authentication in the system, this enforce implementation of revocation schemes.

In order to propose revocation models for Feide, it is necessary to define the framework and the requirements for the analysis.

2.1   Reference Model for Feide

We refer to IETF standardization framework [14] and do some modification,
Fig. 1. The adjustments are end entity and Feide log-in. The end entities are
the institutions such as universities, colleges or high schools. The user of a PKI
certificate belongs to an end entity with unique DN (distinguished name) in
Feide. The DN is <username@institution> and used for local applications at
their own institution as well as for national applications. Feide is a central log-in
service which establishes a SSL/TLS connection to the end users. The end users
choose the institution they belong to and the institution authenticate the users
[13]. A ticket is delivered to the Feide login-in service and the user can utilize
the Feide services.

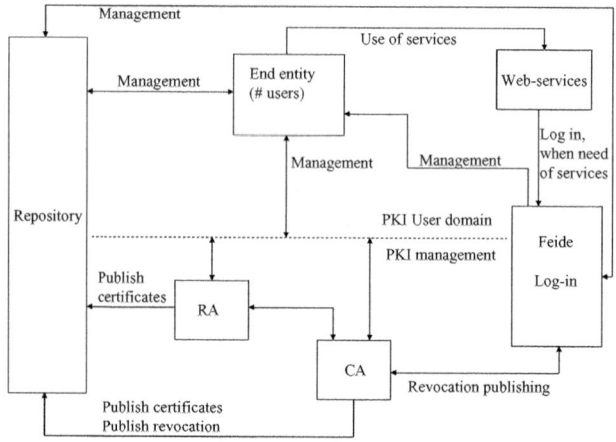

Fig. 1. Reference model for Feide

2.2   Requirements

In order to perform an analysis of revocation schemes, the criteria must be
defined and relevant for the PKI environment. The focus will be the three requirements: security, cost and scalability.

   Security: In general, the security properties of the revocation schemes shall
not be weaker than the rest of the system. The authenticity and integrity are
ensured when a trusted entity has signed the revoked information. Freshness is
the time between the actual revocation and when the revocation information is
available to the end entities.

   Cost: The bandwidth and operating costs are important consideration. The
bandwidth cost is link capacity between CA and relying parties. The operating
cost is the maintaining of revocation information on CA, the repository, renewing
and issuing of certificates.

Scalability: The revocation schemes must scale to European countries and wield the number of certificate users, end entities, revocation information and prevent the bottlenecks in the network. The revocation information must be distributed in a bandwidth efficient way.

3   Empirical Data

The analysis is based on empirical data which is collected from the database for higher education [15]. The end users are: teachers, part-time teachers, visiting lectures, professors, students, PhD students, administration staff and other staff. We propose to classify the end users into three categories: 1) students, 2) temporary employees (e.g. visiting lectures, PhD students) and 3) permanent employees (e.g. teachers, professors, administration staff). The number of students (S), temporary employees (T_emp), permanent employees (P_emp), new registered students (N) and students who finish their study program (P) is collected and presented in Table 1. The notation is listed in Table 2.

Table 1. Students and employees

i	N_i	S_i	P_i	P_emp_i	T_emp_i
03/04	68519	208504	59623	18783	8510
04/05	70729	209496	56552	18974	8924
05/06	70453	208863	57227	19253	9306
06/07	72012	205414	56732	19695	9448
07/08	72444	209009	56323	20421	9885

Table 2. Notation

Parameter	Meaning of Parameter
S	The number of students
M	Master students
B	Bachelor students
A	Students on annual programs
O	Other students on two years programs
T_emp	Temporary employees
P_emp	Permanent employees
P	Numbers of students who finish a study program
N	New students
i	Study year (autumn and spring semester)
n	Counter
E	Number of End Entities within a member in European student Union
#Uni_Rev	Number of revocation when uniform distributed
#NegExp_Rev	Number of revocation when neg exp distributed

4   Analysis

We analyze the revocation mechanisms based on the three requirements (security, scalability and cost) for each of the three user categories (S, T_emp, P_emp). These user categories behave differently: they stay in the system for various periods, apply different Web-services and have different reasons for revoking the certificates. These are important parameters for the design of revocation schemes. The three revocation mechanisms are: push which provide retrieving of revocation information lists from CA, pull mechanisms which are on-demand validation of the certificates and short validity period which is certificates with short lifetime without any validation of the certificates.

4.1   Students

In Norway, the students apply for a specific study program (P): annual program (A), two-year program (O), three-year program (B) or five-year program (M). In order to find a formula for S, we suggest:

$$S_i = A_i + O_i + B_i + M_i, \tag{1}$$

where A_i, O_i, B_i, M_i is shown in (Table 3), [16];

Table 3. Students per study programs

i	A_i	O_i	B_i	M_i
03/04	60466	27106	91742	29190
04/05	61757	26905	92040	28794
05/06	63367	23514	92599	29383
06/07	63622	20290	93131	28371
07/08	70127	16337	94172	28373

We investigate the revocation reasons: 1) when they quit before graduating 2) they change IDs. From Tables 1 and 3, the number of students who quit before graduating varies from 16,000 to 19,000. Uninett reports that 1,000 students change IDs. This means that in the worst case 20,000 revoked certificates or 9.5% of S. The numbers of revocation for the students are expressed in the following formulas:

$$rev_{S_i} = S_i * 0.095. \tag{2}$$

and,

$$rev_{A_i} = A_i * 0.095, \quad rev_{O_i} = O_i * 0.095, \quad rev_{B_i} = B_i * 0.095 \text{ and } rev_{M_i} = M_i * 0.095 \tag{3}$$

Security. The challenge is the freshness of the revocation information, except for the pull mechanisms. Those are online on-demand validation-based systems which ensure freshness.

The push mechanisms ensure the integrity or authenticity by using a digital signature on the revocation lists, in which the relying party verifies the lists. The signer of the revocation list is the same CA signer who signs the certificates in the list, except for indirect CRL. The freshness depends on how often the relying parties retrieve the revocation information.

For short lifetime validation certificates the freshness depends on the validity period of the certificates. The vulnerability is if someone else uses the certificate after it is revoked. This vulnerability depends on the Web-services. For instance, using the Web-services for e-voting or obtaining student loan has a high risk if someone else uses the certificate, but borrowing books from the library is not that critical. For services that require strong security, the solution can be supplementary protocols or policies. Example of that can be non-repudiation protocol for services that require strong authentication such as e-voting. Another example can be policy such as connecting the name of the certificate owner to the owner's home address and correct bank account for supporting the services that require strong security such as the disbursement of student loan.

Scalability. The pull mechanisms are on-demand validation systems, in which the frequency of the revocation request depends on how often the students make use of the Web-services. This means that the revocation requests will increase at the same rate as students make service requests, which can cause a bottleneck between the Web service, Feide log-in and CA, see Fig. 1. Scalability suffers from this bottleneck.

The push lists can be voluminous and the retrieving from CA can cause bottlenecks in the network. This depends on the number of students and the number of revocation within the certificate's lifetime. The number of students is presented in Tables 1 and 3, and the number of revocations can be calculated based on equations 2 and 3.

We will investigate the amount of revoked certificates in different cases. The worst case is such that revocation occurs in the first year after being issued, and with a long certificate lifetime. If all students have the same lifetime period such as master students (five years), the revocation amount is approximately 98,822 revoked certificates in 2008, $(\sum_{n=1}^{5} rev_{S_{(i-n+1)}}, i=07/08)$. If the certificate's lifetime is the same as the length of the study program, the amount of revocation information is calculated to 50,424 $(rev_{A_{(i)}} + \sum_{n=1}^{2} rev_{O_{(i-n+1)}} + \sum_{n=1}^{3} rev_{B_{(i-n+1)}} + \sum_{n=1}^{5} rev_{M_{(i-n+1)}}, i=07/08)$. This is nearly 50 % less than the amount of revoked certificates when the certificate's lifetime is the same as the length of the study program (annual, two-year, bachelor and master).

The probability is very low that all revocations will occur in the first year. Therefore, we consider revocation occurrence as being either: 1) uniform distributed or 2) negative exponential distributed. A certificate's lifetime is equal to the period of the study program.

Uniform distribution is the number of revoked certificates in a study program divided by the number of study year $(rev_{A_i}, \frac{rev_{O_i}}{2}, \frac{rev_{B_i}}{3}, \frac{rev_{M_i}}{5})$, see Table 4. The total amount of revoked certificates in 2008 was 35,296.

Table 4. Revocation per study program, Uniform distribution

i	$\frac{rev_{M_{03/04}}}{5}$	$\frac{rev_{M_{04/05}}}{5}$	$\frac{rev_{M_{05/06}}}{5}$	$\frac{rev_{M_{06/07}}}{5}$	$\frac{rev_{M_{07/08}}}{5}$
03/04	555	555	555	555	555
04/05	-	547	547	547	547
05/06	-	-	558	558	558
06/07	-	-	-	539	539
07/08	-	-	-	-	539

i	$\frac{rev_{B_{03/04}}}{3}$	$\frac{rev_{B_{04/05}}}{3}$	$\frac{rev_{B_{05/06}}}{3}$	$\frac{rev_{B_{06/07}}}{3}$	$\frac{rev_{B_{07/08}}}{3}$
03/04	2905	2905	2905	-	-
04/05	-	2915	2915	2915	-
05/06	-	-	2932	2932	2932
06/07	-	-	-	2949	2949
07/08	-	-	-	-	2982

i	$\frac{rev_{O_{03/04}}}{2}$	$\frac{rev_{O_{04/05}}}{2}$	$\frac{rev_{O_{05/06}}}{2}$	$\frac{rev_{O_{06/07}}}{2}$	$\frac{rev_{O_{07/08}}}{2}$
03/04	1289	1289	-	-	-
04/05	-	1278	1278	-	-
05/06	-	-	1117	1117	-
06/07	-	-	-	964	964
07/08	-	-	-	-	776

The summary from Table 4 can be expressed in a more formally expression: *Uniform distribution*

$$\#Uni\_Rev_i = rev_{A_{(i)}} + \sum_{n=1}^{2} \frac{1}{2} * rev_{O_{(i-n+1)}} * n +$$

$$\sum_{n=1}^{3} \frac{1}{3} * rev_{B_{(i-n+1)}} * n + \sum_{n=1}^{5} \frac{1}{5} * rev_{M_{(i-n+1)}} * n. \tag{4}$$

For calculating the negative exponential distribution, we assume a different distribution for the master, bachelor and two-year programs. For the two-year programs (O), we make the assumption 2/3 of all certificate revocations will occur in the first year and 1/3 in the last year. For the bachelor's program (B), we assume that (3/6) of the certificate revocations will occur in the first year, (2/6) in the second year and (1/6) in the last year. For the master's program (M), we make the assumption that (5/15) of all revoked certificates will occur the first year, (4/15) in the second year, (3/15) in the third year, (2/15) in the

Table 5. Revocation per study program, neg. exp. distribution

i	$\frac{5*rev_{M_i}}{15}$	$\frac{4*rev_{M_{i+1}}}{15}$	$\frac{3*rev_{M_{i+2}}}{15}$	$\frac{2*rev_{M_{i+3}}}{15}$	$\frac{rev_{M_{i+4}}}{15}$
03/04	924	739	555	370	185
04/05	912	729	547	365	-
05/06	930	744	558	-	-
06/07	898	719	-	-	-
07/08	898	-	-	-	-

i	$\frac{3*rev_{B_i}}{6}$	$\frac{2*rev_{B_{i+1}}}{6}$	$\frac{rev_{B_{i+2}}}{6}$
05/06	4398	2932	1466
06/07	4424	2949	-
07/08	4473	-	-

i	$\frac{2*rev_{O_i}}{3}$	$\frac{rev_{O_{i+1}}}{3}$
06/07	1285	643
07/08	1035	-

fourth year and (1/15) in the fifth year. The total amount of revoked certificates in 2008 was $40,340 (= \#NegExp\_Rev_{07/08})$, the sum of Table 5 and $rev_{A_{07/08}}$.

For instance, a CRL contains the complete list of all revocation information until the certificate's lifetime expiry. It has been criticized to not scale [2,3,4,5]. This criticism is general and we will investigate the scalability of the CRL in our environment.

CRLs have various formats such as PEM CRL, X.509 CRL or ANSI X9.30 CRL [1]. The X.509 CRL [14,17] allows for revocation from different CAs and best represents our PKI environment. The fields in the X.509 CRL are: the issuer's distinguished name which is O (organizations name), OU (organizations unit name) and C (country)[18,19] (130 bytes [17]), the issue date (6 bytes), the date of the next issue (6 bytes) and the revoked certificate list. This means the CRL overhead is 142 bytes. The revoked certificates have serial number (20 bytes, [17]) and the revocation date (6 bytes). This means that the revocation information per revoked certificates is 26 bytes. In addition to all these fields, X.509 CRLs must be signed by the issuer's signature (256 bytes).

The bandwidth consumption for $\#Uni\_Rev_{07/08} = 35,296$ is 0.9MB and for $\#NegExp\_Rev_{07/08} = 40,340$ is 1.1 MB, (142 byte overhead + 26 byte revocation information per revoked certificates + 256 byte digital signature). This means that the transmission delay is approximately 1 second on 1 Gbps link. This is acceptable for our environment in Norway.

The challenge is scaling to all 49 members in the European students' union, a total of 10 million students. CRL size will be approximately 45 MB and 55 MB, respectively. The Geant2 research and educational network has a backbone of 2.5 Gbps and some links have a planned upgrade to 10 Gbps, except for some islands as such as Malta, Cyprus and Iceland which have only 34-310 Mbps links.

The amount of revocation information is acceptable. For instance, the Segmented CRL loads the network more than a traditional CRL. A Segmented CRL usually reduces the size of each CRL, but the size is not enough in a scalable situation. The total amount of data is larger for segmented CRL than CRL because of overhead and a digital signature on each segment. The main problem is the load of multiple revocations lists on the link to the CA. This can cause in a bottleneck between the CA and relying parties. The Multicast groups contribute to load reduction, and we will talk more about this in the cost analysis part.

For short period validation mechanism, it is two parameters which determine the period of lifetime: the amount of revocation information and the frequency of certificates renewing. For example, in the study year 07/08, there were 19886 ($rev_{S_{07/08}}$) revoked certificates with a one year lifetime for all students. This is approximately a 40 % to 50 % data reduction compare to certificates with lifetime which is the same as the length of the study program, there were 35,296 ($\#Uni\_Rev_{07/08}$) and 40,340 ($\#NegExp\_Rev_{07/08}$) revoked certificates . This can be reduced even more based on a shorter lifetime. The drawback is when the lifetime becomes too short: then 10 million students must renew their certificates often. The current students must pay the register fee every semester, and we suggest that the lifetime period should be connected to the semester.

Cost. The pull mechanisms have a high operational cost when the CA responds on each certificate status request. In addition, a CA issues the certificates. A VA can reduce this cost, but bandwidth consumption will be the same.

The costs of using push mechanisms are maintenance and the distribution of the lists. The distribution depends on, how often the relying parties retrieve the revocation data. The bandwidth cost depends on the distribution method such as the addressing type e.g. Unicast or Multicast. The maintenance of Multicast groups has an operational cost, but the gain is lower bandwidth consumption. For example, the size of CRLs is 0.9 MB when $\#Uni\_Rev_{07/08} = 35,296$ and 1.1 MB when $\#NegExp\_Rev_{07/08} = 40,340$. Uninett has 147 end entities and if all of them retrieve the revocation list, the data amount on the link to the CA will be 132.3 MB (147 end entities * 0.9 MB) and 161 MB (147 end entities * 1.1 MB). There are six universities in Uninett, and if each of them establishes a Multicast group, the amount of data on the same link will be 5.4 MB (6 relying parties * 0.9 MB) or 6.6 MB (6 relying parties * 1.1 MB). This is approximately a 95 % data reduction. The reduction increases in large scale systems with many hops and many end entities during large Multicast groups.

In addition to reducing the amount of data during Multicast groups, unnecessary revocation information should be reduced. For instance, Norwegian students in most part request for services at Norwegian universities/colleges and the Italian students requesting at the Italian universities/colleges etc. A CA domain per member reduces number of revocation distributions, from $\sum_{n=1}^{49} \sum_{m=1}^{E} End\ entity_{(n,m)}$ to $\sum_{m=1}^{E} End\ entity_m$. If members in European student Union want co-operate and use each other Web-services, the revocation lists can easily exchanged among the co-operated members. In such case the student must request for a new certificate in others CA domains.

The short validity certificates do not have any revocation costs. The only operational cost is to renew the certificates. Renewing means that all attributes of the certificate are the same except the validity period. For instance, students who only want the student discount for buying cheap train/flight tickets may never want the certificate. In those cases, policy such as requesting a certificate issuing will reduce the number of certificates in the infrastructure.

4.2 Comparison of Revocation Mechanisms for the Student Group

As shown in the previous section, the different revocation mechanisms have different properties. The summary of weaknesses based on the analysis is presented in Table 6.

Table 6. Pull, push and short lifetime validation comparison

	Pull mechanisms	Push mechanisms	Short lifetime validation
Security	Good	Freshness depends on the revocation release	Vulnerable
Scalable	Bottleneck problems	Bottleneck problems	High certificate request at CA
Cost	High operational cost	High bandwidth cost	High operational cost

The analysis makes improvements to the weaknesses of the pull, push and short validity period mechanisms, Table 6: for the pull mechanisms we propose to implement a VA to reduce the high operational costs, but it suffer from scalability. The push mechanisms have challenges such as scalability and high costs. Implementation of Multicast groups reduces the bandwidth consumption and increase scalability. Further, reduces unnecessary revocation distribution in the infrastructure by implementation of a CA per member in European student Union. For the short validity period we proposed some policies to increase the security and reduce the number of certificates.

4.3 Revocation Model for Students

The design of the revocation mechanisms is driven by the applications, the network topology and the requirements of the PKI environment. None of the three revocation mechanisms fulfill all the requirements. Pull mechanisms suffer from scalability and high costs. Push and short validity period have the challenges such as freshness, scalability and high costs, but a combination of those mechanisms will satisfy the requirements (security, scalability and costs) based on the improvements. We recommend short lifetime certificates combined with CRLs, and specify architecture, policies and network aspects:

1. The architecture:
   (a) a CA domain is a member or country in the European students' union
   (b) a VA to each CA
2. The policies:
   (a) the lifetime of certificates is equal to the semester period
   (b) issue the certificates after the registration fee is paid
   (c) the students who want access to Web-services in another CA domain must put in a request for a new certificate
3. The network aspects:
   (a) distribute the revocation lists using Multicast addressing
   (b) the Multicast group is preferred to be large, with a maximum CA domain

4.4   Employees

Public statistical databases do not have any statistics on employee resignation. The collection of empirical data is for the population at the University of Trondheim (NTNU). It is an exhaustive, non-random sample of the second largest university in Norway and PhD admissions are only at the universities. We consider the differences between the sample (NTNU) and study population in Norway [20], selection bias [21,22]. The variables of age and gender described in the sample have the same characteristics as the study population. The difference in proportion between the sample and population is measured in relative frequency. The bias for the ages is approximately 0.02 % - 2% except for the age group between 25-29, which is overestimated by 6 %. For the gender, the bias is underestimated by 10% for women compared to the overall population. The reason for this can be that NTNU has a high degree of technology studies, in which men are more highly represented than women. Therefore, the internal validity of the NTNU sample in terms of the selection bias variables of age and gender, can be generalized for all employees in the Norwegian educational system [23].

Temporary employees. The temporary employee group is presented in Table 1: temporary, part-time teachers and PhD students. We can assume 9,000-10,000 employees, in which less than 3% resign from their job or job position. This means 270-300 certificates are revoked every year.

In Norway, PhD students sign an employment contract for three or four years, but it is possible to be a PhD student for up to six years. The common criteria are that all temporary employees sign a contract for a the short-term work period with a maximum of four years. The reason for this is that after four years as a temporary government employee, you can make a claim for a permanent position.

Security. The push mechanisms assume that the revocation information is released each time an employee or employer terminates employee's contract before the lifetime of certificate is expired. Temporary employees have a termination notice of between 14 days to three months, which is a long period to prepare the registration of revocation information so it will be fresh at the revocation date.

For temporary employees who have a very short period of employment of one to two months, the short lifetime certificates can be a good option. This depends on the job position and security risk when using Web-services in the system. For instance, the cleaners do not need access to critical Web-services such as salary system, marks, account, etc. The visiting professors may need access to the student database for the marks. Job positions such as cleaners can use the short lifetime certificates, but do not offer freshness for the revocation information, though the pull mechanisms do (same analysis such as for the students).

Scalability. It is not an option to scale to European countries because of various laws and Working Environment Acts among the countries. This means the maximum amount of revocation is within a country. We can assume 1,080-1,200 revoked certificates in a four years period or 30-32 KB. In Uninett, the amount of revocation information will be 4-5 MB when using Unicast distribution to the current 147 end entities.

Cost. The operational cost depends on the certificate's lifetime, the number of revoked certificates and maintenance of the revocations information. A short lifetime increases the issuing of certificates at CA, and too long of a lifetime increases the revocation amount. For example, if the temporary employees have certificates with three years lifetime, there is 810-900 revoked certificates contra 1080-1200 revoked certificates with four years lifetime. The amount of revocations is not very large, but for each year that the lifetime increase will the amount of revocations increase approximately 25 %. Therefore, to choose an optimal lifetime is important. The lifetime should be connected to the period stated in the employment contract. In addition, the number of revoked certificates can be reduced with one CA in Uninett. For example, some professors advise students or lecture at several universities/colleges. In those cases, a CA domain should reduces unnecessary certificate issuing.

Pull mechanims have high operational cost, same evaluation of the cost as we did for the students.

Permanent employees. The number of permanent employees is shown in Table 1. We can assume 18,000 to 20,000 employees at the universities and colleges in Norway. The number of employees increases each year, but employees who resign is constant at under 5 % and smoothly distributed throughout the year. This means that revocation occurrence is uniformly distributed.

Security: The difference between temporary and permanent employees is the period of the employment contract and that the notice period starts counting on the first day of the month. The revocation information should be released on the first day of every month because of freshness. The rest of the evaluation of the security aspect will be the same as we did for the temporary employees.

Scalability. The various laws and the Working Environment Act among the countries reduces the number of certificates being issued. The amount of revocation information can be calculated to 3,000 if the certificate's lifetime is three years and 4,000 revoked certificates if the lifetime is four years. The amount of revocation information to 147 end entities is 15.3 MB with Unicast distribution, and even when merging the temporary and permanent employees, the amount of revocation information is acceptable.

Cost. The difference between temporary and permanent employees is the amount of revocation. It is three times more than amount of revocations for temporary employees, but very few revocations. Therefore, the evaluation of the cost analysis will be the same as we did for the temporary employee group.

4.5   Comparison of Revocation Mechanisms for Employee Groups

The summary of weaknesses for both employee groups are based on the analysis is presented in Table 7, except for the criteria scalability. This is because of the various laws and Working Environment Acts among the countries.

Table 7. Pull, push and short lifetime validation comparison for employee groups

	Pull mechanisms	Push mechanisms	Short lifetime validation
Security	Good	Good	Vulnerable
Cost	High operational cost	Good	High operational cost

4.6   Revocation Model for Employees

We propose to use the common architecture with the students, section 4.3. This will reduce the costs when implementing PKI in a small country such as Norway. From the analysis and Table 7, we propose common CRLs for temporary and permanent employees which will reduce the operational and bandwidth costs. The architecture, policies and network aspects based on the analysis proposes to:

1. The architecture:
   (a) common with the students
2. The policies:
   (a) the certificates are valid for the same period as the employment contract with a maximum of four years
   (b) visiting employees must issue a new certificate for the visiting CA domain
3. The network aspects:
   (a) optional between Multicast or Unicast

5   Conclusion

In this paper we have presented two revocation models based on a CRL scheme which scales. A CRL does not scale itself, but with cost reduction it does. The proposals to cost reductions are: 1) Reduce number of certificates issuing by policy. This contributes to reducing the amount of certificates and increases the scalability. 2) Reduce the number of CA domains. This reduces the unnecessary revocation distribution, the operational costs and the bandwidth costs. 3) Offer different lifetime to the different user groups in the same PKI environment. This reduces amount of revocation, the operational costs and increases the scalability. 4) Implementation of Multicast groups. Multicast sends only one transmission per link and reduces unnecessary traffic load in the network, the bandwidth cost and increase the scalability. The segmented CRLs using Unicast will distribute more loads in the network than traditional CRLs using Multicast addressing.

References

1. Berkovits, S., Chokhani, S., Furlong, J.A., Geiter, J. A., Guild J.C.: Public Key Infrastructure Study: Final Report. Produced by MITRE Corporation for NIST (1994)
2. Adams, C., Lloyd, S.: Understanding PKI - concepts, standards and deployment considerations, 2nd edn. Addison-Wesley, Reading (2003)
3. Cooper, D.A.: A Model of Certificate Revocation. In: Proceedings of the Fifteenth Annual Computer Applications Conference, pp. 256–264 (1999)
4. Aarnes, A.: Public key Certificate Revocation schemes. Degree of Sivilingeniør at NTNU, Trondheim Norway (2000)
5. McDaniel, P., Rubin, A.: A response to Can we eliminate certificate revocation lists? In: Frankel, Y. (ed.) FC 2000. LNCS, vol. 1962, pp. 245–258. Springer, Heidelberg (2001)
6. Micali, S.: NOVOMODO - scalable certificate validation and simplified PKI management. In: Proceedings - 1st annual PKI research workhop (2002)
7. Cvrcek, D.: Real-world problems of PKI hierarchy. In: Proceedings of the SPI Conference, Brno Czech, pp. 39–46 (2001)
8. Zheng, P.: Tradeoffs in certificate revocation schemes. In: ACM SIGCOMM Computer Communication Review, pp. 103–112. ACP Press, New York (2003)
9. Wohlmacher, P.: Digital Certificates: A survey of Revocation Methods. In: Proceedings of the 2000 ACM workshops on Multimedia, pp. 111–114. ACM Press, New York (2000)
10. Jain, G.: Certificate revocation - A survey Computer Science Department. University of Pennsylvania (2000)
11. Rivest, R.L.: Can we eliminate certificate revocation lists? In: Hirschfeld, R. (ed.) FC 1998. LNCS, vol. 1465, pp. 178–183. Springer, Heidelberg (1998)
12. Ma, C., Yingjiu Li, N.H.: On the Release of CRL in Public Key Infrastructure. In: Proceedings 15th Usenix Security Symposium, Vancouver Canada, pp. 17–28 (2006)
13. Feide.: FEIDE System Architecture. version 1.2 - 2007. This handbook is in Norwegian. For English, http://www.feide.no
14. Cooper, D., Santesson, S., Farrell, S., Boeyen, S., Housley, R., Polk, W.: PKIX Certificate and CRL Profile. RFC5280 (2008)
15. Database for statistic on higher degree, The ministry of Knowledge in Norway,http://dbh.nsd.uib.no/dbhvev/ (in Norwegian)
16. Survey report for higher education, The ministry of Knowledge in Norway (2009), http://www.regjeringen.no (in Norwegian)
17. Housley, R., Polk, W., Ford, W., Solo, D.: Internet X.509 Public Key Infrastructure: Certificate and Certificate Revocation List (CRL) Profile. RFC3280 (2002)

18. Zheilenga, K.: Lightweight Directory Access Protocol (LDAP): String Representation of Distinguished Names. RFC4514 (2006)
19. Sciberras, A.: Lightweight Directory Access Protocol (LDAP): Schema for User Applications. RFC 4519 (2006)
20. Kazeronni, E.A.: Population and Sample. American Journal of Roentgenology, AJR2001 177, 993–999 (2006)
21. Battacharyya, G.K., Johnson, R.A.: Statistical concepts and methods. John Wiley & Sons, Chichester (1977)
22. Sica, G.T.: Bias in Research Studies. Journal of Radiological Society of North America, Radiology 238, 780–789 (2006)
23. Fletcher, R., Suzanne: Clinical empidemiology - The essentials, 4th edn. Lippincott Williams & Wilkins (2005)

Automatic Generation of Sigma-Protocols⋆

Endre Bangerter[1], Thomas Briner[2], Wilko Henecka[3],
Stephan Krenn[4], Ahmad-Reza Sadeghi[3], and Thomas Schneider[3]

[1] Bern University of Applied Sciences, Biel-Bienne, Switzerland
endre.bangerter@bfh.ch
[2] Abraxas Informatik AG, Zürich, Switzerland
thomas.briner@gmail.com
[3] Horst Görtz Institute for IT Security, Ruhr-University Bochum, Germany
wilko.henecka@rub.de, {ahmad.sadeghi,thomas.schneider}@trust.rub.de
[4] Bern University of Applied Sciences, Biel-Bienne, Switzerland, and
University of Fribourg, Switzerland
stephan.krenn@bfh.ch

Abstract. Efficient zero-knowledge proofs of knowledge (ZK-PoK) are
basic building blocks of many cryptographic applications such as identification schemes, group signatures, and secure multi-party computation. Currently, first applications that essentially rely on ZK-PoKs are
being deployed in the real world. The most prominent example is the Direct Anonymous Attestation (DAA) protocol, which was adopted by the
Trusted Computing Group (TCG) and implemented as one of the functionalities of the cryptographic chip Trusted Platform Module (TPM).

Implementing systems using ZK-PoK turns out to be challenging,
since ZK-PoK are significantly more complex than standard crypto primitives (e.g., encryption and signature schemes). As a result, the design-
implementation cycles of ZK-PoK are time-consuming and error-prone.

To overcome this, we present a compiler with corresponding languages
for the automatic generation of sound and efficient ZK-PoK based on Σ-
protocols. The protocol designer using our compiler formulates the goal
of a ZK-PoK proof in a high-level protocol specification language, which
abstracts away unnecessary technicalities from the designer. The compiler then automatically generates the protocol implementation in Java
code; alternatively, the compiler can output a description of the protocol
in LaTeX which can be used for documentation or verification.

Keywords: Zero-Knowledge, Protocol Compiler, Language Design.

1 Introduction

A zero-knowledge proof of knowledge (ZK-PoK) is a two-party protocol between
a prover and a verifier, which allows the prover to convince the verifier that he
knows some secret values (proof of knowledge property), without the verifier

---

⋆ This work was in part funded by the European Community's FP7 projects CACE
and ECRYPT II under grant agreements no. 216499 and 216676.

F. Martinelli and B. Preneel (Eds.): EuroPKI 2009, LNCS 6391, pp. 67–82, 2010.

learning anything about them beyond what was known before the protocol run (zero-knowledge property). There are fundamental results showing that all relations in NP have ZK-PoK [1,2,3]. The corresponding protocols are of theoretical relevance, but much too inefficient to be used in practical applications.

In contrast to these generic protocols for arbitrary NP statements we concentrate on a subset of practically relevant relations that can be proven with practically efficient protocols. Essentially, all efficient ZK-PoK protocols used in practice today are based on a class of three move protocols, called Σ-protocols.

Basic Σ-protocols allow to prove knowledge of a secret preimage under a homomorphism (e.g., a discrete exponentiation or an RSA function). There are numerous variations of these preimage proofs. For instance, "AND-proofs" allow to prove simultaneous knowledge of multiple preimages under different homomorphisms. Similarly there are "OR-proofs" and proofs to show that different preimages fulfill a set of linear relations.

ZK-PoK proof techniques based on Σ-protocols play an important role in applied cryptography. In fact, many practically oriented applications use such proofs as basic building blocks. Examples therefore include identification schemes [4], interactive verifiable computation [5], group signatures [6], secure watermark detection [7], and efficient secure multiparty computation [8].

While many of these applications typically only exist on a specification level, a direction of applied research has produced first real-world applications using ZK-PoKs. One prominent example is the Direct Anonymous Attestation (DAA) protocol [9], which was adopted by the Trusted Computing Group (TCG) – an industry consortium of many IT enterprises – as a privacy enhancing mechanism for remote authentication of computing platforms. Another example is the identity mixer anonymous credential system [10], which was released by IBM into the Eclipse Higgins project, an open source effort dedicated to developing software for "user-centric" identity management.

Up to now, the design and implementation of practical ZK-PoK protocols is done "by hand". The security proofs of these protocols consist of, loosely speaking, a handful of standard arguments and tricks which are repeated in different constellations over and over again. In fact, past experiences, e.g., during the development of the previous two examples have shown the following:

– Implementation cycles of ZK-PoK are time-consuming and error-prone.
– Minor changes in the protocol specification can result in substantial implementation work, i.e., it is hard to achieve resilience against design modifications.
– Protocols are often designed by cryptographers and implemented by software engineers. The former typically are not skilled in implementation matters and the latter have a hard time understanding details and subtleties of ZK-PoK protocols, which are sometimes rather complex. This can lead to a rupture between design and implementation, resulting in implementation errors.

Our Contributions. To overcome the mentioned challenges, we have designed and implemented a language and a corresponding compiler. Given a high-level

ZK-PoK protocol specification in our language, the compiler automatically generates the implementation of the corresponding Σ-protocol.

The design of the language is inspired by the widely used Camenisch-Stadler notation [11]. It allows to specify Σ-protocols and compositions (e.g. *AND*, *OR*) thereof, while it abstracts away details that are unnecessary at a protocol design level. Since the Camenisch-Stadler notation is informal and incomplete, our language contains additional elements, denoting, e.g., the algebraic setting in which the proofs are carried out.

ZK-PoK protocol specifications in this language are then translated by the compiler either into Java or LaTeX code. The group operations in the generated code are expressed in terms of abstract interfaces. This allows users of the code to plug their preferred libraries or favorite algebraic groups into the protocol code by implementing our abstract interfaces. The LaTeX code can be used for documenting the protocols and also for verification purposes. To the best of our knowledge, this is the first compiler suite to support automatic generation of sound ZK-PoK protocols.

The current version of the compiler allows to generate a large number of protocols found in the literature, including Pedersen Commitments/Verifiable Secret Sharing [12], Schnorr Authentication/Signatures [4], proof showing that a number is the product of two safe primes [5], Electronic Cash [13,14,15], Group Signatures [16], and Ring Signatures [17]. Also supported are ZK-PoKs of a plaintext corresponding to a ciphertext or relations between plaintexts under various asymmetric encryption schemes such as, RSA [18], Paillier [19], or Damgård-Jurik [20]; these homomorphic encryption schemes are widely used in e-voting and secure multiparty computation.

The existing theory and collection of ZK-PoK proof techniques using Σ-protocols is vast, and a satisfactory unified theory underlying these techniques is missing. In fact, for some of these techniques it is not clear whether and how they can be combined in a modular way. To design the input language and compiler on solid theoretical grounds, we have put together a unified framework of existing proof techniques. This framework is simple to understand, modular and encompasses a large number of existing ZK-PoK. The basis of the framework are simple proofs of knowledge of preimages under homomorphisms. For these basic proofs, we have incorporated the theory by Cramer [21] on special homomorphisms, which are essentially homomorphisms with a known order codomain as well as RSA and Paillier-type of homomorphisms. Our framework then describes how the basic protocols can be composed to obtain "AND" and "AND-OR" proofs, and to prove linear relations among preimages.

Related Work. This paper describes ongoing work on the zero-knowledge compiler initiated by [22] which focused mainly on the implementation details of the compiler. The motivation for having a compiler framework for zero-knowledge protocols was described in [23]. In this paper we describe the underlying theoretical framework and how to use the fixed and slightly extended (e.g., native support of groups $\mathbb{Z}_n^*$) compiler based on a concrete running-example. An earlier draft of this paper was presented at the poster session of Eurocrypt 2009 [24].

An analysis of Σ-protocols for special homomorphisms can be found in [21], and the used composition rules are explained in [17]. A first framework for Boolean formulae containing linear relations was done by Brands [25] and extended in [26] to a larger class of predicates. The idea underlying our proofs for linear relations is the same as in [27]. A unified theory for exponentiation homomorphisms in arbitrary groups has recently been published [28] which we plan to incorporate into future versions of the compiler. Yet, this does not influence proofs for special homomorphisms, for which our compiler is currently designed.

In principle, zero-knowledge can be obtained from secure multiparty computation (SMPC) by evaluating the corresponding verification relation securely [2]. While this allows to prove arbitrary NP statements in zero-knowledge in communication and computation complexity which is linear in the circuit size, this approach is limited in practice by the circuit size (today's implementations of generic SMPC techniques can evaluate circuits with a few million gates only [8,29,30]). The Σ-protocols generated by our compiler are much more efficient but limited to a smaller, yet useful, class of statements that can be proven.

Provably secure protocols for two-party secure function evaluation (SFE) based on homomorphic encryption [31] respectively circuits [29,32,33] can be generated automatically. Similar to what our compiler does in the context of ZK-PoK protocols, these compilers allow to specify the function to be evaluated in a high-level language and automatically compile this into an executable protocol. In order to achieve security against malicious participants, cut-and-choose techniques together with efficient zero-knowledge proofs are added to prove that parties behave honestly [8,34]. Recently, highly efficient protocols combining subprotocols based on homomorphic encryption with such based on circuits were proposed. To secure the conversion between both domains against malicious players they make use of efficient ZK-PoK [35]. Our compiler can be used to generate these ZK-PoK protocols at the interfaces between different protocols.

A specification language at the implementation level of cryptographic primitives is Cryptography Aware Language and Compiler (CAO) [36]. This framework provides compiler support for efficient and secure implementation of cryptographic primitives resistant against software side-channels [37] and applications to elliptic curve cryptography [38]. In future versions of our compiler we plan to automatically generate implementations of our generated protocols also in CAO.

Overall, our compiler for automatic generation of sound ZK-PoK protocols can be positioned in between the (high-level) compilers for secure computation [31,29,33] and the (low-level) compilers to automatically generate implementations of cryptographic primitives [36].

Outline. In §2 we describe the theoretical framework of Σ-protocols underlying our compiler. In §3 we describe the compiler and its input language. Particularly, we give a detailed example showing how our compiler can be used to prove relations among messages encrypted with the Damgård-Jurik [20] cryptosystem.

2   General Framework Description

Our compiler can be used to generate protocols for honest-verifier zero-knowledge (HVZK) proofs of knowledge of preimages under homomorphisms. These proofs can be combined arbitrarily using the Boolean operators AND and OR, which allows proving knowledge of certain subsets of preimages. Further, homogeneous linear relations among the preimages can be proven. In this section we want to briefly recap the theory underlying the compiler as well as the techniques we've implemented. After giving some basic notation and definitions in §2.1, we will formally describe the class of proofs for which the compiler produces HVZK proofs of knowledge in form of Σ-protocols in §2.2 and review the techniques we implemented together with sufficient conditions guaranteeing soundness in §2.3. Finally in §2.4 we will conclude by showing how these results can be used to prove more complex relations among the preimages, such as multiplicative or polynomial ones.

2.1   Preliminaries

By $s \in_R S$ we denote a uniform random choice of element s from set S. The cardinality of S is denoted by $\#S$. A mapping $\phi : \mathcal{G} \rightarrow \mathcal{H}$ from an additive group $(\mathcal{G}, +)$ into a multiplicative group $(\mathcal{H}, \cdot)$ is called *homomorphism*, iff for all $a, b \in \mathcal{G}$ we have $\phi(a + b) = \phi(a) \cdot \phi(b)$. By Im ϕ we denote the *image of ϕ*, i.e., Im $\phi = \{z \in \mathcal{H} : \exists w \in \mathcal{G} : z = \phi(w)\}$, which is a subgroup of $\mathcal{H}$.

Next we briefly recap the notion of zero-knowledge proofs of knowledge, and that of Σ-protocols which our compiler uses to implement them.

Let R be a binary relation and let $(x, w) \in R$, where w is a witness and x an element of the associated language L_R. Informally, a *proof of knowledge* with *knowledge error* κ for R is a pair of interactive algorithms (P, V), such that every (potentially dishonest) prover P^* who on input x can make verifier V accept with probability more than $\kappa(x)$, has to know a w', such that $(x, w') \in R$; further, V always accepts for the honest prover P. A formal definition is given in [39].

All protocols generated by our compiler are Σ-protocols. Informally, a Σ-protocol is a protocol with 3 messages being exchanged: the prover sends a *commitment* t to V, who replies with a random *challenge* c from a predefined challenge set $\mathcal{C}$. Then P computes a *response* s, which V uses to decide whether to accept or to reject the proof. The protocol must satisfy three properties: First, the verifier always accepts for an honest prover. Second, having two tuples (t, c, s), (t, c', s') with $c \neq c'$ for which the verifier accepts, it's possible to efficiently compute a witness. Finally, the protocol is HVZK. It turns out that from the form of the protocol and the first two properties, the proof of knowledge property can be implied. For a more detailed discussion of Σ-protocols see, e.g., [21].

Notation of ZK-PoKs. Using the notation introduced in [11] to denote ZK-PoKs, a term like

$$\mathsf{ZPK}\left[(\omega_1, \omega_2) : x_1 = \phi_1(\omega_1) \quad \wedge \quad x_2 = \phi_2(\omega_2) \quad \wedge \quad \omega_1 = a\omega_2\right]$$

means "*proof of knowledge of w_1, w_2 such that $x_1 = \phi_1(w_1)$, $x_2 = \phi_2(w_2)$ and $w_1 = aw_2$*". We will stick to the common convention that knowledge of variables denoted by Greek letters has to be proven, whereas all other quantities are assumed to be known to both parties, i.e. P and V. Note that this notation specifies a *proof-goal* rather than a protocol: it describes what actually has to be proven, but there may be many differently efficient protocols for the same proof-goal.

2.2   Proof-Goals Supported by Our Compiler

The compiler described in §3 can be used to generate implementations for HVZK proofs of knowledge of preimages under homomorphisms. The proofs can be combined arbitrarily using the Boolean operators "AND" and "OR", which allows proving knowledge of sets respectively subsets of preimages. Also homogeneous linear relations among the preimages can be proven.

That is, the class of proof-goals that can be handled by our compiler consists of all expressions that can be expressed in one of the following two forms:

$$\mathsf{ZPK}\left[(\omega_1, \ldots, \omega_m) : \bigvee \bigwedge y_i = \phi_i(\omega_i)\right] \tag{1}$$

or

$$\mathsf{ZPK}\left[(\omega_1, \ldots, \omega_m) : \bigwedge y_i = \phi_i(\omega_1, \ldots, \omega_m) \wedge HLR(\omega_1, \ldots, \omega_m)\right] \tag{2}$$

Here, $HLR(w_1, \ldots, w_m)$ denotes a system of homogeneous linear relations among the preimages. That is, it consists of a set of equations of the following form:

$$w_i = \sum_{j>i} a_{ij} w_j \qquad \text{with} \qquad a_{ij} \in \mathbb{Z}.$$

We want to make some remarks on the specification on the proof-goals: first, in (1), the proof-goal does not necessarily have to be given in disjunctive normal form (DNF), but also as arbitrary monotone Boolean formula, i.e. a Boolean formula containing arbitrarily many $\wedge$ and $\vee$ with predicates of the form $y_j = \phi_j(\omega_j)$. Second, in (1) as well as in (2), linear relations can also be proven *implicitly*: for instance, it's easy to see that $\mathsf{ZPK}\left[(\omega_1, \omega_2) : y = \phi(\omega_1, \omega_2) \wedge \omega_1 = 2\omega_2\right]$ is equivalent to $\mathsf{ZPK}\left[(\omega) : y = \phi(2\omega, \omega)\right]$ by setting $w := w_2$. Finally, note that the group w_i lies in can decompose into a product of groups. That is, w_i can denote a vector $(w_{i1}, \ldots, w_{ik_i})$ of elements.

2.3   Implemented Techniques and Soundness Conditions

In this section we briefly describe which techniques we implemented in our compiler, and point out when our compiler makes use of them.

AND-proofs. An *AND-proof* allows to prove knowledge of multiple preimages, i.e., it is used to prove a semantic goal like (2) without linear relations. Such a proof can be realized by considering the product homomorphism of the ϕ_i, and proving knowledge of a preimage of this as follows:

- The compiler defines $\mathcal{G} := \mathcal{G}_1 \times \cdots \times \mathcal{G}_m$, and $\mathcal{H} := \mathcal{H}_1 \times \cdots \times \mathcal{H}_m$.
- It sets $\phi : \mathcal{G} \to \mathcal{H}$, $\phi(w_1, .., w_m) := (\phi_1(w_1, .., w_m), .., \phi_m(w_1, .., w_m))$.
- Further, it defines $w := (w_1, \ldots, w_m)$ and $x := (x_1, \ldots, x_m)$.
- Finally, it performs the following proof: $\mathsf{ZPK}\big[(\omega) : x = \phi(\omega)\big]$.

AND-OR-Proofs. An *AND-OR-proof* is capable of proving knowledge of preimages corresponding to one out of a family of given subsets of $\{x_1, \ldots, x_m\}$. That is, it can be used to proof expressions like (1). In this case, the proof goal is first translated into disjunctive normal form (DNF), and then each conjunctive term is proved using the technique described before. The OR-proof is then performed using the technique of [17] based on Shamir's secret sharing scheme [40].

Linear Relations. If linear constraints occur in (2), the compiler uses a technique which is very similar to that for "AND"-proofs [27]. It is based on the observation that the set of all elements in $\mathcal{G} := \mathcal{G}_1 \times \cdots \times \mathcal{G}_m$ satisfying the linear constraints in (2) is a subgroup of $\mathcal{G}$. Thus, by denoting this set by $\hat{\mathcal{G}}$ the same technique as for AND-proofs can be used with $\hat{\mathcal{G}}$ instead of $\mathcal{G}$.

We stress that because of the form of the equation system random choices in $\hat{\mathcal{G}}$ can be drawn efficiently by forward substitution.

Sufficient conditions to guarantee soundness. It is a well known result that all Σ-protocols for preimage proofs under homomorphisms with finite domain are HVZK proofs of knowledge for the challenge set $\mathcal{C} = \{0, 1\}$ [21] . Yet, this only guarantees a knowledge error of $\kappa = 1/2$ and many repetitions are necessary to reach a sufficiently small knowledge error in most applications.

It turns out that for certain homomorphisms we can obtain much more efficient proofs, since they allow to obtain a small knowledge error in a single protocol run. Consider an homomorphism ϕ, for which a non-zero multiple v of the order of Im ϕ is known: then we have that $x^v = 1 = \phi(0)$ for all $x \in$ Im ϕ. Especially, if $\mathrm{ord}(\mathcal{H})$ is known, one can set $v := \mathrm{ord}(\mathcal{H})$. Such homomorphisms are used in [4]. The authors of [41] use power homomorphisms $\phi : \mathbb{Z}_n^* \to \mathbb{Z}_n^*, x \mapsto x^e$ where n is an RSA modulus and $e \in \mathbb{Z}$. There we have $x^e = \phi(x)$ for all x. In both cases it's feasible to find a preimage of a power of x for each $x \in$ Im ϕ. This property is caught by the following definition:

Definition 1 (Special Homomorphism [21]). *A homomorphism ϕ is called special, if there is a probabilistic polynomial time algorithm that on input ϕ : $\mathcal{G} \to \mathcal{H}$ and $x \in$ Im ϕ outputs $(u, v) \in \mathcal{G} \times \mathbb{Z} \setminus \{0\}$, such that $x^v = \phi(u)$. For a fixed ϕ, the special exponent v being output has to be the same for all x.*

Building on this definition, we get the following theorem giving conditions for the Σ-protocols produced by our compiler to be sound:

Theorem 1. *The composition techniques described above result in HVZK proofs of knowledge with knowledge error $1/\#\mathcal{C}$ for (1) or (2), if the following conditions are satisfied:*

- All ϕ_i, $i = 1, \ldots, m$ are special, and the special exponent v_i of ϕ_i satisfies $v_i \leq \max(\mathcal{C})$.
- If the preimage of ϕ_j occurs in one of the homogeneous linear relations in (2), the special exponent of ϕ_j is a non-zero multiple of the order of Im ϕ_j.

Proof (Sketch). The case of proving knowledge of only one preimage is handled in, e.g., [21,42], by using Shamir's trick. By observing that the product of special homomorphisms is again special with a special exponent equal to the product of the special exponents of its factors, the correctness of the AND-composition follows. With a similar argument, the soundness for the case of linear equations can be inferred [27]. Finally, the proof for proof goals containing ORs can be found in [17]. □

2.4   Proving More Complex Relations

Using our compiler even more complex proof goals than pure preimage proofs (optionally containing homogeneous linear relations) can be realized. On a high level, all proof goals having an equivalent representation as preimage proofs containing only homogeneous linear relations can be handled. Yet, this rewriting has to be manually by the user of our compiler. We thus illustrate on hand of two practically important classes of relations how this can be done.

Example 1 (Multiplicative Relations modulo ord(Im ϕ)). To prove knowledge of the discrete logarithms w_1, w_2, w_3 of x_1, x_2, x_3 in base g, satisfying $w_1 w_2 = w_3$ mod ord(Im ϕ) one can perform the following "AND"-proof with one implicit linear relation:

$$\mathsf{ZPK}\left[(\omega_1, \omega_2) : x_1 = g^{\omega_1} \wedge x_2 = g^{\omega_2} \wedge x_3 = x_1^{\omega_2}\right].$$

If P can convince V that he knows such w_1, w_2, it is clear that he knows the discrete logarithms of x_1 and x_2. Further, we can infer the following: $x_3 = x_1^{w_2} = (g^{w_1})^{w_2} = g^{w_1 w_2}$. Hence, P knows the discrete logarithm of x_3 in base g, and it is equal to $w_1 w_2$. That is what had to be proven.

Example 2 (Inhomogeneous Linear Relations). Inhomogeneous linear relations can easily be homogenized [25] by using the homomorphic property of ϕ: for instance, proving knowledge of w_1, w_2 such that $x_i = \phi(w_i)$, and $w_1 = w_2 + c$ for a fixed $c \in \mathcal{G}$ is equivalent to performing

$$\mathsf{ZPK}\left[(\omega) : x_1 = \phi(\omega) \wedge x_2 \cdot \phi(c)^{-1} = \phi(\omega)\right].$$

We remark that by combining these two techniques, arbitrary polynomial relations modulo the order of Im ϕ among the secret preimages can be proved. Finally, we note that proving that a certain relation is *not* satisfied, e.g., that two discrete logarithms are not equal, requires a little more effort, as no equivalent representations in form of pure preimage proofs are known for such proof goals. Thus, the source code of the last round of the verifier has to be edited, and a simple check for inequality of two values has to be added manually. For a description of techniques handling such proof goals see, e.g., [26].

In the next section we describe how our current compiler implements the described general framework and give a practical example.

3   Implementation of Our ZK-PoK Compiler

We have implemented a compiler that can automatically generate Σ-protocols according to the theoretical framework described in §2. The initial version of the compiler was started in [22,23]. In this work we describe how to use the compiler with a concrete example.[1] The compiler is used as follows (cf. Fig. 1):

- The user formulates the *Protocol Specification* of the intended Σ-protocol in our high-level *input language*. This language abstracts away all implementation details, e.g., how to combine protocols, operations performed within algorithms, or messages to be exchanged. It allows to describe all expressions of the language discussed in §2 and is inspired by the Camenisch-Stadler notation [11], but augmented so that one can actually generate code. This is impossible directly from the Camenisch-Stadler notation as it does not contain information on the underlying algebraic structures. More details on the input language will be given later in §3.1.
- Then, the *Protocol Compiler* automatically transforms this protocol specification into the corresponding implementation of the protocol.
- This protocol implementation can be output as JAVA-code which can easily be incorporated into other applications that use the corresponding ZK-PoK protocol. Alternatively, a LATEX documentation which shows the detailed steps (e.g., inputs, algorithms, operations, messages) of the protocol can be generated. The compiler was designed modularly to be easily extendible with other back-ends, e.g., to produce C-code for embedded platforms.

3.1   Input Language

Below, we describe the rationale underlying the input language and how to use it to formulate a proof goal based on the following running example:

Many protocols for secure computation use the semantically-secure, additively-homomorphic encryption scheme of Paillier [19] which was extended by Damgård and Jurik [20]. Recall, in this scheme encryption is performed as $E(m, r) = g^m \cdot r^n$ mod n^2 with message $m \in \mathbb{Z}_n$, randomness $r \in_R \mathbb{Z}_n^*$, and public key n, where n is a RSA modulus and $g := n + 1 \in \mathbb{Z}_{n^2}^*$. This scheme allows to add values under encryption, i.e., $E(a)E(b) = E(a + b)$, where the operations are performed in the ciphertext group $\mathbb{Z}_{n^2}^*$ respectively plaintext group $\mathbb{Z}_n$. This property allows to compute linear operations on ciphertexts (crypto-computing) and is used in many protocols such as [35,43,44] - just to name a few. The security against

---

[1] The compiler together with a formal syntactic definition of the input language as EBNF is available at http://zkc.cace-project.eu.

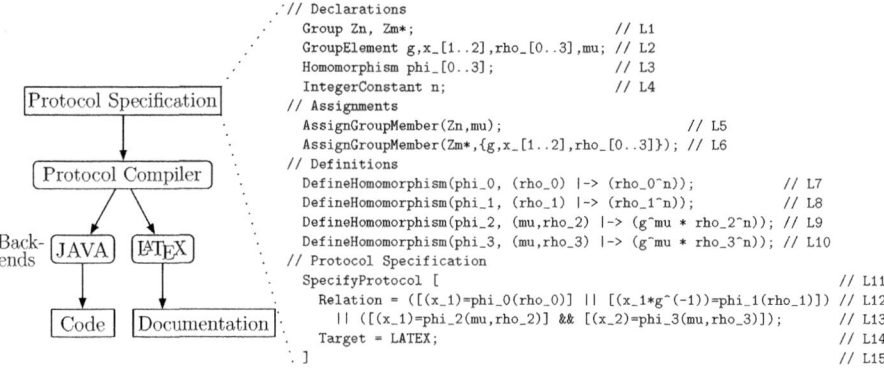

```
// Declarations
   Group Zn, Zm*;                                      // L1
   GroupElement g,x_[1..2],rho_[0..3],mu;  // L2
   Homomorphism phi_[0..3];                            // L3
   IntegerConstant n;                                  // L4
// Assignments
   AssignGroupMember(Zn,mu);                           // L5
   AssignGroupMember(Zm*,{g,x_[1..2],rho_[0..3]});  // L6
// Definitions
   DefineHomomorphism(phi_0, (rho_0) |-> (rho_0^n));            // L7
   DefineHomomorphism(phi_1, (rho_1) |-> (rho_1^n));            // L8
   DefineHomomorphism(phi_2, (mu,rho_2) |-> (g^mu * rho_2^n));  // L9
   DefineHomomorphism(phi_3, (mu,rho_3) |-> (g^mu * rho_3^n));  // L10
// Protocol Specification
   SpecifyProtocol [                                           // L11
      Relation = (([(x_1)=phi_0(rho_0)] || [(x_1*g^(-1))=phi_1(rho_1)]) // L12
         || ([(x_1)=phi_2(mu,rho_2)] && [(x_2)=phi_3(mu,rho_3)]);  // L13
      Target = LATEX;                                          // L14
   ]                                                           // L15
```

Fig. 1. Architecture and Example for Protocol Specification in Input Language

honest-but-curious adversaries of such protocols follows from the semantic security of the encryption scheme, whereas for security against malicious adversaries each party usually needs to prove in zero-knowledge that it behaved correctly.

The following example is inspired by the application scenario described above. It does not correspond to a published protocol but is rather chosen to demonstrate many features of our compiler. One party proves in ZK that a generated ciphertext x_1 is either an encryption of 0 or 1 (this need arises for example in oblivious transfer protocols based on Paillier encryption [45]), or it encrypts the same plaintext μ encrypted as another ciphertext x_2 (this could be used to prove that the encrypted message is consistent with a previous encrypted message). More formally, this proof goal is written in Camenisch-Stadler notation [11] as

$$ZPK\Big[(\mu, \rho_{0..3}) : (x_1 = E(0, \rho_0) \vee x_1 = E(1, \rho_1))$$

$$\vee(x_1 = E(\mu, \rho_2) \wedge x_2 = E(\mu, \rho_3))\Big].$$

Plugging in the explicit definitions of the encryption function yields

$$ZPK\Big[(\mu, \rho_{0..3}) : (x_1 = \rho_0^n \vee x_1 g^{-1} = \rho_1^n) \vee (x_1 = g^\mu \rho_2^n \wedge x_2 = g^\mu \rho_3^n)\Big]. \qquad (3)$$

However, the proof goal given in Camenisch-Stadler notation is not yet explicit enough for automatic generation of protocols as it is a semi-formal notation which does not contain the involved algebraic structures which is essential for the generation. For this, the input language of our compiler requires explicit Declarations of the involved algebraic objects (groups, elements, homomorphisms, constants), Assignments from group elements to the group they live in, as well as Definitions of homomorphisms which encapsulate functions with homomorphic properties as described next. In the following we refer to the line numbers (L...) of the example given in Fig. 1. These line numbers are comments which are separated with // in our input language.

Declarations (L1-L4): In the beginning the name of each group (L1), group element (L2), homomorphism (L3), and integer constant (L4) used in the protocol must be declared. As in L1, multiple elements can be separated with a comma. For convenience, multiple elements can be grouped together with array notation, e.g., in L2 where x_[1..2] is a shortcut for x_1,x_2. The integer constant n in L4 will later be set to the RSA modulus n in the implementation.

The compiler supports additive groups $(\mathbb{Z}_n, +)$ defined as Zn as well as multiplicative groups $(\mathbb{Z}_m^*, *)$ defined as Zm* (L1). The single letter following the capital Z is the name of the modulus which must be set to the corresponding value during runtime. In our example, n would be set to the RSA modulus n, whereas m would be set to n^2. Future versions of the compiler will allow to express such relations as arbitrary expressions already in the input language.

Assignments (L5-L6): Each group element declared before must be assigned to a group in this section, i.e. mu to Zn in L5. To assign multiple group elements to the same group, they can be put in curly braces (L6).

Definitions (L7-L10): As described in §2, efficient Σ-protocols can be generated to prove knowledge of preimages under homomorphisms. To allow automatic generation of such Σ-protocols, the user identifies the homomorphisms in the proof goal in equation (3) and writes it as

$$\mathsf{ZPK}\Big[(\mu, \rho_{0..3}) : (x_1 = \phi_0(\rho_0) \vee x_1 g^{-1} = \phi_1(\rho_1))$$

$$\vee (x_1 = \phi_2(\mu, \rho_2) \wedge x_2 = \phi_3(\mu, \rho_3))\Big], \qquad (4)$$

where e.g., $\phi_2 : (\mu, \rho_2) \mapsto g^\mu \rho_2^n$. This homomorphism is specified in our input language (L9), where the first parameter is the name of the homomorphism phi_2 followed by the list of preimages (mu,rho_2) and finally the mapping from preimages to images as term g^mu * rho_2^n. The compiler automatically infers domain and co-domain of the homomorphism from the involved group elements which have been assigned to groups in the Assignments section. Using this information, the compiler checks that the group operations in the mapping are written correctly to avoid errors in the input specification. In additive groups, + denotes the group-operation, and * the multiplication with a scalar. In multiplicative groups (as Zm* in the example), * and ^ are handled analogously.

Protocol Specification (L11-L15): After having declared, assigned and defined all needed components, the protocol to be generated can be specified in the SpecifyProtocol [...] block (L11-L15):

For this, the relation to be proven - rewritten to use homomorphisms (4) - is formulated one-to-one in the input language (L12-L13). Boolean compositions are written as in the C language, i.e., AND composition as && and OR composition as ||. If this expression is not explicitly given in the disjunctive normal form (DNF) as in (1) the compiler transforms it automatically into this form.

Finally, a back-end of the compiler is chosen by specifying the output target. In the example, we chose the LATEX back-end in L14 to automatically generate the LaTeX documentation given in §A from the protocol specification in Fig. 1.

Alternatively, setting the target to JAVA would produce Java source code for the generated Σ-protocol. The Java code corresponds to the algorithms of the Σ-protocol for prover and verifier (P_1, P_2, V) that can easily be integrated into user applications. Some parameters that can not yet be inferred by the compiler automatically (like the size of the challenge set) must be chosen by the user according to the theory described in §2 and provided as constructor arguments.

Yet, this does not cause much effort to the user: for instance, for every $x \in$ Im ϕ_2 we have that $(0, x)$ satisfies $x^n = \phi_2(0, x)$, and thus ϕ_2 is special with special exponent n, cf. Def. 1. The same holds for ϕ_0, ϕ_1, ϕ_3. Hence, the maximum c^+ of the challenge set has only to be chosen smaller than any prime divisor of n. But as n is an RSA-modulus, all its divisors have some hundred bits, and c^+ should have about 80 bits in practical applications. Hence, choosing $c^+ := 2^{80}$ satisfies the conditions of Th. 1, and one gets an HVZK proof of knowledge.

Easy Extendability with Further Groups: While the two most common groups $(\mathbb{Z}_n, +)$ and $(\mathbb{Z}_m, *)$ are natively supported by our toolbox already, a user can easily add arbitrary self-defined groups. This allows to easily enhance the toolbox, e.g., with groups over elliptic curves that allow high performance and are ideally suited for constraint devices such as embedded systems. To extend the compiler with such a self-defined group, the user would declare an abstract group $(G, +)$ as `Group (G,+);` in the `Declarations` part of the input language. The compiler treats this group called G as an additive group which is also output into the LaTeX documentation. The JAVA back-end automatically generates an abstract class for this group which the user can instantiate with the corresponding implementation of the operations in the intended group.

Future Work. We are currently working on a new version of the compiler which supports efficient proofs in hidden-order groups and automatic transformation of the generated Σ-protocols into non-interactive zero-knowledge proofs (NIZK).

References

1. Goldreich, O., Micali, S., Wigderson, A.: Proofs that yield nothing but their validity or all languages in NP have zero-knowledge proof systems. Journal of the ACM 38(1), 691–729 (1991), Preliminary version in FOCS 1986
2. Ishai, Y., Kushilevitz, E., Ostrovsky, R., Sahai, A.: Zero-knowledge from secure multiparty computation. In: STOC 2007, pp. 21–30. ACM Press, New York (2007)
3. Kilian, J.: A note on efficient zero-knowledge proofs and arguments (extended abstract). In: STOC 1992, pp. 723–732. ACM Press, New York (1992)
4. Schnorr, C.: Efficient signature generation by smart cards. Journal Of Cryptology 4(3), 161–174 (1991)
5. Camenisch, J., Michels, M.: Proving in zero-knowledge that a number is the product of two safe primes. In: Stern, J. (ed.) EUROCRYPT 1999. LNCS, vol. 1592, pp. 107–122. Springer, Heidelberg (1999)

6. Camenisch, J.: Group Signature Schemes and Payment Systems Based on the Discrete Logarithm Problem. PhD thesis, ETH Zurich, Konstanz (1998)
7. Adelsbach, A., Rohe, M., Sadeghi, A.-R.: Complementing zero-knowledge watermark detection: Proving properties of embedded information without revealing it. Multimedia Systems 11, 143–158 (2005)
8. Lindell, Y., Pinkas, B., Smart, N.: Implementing two-party computation efficiently with security against malicious adversaries. In: Ostrovsky, R., De Prisco, R., Visconti, I. (eds.) SCN 2008. LNCS, vol. 5229, pp. 2–20. Springer, Heidelberg (2008)
9. Brickell, E., Camenisch, J., Chen, L.: Direct anonymous attestation. In: CCS 2004, pp. 132–145. ACM Press, New York (2004)
10. Camenisch, J., Herreweghen, E.V.: Design and implementation of the idemix anonymous credential system. In: CCS 2002, pp. 21–30. ACM Press, New York (2002)
11. Camenisch, J., Stadler, M.: Efficient group signature schemes for large groups. In: Kaliski Jr., B.S. (ed.) CRYPTO 1997. LNCS, vol. 1294, pp. 410–424. Springer, Heidelberg (1997)
12. Pedersen, T.P.: Non-interactive and information-theoretic secure verifiable secret sharing. In: Feigenbaum, J. (ed.) CRYPTO 1991. LNCS, vol. 576, pp. 129–140. Springer, Heidelberg (1992)
13. Brands, S.: Untraceable off-line cash in wallet with observers. In: Stinson, D.R. (ed.) CRYPTO 1993. LNCS, vol. 773, pp. 302–318. Springer, Heidelberg (1994)
14. Chan, A., Frankel, Y., Tsiounis, Y.: Easy come - easy go divisible cash. Technical Report TR-0371-05-98-582, GTE (1998), updated version with corrections
15. Okamoto, T.: An efficient divisible electronic cash scheme. In: Coppersmith, D. (ed.) CRYPTO 1995. LNCS, vol. 963, pp. 438–451. Springer, Heidelberg (1995)
16. Camenisch, J., Lysyanskaya, A.: Signature schemes and anonymous credentials from bilinear maps. In: Franklin, M. (ed.) CRYPTO 2004. LNCS, vol. 3152, pp. 56–72. Springer, Heidelberg (2004)
17. Cramer, R., Damgård, I., Schoenmakers, B.: Proofs of partial knowledge and simplified design of witness hiding protocols. In: Desmedt, Y.G. (ed.) CRYPTO 1994. LNCS, vol. 839, pp. 174–187. Springer, Heidelberg (1994)
18. Rivest, R.L., Shamir, A., Adleman, L.: A method for obtaining digital signatures and public-key cryptosystems. CACM 21(2), 120–126 (1978)
19. Paillier, P.: Public-key cryptosystems based on composite degree residuosity classes. In: Stern, J. (ed.) EUROCRYPT 1999. LNCS, vol. 1592, pp. 223–238. Springer, Heidelberg (1999)
20. Damgård, I., Jurik, M.: A generalisation, a simplification and some applications of Paillier's probabilistic public-key system. In: Kim, K.-c. (ed.) PKC 2001. LNCS, vol. 1992, pp. 119–136. Springer, Heidelberg (2001)
21. Cramer, R.: Modular Design of Secure yet Practical Cryptographic Protocols. PhD thesis, CWI and University of Amsterdam (1996)
22. Briner, T.: Compiler for zero-knowledge proof-of-knowledge protocols. Master's thesis, ETH Zurich (2004)
23. Camenisch, J., Rohe, M., Sadeghi, A.-R.: Sokrates - a compiler framework for zero-knowledge protocols. In: WEWoRC 2005 (2005)
24. Bangerter, E., Camenisch, J., Krenn, S., Sadeghi, A.R., Schneider, T.: Automatic generation of sound zero-knowledge protocols. Cryptology ePrint Archive, Report 2008/471 (2008); Poster session of EUROCRYPT (2009)
25. Brands, S.: Rapid demonstration of linear relations connected by boolean operators. In: Fumy, W. (ed.) EUROCRYPT 1997. LNCS, vol. 1233, pp. 318–333. Springer, Heidelberg (1997)

26. Bresson, E., Stern, J.: Proofs of knowledge for non-monotone discrete-log formulae and applications. In: Chan, A.H., Gligor, V.D. (eds.) ISC 2002. LNCS, vol. 2433, pp. 272–288. Springer, Heidelberg (2002)
27. Camenisch, J., Stadler, M.: Proof systems for general statements about discrete logarithms. Technical Report 260, Institute for Theoretical Computer Science, ETH Zürich (1997)
28. Camenisch, J., Kiayias, A., Yung, M.: On the portability of generalized Schnorr proofs. In: Joux, A. (ed.) EUROCRYPT 2009. LNCS, vol. 5479, pp. 425–442. Springer, Heidelberg (2010)
29. Malkhi, D., Nisan, N., Pinkas, B., Sella, Y.: Fairplay — a secure two-party computation system. In: USENIX Security 2004 (2004)
30. Damgård, I., Geisler, M., Krøigaard, M., Nielsen, J.B.: Asynchronous multiparty computation: Theory and implementation. In: Jarecki, S., Tsudik, G. (eds.) Public Key Cryptography – PKC 2009. LNCS, vol. 5443, pp. 160–179. Springer, Heidelberg (2009)
31. MacKenzie, P., Oprea, A., Reiter, M.K.: Automatic generation of two-party computations. In: ACM CCS 2003, pp. 210–219. ACM, New York (2003)
32. Ben-David, A., Nisan, N., Pinkas, B.: FairplayMP: a system for secure multi-party computation. In: ACM CCS 2008, pp. 257–266. ACM Press, New York (2008)
33. Paus, A., Sadeghi, A.-R., Schneider, T.: Practical secure evaluation of semi-private functions. In: Abdalla, M., Pointcheval, D., Fouque, P.-A., Vergnaud, D. (eds.) ACNS 2009. LNCS, vol. 5536, pp. 89–106. Springer, Heidelberg (2009)
34. Lindell, Y., Pinkas, B.: An efficient protocol for secure two-party computation in the presence of malicious adversaries. In: Naor, M. (ed.) EUROCRYPT 2007. LNCS, vol. 4515, pp. 52–78. Springer, Heidelberg (2007)
35. Brickell, J., Porter, D.E., Shmatikov, V., Witchel, E.: Privacy-preserving remote diagnostics. In: ACM CCS 2007, pp. 498–507. ACM Press, New York (2007)
36. Barbosa, M., Noad, R., Page, D., Smart, N.: First steps toward a cryptography-aware language and compiler. Cryptology ePrint Archive, Report 2005/160 (2005)
37. Barbosa, M., Page, D.: On the automatic construction of indistinguishable operations. Cryptology ePrint Archive, Report 2005/174 (2005)
38. Barbosa, M., Moss, A., Page, D.: Compiler assisted elliptic curve cryptography. In: Meersman, R., Tari, Z. (eds.) OTM 2007, Part II. LNCS, vol. 4804, pp. 1785–1802. Springer, Heidelberg (2007)
39. Bellare, M., Goldreich, O.: On defining proofs of knowledge. In: Brickell, E.F. (ed.) CRYPTO 1992. LNCS, vol. 740, pp. 390–420. Springer, Heidelberg (1993)
40. Shamir, A.: How to share a secret. Communications of ACM 22, 612–613 (1979)
41. Guillou, L., Quisquater, J.: A practical zero-knowledge protocol fitted to security microprocessor minimizing both transmission and memory. In: Günther, C.G. (ed.) EUROCRYPT 1988. LNCS, vol. 330, pp. 123–128. Springer, Heidelberg (1988)
42. Bangerter, E.: Efficient Zero-Knowledge Proofs of Knowledge for Homomorphisms. PhD thesis, Ruhr-University Bochum (2005)
43. Brickell, J., Shmatikov, V.: Privacy-preserving classifier learning. In: Dingledine, R., Golle, P. (eds.) FC 2009. LNCS, vol. 5628, pp. 128–147. Springer, Heidelberg (2009)
44. Piva, A., Caini, M., Bianchi, T., Orlandi, C., Barni, M.: Enhancing privacy in remote data classification. In: New Approaches for Security, Privacy and Trust in Complex Environments, SEC 2008 (2008)
45. Lipmaa, H.: Verifiable homomorphic oblivious transfer and private equality test. In: Laih, C.-S. (ed.) ASIACRYPT 2003. LNCS, vol. 2894, pp. 416–433. Springer, Heidelberg (2003)

A Generated Output for Example in Fig. 1

A.1 Protocol Inputs

Homomorphisms defined in Input File

$\phi_0 : \mathbb{Z}_m^* \to \mathbb{Z}_m^*, \rho_0 \mapsto \rho_0{}^n$

$\phi_1 : \mathbb{Z}_m^* \to \mathbb{Z}_m^*, \rho_1 \mapsto \rho_1{}^n$

$\phi_2 : \mathbb{Z}_n \times \mathbb{Z}_m^* \to \mathbb{Z}_m^*, (\mu, \rho_2) \mapsto g^\mu \cdot \rho_2{}^n$

$\phi_3 : \mathbb{Z}_n \times \mathbb{Z}_m^* \to \mathbb{Z}_m^*, (\mu, \rho_3) \mapsto g^\mu \cdot \rho_3{}^n$

Homomorphisms used in Protocol

$\phi_0, \phi_1, \psi_2 = \phi_2 \times \phi_3$

Common Input

$\mathbb{Z}_m^*, \mathbb{Z}_n$

$\mathbb{Z} : c^+, n$

$\mathbb{Z}_m^* : g, x_1, x_2$

Preimage Input

$\mathbb{Z}_n : \mu$

$\mathbb{Z}_m^* : \rho_0, \rho_1, \rho_2, \rho_3$

Access Structure

$$\Big((\rho_0)\Big) \vee \Big((\rho_1)\Big) \vee \Big((\mu, \rho_2) \wedge (\mu, \rho_3)\Big)$$

Constraints on Preimages

$\mu_{\phi_3} = 1 \cdot \mu_{\phi_2}$

Relation

$\phi_0 : x_1 = \rho_0{}^n$

$\phi_1 : x_1 \cdot g^{-1} = \rho_1{}^n$

$\phi_2 : x_1 = g^\mu \cdot \rho_2{}^n$

$\phi_3 : x_2 = g^\mu \cdot \rho_3{}^n$

A.2 Protocol

Round 1, Prover:

if secret ρ_0 is known:

      $r_{0,0} \in_R \mathbb{Z}_m^*$

      $t_{0,0} := (r_{0,0}{}^n)$

else:

      $s_{0,0} \in_R \mathbb{Z}_m^*$

      $c_0 \in_R [0, c^+]$

      $t_{0,0} := (s_{0,0}{}^n) \cdot x_1{}^{c_0}$

if secret ρ_1 is known:

      $r_{1,0} \in_R \mathbb{Z}_m^*$

      $t_{1,0} := (r_{1,0}{}^n)$

else:

$s_{1,0} \in_R \mathbb{Z}_m^*$
$c_1 \in_R [0, c^+]$
$t_{1,0} := (s_{1,0}{}^n) \cdot (x_1 \cdot g^{-1})^{c_1}$
if secret $(\mu, \rho_2, \mu, \rho_3)$ is known:
$r_{2,0} \in_R \mathbb{Z}_n, r_{2,1} \in_R \mathbb{Z}_m^*, r_{2,3} \in_R \mathbb{Z}_m^*$
$r_{2,2} := r_{2,0} \cdot 1$
$t_{2,0} := (g^{r_{2,0}} \cdot r_{2,1}{}^n)$
$t_{2,1} := (g^{r_{2,2}} \cdot r_{2,3}{}^n)$

else:

$s_{2,0} \in_R \mathbb{Z}_n, s_{2,1} \in_R \mathbb{Z}_m^*, s_{2,3} \in_R \mathbb{Z}_m^*, s_{2,2} := s_{2,0} \cdot 1$
$c_2 \in_R [0, c^+]$
$t_{2,0} := (g^{s_{2,0}} \cdot s_{2,1}{}^n) \cdot x_1{}^{c_2}$
$t_{2,1} := (g^{s_{2,2}} \cdot s_{2,3}{}^n) \cdot x_2{}^{c_2}$

$$t_{0,0}, t_{1,0}, t_{2,0}, t_{2,1}$$

Round 2, Verifier:
$c \in_R [0, c^+]$

$$c$$

Round 3, Prover:
$(c_0, c_1, c_2) := \text{complete}(c, \{c_0, c_1, c_2\})$
if secret ρ_0 is known:
$$s_{0,0} := r_{0,0} \cdot ((\rho_0)^{-1})^{c_0}$$
if secret ρ_1 is known:
$$s_{1,0} := r_{1,0} \cdot ((\rho_1)^{-1})^{c_1}$$
if secret $(\mu, \rho_2, \mu, \rho_3)$ is known:
$$(s_{2,0}, s_{2,1}) := (r_{2,0}, r_{2,1}) + (-(\mu, \rho_2)) \cdot c_2$$
$$(s_{2,2}, s_{2,3}) := (r_{2,2}, r_{2,3}) + (-(\mu, \rho_3)) \cdot c_2$$

$$s_{0,0}, s_{1,0}, s_{2,0}, s_{2,1}, s_{2,2}, s_{2,3}, c_0, c_1, c_2$$

Round 4, Verifier:
Check whether:

$\text{isConsistent}(c, \{c_0, c_1, c_2\}) \stackrel{?}{=} \text{true}$

$s_{2,2} \stackrel{?}{=} 1 \cdot s_{2,0}$

$t_{0,0} \stackrel{?}{=} (s_{0,0}{}^n) \cdot x_1{}^{c_0}$

$t_{1,0} \stackrel{?}{=} (s_{1,0}{}^n) \cdot (x_1 \cdot g^{-1})^{c_1}$

$t_{2,0} \stackrel{?}{=} (g^{s_{2,0}} \cdot s_{2,1}{}^n) \cdot x_1{}^{c_2}$

$t_{2,1} \stackrel{?}{=} (g^{s_{2,2}} \cdot s_{2,3}{}^n) \cdot x_2{}^{c_2}$

A Secure and Efficient Authenticated Diffie–Hellman Protocol

Augustin P. Sarr[1,2], Philippe Elbaz–Vincent[2], and Jean–Claude Bajard[3]

[1] Netheos R&D
[2] Institut Fourier – CNRS, Université Grenoble 1
[3] LIP6 – CNRS, Université Pierre et Marie Curie

Abstract. The Exponential Challenge Response (XRC) and Dual Exponential Challenge Response (DCR) signature schemes are the building blocks of the HMQV protocol. We propose a complementary analysis of these schemes; on the basis of this analysis we show how impersonation and man in the middle attacks can be mounted against HMQV, when some session specific information leakages happen. We define the Full Exponential Challenge Response (FXRC) and Full Dual Exponential Challenge Response (FDCR) signature schemes; using these schemes we propose the Fully Hashed MQV protocol, which preserves the performance and security attributes of the (H)MQV protocols and resists the attacks we present.

Keywords: security model, (H)MQV, vulnerability, security reduction.

1 Introduction

Implicitly authenticated key exchange protocols have gained wide acceptance; in addition to provide implicit authentication, these protocols are usually more efficient than the explicitly authenticated ones. The HMQV protocol [5], inspired by the famous MQV protocol [7,4], was proposed with security arguments in the Canetti–Krawczyk model [2]. HMQV was designed in accord with the principle that "a good security system is not one that denies the possibility of failures but rather one designed to confine the adverse effects of such failures to the possible minimum" [5]. Session secret leakages may happen; in that case the exposed session may be compromised, but this should have no effect on the security of any other unexposed session.

In this paper, we propose a complementary analysis of the Exponential Challenge Response (XCR) and Dual Exponential Challenge Response (DCR) signature schemes. On the basis of this analysis we show how impersonation and man in the middle attacks can be performed against, HMQV when some session specific information leakages happen. We propose the Full Exponential Challenge Response (FXRC) and Full Dual Exponential Challenge Response (FDCR) signature schemes. With these schemes we define the Fully Hashed MQV protocol, which resists the attacks we present and preserves the remarkable performance of the (H)MQV protocols.

F. Martinelli and B. Preneel (Eds.): EuroPKI 2009, LNCS 6391, pp. 83–98, 2010.

This paper is organized as follows. In section 2 we propose a complementary analysis of the XCR and DCR signatures schemes; we also show how session specific information leakages lead to impersonation and man in the middle attacks against (H)MQV. In section 3 we define a Canetti–Krawczyk type security model [2,6] for the (H)MQV family protocols. Section 4, deals with the FHMQV protocol and its design elements, namely the FXCR, FDCR, and Hashed FDCR signature schemes and their security arguments. We conclude in section 5.

The following notations are used in this paper: $\mathcal{G}$ is a multiplicatively written cyclic group of prime order q generated by G, $|q|$ is the bit length of q. $\mathcal{G}^*$ is the set of non–identity elements in $\mathcal{G}$. For $X \in \mathcal{G}$, the lowercase x denotes the discrete logarithm of X in base G. The identity of an entity with public key A is denoted $\hat{A}$; for two parties $\hat{A} \neq \hat{B}$, we suppose that no substring of $\hat{A}$ equals $\hat{B}$. H is a λ–bit hash function where λ is the length of the session keys, and $\bar{H}$ is a l–bit hash function where $l = (\lfloor \log_2 q \rfloor + 1)/2$ (see [5, section 4.2] for a discussion on the value of l). The concatenation of n strings $s_1, \cdots, s_n$ is denoted $(s_1, \cdots, s_n)$. The symbol "$\in_R$" stands for "chosen uniformly at random in"; $\{0,1\}^\varepsilon$ denotes the set of binary strings of length ε, and $\{0,1\}^*$ is the set of finite binary strings. The Computational Diffie–Hellman (CDH) assumption is supposed to hold in $\mathcal{G}$, i.e. given $U = G^u$ and $V = G^v$ with $U, V \in_R \mathcal{G}^*$, computing $CDH(U, V) = G^{uv}$ is infeasible.

2   Complementary Analysis of the HMQV Design

We show in this section how session specific information leakages, can be used for impersonation and man in the middle attacks against HMQV. Notice that in our description of HMQV, the ephemeral public keys are tested for membership in $\mathcal{G}^*$; public key validation is voluntarily omitted in [5], but (H)MQV is known to be insecure if the incoming ephemeral keys are not correctly validated [10,9].

Definition 1 (XCR signature [5]). *Let $\hat{B}$ be a party with public key $B \in \mathcal{G}^*$, and $\hat{A}$ a verifier. $\hat{B}$'s signature on a message m and a challenge X provided by $\hat{A}$ ($X = G^x$, $x \in_R [1, q-1]$ is chosen and kept secret by $\hat{A}$) is $Sig_{\hat{B}}(m, X) = (Y, X^{s_B})$, where $Y = G^y$, $y \in_R [1, q-1]$ is chosen by $\hat{B}$, and $s_B = y + \bar{H}(Y, m)b$. And $\hat{A}$ accepts a pair (Y, σ_B) provided by $\hat{B}$ as a valid signature if $Y \in \mathcal{G}^*$ and $(Y B^{\bar{H}(Y,m)})^x = \sigma_B$.*

In this scheme, the information s_B "allows" an attacker to generate valid signatures. Indeed, given the s_B, "corresponding" to some message m and some challenge Y, one can generate a valid signature on any message–challenge pair (m, X_1) (X_1 is a new challenge and the message is unchanged). In a (H)MQV[1] session between $\hat{A}$ and $\hat{B}$, the identity of the entity $\hat{B}$ is $\hat{A}$'s message to $\hat{B}$, and thus does not change from one session (between $\hat{A}$ and $\hat{B}$) to another. This can be exploited when s_B leakage happens.

---

[1] When regarded through XCR schemes, the XCR variant corresponding to MQV does not use the message in the computation of s_B, and thus can be analyzed as if it takes a constant message.

Proposition 1. *Let $\hat{B}$ be an entity, with public key $B \in \mathcal{G}^*$, signing a message–challenge pair (m, X). If an attacker learns the β most significant bits of s_B, it can generate a valid signature, with respect to $\hat{B}$'s public key, on any message–challenge pair (m, X_1) (the message is unchanged). This requires $\mathcal{O}\big(2^{\frac{|q|-\beta}{2}}\big)$ time complexity and $\mathcal{O}\big(2^{\frac{|q|-\beta}{2}}\big)$ space complexity.*

Proof. From Shank's Baby Step Giant Step (BSGS) lemma [15], given $\sigma_B = X^{s_B}$, $X \in \mathcal{G} = \langle G \rangle$, and the β most significant bits of s_B, one can compute s_B in $\mathcal{O}\big(2^{\frac{|q|-\beta}{2}}\big)$ time complexity and $\mathcal{O}\big(2^{\frac{|q|-\beta}{2}}\big)$ space complexity. And given a message–challenge (m, X_1), the attacker replays Y (since Y is chosen by the signer) and produces $(Y, X_1^{s_B})$ as a signature. The signature is a valid one; Proposition 1 holds.

Shanks method is deterministic, but requires a large storage; with Pollard's Kangaroo method [13,15] one can obtain s_B with negligible storage, in probabilistic run time $\mathcal{O}\big(2^{\frac{|q|-\beta}{2}}\big)$.

Definition 2 (DCR signature [5]). *Let $\hat{A}$ and $\hat{B}$ be two parties with public keys $A, B \in \mathcal{G}$. The DCR signature of $\hat{A}$ and $\hat{B}$ on two messages m_1 and m_2 is $DSig_{\hat{A}, \hat{B}}(m_1, m_2, X, Y) = G^{(x+da)(y+eb)}$, where $X = G^x$, $Y = G^y \in_R \mathcal{G}^*$ are respectively chosen by $\hat{A}$ and $\hat{B}$, $d = \bar{H}(X, m_1)$ and $e = \bar{H}(Y, m_2)$.*

The DCR signature of $\hat{A}$ and $\hat{B}$ on messages m_1, m_2 is an XCR of $\hat{A}$ on m_1 and challenge YB^e. Hence, an attacker which learns the β most significant bits of $s_A = x + da$ can, for any message m_2', and any challenge Y' from $\hat{B}$, compute a valid DCR signature of $\hat{A}$ and $\hat{B}$ on messages m_1, m_2' and challenges X, Y'. This requires $\mathcal{O}\big(2^{\frac{|q|-\beta}{2}}\big)$ time complexity and $\mathcal{O}\big(2^{\frac{|q|-\beta}{2}}\big)$ space complexity.

The HMQV security arguments follows from the XCR security. An execution of HMQV is as in Protocol 1 (if any verification fails, the execution aborts). The secret shared between $\hat{A}$ and $\hat{B}$ is a DCR signature with messages fixed to $\hat{A}$ and $\hat{B}$. In [5], Krawczyk presents the XCR scheme as a new exponential variant of the Schnorr's identification scheme wherein:
(a) $\hat{B}$ chooses $y \in_R [1, q-1]$ and sends $Y = G^y$ to $\hat{A}$;
(b) the verifier $\hat{A}$ chooses $e \in_R [1, q-1]$ and sends e to $\hat{B}$;
(c) $\hat{B}$ computes $s = y + eb$ and sends s to $\hat{A}$; and $\hat{A}$ accepts s as a valid signature if $Y \in \mathcal{G}^*$ and $G^s = YB^e$.

However, there is a subtlety: in Schnorr's scheme, the random element e used by $\hat{B}$ is *always* provided by the verifier; while in the XCR and DCR schemes, when $\hat{A}$'s message m_1 is fixed (to $\hat{B}$, as in all HMQV sessions between $\hat{A}$ and $\hat{B}$) the value of e depends only on the ephemeral key Y provided by (the signer) $\hat{B}$. This makes replay attacks possible against the XCR and DCR schemes, and the (H)MQV(–C) protocols, when s_A or s_B leakage happens.

Impersonation and Man in the Middle Attacks using Session Secret Leakages. We show here how ephemeral secret exponent (s_A or s_B) leakages can be used

---

Protocol 1. HMQV key exchange

I) The initiator $\hat{A}$ does the following:
    (a) Choose $x \in_R [1, q-1]$ and compute $X = G^x$.
    (b) Send $(\hat{A}, \hat{B}, X)$ to $\hat{B}$.
II) At receipt of $(\hat{A}, \hat{B}, X)$, $\hat{B}$ does the following:
    (a) Verify that $X \in \mathcal{G}^*$.
    (b) Choose $y \in_R [1, q-1]$ and compute $Y = G^y$.
    (c) Send $(\hat{B}, \hat{A}, Y)$ to $\hat{A}$.
    (d) Compute $d = \bar{H}(X, \hat{B})$ and $e = \bar{H}(Y, \hat{A})$.
    (e) Compute $s_B = y + eb \bmod q$, $\sigma_B = (XA^d)^{s_B}$, and $K = H(\sigma_B)$.
III) At receipt of $(\hat{B}, \hat{A}, Y)$, $\hat{A}$ does the following:
    (a) Verify that $Y \in \mathcal{G}^*$.
    (b) Compute $d = \bar{H}(X, \hat{B})$ and $e = \bar{H}(Y, \hat{A})$.
    (c) Compute $s_A = x + da \bmod q$, $\sigma_A = (YB^e)^{s_A}$, and $K = H(\sigma_A)$.
IV) The shared session key is K.

---

for impersonation[2] and man in the middle attacks . The following definition gives a broader view of the points needed for impersonation attack; these points are recalled to make the analysis reading easier.

Definition 3 (Point for impersonation attack, i–point). *Let $\hat{A}$ and $\hat{B}$ be two entities with respective public keys $A, B \in \mathcal{G}^*$. A group element $R \in \mathcal{G}^*$ is said to be a HMQV i–point for $\hat{A}$ to $\hat{B}$ if there exists some $k \in [1, q-1]$ such that $R = G^k A^{-\bar{H}(R, \hat{B})}$; k is said to be the decomposition.*

It can be shown that if $\hat{A}$ and $\hat{B}$'s public keys belong to $\mathcal{G}^*$, there exists at least $(q - 2^l - 1)$ HMQV i–points for $\hat{A}$ to $\hat{B}$. The important aspect for succeeding in impersonation attack is knowing the decomposition of an i–point. Given a HMQV i–point for $\hat{A}$ to $\hat{B}$ X' and its decomposition k, one can indefinitely impersonate $\hat{A}$ to $\hat{B}$. The attack is described in Algorithm 2.

Algorithm 2. HMQV impersonation of $\hat{A}$ to $\hat{B}$

Require: A HMQV i–point for $\hat{A}$ to $\hat{B}$ X' and its decomposition k.
    (a) Send $(\hat{A}, \hat{B}, X')$ to $\hat{B}$.
    (b) Intercept $\hat{B}$'s response $(\hat{B}, \hat{A}, Y)$.
    (c) verify that $Y \in \mathcal{G}^*$.
    (d) Compute $e = \bar{H}(Y, \hat{A})$, $\sigma_A = (YB^e)^k$, and $K = H(\sigma_A)$.
    (e) Use K to communicate with $\hat{B}$ on behalf of $\hat{A}$.

Proposition 2. *Let $\hat{A}$ be a party executing the HMQV protocol with some peer $\hat{B}$. If an attacker learns the β most significant bits of the ephemeral secret exponent at $\hat{A}$, it can indefinitely impersonate $\hat{A}$ to $\hat{B}$. This requires $\mathcal{O}\bigl(2^{\frac{|q|-\beta}{2}}\bigr)$ time complexity and $\mathcal{O}\bigl(2^{\frac{|q|-\beta}{2}}\bigr)$ space complexity.*

---

[2] The impersonation attack is also reported in [1] (Appendix C). This work is however independent from [1], as we submitted at WCC 2009 (on February 9th, 2009) a paper (#1569187679), which describes this attack; therefore before [1] was posted at http://eprint.iacr.org/2009/079 (on February 18, 2009).

Proof. From the BSGS lemma, given the β most significant bits of s_A, computing s_A requires $\mathcal{O}(2^{\frac{|q|-\beta}{2}})$ time complexity and $\mathcal{O}(2^{\frac{|q|-\beta}{2}})$ space complexity. And an attacker which learns s_A, knows an i–point for $\hat{A}$ to $\hat{B}$ and its decomposition $(XA^{\bar{H}(X,\hat{B})} = G^{s_A}$ i.e. $X = G^{s_A}A^{-\bar{H}(X,\hat{B})})$; it can then (indefinitely) impersonate $\hat{A}$ to $\hat{B}$, using Algorithm 2.

Remark 1. *(i)* For the MQV(–C) protocols, if an attacker learns the ephemeral secret exponent, in some session at $\hat{A}$, it can not only impersonate $\hat{A}$ to $\hat{B}$ (as in (C, H)MQV), but also to *any* other entity. *(ii)* To meet the two–and–half exponentiations per party performance, which partly makes the attractiveness of the (H)MQV protocols, s_A has to be computed, and the exponentiation $(YB^e)^{s_A}$ has to be performed, and then s_A leakage may happen (through side channel attacks for instance), independently of the ephemeral private keys. *(iii)* We do not discuss leakages on consecutive middle part bits of ephemeral secret exponents, but with tools from [3], a similar analysis can be performed in this case.

Ephemeral secret exponent leakage does not imply static or ephemeral private key leakage. Indeed, one can show that from any algorithm $\mathcal{A}$ with complexity $C_{\mathcal{A}}$, which given s_A, X, A and $\hat{B}$, finds $\hat{A}$'s ephemeral private key x or the static one a, one can derive an algorithm which solves two instances of the DLP in $\mathcal{G}^*$, in $C_{\mathcal{A}} + C_{DLP}$ time complexity where C_{DLP} is the complexity for solving one instance of the DLP in $\mathcal{G}$. Hence ephemeral secret exponent leakage implies (but is not equivalent to) *session key reveal*, and does imply neither *static key reveal* nor *ephemeral key reveal*. (Both ephemeral secret exponent and ephemeral key leakages on the *same* session imply a discloser of the session owner's static key.)

If in addition to s_A, an attacker learns s_B in a session at $\hat{B}$, it can perform man in the middle attacks, between $\hat{A}$ and $\hat{B}$, as in Algorithm 3. We denote by $s_A^{(l)}$ and $s_B^{(l)}$ the ephemeral secret exponents the attacker learned at $\hat{A}$ and $\hat{B}$ respectively; $X^{(l)}$ and $Y^{(l)}$ are $\hat{A}$ and $\hat{B}$'s outgoing ephemeral keys in the sessions in which leakages happened. Notice that it is *not* required that the (s_A and s_B) leakages happened in matching sessions.

Algorithm 3 is merely a simultaneous impersonation of $\hat{A}$ to $\hat{B}$, and $\hat{B}$ to $\hat{A}$. The session key that $\hat{A}$ derives is $K_A = H((Y^{(l)}B^{e_A})^{x+d_A a}) = H((XA^{d_A})^{s_B^{(l)}})$, where $e_A = H(Y^{(l)}, \hat{A})$ and $d_A = H(X, \hat{B})$. This is the K_A the attacker computes at step (e). Similarly, the session key that $\hat{B}$ derives is $K_B = H((YB^{e_B})^{s_A^{(l)}})$.

Algorithm 3. Man in the middle attack

(a) Send $(\hat{A}, \hat{B}, X^{(l)})$ to $\hat{B}$.

(b) Intercept $\hat{B}$'s response to $\hat{A}$ $(\hat{B}, \hat{A}, Y)$.

(c) Send $(\hat{B}, \hat{A}, Y^{(l)})$ to $\hat{A}$.

(d) Intercept $\hat{A}$'s response to $\hat{B}$, $(\hat{A}, \hat{B}, X)$.

(e) Compute $d_A = H(X, \hat{B})$ and $K_A = H((XA^{d_A})^{s_B^{(l)}})$.

(f) Compute $e_B = H(Y, \hat{A})$ and $K_B = H((YB^{e_B})^{s_A^{(l)}})$.

(g) Use K_B to communicate with $\hat{B}$ on behalf of $\hat{A}$.

(h) Use K_A to communicate with $\hat{A}$ on behalf of $\hat{B}$.

Notice that the attack remains possible when communications are initiated by $\hat{A}$ (or $\hat{B}$).

3   Security Model

We define a security model, inspired by the (extended) Canetti–Krawczyk models [2,6], for the (H)MQV type protocols. We aim to a better capture of session specific information leakages. While both ephemeral secret exponent and ephemeral key leakages on the *same* session imply the session owner's private key disclosure, resistance ephemeral secret exponent leakage is a desirable security attribute.

Rationale of the model. In the extended Canetti–Krawczyk (eCK) model [6] the *ephemeral key* of a session is required to contain *all* session specific information. When this requirement is fully satisfied, it becomes difficult to consistently simulate information leakages; in practice, the ephemeral key is not always defined to contain *all* session specific information. In [16,6], for instance, the ephemeral key is not defined to contain the ephemeral Diffie–Hellman exponent.

A session key derivation generally involves some intermediate results, on which leakages may happen; these intermediate results cannot always be computed, given only the session's ephemeral private key. Leakages on these intermediate results are not necessarily captured through *ephemeral key reveal*. In the CMQV protocol [16] (shown eCK–secure), an ephemeral secret exponent leakage allows an attacker to impersonate indefinitely the session owner to its peer in the leaked session.

In the Canetti–Krawczyk (CK) model(s) [2,5], a *session state* is defined to contain the ephemeral information in a session; session state leakage is modeled using a *session state reveal* query. However, the model does not define the ephemeral information contained in a session state; this is left to be specified by each protocol. As a consequence, it is not always clear, which information in a session can be revealed. In addition it is difficult to figure out the practical meaning of the CK–security, as a protocol may be both secure and insecure, depending on the definition of the session state.

Moreover, the ephemeral information that can be available in a session state depends on the reached step in the session's tree of computations. To capture precisely ephemeral information leakages, one has to consider sessions' tree of computations. In the model we propose, the eCK model is completed with reveal queries on intermediate results. We aim to capture both intermediate results and ephemeral key leakages. It is however difficult to simultaneously and consistently simulate leakages on both ephemeral keys and intermediate results. This is the reason why our model follows two stages. In the first, leakages on the intermediate results are considered; the second deals with ephemeral private keys leakages.

Session. We suppose $n \leqslant \mathcal{P}(|q|)$ (for some polynomial $\mathcal{P}$) parties $\hat{P}_{i,i=1,\cdots,n}$ modeled as probabilistic polynomial time machines, and a certification authority (CA) trusted by all parties. All static public keys are supposed to belong to

$\mathcal{G}^*$ (the CA is required to test public keys for membership in $\mathcal{G}^*$ at certificate issuance). Each party has a static public key together with a certificate binding his identity to his public key.

A session is an instance of a protocol run at a party. A session at $\hat{A}$, with peer $\hat{B}$, can be created with parameter $(\hat{A}, \hat{B})$ or $(\hat{B}, \hat{A}, Y)$; $\hat{A}$ is the initiator if the creation parameter is $(\hat{A}, \hat{B})$, otherwise the responder. At session activation, a session state is created to contain the information specific to the session. Each session is identified with a quadruple $(\hat{A}, \hat{B}, X, \star)$, where $\hat{A}$ is the session owner, $\hat{B}$ is the peer, X is the outgoing ephemeral key, and $\star$ is the incoming key Y if it exists, otherwise a special symbol meaning that an incoming ephemeral key is not received yet; in that case when $\hat{A}$ receives an ephemeral key Y from $\hat{B}$, it updates the identifier to $(\hat{A}, \hat{B}, X, Y)$. Two sessions with identifiers $(\hat{B}, \hat{A}, Y, X)$ and $(\hat{A}, \hat{B}, X, Y)$ are said to be matching. Notice that the session matching $(\hat{B}, \hat{A}, Y, X)$ can be any session $(\hat{A}, \hat{B}, X, \star)$; as the ephemeral keys X and Y are chosen uniformly at random in $\mathcal{G}^*$, a session cannot have (except with negligible probability) more than one matching session.

Adversary. The adversary, denoted $\mathcal{A}$, is a probabilistic polynomial time machine. It is a common assumption that an adversary is able to eavesdrop, modify, delete any message sent in a cryptographic protocol, or inject its own messages. This is captured through the assumption that outgoing messages are submitted to $\mathcal{A}$ for delivery ($\mathcal{A}$ decides about messages delivery); $\mathcal{A}$ is also supposed to control session activations at each party $\hat{P}_i$ via the $Send(\hat{P}_i, \hat{P}_j)$ and $Send(\hat{P}_j, \hat{P}_i, Y)$ queries, which make $\hat{P}_i$ initiate a session with peer $\hat{P}_j$ or respond to $\hat{P}_j$.

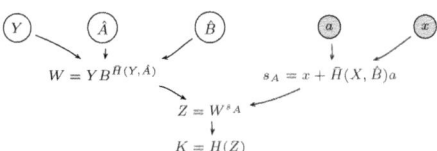

Fig. 1. Tree of computations in a HMQV session

The adversary is also provided with the reveal queries from one of the following sets. At the beginning of its run, the adversary adopts one of the sets of queries; it can then perform queries from the selected set (and only those queries).

In **Set 1**, the following queries are allowed.
- *StaticKeyReveal(party)* to obtain the static private key of a party.
- *SessionKeyReveal(session)* to obtain the derived key in a session.
- *SecretExponentReveal(session)* to obtain the ephemeral secret exponent ($s = x + da$ or $y + eb$) in a session.
- *SecretGroupElementReveal(session)* to obtain the session signature $Z = W^{s_A}$.
- *EstablishParty(party)* to register a static public key on behalf of a party; from there, the party is supposed totally controlled by $\mathcal{A}$. A party against which this query is not issued is said *honest*.

Notice that, we consider only the intermediate values which evaluation requires a secret information; as the attacker is supposed to control the communication links between parties, considering leakages on the other intermediate values is superfluous. We also implicitly assume that the considered protocol has a tree of computations "matching" that of the (H)MQV protocols; otherwise some queries (*SecretExponentReveal* for instance) may become meaningless.

In **Set 2**, the allowed queries are the following; the definitions remain unchanged for the queries belonging also to Set 1.

- *EphemeralKeyReveal(session)* to obtain the ephemeral private key used by the session owner.
- *StaticKeyReveal(party)*.
- *SessionKeyReveal(session)*.
- *EstablishParty(party)*.

Definition 4 (session freshness). *Let sid be the identifier of a completed session at an honest party $\hat{A}$, with some honest peer $\hat{B}$, and sid^* the matching session's identifier. The session sid is said to be* ck–fresh, *if none of the following conditions hold:*

- *$\mathcal{A}$ issues a SecretExponentReveal query on sid or sid^* (if sid^* exists);*
- *$\mathcal{A}$ issues a SecretGroupElementReveal query on sid or sid^*;*
- *$\mathcal{A}$ issues a SessionKeyReveal query on sid or sid^*;*
- *sid^* does not exist and $\mathcal{A}$ makes a StaticKeyReveal query on $\hat{B}$.*

And sid is said to be eck–fresh, *if none of the following conditions hold:*

- *$\mathcal{A}$ issues a SessionKeyReveal query on sid or sid^* (if sid^* exists);*
- *$\mathcal{A}$ issues a StaticKeyReveal query on $\hat{A}$ and an EphemeralKeyReveal query on sid;*
- *sid^* exists and $\mathcal{A}$ makes a StaticKeyReveal query on $\hat{B}$ and an EphemeralKeyReveal query on sid^*;*
- *sid^* does not exist and $\mathcal{A}$ makes a StaticKeyReveal query on $\hat{B}$.*

Definition 5 (security). *Let Π be a key agreement protocol, such that if two honest parties complete matching sessions, then they both compute the same session key.*

- *The protocol Π is said to be* ck–secure, *if no polynomially bounded adversary (performing queries from Set 1) can distinguish a ck–fresh session key from a random value, chosen under the distribution of session keys, with probability (taken over the random coins of the adversary and the choices of static and ephemeral public keys in $\mathcal{G}$) significantly greater than $1/2$.*
- *Π is said to be* eck–secure, *if no polynomially bounded adversary (performing queries from Set 2) can distinguish an eck–fresh session key from a random value, chosen under the distribution of session keys, with probability significantly greater than $1/2$.*
- *And Π is said to be* secure, *if it is both ck–secure and eck–secure.*

4 A New Authenticated Diffie–Hellman Protocol

In this section, we define the FXCR and FDCR signature schemes, which confine to the minimum the consequences of ephemeral secret exponent leakage. With these schemes, we define the Fully Hashed MQV (FHMQV) protocol, which preserves the HMQV performance and security attributes, in addition to being ephemeral secret exponent leakage resilient.

4.1 Building Blocks

Definition 6 (FXCR signature). *Let $\hat{B}$ be an entity with public key $B \in \mathcal{G}^*$, and $\hat{A}$ a verifier; $\hat{B}$'s signature on message m and challenge X provided by $\hat{A}$ ($X = G^x$, $x \in_R [1, q-1]$ is chosen and kept secret by $\hat{A}$) is $FSig_{\hat{B}}(m, X) = (Y, X^{s_B})$, where $Y = G^y$, $y \in_R [1, q-1]$ is chosen by $\hat{B}$, and $s_B = y + \bar{H}(Y, X, m)b$. And $\hat{A}$ accepts the pair (Y, σ_B) as a valid signature if $Y \in \mathcal{G}^*$ and $(YB^{\bar{H}(Y,X,m)})^x = \sigma_B$.*

The "replay attack" we present in section 2 does not hold against the FXCR scheme. Suppose an attacker which has learned some $s_B^{(l)} = y^{(l)} + \bar{H}(Y^{(l)}, X^{(l)}, m)b$. When it is provided with a new challenge X, chosen at random, and the same message m, except with negligible probability, $X \neq X^{(l)}$ (and $\bar{H}(Y^{(l)}, X^{(l)}, m) \neq \bar{H}(Y^{(l)}, X, m)$). Hence, to replay $Y^{(l)}$ at signature query on the message–challenge pair (m, X), the attacker has to find $s_B = y^{(l)} + \bar{H}(Y^{(l)}, X, m)b$. It is not difficult to see that if it can find s_B from $s_B^{(l)}$, it can also find b from s_B (which is not feasible).

Recall that a function f, with parameter λ, is said to be negligible (in λ) if for every polynomial p, $f(k) < (|p(k)|)^{-1}$ for k large enough; otherwise, f is said to be non–negligible.

Definition 7 (FXCR scheme security). *The FXCR scheme is said to be secure, if given a public key B, a challenge X_0 ($B, X_0 \in_R \mathcal{G}^*$), and hashing and signing oracles, no adaptive probabilistic polynomial time attacker can output with non negligible success probability a triple (m_0, Y_0, σ_0) such that:*
– (Y_0, σ_0) is a valid signature with respect to the key B, and the message–challenge pair (m_0, X_0);
– (Y_0, σ_0) was not obtained from the signing oracle with a query on (m_0, X_0) (freshness).

Contrary to the XCR security definition [5, section 4.1], which requires that "the pair (Y_0, m_0) did not appear in *any* of the responses of $\hat{B}$", we only use the minimal requirement that (Y_0, σ_0) was not produced by $\hat{A}$ as a signature on (m_0, X_0).

Proposition 3. *Under the CDH assumption in $\mathcal{G}$ and the RO model, the FXCR signature scheme is secure in the sense of Definition 7.*

Proof. Suppose an attacker $\mathcal{A}$, which given $B, X_0 \in_R \mathcal{G}^*$ succeeds with non–negligible probability in forging a FXCR signature, with respect to the public key B and the challenge X_0. Using $\mathcal{A}$ we build a polynomial time CDH solver $\mathcal{S}$ which succeeds with non–negligible probability. The solver $\mathcal{S}$ provides $\mathcal{A}$ with random coins, and simulates the digest and signature queries. The interactions between $\mathcal{S}$ and $\mathcal{A}$ are described in Figure 4.

Figure 4. A CDH solver from $\mathcal{A}$

Run of $\mathcal{A}$:

(a) At $\mathcal{A}$'s digest query on (Y, X, m), $\mathcal{S}$ responds as follows: *(i)* if a value is already assigned to $\bar{H}(Y, X, m)$, $\mathcal{S}$ returns $\bar{H}(Y, X, m)$; *(ii)* otherwise $\mathcal{S}$ responds with $e \in_R \{0, 1\}^l$, and sets $\bar{H}(Y, X, m) = e$.

(b) At $\mathcal{A}$'s signature query on (m, X), $\mathcal{S}$ responds as follows: *(i)* $\mathcal{S}$ chooses $s_B \in_R [1, q-1]$, $e \in_R \{0, 1\}^l$, sets $Y = G^{s_B} B^{-e}$ and $\bar{H}(Y, X, m) = e$. If $\bar{H}(Y, X, m)$ was previously defined, $\mathcal{S}$ aborts. *(ii)* Else, $\mathcal{S}$ responds with (Y, X^{s_B}).

(c) At $\mathcal{A}$'s halt, $\mathcal{S}$ verifies that $\mathcal{A}$'s output $(m_0, Y_0, \sigma_0^{(1)})$ (if any) satisfies the following conditions. If not, $\mathcal{S}$ aborts.
  - $Y_0 \in \mathcal{G}^*$ and $\bar{H}(Y_0, X_0, m_0)$ was queried from $\bar{H}$.
  - $(Y_0, \sigma_0^{(1)})$ was not returned by $\hat{B}$ at signature query on (m_0, X_0).

Repeat: $\mathcal{S}$ executes a new run of $\mathcal{A}$, using the same input and coins; and answering to all the digest queries before $\bar{H}(Y_0, X_0, m_0)$ with the same values as in the previous run. The new query of $\bar{H}(Y_0, X_0, m_0)$ and subsequent $\bar{H}$ queries are answered with new random values.

Output: If $\mathcal{A}$ outputs a second forgery $(m_0, Y_0, \sigma_0^{(2)})$ satisfying the conditions of step (c), with a hash value $\bar{H}(Y_0, X_0, m_0)_2 = e_0^{(2)} \neq e_0^{(1)} = \bar{H}(Y_0, X_0, m_0)_1$, then $\mathcal{S}$ outputs $(\sigma_0^{(1)}/\sigma_0^{(2)})^{(e_0^{(1)} - e_0^{(2)})^{-1}}$ as a guess for $CDH(B, X_0)$.

Under the RO model, the distribution of simulated signatures is indistinguishable from the that of real signatures generated by $\hat{B}$, except the deviation that happens when $\bar{H}(Y, X, m)$ was queried before. Let Q_h and Q_s be respectively the number of queries that $\mathcal{A}$ asks to the hashing and signing oracles. Since the number of queries to the oracles is less than $(Q_h + Q_s)$, and Y is chosen uniformly at random in $\mathcal{G}$, this deviation happens with probability less than $(Q_h + Q_s)/q$, which is negligible. Hence this simulation is perfect, except with negligible probability. Moreover the probability of producing a valid forgery without querying $\bar{H}(Y_0, X_0, m_0)$ is 2^{-l}. Thus under this simulation, $\mathcal{A}$ outputs with non–negligible probability a valid forgery $(m_0, Y_0, \sigma_0^{(1)})$; we denote $\bar{H}(Y_0, X_0, m_0)$ by $e_0^{(1)}$. From the Forking lemma [12], the repeat experiment produces with non–negligible probability a valid forgery $(m_0, Y_0, \sigma_0^{(2)})$ with a digest $e_0^{(2)}$, which with probability $1 - 2^{-l}$, is different from $e_0^{(1)}$. Then the computation

$$\left(\frac{\sigma_0^{(1)}}{\sigma_0^{(2)}}\right)^{\left(e_0^{(1)} - e_0^{(2)}\right)^{-1}} = \left(\frac{\left(Y_0 B^{e_0^{(1)}}\right)^{x_0}}{\left(Y_0 B^{e_0^{(2)}}\right)^{x_0}}\right)^{\left(e_0^{(1)} - e_0^{(2)}\right)^{-1}} = B^{x_0}$$

gives $CDH(B, X_0)$ with non–negligible success probability.

Definition 8 (FDCR signature scheme). *Let $\hat{A}$ and $\hat{B}$ be two entities with public keys $A, B \in \mathcal{G}^*$, and m_1, m_2 two messages. The FDCR signature of $\hat{A}$ and $\hat{B}$ on messages m_1, m_2 is $FDSig_{\hat{A},\hat{B}}(m_1, m_2, X, Y) = (XA^d)^{y+eb} = (YB^e)^{x+da}$, where $X = G^x$ and $Y = G^y$ $(x, y \in_R [1, q-1])$ are chosen respectively by $\hat{A}$ and $\hat{B}$, $d = \bar{H}(X, Y, m_1, m_2)$, and $e = \bar{H}(Y, X, m_1, m_2)$.*

Notice that contrary to the DCR and XCR schemes, the FDCR signature of $\hat{A}$ and $\hat{B}$ on messages m_1, m_2 and challenges X, Y, is not a FXCR signature of $\hat{A}$ on the message m_1 and challenge YB^e.

Definition 9 (Security of the FDCR scheme). *Let $A = G^a, B, X_0 \in_R \mathcal{G}^*$ $(A \neq B)$. The FDCR scheme is said to be secure in $\mathcal{G}$, if given a, A, B, X_0, and a message m_{1_0}, together with hashing and signing oracles, no adaptive probabilistic polynomial time attacker can output with non negligible success probability a triple (m_{2_0}, Y_0, σ_0) such that:*

- *$(m_{1_0}, m_{2_0}, X_0, Y_0, \sigma_0)$ is a valid FDCR signature with respect to the public keys A, B.*
- *(Y_0, σ_0) was not obtained from the signing oracle with a query on a message–challenge pair (m_1', X_0) such that $(m_1', m_2') = (m_{1_0}, m_{2_0})$, where (m_{1_0}, m_{2_0}) denotes the concatenation of m_{1_0} and m_{2_0}, and m_2' is the message returned at signature query on (m_1', X_0) (if any).*

Remark 2. Since we suppose that if $\hat{A} \neq \hat{A}'$, no substring of $\hat{A}$ equals $\hat{A}'$ (and conversely), if $\hat{A} \neq \hat{A}'$ or $\hat{B} \neq \hat{B}'$ then $(\hat{A}, \hat{B})$ cannot equal $(\hat{A}', \hat{B}')$.

Proposition 4. *Under the RO model, and the CDH assumption in $\mathcal{G}$, the FDCR scheme is secure in the sense of Definition 9.*

Proof. Suppose an attacker $\mathcal{A}$, which given a, A, B, X_0, m_{1_0} $(A \neq B)$ outputs with non–negligible probability a valid and fresh FDCR forgery (m_{2_0}, Y_0, σ_0). Using $\mathcal{A}$ we build a polynomial time FXCR forger which succeeds with non–negligible probability. The forger $\mathcal{S}$ provides $\mathcal{A}$ with random coins, a, A, B , X_0, m_{1_0}, and simulates $\hat{B}$'s role as follows.

(a) At $\mathcal{A}$'s digest query on (X, Y, m_1, m_2), $\mathcal{S}$ responds as follows: *(i)* if a value is already assigned to $\bar{H}(X, Y, m_1, m_2)$, $\mathcal{S}$ returns $\bar{H}(X, Y, m_1, m_2)$; *(ii)* else $\mathcal{S}$ responds with $d \in_R \{0, 1\}^l$, and sets $\bar{H}(X, Y, m_1, m_2) = d$.
(b) At signature query on (m_1, X), $\mathcal{S}$ responds as follows: *(i)* $\mathcal{S}$ chooses $m_2 \in_R \{0, 1\}^*$, $s_B \in_R [1, q-1], d, e \in_R \{0, 1\}^l$, computes $Y = G^{s_B} B^{-e}$, and sets $\bar{H}(X, Y, m_1, m_2) = d$ and $\bar{H}(Y, X, m_1, m_2) = e$; if $\bar{H}(X, Y, m_1, m_2)$ or $\bar{H}(Y, X, m_1, m_2)$ was previously defined, $\mathcal{S}$ aborts. *(ii)* $\mathcal{S}$ provides $\mathcal{A}$ with the signature $(m_2, Y, (XA^d)^{s_B})$.

The simulated environment is perfect, except with negligible probability. The deviation happens when the same message–challenge pair (m_2, Y) is chosen twice in two signature queries on the same pair (m_1, X). Since Y is chosen uniformly at random in $\mathcal{G}$, this deviation happens with negligible probability. Then, if $\mathcal{A}$ succeeds with non–negligible probability in FDCR forging attack, it succeeds also with non–negligible probability under this simulation. And since $\mathcal{S}$ knows a, it outputs from any valid forgery σ_0

$$\sigma_0(Y_0 B^e)^{-da} = (Y_0 B^e)^{x_0 + da}(Y_0 B^e)^{-da} = X_0^{y_0 + eb}.$$

This is valid FXCR forgery on the message (m_{1_0}, m_{2_0}) (the concatenation of m_{1_0} and m_{2_0}) and challenge X_0 with respect to the public key B. And if $\mathcal{A}$ succeeds with non–negligible probability, so does $\mathcal{S}$, contradicting Proposition 3.

Definition 10 (Hashed FDCR (HFDCR) scheme). *Let $\hat{A}$ and $\hat{B}$ be two entities with public keys $A, B \in_R \mathcal{G}^*$. The HFDCR signature of $\hat{A}$ and $\hat{B}$ on messages m_1, m_2 and challenges X, Y is $HFDCR_{A,B}(X, Y, m_1, m_2) = H(\sigma, m_1, m_2, X, Y)$, where $\sigma = FDSig_{\hat{A},\hat{B}}(m_1, m_2, X, Y)$.*

Definition 11 (Security of the HFDCR scheme). *Let $\hat{A}$ and $\hat{B}$ be two entities with public keys $A, B \in_R \mathcal{G}^*$. The HFDCR scheme is said to be secure, if given A, B, $x_0, y_0 \in_R [1, q-1]$, together with hashing and signing oracles, no adaptive probabilistic polynomial time attacker can output with non negligible success probability a triple $(m_{1_0}, m_{2_0}, \pi_0)$ such that: $HFDCR_{A,B}(X_0, Y_0, m_{1_0}, m_{2_0}) = \pi_0$, and π_0 was not obtained from the signing oracle with a query on a quadruple (X_0, Y_0, m'_1, m'_2) such that $(m_{1_0}, m_{2_0}) = (m'_1, m'_2)$.*

For the HFDRC security arguments, we need the Gap Diffie–Hellman (GDH) assumption [11]. An algorithm is said to be a *Decisional Diffie–Hellman Oracle* (DDHO) for $\mathcal{G}$, if on input $G, X = G^x, Y = G^y$, and $Z \in \mathcal{G}$, it outputs 1 if and only if $Z = G^{xy}$. The *Gap Diffie–Hellman* (GDH) assumption is said to hold in $\mathcal{G}$, if given a DDHO for $\mathcal{G}$, there exists no polynomially bounded algorithm which solves the CDH problem in $\mathcal{G}$, with non–negligible success probability.

Proposition 5. *Under the GDH assumption, and the RO model, the HFDCR scheme is secure in the sense of Definition 11.*

Proof. Suppose a polynomially bounded attacker $\mathcal{A}$, which given a DDHO, $A, B \in_R \mathcal{G}^*$, and $x_0, y_0 \in_R [1, q-1]$, outputs with non–negligible success probability a valid and fresh $HFDCR_{A,B}$ signature on some messages m_{1_0}, m_{2_0} with respect to the challenges $X_0 = G^{x_0}, Y_0 = G^{y_0}$.

Non–matching HFDCR signature queries cannot have the same signature value, except with negligible probability; and (under th RO model) guessing the output of a hash function cannot be done with non–negligible success probability. We thus suppose that $\mathcal{A}$ succeeds with non–negligible probability in forging attack. Using $\mathcal{A}$ and a DDHO, we build a polynomial time CDH solver $\mathcal{S}$ which succeeds with non–negligible probability. The solver $\mathcal{S}$ provides $\mathcal{A}$ with random coins and simulates the signature queries; it takes as input $A, B \in_R \mathcal{G}^*$, $x_0, y_0 \in_R [1, q-1]$, and outputs $CDH(A, B)$ with non–negligible success probability. The interactions between $\mathcal{A}$ and $\mathcal{S}$ are as follows.

(1) At $\mathcal{A}$'s $\bar{H}$ digest query on (X, Y, m_1, m_2), $\mathcal{S}$ does the following: if a value is already assigned to $\bar{H}(X, Y, m_1, m_2)$, $\mathcal{S}$ provides $\mathcal{A}$ with the value of $\bar{H}(X, Y, m_1, m_2)$; else $\mathcal{S}$ chooses $d \in_R \{0, 1\}^l$, sets $\bar{H}(X, Y, m_1, m_2) = d$, and provides $\mathcal{A}$ with d.

(2) At $\mathcal{A}$'s signature query on (X, Y, m_1, m_2), $\mathcal{S}$ responds as follows.
  - If same query was performed previously, $\mathcal{S}$ returns the previously returned value.
  - Else $\mathcal{S}$ chooses $\pi \in_R \{0,1\}^\lambda$, sets $HFDCR_{A,B}(X, Y, m_1, m_2) = \pi$, and provides $\mathcal{A}$ with π.
  - If no value is assigned to $h_1 = \bar{H}(X, Y, m_1, m_2)$ (resp. $h_2 = \bar{H}(Y, X, m_1, m_2)$), $\mathcal{S}$ chooses $d \in_R \{0,1\}^l$ and sets $h_1 = d$ (resp. $h_2 = d$).
(3) At $\mathcal{A}$'s digest query on (σ, m_1, m_2, X, Y), $\mathcal{S}$ does the following.
  - If a value is already assigned to $HFDCR_{A,B}(X, Y, m_1, m_2)$ (in this case, $d = \bar{H}(X, Y, m_1, m_2)$ and $e = \bar{H}(Y, X, m_1, m_2)$ are already defined), and if $\sigma = CDH(XA^d, YB^e)$, $\mathcal{S}$ returns $HFDCR_{A,B}(X, Y, m_1, m_2)$.
  - Else, (i) if the same query was issued previously, $\mathcal{S}$ returns the previously returned value; (ii) else $\mathcal{S}$ chooses $\pi \in_R \{0,1\}^\lambda$, sets $H(\sigma, m_1, m_2, X, Y) = \pi$, and provides $\mathcal{A}$ with π.
  - If no value is assigned to $h_1 = \bar{H}(X, Y, m_1, m_2)$ (resp. $h_2 = \bar{H}(Y, X, m_1, m_2)$), $\mathcal{S}$ chooses $d \in_R \{0,1\}^l$ and sets $h_1 = d$ (resp. $h_2 = d$); and if $\sigma = CDH(XA^d, YB^e)$, $\mathcal{S}$ sets $HFDCR_{A,B}(X, Y, m_1, m_2) = \pi$.
(4) If $\mathcal{A}$ halts with a forgery $(m_{1_0}, m_{2_0}, \pi_0)$, $\mathcal{S}$ verifies that the digest value π_0 was issued from the random oracle, as $H(\sigma_0, m_{1_0}, m_{2_0}, X_0, Y_0)$ for some σ_0, and that $\sigma_0 = CDH(X_0 A^{d_0}, Y_0 B^{e_0})$, where $d_0 = \bar{H}(X_0, Y_0, m_{1_0}, m_{2_0})$, and $e_0 = \bar{H}(Y_0, X_0, m_{1_0}, m_{2_0})$ (if π_0 was issued from the hashing oracle, d_0 and e_0 are defined, an the verification is performed using the DDHO).

Under the RO model, $\mathcal{A}$'s simulated environment is perfect except with negligible probability; hence if $\mathcal{A}$ succeeds with non–negligible probability in forging attack, except a negligible difference, it succeeds with the same probability under this simulation. Since $\mathcal{S}$ knows x_0, y_0, and $\mathcal{A}$ succeeds with non–negligible probability, $\mathcal{S}$ outputs with non–negligible probability

$$\left(\left((\sigma_0)(Y_0 B^e)^{-x_0}\right)^{d^{-1}} A^{-y_0}\right)^{e^{-1}} = \left(\left((Y_0 B^e)^{x_0 + da}(Y_0 B^e)^{-x_0}\right)^{d^{-1}} A^{-y_0}\right)^{e^{-1}}$$
$$= \left(\left((Y_0 B^e)^{da}\right)^{d^{-1}} A^{-y_0}\right)^{e^{-1}} = CDH(A, B);$$

contradiction the GDH assumption.

4.2   The Fully Hashed MQV Protocol

We can now derive the FHMQV protocol, which provides the efficiency and security attributes of the (H)MQV protocols, in addition to being ephemeral secret exponent leakage resilient.

The FHMQV protocol is secure in the sense of Definition 5 under the GDH assumption and the RO model. (Please, refer to the extended version of this paper [14], which discusses in detail the security arguments.). The ck–security arguments follow from the FDCR signature scheme security. Indeed, under the CDH assumption and the RO model, from any attacker which succeeds with non–negligible probability in distinguishing a ck–fresh session key from a

---

Protocol 5. FHMQV key exchange

I) The initiator $\hat{A}$ does the following:
   (a) Choose $x \in_R [1, q - 1]$ and compute $X = G^x$.
   (b) Send $(\hat{A}, \hat{B}, X)$ to $\hat{B}$.
II) At receipt of $(\hat{A}, \hat{B}, X)$, $\hat{B}$ does the following:
   (a) Verify that $X \in \mathcal{G}^*$.
   (b) Choose $y \in_R [1, q - 1]$ and compute $Y = G^y$.
   (c) Send $(\hat{B}, \hat{A}, Y)$ to $\hat{A}$.
   (d) Compute $d = \bar{H}(X, Y, \hat{A}, \hat{B})$ and $e = \bar{H}(Y, X, \hat{A}, \hat{B})$.
   (e) Compute $s_B = y + eb \bmod q$, $\sigma_B = (XA^d)^{s_B}$, and $K = H(\sigma_B, \hat{A}, \hat{B}, X, Y)$.
III) At receipt of $(\hat{B}, \hat{A}, Y)$, $\hat{A}$ does the following:
   (a) Verify that $Y \in \mathcal{G}^*$.
   (b) Compute $d = \bar{H}(X, Y, \hat{A}, \hat{B})$ and $e = \bar{H}(Y, X, \hat{A}, \hat{B})$.
   (c) Compute $s_A = x + da \bmod q$, $\sigma_A = (YB^e)^{s_A}$, and $K = H(\sigma_A, \hat{A}, \hat{B}, X, Y)$.
IV) The shared session key is K.

Protocol 6. FHMQV–C key exchange

I) $\hat{A}$ does the following:
   (a) Choose $x \in_R [1, q - 1]$ and compute $X = G^x$.
   (b) Send $(\hat{A}, \hat{B}, X)$ to $\hat{B}$.
II) At receipt of $(\hat{A}, \hat{B}, X)$, $\hat{B}$ does the following:
   (a) Verify that $X \in \mathcal{G}^*$.
   (b) Choose $y \in_R [1, q - 1]$ and compute $Y = G^y$.
   (c) Compute $d = \bar{H}(X, Y, \hat{A}, \hat{B})$ and $e = \bar{H}(Y, X, \hat{A}, \hat{B})$.
   (d) Compute $s_B = y + eb \bmod q$, $\sigma_B = (XA^d)^{s_B}$.
   (e) Compute and $K_1 = KDF_1(\sigma_B, \hat{A}, \hat{B}, X, Y)$ and $t_B = MAC_{K_1}(\hat{B}, Y)$.
   (f) Send $(\hat{B}, \hat{A}, Y, t_B)$ to $\hat{A}$.
III) At receipt of $(\hat{B}, \hat{A}, Y, t_B)$, $\hat{A}$ does the following:
   (a) Verify that $Y \in \mathcal{G}^*$.
   (b) Compute $d = \bar{H}(X, Y, \hat{A}, \hat{B})$ and $e = \bar{H}(Y, X, \hat{A}, \hat{B})$.
   (c) Compute $s_A = x + da \bmod q$ and $\sigma_A = (YB^e)^{s_A}$.
   (d) Compute $K_1 = KDF(\sigma_A, \hat{A}, \hat{B}, X, Y)$.
   (e) Verify that $t_B = MAC_{K_1}(\hat{B}, Y)$.
   (f) Compute $t_A = MAC_{K_1}(\hat{A}, X)$ and send t_A to $\hat{B}$.
   (g) Compute $K_2 = KDF_2(\sigma_B, \hat{A}, \hat{B}, X, Y)$
IV) At receipt of t_A, $\hat{B}$ does the following:
   (a) Verify that $t_A = MAC_{K_1}(\hat{A}, X)$.
   (b) Compute $K_2 = KDF_2(\sigma_B, \hat{A}, \hat{B}, X, Y)$.
V) The shared session key is K_2.

---

random value, one can build a polynomial time machine, which succeeds with non–negligible probability in forging a valid FDCR signature or solving the CDH problem. The eck–security attribute is achieved under the GDH assumption and the RO model; this can be shown basing on the security of the HFDCR scheme.

When needed, FHMQV can be added with a third message, yielding the FHMQV–C protocol (the 'C' stands for *key confirmation*), we describe in Protocol 6; KDF_1 and KDF_2 are key derivation functions, and MAC is a message authentication code. (As in FHMQV, if any verification fails, the execution aborts.) When a party completes a FHMQV–C session with some honest peer, and with incoming ephemeral key Y, he is guaranteed that the incoming ephemeral key was chosen and authenticated by the peer, and that the peer can compute the session key it derives. The FHMQV–C protocol provides also perfect forward secrecy, the compromise of $\hat{A}$'s static private key, does not compromise the session keys established in previous runs. This can be shown when the analysis of FHMQV [14] is completed with the *session–key expiration* notion [2].

5   Concluding Remarks

We proposed a complementary analysis of the XCR and DCR schemes, which are the building blocks of the HMQV protocol. We showed how impersonation and man in the middle attacks can be performed against the (H)MQV protocols, when ephemeral secret exponent leakages happen.

We proposed the FXCR and FDCR signature schemes, with security arguments. Using these schemes, we defined the Fully Hashed MQV (FHMQV) protocol, which preserves the efficiency and security attributes of the (H)MQV protocols, in addition to being ephemeral secret exponent leakage resilient. We defined, for the MQV type protocols, a Canetti–Krawczyk type security model based on session's tree of computations, which aims to an exhaustive capture of session specific information leakages. The FHMQV protocol can be shown secure in this model.

In a forthcoming stage, we will be interested in the analysis of relations between the security model we propose and the Canetti–Krawczyk and extended Canetti–Krawczyk security models. We will also be interested in the generalization of the security model we propose to the Diffie–Hellman protocols.

Acknowledgments. The authors would like to thank Netheos R&D for supporting this work. We would like also to thank the EuroPKI 2009 reviewers for their useful comments.

References

1. Basin, D., Cremers, C.: From Dolev–Yao to Strong Adaptive Corruption: Analyzing Security in the Presence of Compromising Adversaries. Cryptology ePrint Archive, Report 2009/079 (2009)
2. Canetti, R., Krawczyk, H.: Analysis of Key–Exchange Protocols and Their Use for Building Secure Channels. Cryptology ePrint Archive, Report 2001/040 (2001)
3. Gopalakrishnan, K., Thériault, N., Yao, C.Z.: Solving Discrete Logarithms from Partial Knowledge of the Key. In: Srinathan, K., Rangan, C.P., Yung, M. (eds.) INDOCRYPT 2007. LNCS, vol. 4859, pp. 224–237. Springer, Heidelberg (2007)

4. Hankerson, D., Menezes, A., Vanstone, S.: Guide to Elliptic Curve Cryptography. Springer, Heidelberg (2003)
5. Krawczyk, H.: HMQV: A Hight Performance Secure Diffie–Hellman Protocol. Cryptology ePrint Archive, Report 2005/176 (2005)
6. LaMacchia, B.A., Lauter, K., Mityagin, A.: Stronger Security of Authenticated Key Exchange. In: Susilo, W., Liu, J.K., Mu, Y. (eds.) ProvSec 2007. LNCS, vol. 4784, pp. 1–16. Springer, Heidelberg (2007)
7. Law, L., Menezes, A., Qu, M., Solinas, J., Vanstone, S.: An Efficient Protocol for Authenticated Key Agreement. Designs, Codes and Cryptography 28(2), 119–134 (2003)
8. Maurer, U.M., Wolf, S.: Diffie–Hellman Oracles. In: Koblitz, N. (ed.) CRYPTO 1996. LNCS, vol. 1109, pp. 268–282. Springer, Heidelberg (1996)
9. Menezes, A.: Another Look at HMQV. Journal of Mathematical Cryptology 1, 148–175 (2007)
10. Menezes, A., Ustaoglu, B.: On the Importance of Public-Key Validation in the MQV and HMQV Key Agreement Protocols. In: Barua, R., Lange, T. (eds.) INDOCRYPT 2006. LNCS, vol. 4329, pp. 133–147. Springer, Heidelberg (2006)
11. Okamoto, T., Pointcheval, D.: The Gap–Problems: A new class of problems for the security of cryptographic schemes. In: Kim, K.-c. (ed.) PKC 2001. LNCS, vol. 1992, pp. 104–118. Springer, Heidelberg (2001)
12. Pointcheval, D., Stern, J.: Security Arguments for Digital Signatures and Blind Signatures. Journal of Cryptology 13, 361–396 (2000)
13. Pollard, J.M.: Kangaroos, Monopoly and Discrete Logarithms. Journal of Cryptology 13, 437–447 (2000)
14. Sarr, A.P., Elbaz–Vincent, P., Bajard, J.C.: A Secure and Efficient Authenticated Diffie–Hellman Protocol. Cryptology ePrint Archive, Report 2009/408 (2009)
15. Teske, E.: Square-root Algorithms for the Discrete Logarithm Problem (A survey). In: Public Key Cryptography and Computational Number Theory, pp. 283–301. Walter de Gruyter, Berlin (2001)
16. Ustaoglu, B.: Obtaining a secure and efficient key agreement protocol from (H)MQV and NAXOS. Designs, Codes and Cryptography 46(3), 329–342 (2008)

Key Management for Large-Scale Distributed Storage Systems

Hoon Wei Lim

SAP Research, Sophia Antipolis, France
hoon.wei.lim@sap.com

Abstract. Petabyte-scale file systems are often extremely large, containing gigabytes or terabytes of data that can be spread across hundreds or thousands of storage devices. Hence, the cost of security operations can be very high. Recent security proposals for large-scale file systems have been focussing on the use of hybrid symmetric and asymmetric key cryptographic techniques, in order to strive for a balance between security and performance. However, key management issues, such as distribution, renewal and revocation of keys, have not been explicitly addressed. In this paper, we first show that key management can be very challenging and costly in large-scale systems, and can have significant impact on the scalability of the systems. We then propose a file system security architecture which makes use of lightweight key management techniques. Our approach not only addresses essential key management concerns, it also improves existing proposals with stronger security and better usability.

1 Introduction

Cryptographic key management, such as generation, distribution, storage, renewal and revocation of keys, is the foundation for securing a system. It can be very challenging, particularly for petabyte-scale, open distributed file systems because the cost of managing keys may be far higher than the cost of executing security mechanisms or protocols in which the keys are used. Files in such systems are often extremely large, containing terabytes of data, which can be spread across thousands of devices and accessed by thousands of clients [14,23]. While it is possible that the authenticated public key of each storage device is made available to all clients within the system, it can be very difficult and costly for the clients to manage such large sets of public keys, particularly in terms of key renewal and revocation.

Most prior work on large-scale file systems, particularly those based on object storage devices or network-attached disks [2,19], presupposes that all keys required to perform security protocols are held by all the relevant parties. For example, Leung et al. [16] recently proposed Maat, a set of security protocols designed to provide strong and scalable security for petabyte-scale file systems by making use of various state-of-the-art techniques, such as extended capabilities, automatic revocation and secure delegation. While Maat appears to be currently the most efficient and scalable proposal, Leung et al. assumed that each client knows the

F. Martinelli and B. Preneel (Eds.): EuroPKI 2009, LNCS 6391, pp. 99–113, 2010.

authenticated public key of all other entities in the system. This is a rather strong assumption which has significant impact on the overall performance and scalability of the system. We further explain why this is the case. In Maat, each storage device within a file system possesses a public/private key pair, of which the public component is assumed to be available to all clients in the system. A client must then, using the relevant storage device public keys, establish shared symmetric keys with storage devices on which the client stores its files. (This is necessary so that the client can subsequently access its files in a secure and efficient manner.) We note that the process of establishing a shared key has to be repeated thousands of times if the client has many large files stored across thousands of storage devices. A more worrying concern is that if a storage device is compromised or corrupted, and thus so as its private key and the symmetric keys that the device shares with its clients, revocation and replacement of these keys can be extremely tedious and costly. Similarly, when new storage devices are added to the system, it may also be costly to distribute new public keys to all the clients. Other recent proposals, such as [15,21], also assumed the existence of all necessary authenticated public keys and did not address issues related to key distribution, key renewal and revocation either. They focussed on other security aspects instead, for example issuance and revocation of coarse-grained capabilities.

In this paper, we propose a file system security architecture (FSSA) which not only addresses the aforementioned key management issues, but also has stronger security and better usability in comparison with the recent proposals. In large-scale and highly distributed file systems, storage devices can be vulnerable to various attacks and may encounter hardware or software failure, and thus this may lead to exposure of secret cryptographic keys or data stored on the devices. However, this has not been explicitly taken into consideration in the existing security model, although it has significant impact on not only key management, but also the data protected by the relevant keys. Hence, we first propose a stronger security model for large-scale object storage systems by considering *forward secrecy*, an essential security property for shared key establishment between two parties [18]. In our security model, we assume that a long-term secret key stored on a storage device can be corrupted or exposed, and that even when the key is revealed to an adversary, past session keys derived using the long-term key are still protected from the adversary.

Our proposal of FSSA then employs lightweight key management techniques suitable for petabyte-scale object storage file systems. In our approach, clients make use of only short-lived cryptographic keys in order to negotiate shared symmetric keys with storage devices. Thus this obviates many difficulties in public key management, such as key revocation and renewal. We develop an authenticated key agreement protocol using the classic Diffie-Hellman key exchange technique [8]. Our protocol is not only lightweight, but also shown to be secure in the stronger security model.

Managing public keys, such as authenticating public keys and checking for their validity, can be complicated for a non-IT savvy. Even an IT savvy may not have general understanding of the security implication of inappropriate public key management. Therefore, unlike many existing proposals, our approach is very user-friendly, since users do not possess large sets of storage device public keys. All is required for a user is to remember a password which she shares with her metadata server and has access to the server's public key. The server's public key is needed so that essential security features for a large-scale distributed file system, for example extended capabilities and delegation [16], can be provided.

In the next section, we provide related work in large-scale file system security. In Section 3, we present our proposal for a file system security architecture. We also describe a security model, key management, an authenticated key agreement protocol and its security and performance analyses. We conclude in Section 4.

2   Related Work

Most earlier work in securing large-scale distributed file systems, for example [11,12], employed Kerberos [20] for performing authentication and enforcing access control. Kerberos, being based on symmetric key cryptography, is usually regarded as a very efficient approach. However, it is generally believed to be more suitable for rather closed, well-connected distributed environments.

On the other hand, data grids and file systems such as, OceanStore [14], LegionFS [24] and FARSITE [1], make use of public key cryptographic techniques and public key infrastructure (PKI) to perform cross-domain user authentication. Independently, SFS [17], also based on public key cryptographic techniques, was designed to enable inter-operability of different key management schemes. Each user of these systems is assumed to possess a certified public/private key pair. However, these systems were not designed specifically with usable and scalable security in mind. Furthermore, they did not address key management issues that we highlighted in the previous section.

With the increasing deployment of highly distributed and network-attached storage systems, subsequent work, such as [2,10,26], focussed on scalable security. Nevertheless, these proposals assumed that a metadata server shares a group secret key with each distributed storage device. The group key is used to produce capabilities in the form of message authentication codes [18]. However, compromise of the metadata server or any storage device allows the adversary to impersonate the server to any other entities in the file system. This issue can be alleviated by requiring that each storage device shares a different secret key with the metadata server. Nevertheless, such an approach restricts a capability to authorising I/O on only a single device, rather than larger groups of blocks or objects which may reside on multiple storage devices.

More recent proposals, which adopted a hybrid symmetric key and asymmetric key method, allow a capability to span any number of storage devices, while maintaining a reasonable efficiency-security ratio [15,16,21]. Among these proposals, Maat [16] appears to be currently the most refined set of security protocols which consider various security issues identified and lessons learned from other existing work.

Briefly, Maat encompasses a set of protocols that facilitate (i) authenticated key establishment between clients and storage devices, (ii) capability issuance and renewal, and (iii) delegation between two clients. The authenticated key establishment protocol allows a client to establish a shared (session) key with a storage device by performing the following steps:

1. generates a public/private key pair;
2. requests for a ticket, which certifies the newly created public key, from the metadata server;
3. creates and transports a session key to the storage device using the device's public key;

Note that the above protocol presupposes that the client has access to all the relevant storage device public keys, which are required for the key establishment. Moreover the client's and the device's public/private key pairs, and their shared session key, are considered reasonably long-term and updated infrequently. The main reason for this is that in a large-scale file system, establishing session keys with thousands of storage devices can be extremely computationally expensive. Therefore, the strategy is to use asymmetric cryptographic techniques to setup symmetric session keys, which in turn, are used for a relatively long period.

In order to access files on specific storage devices, the client then obtains a short-term capability from the metadata server. The capability specifies the client's I/O request and access permissions, which allow the storage devices to evaluate whether or not the client is authorised to access the requested data[1]. The data transmitted between the client and storage devices are protected using the shared keys established earlier. Maat makes use of relatively short-lived capabilities, typically 5 minutes, so that they are not required to be revoked explicitly using a revocation mechanism, but simply allowing the capabilities to expire automatically. Should a client require access to files longer than 5 minutes, Maat allows the client to request for capability renewal from the metadata server. In addition, secure file sharing between clients through delegation is also supported by Maat. Description about how delegation is performed in Maat can be found in [16].

Nevertheless, the assumption of Maat and other proposals which requires user public keys to be made available to all storage devices seems impractical. This is because users may join or leave the systems over time, and thus new public keys would be generated or existing public keys would be revoked. It is not clear how new or revoked public keys can be communicated to all users in the systems on a timely basis.

3   File System Security Architecture

Our proposal of a file system security architecture (FSSA) is based on the current model for object storage devices or network-attached disks [2,19]. Unlike existing

---

[1] We note that a capability is typically associated with one client and a single file, which may be composed of object blocks distributed across multiple storage devices. On the other hand, an extended capability is associated with multiple clients and files. A metadata servers produces and caches extended capabilities in order to reduce its workload.

proposals, however, we emphasise simplified, lightweight key management and improved usability in our approach. In FSSA, a client does not make use of long-term cryptographic keys when accessing data on storage devices. All is assumed, from the client's perspective, is that it needs to share a secret, *i.e.* password, with its metadata server. The client then interacts with the storage devices using only short-term cryptographic keys, which in turn, will be destroyed at the end of a session. We also assume that each storage device pre-distributes some keying material to the metadata server when it is first added to the system. Figure 1 gives an overview of our security architecture. We will explain the steps involved in requesting and accessing files using FSSA in Section 3.3.

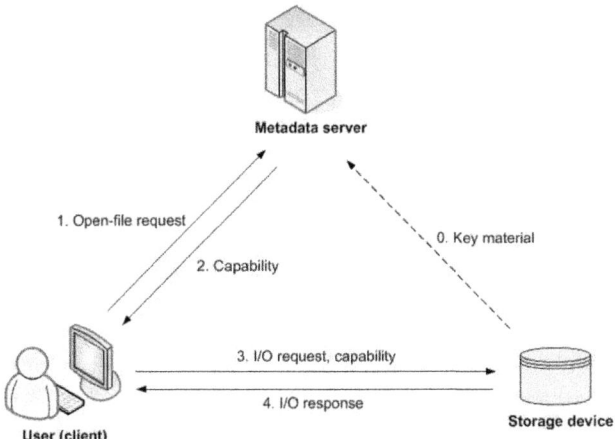

Fig. 1. Architectural view of FSSA

Notice that for simplicity of exposition, in this section, we only consider the case of a single metadata server handling metadata and facilitating clients' access to storage devices. Our approach can be extended straightforwardly to cope with multiple servers. We also assume that each client can access to a relatively large number of storage devices, *i.e.* on the orders of hundreds or thousands.

In what follows, we first refine existing security assumptions and provide a stronger security model which reflects more realistic security requirements of large-scale distributed file systems. We then highlight existing key management issues and present our approach to alleviating these issues. We also present our authenticated key agreement protocol between a metadata server, a client and a storage device, in order to establish a session key shared between the client and the storage device. The protocol is developed using our simplified key management techniques and after taking into consideration the refined security assumptions.

3.1 Security Model

The security model used in existing proposals assumes that both a metadata server and storage devices are trusted entities [10,15,16,21]. The former is trusted to act as a reference monitor and issue valid capabilities, while the latter are trusted to store data and only perform I/O operations upon authorised requests. On the other hand, no implicit trust is placed on clients.

A large-scale file system may have thousands of storage devices which are geographically distributed. Thus it may not be feasible to provide strong physical security and network protection for all the devices. This implies that storage devices are at a higher risk of being compromised compared to a metadata server, which can usually be physically secured and protected. Furthermore, storage devices may encounter hardware or software failure, causing the data stored on them no longer accessible. We believe that these risks are serious and have significant impact on the design of security protocols and their associated key management.

We, therefore, raise the security bar of protocols for large-scale object storage systems by considering forward secrecy, which has already been an important part of the security requirements for most modern security protocols [5]. The idea of forward secrecy is that previous encrypted data is securely locked in the past [18]. For example, if a key establishment protocol performed between a client and a storage device provides forward secrecy, past session keys shared between the client and the storage device will not be exposed even if one of their long-term private key (or secret component) has been compromised. This is to ensure that all data encrypted under past session keys and exchanged between the two parties will not be revealed. This is clearly a very desirable security property, particularly if we assume that cryptographic keys stored in a storage device can be vulnerable to exposure.

We now sketch the definition of the security of our authenticated key agreement protocol, which will be discussed in Section 3.3. Our protocol is based on the Diffie-Hellman key exchange technique [8]. In our security model, we assume that the entire communication network is managed by an adversary, who may schedule interactions arbitrarily, and who may inject, modify and drop messages arbitrarily.

Computational Diffie-Hellman (CDH) Problem. Given $g^a, g^b \in \mathbb{G}$, where $\mathbb{G}$ is a cyclic group of prime order q generated by g, and a, b are randomly chosen from $\{1, \ldots, q-1\}$, the CDH problem in $\mathbb{G}$ is to compute g^{ab}.

The CDH assumption then says it is computationally intractable to compute the value g^{ab} within polynomial time.

Definition 1 (Informal). *We say that the authenticated key agreement protocol between a client, a metadata server and a storage device is secure if all the following conditions are satisfied, assuming the CDH problem is hard.*

1. *The client and the storage device are mutually authenticated.*
2. *No useful information about the session key between the client and the storage device is revealed to the adversary during a successful protocol run.*
3. *The exposure of the current session key does not leak any information about past session keys.*

4. The exposure of either the client's, metadata server's or storage device's long-term credential does not leak any information about past session keys, thus achieving forward secrecy.

We remark that formal specification of the security model and definitions, such as those used in [3], is beyond the scope of this paper since we focus on addressing key management issues.

3.2   Key Management

As explained before, Maat and other large-scale file systems, such as [1,14,24], presuppose that each client has knowledge of all the required authenticated public keys that can be used "on-the-fly". However, in reality, managing long-term public keys can be very problematic and costly [9,22]. This is particularly true for large-scale file systems. Furthermore, Maat and recent proposals, for example [15,16,21], adopt the use of long-term (symmetric) session keys in order to reduce cryptographic operation costs. This increases the risk of exposing sensitive data transmitted between the clients and the storage devices.

In FSSA, we employ a lightweight and "just-in-time" key management approach, in which the client is not required to possess long-term public keys of storage devices, but makes use of only ephemeral key materials in order to establish a session key with each storage device. These short-lived key materials are generated as needed, and destroyed at the end of a security session, and therefore the client can avoid long-term key management and its associated issues. Furthermore, the client does not perform any asymmetric cryptographic operations during key establishment with the storage devices. More importantly, our simplified key management approach suits perfectly the stronger security model defined in Section 3.1 that ensures forward secrecy. Further details of our approach are as follows.

Pre-distribution of keys. As mentioned earlier, we assume that the metadata server is the root of trust, and thus is trusted by the clients and the storage devices to issue authenticated and valid capabilities. In order to verify these capabilities, all the clients and devices must be in possession of the server's public key. We assume this can be achieved by bootstrapping the server public key into the system, or by making the public key available to the clients and devices during a one-off registration process. Note that this is a much weaker assumption than having to assume that each client has knowledge of the authenticated public key of every storage device[2].

In addition, our approach requires that each storage device distributes key material in the form of a Diffie-Hellman component, $g^{d_0} \in \mathbb{G}$, to the server through an authenticated channel. This can also be achieved during the registration process. Here $\mathbb{G}$ is a group generated by g and d_0 is a randomly

---

[2] It is also reasonable to assume that the metadata server is less likely to be compromised (and thus so is its private key) and more reliable than distributed storage devices.

chosen number. The Diffie-Hellman component is relatively long-term and will not be renewed frequently, unless the value d_0, which is supposed to be known only to the storage device, is exposed.

Ephemeral key generation. For each file access request, the client generates a new Diffie-Hellman component g^c, where c is randomly chosen. The Diffie-Hellman value is then used by the client to request a capability from the metadata server.

It is worth noting that a storage device's key material (g^{d_0}) is distributed to a client as part of the capability issued to the client. This way, the task of obtaining and validating the storage device's key material has been transferred from the client to the server. We remark that this eases significantly the problem of revoking the key material if the associated secret component (d_0) is compromised. This is because it is much easier and sensible for *only the server* to obtain an up-to-date revocation list on a timely basis, instead of relying on *all clients* to update their respective revocation lists regularly and check for revoked key materials[3].

Session key generation. In our FSSA approach, a fresh shared key is used between the client and a storage device for each new security session. Both the client and the storage device shares a session key by exchanging their respective fresh Diffie-Hellman components, from which a composite Diffie-Hellman value can be computed and used to derive the session key. More details on the Diffie-Hellman key agreement technique will be provided in Section 3.3.

Deletion of keys. At the end of each file access session between the client and the storage device, all ephemeral Diffie-Hellman values and key materials, for example c and g^c, are deleted from the memory upon completion of a protocol run. The session key is also destroyed. This implies that the client uses only short-term key materials and fresh session keys. Hence, key revocation is not a major concern from the client's perspective. We note that deletion of short-term key materials and session keys is essential in order to achieve forward secrecy.

We are now ready to show how our simplified key management techniques influence the design of our key agreement protocol, particularly in order to achieve forward secrecy.

3.3 Authenticated Key Agreement

In our simplified key management approach, users make use of only short-term key materials and it is possible for a client and a storage device to agree on a session key based on the key materials in a lightweight manner. (Recall that Maat requires the storage device's public key to transport a session.) Our authenticated

---

[3] Notice that this approach can be adopted by Maat to alleviate the problem of revoking storage devices' public keys. However Maat still needs to cope with the problem of revoking clients' long-term public keys of which the private keys have been exposed.

key agreement protocol not only retains features provided by Maat, such as the use of extended capabilities, but also meets the stronger security requirements defined in Section 3.1. We now present our 3-party authenticated key agreement protocol in FSSA between a client, a metadata server and a storage device. This is shown in Figure 2.

Notation. We use C and S to denote a client and a metadata server, respectively, while D denotes a storage device or disk. We then use $\mathsf{Sig}_S(\cdot)$ to indicate signing using S's signing key SK_S, and MAC_S to denote a message authentication code produced using S's secret key K_S. Both the signature and MAC schemes are assumed to be secure against existential forgeability under adaptive chosen-message attacks [18]. Other notations will be introduced as they are needed.

$$
\begin{aligned}
&(1)\ C \rightarrow S:\ \mathtt{open(path, mode)}, g^c, T_C,\\
&\qquad\qquad \mathsf{MAC}_{CS}(\mathtt{open(path, mode)}, g^c, T_C)\\
&(2)\ S \rightarrow C:\ \mathtt{access\_info}, \mathsf{Sig}_S(\mathtt{access\_info}, g^c, T_C)\\
&(3)\ C \rightarrow D:\ \mathtt{operate(object\_id)}, \mathtt{access\_info}, g^c, T_C\\
&\qquad\qquad \mathsf{MAC}_{CD_0}(\mathtt{operate(object\_id)}),\\
&\qquad\qquad \mathsf{Sig}_S(\mathtt{access\_info}, g^c, T_C)\\
&(4)\ D \rightarrow C:\ g^d, \mathsf{MAC}_{CD_0}(g^d, T_C)
\end{aligned}
$$

Fig. 2. Authenticated key agreement protocol in FSSA

We assume that the client (acting on a user's behalf) and the server can authenticate each other and establish a session key K_{CS} using the classic hybrid username/password and TLS/SSL handshake method, for example. (Note that the server-authenticated TLS handshake does not require a client public key certificate [7].) Alternatively, Kerberos or any well-studied password-based authenticated key agreement protocol, such as [4,25], can be used.

In order to access the data stored on a storage device, a client, as with other proposals, must first obtain a valid capability from its metadata server. In step (1), the client submits an $\mathtt{open()}$ request to the metadata server, where $\mathtt{path}$ specifies a file's namespace and $\mathtt{mode}$ specifies the access mode: read, write, or both. The client also computes and sends a fresh Diffie-Hellman value g^c, where c is randomly chosen, and a lifetime T_C to the server. The integrity of the information that the client transmits to the server is protected through a MAC value computed using the session key K_{CS}.

In step (2), the metadata server checks if the lifetime T_C is valid and the client is permitted to access the file. If so, the server retrieves information required to generate a capability, which is in the form of a signature

$$\mathsf{Sig}_S(\mathtt{access\_info}, g^c, T_C),$$

generated using the server's long-term private key. Here, $\mathtt{access\_info}$ specifies the long-term Diffie-Hellman component of the relevant storage device, g^{d_0}, and other access details such as, the client's identity, the file handle (which lists objects or physical blocks that compose the file), file identifier, access mode and capability identifier [2,21]. The capability is then returned to the client, so that it can later be used by the client to prove its access rights for the specified file. Note that the capability can be verified by any party who possesses an authentic copy of the metadata server's public key.

Upon receiving the capability, the client extracts the Diffie-Hellman component g^{d_o} and computes a pre-session key

$$K_{CD_0} = F(C, D, g^{cd_o}, T_C),$$

where F is a key derivation function based on a secure hash function, for example. (Further details and examples on key derivation can be found in [13].) The client then issues an I/O operation request to the relevant storage device. As shown in step (3), the request contains the necessary information which allows the client to communicate to the storage device the target objects to be accessed, as well as to convince the storage device that the client is indeed authorised for the access. (We assume that the object_id can be extracted from the access_info.) The pre-session key K_{CD_0} is used by the client to compute a MAC on the request, in order to authenticate itself to the storage device.

In the last step of the protocol, the storage device verifies the validity of the client's capability and the MAC value. Note that the storage device could compute the key K_{CD_0} because it knows the secret value d_0, which in turn, is applied on the client's chosen Diffie-Hellman value g^c. The storage device then generates a fresh Diffie-Hellman value g^d, where d is randomly chosen. The session key, K_{CD}, between the client and the storage device is then set to be

$$F(C, D, g^{cd_o}, g^{cd}, T_C).$$

We have so far considered only the case of a client accessing a single storage device. Nevertheless, note that a capability can be used by a client to establish secure connections with multiple storage devices if a large file is spread across different locations. Moreover, our approach can be extended straightforwardly to cope with the concept of extended capabilities of Maat by explicitly specifying all authorised users and file identifiers in a capability. For example, authorised users and file identifiers are specified using hash (Merkle) trees so that they can be aggregated into fixed size data structures and embedded into a single capability [16]. Similarly, we can also employ the capability renewal techniques used in Maat in our protocol. Briefly speaking, the client renews its expiring capability by sending it to its metadata server, which then issues a new capability with an extended lifetime. Since a capability usually has a short validity period, capability revocation is not a major concern.

To summarise, our authenticated key agreement protocol makes use of Diffie-Hellman key agreement techniques and it does not rely on computationally expensive public key encryption. Moreover, our approach has the luxury of using a fresh session key between a client and a storage device for each new security session (rather than re-using a session key for many different security sessions).

3.4   Security Analysis

We now provide heuristic security analysis of our authenticated key agreement protocol based on the security definition given in Section 3.1.

The value $\mathsf{MAC}_{CS}(\mathtt{open}(\mathtt{path},\mathtt{mode}), g^c, T_C)$ computed by the client in step (1) of our protocol is used to detect illegitimate modification to the Diffie-Hellman component g^c chosen by the client. The client also includes a lifetime T_C in its message in order to prevent a replay attack. Since we assume that the key K_{CS} is an authenticated session key shared between the client and the metadata server, any changes made to the message sent by the client can be detected by the metadata server. The MAC value is also used to prevent a man-in-the-middle attack.

In step (2), we trust the metadata server to issue a valid capability, containing the appropriate file access details required by the client. In particular, we trust that the server will include the correct Diffie-Hellman component of the relevant storage device g^{d_0}. A capability issued by the metadata server can be verified using the server's public key.

The message $\mathsf{MAC}_{CD_0}(\mathtt{operate}(\mathtt{object\_id}))$ of step (3) is used by the client to prove knowledge of the secret value c, which is needed to compute the pre-session key K_{CD_0}. The client is authenticated to the storage device if the MAC value can be verified successfully. This is because the capability issued by the metadata server can be used to verify the binding between the Diffie-Hellman value g^c and the client's identity.

In step (4), the message $\mathsf{MAC}_{CD_0}(g^d, T_C)$ computed by the storage device is used to authenticate itself to the client. Other than the client, the only party who should be able to compute K_{CD_0} is the storage device, which knows the secret value d_0.

It is clear that requirement 1 of Definition 1 is satisfied, assuming that the signature and MAC schemes are secure against existential forgeability under adaptive chosen-message attacks. Moreover, since the session key cannot be computed directly by the adversary (but only by parties who know either the secret value c or d due to the hardness of the CDH problem), requirement 2 is satisfied too.

Each session key of a protocol run is computed based on the Diffie-Hellman value g^{cd}, which in turn, is based on new, ephemeral Diffie-Hellman components g^c and g^d randomly chosen by the client and the storage device, respectively. This implies that, in principle, the computed session key should be indistinguishable from a randomly generated bit string of similar size. Therefore, in the event of exposure of a current session key, the adversary has only a negligible probability of discovering any past session keys through a brute-force search, for example. We then conjecture that the protocol satisfies requirement 3.

On certain rare occasion, the adversary may have access to the client's machine or the storage device, thus their long-term credentials[4] are exposed. However, this does not reveal any useful information about any past session keys. This is because computing a session key requires knowledge of one of the ephemeral

---

[4] In this case, we refer to the client's password which it shares with the metadata server, and the storage device's long-term secret value d_0.

secret values, c or d, which are assumed to be deleted upon completion of each protocol run. Similarly if the metadata server's long-term private key is compromised, it is obvious that past session keys are still protected, even though the adversary can now impersonate the server to the clients and storage devices. Hence, we conclude that requirement 4 on forward secrecy is also satisfied.

3.5   Performance Analysis

We have described how key management is simplified in FSSA in comparison with Maat, and how forward secrecy is achieved using the Diffie-Hellman key agreement technique. We now examine how these changes affect the cost of security operations in large-scale file systems which employ FSSA.

We implemented the protocols for both FSSA and Maat in C++, using the Crypto++ library 5.5 [6]. The codes were compiled with Microsoft Visual C++ 2005 SP1 and run on Intel Core 2/2.20 GHz processor, 2014 MB memory and under Windows Vista in 32-bit mode. We use widely deployed and typical choices of cryptographic algorithms/schemes for our comparison: HMAC (SHA-1), AES (CBC-MAC), RSA-1024 encryption and signature schemes, and DH-1024 key agreement. The implementation of the algorithms/schemes makes use of optimisation techniques to improve their performance, for example, pre-computation of key generation when possible, and the use of the Chinese Remainder Theorem (CRT) method for faster RSA decryption (or signature generation).

Table 1. A comparison of computational cost for one protocol run in milliseconds

	Maat-I	Maat-II	FSSA-KA
Server	1.232	1.316	1.227
Client	1.346	0.085	1.440
Device	1.375	0.070	1.420
Total	3.953	1.470	4.086

Table 1 shows the actual computation times (in ms) incurred by different entities participating in the Maat-I & Maat-II protocols and the FSSA-KA protocol. Here, we use Maat-I to denote the long-term session key establishment protocol of Maat, and Maat-II to represent the secure file access protocol of Maat which makes use of short-term capabilities. In FSSA, we combine these two functionalities into a single key agreement protocol, which we represent by FSSA-KA. Each computation time is the average time for a protocol run over 1000 iterations.

From Table 1, the total time required to perform the FSSA-KA protocol is comparable to that of one round of the combined Maat-I & Maat-II protocols. We note that, in fact, it is difficult to compare the performance of Maat and FSSA using their underlying protocols for obvious reasons. While it is a sensible design strategy that Maat relies on long-term session keys shared between clients and storage devices to improve efficiency and scalability, other key management issues (which we described in earlier sections) have not been addressed. The cost for dealing with these issues may be far higher than the cost of the protocols themselves. Furthermore, the Maat-I & Maat-II protocols do not provide forward secrecy. On the other hand, the design principle of the FSSA-KA protocol takes into consideration various key management limitations in Maat, a stronger security model (providing forward secrecy) and the usability concern.

4   Conclusions and Future Work

Many recent security proposals for large-scale file systems which employ hybrid symmetric and asymmetric key cryptographic techniques did not make use of realistic key management assumptions. In this paper, we considered and addressed key management issues, which could have caused significant efficiency and scalability issues to many existing proposals. In our approach, we adopted lightweight Diffie-Hellman key agreement techniques for session key establishment between a client and a storage device. We also improved the usability of existing security proposals by making use of short-lived credential or key materials. This way, users are not required to manage potentially a large amount of long-term public keys of storage devices. Moreover, we raised the security bar of large-scale distributed file systems by introducing forward secrecy to protect data exchanged in past security sessions.

At the time of writing, Maat is arguably the most efficient security solution for large-scale file systems. Our implementation results show that our protocol is comparable to the Maat protocols in terms of computational cost. More importantly, we get stronger security, improved usability and simplified key management.

For future work, we intend to implement our proposal using a real distributed file system to analyse how much cost savings we can get in terms of key management, and to identify other potential advantages or limitations of our approach.

Acknowledgement. The author would like to thank Philip Robinson for very helpful discussions and the anonymous referees for very useful comments.

References

1. Adya, A., Bolosky, W.J., Castro, M., Cermak, G., Chaiken, R., Douceur, J.R., Howell, J., Lorch, J.R., Theimer, M., Wattenhofer, R.: FARSITE: Federated, available, and reliable storage for an incompletely trusted environment. In: Proceedings of the 5th Symposium on Operating System Design and Implementation (OSDI 2002) (December 2002)
2. Aguilera, M.K., Ji, M., Lillibridge, M., MacCormick, J., Oertli, E., Andersen, D.G., Burrows, M., Mann, T., Thekkath, C.A.: Block-level security for network-attached disks. In: Proceedings of the FAST 2003 Conference on File and Storage Technologies, March 2003, USENIX (2003)

3. Bellare, M., Rogaway, P.: Entity authentication and key distribution. In: Stinson, D.R. (ed.) CRYPTO 1993. LNCS, vol. 773, pp. 232–249. Springer, Heidelberg (1994)
4. Bellare, M., Rogaway, P.: The AuthA Protocol for Password-Based Authenticated Key Exchange. In: Contribution to IEEE P1363 (March 2000)
5. Boyd, C., Mathuria, A.: Protocols for Authentication and Key Establishment. Springer, Berlin (2003)
6. Dai, W.: Crypto++ 5.5 Benchmarks (May 2007), http://www.cryptopp.com/benchmarks.html (last accessed in May 2009)
7. Dierks, T., Allen, C.: The TLS protocol version 1.0. The Internet Engineering Task Force (IETF), RFC 2246 (January 1999)
8. Diffie, W., Hellman, M.E.: New directions in cryptography. IEEE Transactions on Information Theory 22(6), 644–654 (1976)
9. Ellison, C., Schneier, B.: Ten risks of PKI: What you're not being told about public key infrastructure. Computer Security Journal 16(1), 1–7 (2000)
10. Factor, M., Nagle, D., Naor, D., Riedel, E., Satran, J.: The OSD security protocol. In: Proceedings of the 3rd IEEE International Security in Storage Workshop (SISW 2005), pp. 29–39. IEEE Computer Society Press, Los Alamitos (December 2005)
11. Gibson, G.A., Nagle, D.F., Amiri, K., Butler, J., Chang, F.W., Gobioff, H., Hardin, C., Riedel, E., Rochberg, D., Zelenka, J.: A cost-effective, high-bandwidth storage architecture. ACM SIGPLAN Notices 33(11), 92–103 (1998)
12. Howard, J.H., Kazar, M.L., Menees, S.G., Nichols, D.A., Satyanarayanan, M., Sidebotham, R.N., West, M.J.: Scale and performance in a distributed file system. ACM Transactions on Computer Systems (TOCS) 6(1), 51–81 (1988)
13. Krawczyk, H.: SIGMA: The 'SIGn-and-MAc' approach to authenticated Diffie-Hellman and its use in the IKE-protocols. In: Boneh, D. (ed.) CRYPTO 2003. LNCS, vol. 2729, pp. 400–425. Springer, Heidelberg (2003)
14. Kubiatowicz, J., Bindel, D., Chen, Y., Czerwinski, S.E., Eaton, P.R., Geels, D., Gummadi, R., Rhea, S.C., Weatherspoon, H., Weimer, W., Wells, C., Zhao, B.Y.: OceanStore: An architecture for global-scale persistent storage. In: Proceedings of the 9th International Conference on Architectural Support for Programming Languages and Operating Systems (ASPLOS 2000), November 2000, pp. 190–201 (2000)
15. Leung, A.W., Miller, E.L.: Scalable security for large, high performance storage systems. In: Proceedings of the 2006 ACM Workshop on Storage Security and Survivability (StorageSS 2006), October 2006, pp. 29–40. ACM Press, New York (2006)
16. Leung, A.W., Miller, E.L., Jones, S.: Scalable security for petascale parallel file systems. In: Verastegui, B. (ed.) Proceedings of the ACM/IEEE Conference on High Performance Networking and Computing (SC 2007), p. 16. ACM Press, New York (November 2007)
17. Mazières, D., Kaminsky, M., Kaashoek, M.F., Witchel, E.: Separating key management from file system security. In: Proceedings of the 17th ACM Symposium on Operating System Principles (SOSP 1999), pp. 124–139. ACM Press, New York (December 1999)
18. Menezes, A.J., van Oorschot, P.C., Vanstone, S.A.: Handbook of Applied Cryptography. CRC Press, Florida (1997)
19. Miller, E.L., Long, D.D.E., Freeman, W.E., Reed, B.: Strong security for network-attached storage. In: Long, D.D.E. (ed.) Proceedings of the FAST 2002 Conference on File and Storage Technologies, January 2002, pp. 1–13. USENIX (2002)

20. Neuman, B.C., Ts'o, T.: Kerberos: An authentication service for computer networks. IEEE Communications 32(9), 33–38 (1994)
21. Olson, C., Miller, E.L.: Secure capabilities for a petabyte-scale object-based distributed file system. In: Proceedings of the 2005 ACM Workshop on Storage Security and Survivability (StorageSS 2005), November 2005, pp. 64–73. ACM Press, New York (2005)
22. Price, G.: PKI challenges: An industry analysis. In: Zhou, J., Kang, M.-C., Bao, F., Pang, H.-H. (eds.) Proceedings of the 4th International Workshop for Applied PKI (IWAP 2005). FAIA, vol. 128, pp. 3–16. IOS Press, Amsterdam (2005)
23. Wang, F., Xin, Q., Hong, B., Brandt, S.A., Miller, E.L., Long, D.D.E., McLarty, T.T.: File system workload analysis for large scale scientific computing applications. In: Proceedings of the 21st IEEE/12th NASA Goddard Conference on Mass Storage Systems and Technologies (MSST 2004), pp. 139–152 (April 2004)
24. White, B.S., Walker, M., Humphrey, M., Grimshaw, A.S.: LegionFS: A secure and scalable file system supporting cross-domain high-performance applications. In: Proceedings of the ACM/IEEE Conference on Supercomputing (SC 2001), November 2001, p. 59. ACM Press, New York (2001)
25. Wu, T.: The secure remote password protocol. In: Proceedings of Symposium on Network and Distributed System Security (NDSS 1998). The Internet Society (1998)
26. Zhu, Y., Hu, Y.: SNARE: A strong security scheme for network-attached storage. In: Proceedings of the 22nd Symposium on Reliable Distributed Systems, pp. 250–259. IEEE Computer Society Press, Los Alamitos (2003)

Nationwide PKI Testing – Ensuring Interoperability of OCSP Server and Client Implementations Early during Component Tests

Christian Schanes[1], Andreas Mauczka[1], Uwe Kirchengast[1],
Thomas Grechenig[1], and Sven Marx[2]

[1] Vienna University of Technology,
Industrial Software (INSO),
1040 Vienna, Austria
{christian.schanes,andreas.mauczka,
uwe.kirchengast,thomas.grechenig}@inso.tuwien.ac.at
http://www.inso.tuwien.ac.at/
[2] gematik
10117 Berlin, Germany
sven.marx@gematik.de
http://www.gematik.de/

Abstract. Interoperability issues between different implementations in large-scale systems is one of the major reasons for increased effort during system test. This paper addresses this problem in the context of the Online Certificate Status Protocol (OCSP) in a Public Key Infrastructure (PKI), which is part of the certificate verification process of many components. The high interconnection of OCSP clients and server increases the complexity of system tests to ensure interoperation. This paper provides a component based testing method for clients and servers using OCSP exemplified by testing PKI components of a nationwide IT infrastructure. The method ensures high interoperability requirements of large-scale infrastructures during component tests and reduces efforts for test execution.

Keywords: Online Certificate Status Protocol, Interoperability Testing, Public Key Infrastructure.

1   Introduction

Since the Online Certificate Status Protocol (OCSP) is one of the most important protocols to query revocation information of digital certificates, it is used within large-scale public key infrastructures where many OCSP clients have to interoperate with many OCSP servers (OCSP responders). Interoperability tests in those environments are highly complex and thus very time consuming and expensive.

In such systems different components are developed by different teams in different locations. Legal restrictions can cause the unavailability of source code of the implementations. These circumstances raise the need of a black box test method,

F. Martinelli and B. Preneel (Eds.): EuroPKI 2009, LNCS 6391, pp. 114–129, 2010.

which results in a high test coverage, reducing the risk of interoperability issues and thus decreasing error detection costs during the system level testing process.

Systems that integrate OCSP as a method to determine the status of digital certificates have to match a specific set of standards and restrictions fitting special criteria proposed by the current implementation. For high interoperability tightened specifications are required to increase test coverage and ensure standard conformance.

This work shows a test method to ensure high interoperability of OCSP components tested in a nationwide IT infrastructure of the German Health Telematics Infrastructure with multiple different client and server implementations. For this approach we will use a test driver and a simulator for testing. Interoperation between each client with the simulator and between each server with the test driver for the tested functionality of OCSP can be assured which results in reduced complexity for interoperability tests.

In addition in the system test phase interoperability tests are required because some conditions like firewall restrictions or configuration faults can lead to problems. However, with thorough component tests interoperation issues on the protocol level during system tests can be largely reduced.

OCSP is used in the German Health Telematics Infrastructure as the main mechanism for obtaining status information on a certificate. The extensive usage of Public Key Infrastructures (PKI) in many parts of the infrastructure causes interaction of many component implementations with many OCSP responder implementations. After rollout 80 million health insurants and about 200.000 medical professions and pharmacies are part of the infrastructure. About 300 health insurances and several medical profession and pharmacy organizations will be providing infrastructures for issuing certificates and retrieve revocation information.

Due to the size of the infrastructure a continuous integration approach of new services and components was established. To ensure a successful integration different environments for the German Health Telematics Infrastructure are defined. Integration is done in an operational reference environment before the components will be activated in the operational environment. This is required because only limited access for tests in the operational environment is provided. The operating company has to accredit every new component for the infrastructure. During this accreditation tests are performed to ensure functionality and interoperability.

The remainder of this paper is structured as follows: Section 2 lists related work. Section 3 gives an overview of motivation behind using OCSP in large-scale infrastructures. A method how tests for OCSP are executed is given in Section 4. Section 5 gives details about testing of an OCSP responder and Section 6 presents details about the test execution of OCSP clients. The paper finishes with a conclusion in Section 7.

2   Related Work

The Online Certificate Status Protocol was defined by the Internet Engineering Task Force (IETF) in RFC2560 [17] and was tightened in additional specifications like the Common-PKI Specification [1].

A number of academic efforts covering different aspects of protocol testing are introduced in [20,15,24]. Conformance testing of communication protocol implementation has been standardized by ISO 9646-1 [9] and by Moseley and Randall [15]. Kang et al. [12] point out the importance of combining conformance and interoperability tests to test protocol implementations sufficiently.

Nevertheless, our scope is slightly different. Unlike most public key infrastructures, e.g., the EuroPKI project [14], the German Health Telematics Infrastructure includes many different OCSP server implementations. Even though the Online Certificate Status Protocol as defined in RFC 2560 [17] is a protocol by definition, its complexity is not as high compared to others, namely those used in telecommunication (e.g., ATM, GPRS or PPP). Detailed discussion of using OCSP and other protocols for revocation information are given in several publications [8,16,23,13,21].

In [20] Seol et al. claim that during testing of components a lack of information concerning the implementation details is inevitable. This is a known problem and weakens our approach to a certain extent. Therefore, in response to this problem, an important goal was to construct a set of test cases that minimizes the risk of leaving main protocol features uncovered.

Several methods for testing conformance to specific standards or for interoperability exist. All of them are for specific environments or standards like the Common-PKI interoperability certification [3] or the test suites of the Multi-domain PKI Interoperability Framework [11]. For the German Health Telematics Infrastructure a restricted specification [6] is used which gives the possibility to use parts of mentioned test concepts and add domain specific test cases.

3   Customizing OCSP - Reducing Test Complexity for Large Scale Systems

Validating the state of a certificate is an important functionality in an infrastructure to ensure rejection of untrusted certificates. One of the most used protocols in large-scale systems is OCSP. As opposed to Certificate Revocation Lists (CRL) [7], OCSP provides timely accurate information and does not require distribution of lists. By using Server-based Certificate Validation Protocol (SCVP) [5] many parts of the verification process are moved to server side which requires increased processing power. With OCSP only the minimal processing power will be transferred to the server, while the other parts of the verification process are done on client side.

Correct verification of the revocation state of certificates is a security critical aspect in a PKI. Failing this can lead to security problems like accepting untrusted certificates. Problems with interoperability can also lead to errors in the infrastructure and therefore the clients have to reject the verified certificate which yields to reduced availability.

The RFC [17] for OCSP specifies a very open format by allowing many optional fields and extensions. Though the basics of the protocol are clearly described, some considerations on very specific parts of the protocol are still a question of interpretation, and should be taken into account during the design phase of each project involving OCSP. For different environments, additional restrictions are used for the protocol such as Common-PKI specification [1]. Some are given by laws to gain legal binding; others are possible by avoiding optional fields defined by OCSP standards. A tightened specification reduces possible test cases and variations of data for fields which allows higher coverage. Additionally this increases the possible grade of interoperability during component test due to higher standard conformance of the implementations.

For the considered infrastructure in the specification the OCSP usage was clarified in some areas. First a major problem, namely the usage of different algorithms, was specified. In the current specifications only the combination of SHA-1 with RSA 1024 key length and SHA-256 with RSA 2048 key length is allowed. The separation of the responder is done with different CA certificates. The mapping of the CA certificate to the responder is provided by using Trusted-service Status Lists as specified by ETSI [4]. The clients have to configure the allowed algorithms and only accept OCSP responses signed using the configured algorithms. Additionally hash algorithms used for issuerNameHash and issuerKeyHash are limited to SHA-1 and SHA-256. Another important aspect is the interpretation of the status good. For the RFC [17] the status declares that the certificate is not revoked but does not say anything about the existence of the certificate. The Common-PKI specification [1] defines good as the certificate is known and not revoked. In the German Health Telematics Infrastructure both interpretations are available for different certificate types. The Common-PKI approach allows for some types an activation of the certificate. To ease the usage of load balancing OCSP requests are only allowed to contain the request for a single certificate. This provides the possibility to handle and sign the request by a single OCSP responder instance. Some cases are impossible for the used environment and should therefore be restricted. One example is the protocol status sigRequired which an OCSP responder can use to request a signature from the client. If this is allowed a more detailed specification about the signature creation is required. For the considered infrastructure the usage of sigRequired was removed.

Restrictions also have impact on different properties in the infrastructure. For example reducing possible extensions for OCSP can reduce data load. It also makes planning of data load easier because sizes of OCSP requests and responses are known.

Another important aspect is the underlying protocol for OCSP requests and responses. HTTP is a well known protocol and is one of the most used for OCSP. Additional requirements for this protocol layer are required. Missing concretions of these definitions can lead to problems during integration, e.g., missing HTTP headers can lead to a functionally inaccessible OCSP responder. Some clients had problems with responders by using not specified HTTP headers and encoding required headers wrong which leads to interoperability problems. In the German Health Telematics Infrastructure, the transport protocol is limited to OCSP over HTTP as specified in the appendix A of the RFC [17].

Complexity of Interoperability is directly affected by the size of the infrastructure and variability of the used protocols - the more participants, the more different implementations of the protocols combined with possible variations increase the number of required tests.

4   A Method for Component Testing of OCSP Interoperability

Testing theory defines multiple test stages with a different focus on each stage. One of the early stages is the component test, in which interfaces of one component are tested with the help of test drivers and simulators. This stage gives a lot of control and therefore flexibility to testers. Later stages evaluate interoperability aspects of multiple components.

The complexity of interoperability testing is given by a communication matrix. The rows of the matrix are the OCSP clients and the columns are assigned to OCSP responders. With m client implementations and n OCSP responder implementations the size of the communication matrix is $m * n$. The cells define the communication relation between the specific client and the responder. In the German Health Telematics Infrastructure not every client uses every responder. The communication depends on the implemented use cases and the used certificates of the different certificate authorities by the client.

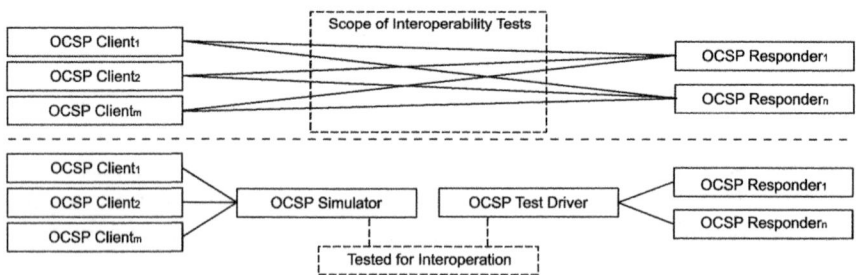

Fig. 1. Interoperability complexity reduction with inclusion of verification instances

The upper part of Figure 1 presents the concept of such a matrix graphically by showing interoperation between client components and OCSP responders. Component test execution can reduce communication matrix complexity by testing the interoperation of components with test drivers and simulators. This is a common approach for component tests [19]. The lower part of Figure 1 visualizes the complexity reduction of multiple communication paths between components and OCSP responders. By splitting communication during test execution servers are tested for interoperation with the test driver and clients with the help of the OCSP responder simulator. This modifies the size of the communication matrix from $m * n$ (every client with every responder) to $m + n$ (every client with the simulator and every responder with the test driver) which is a reduction of the complexity for large m and n. A similar approach was also documented for different protocols by Moseley and Randall [15]. This requires testing the test driver and simulator against each other to ensure interoperation.

The amount of different states OCSP client and server implementations can reside in are very limited. The complexity evolves due to certain extensions and different field values used in the Abstract Syntax Notation One (ASN.1) structure of request and response messages. This problem is countered by tightening the protocol to its minimum but feasible extent, which reduces complexity and therefore interoperability problems. Since the OCSP complexity could be limited within the German Health Telematics Infrastructure by detailed specifications [6], which are publicly available, the focus was to reduce the number of interoperability test cases.

Interoperability testing can be split into organizational, semantical, syntactical and technical aspects [10]. Organizational aspects are not further considered for this test method because these aspects are evaluated by audits. Semantical aspects consider a common processing of the same information. The structure of OCSP requests and responses are considered by validating the syntax. Technical aspects consider lower level protocols for transportation. HTTP as an underlying protocol will be considered for the tests because some components encounter problems in lower level protocols which can lead to interoperation problems.

4.1   Testing the Test Tools

The usage of an OCSP responder simulator and an OCSP test driver offer the possibility to test all specified aspects of OCSP in the infrastructure on different protocol layers. Both tools will be discussed in more detail in Section 5 and Section 6 of this paper. They allow manipulation of OCSP requests and responses on different layers of the OCSP stack and for multiple aspects. Message structure manipulation is possible by ASN.1 alterations. Values of OCSP are all configurable for test cases. For the semantical equivalence partitioning of values for each field is used. For testing underlying protocols the tools provide the possibility to manipulate values of HTTP requests like HTTP header options.

The method is based on the correctness of the used test tools which is ensured by functional testing. Additionally the test driver is tested against the OCSP responder simulator and vice versa. This shows interoperation of the tools. Additionally the tools are tested during implementation against the OCSP client and server implementations of OpenSSL.

5   Server-Side: Implementation Details

The component under test (CUT) [18] in this section is always the OCSP responder - this differs from OCSP client implementations (see Section 6) where the OCSP functionality is only a minor part of the CUT. The OCSP responders are tested using a black box approach by employing a test driver. OCSP requests generated during test execution are sent to the OCSP responder. The returned responses are validated for specification conformance. Depending on the request different aspects of the response are testable. Different variations of certificates are required for the test execution to test the possible response variations of the OCSP responder.

As indicated, a test driver was used for the test execution. This test driver is implemented in Java using BouncyCastle[1] and is integrated into the used test framework (test management, automated test evaluation, etc.). The test driver takes control sequences as input, which can be configured based on the control set of the test driver implementation. It is possible to have the test driver generate a request based on the configuration or to prepare a request directly by using arbitrary ASN.1 tools manipulate the request before sending it to the OCSP responder.

The response sent by the OCSP responder will be evaluated by predefined verification definitions. The test driver provides the possibility to automatically verify the response using the verification definitions (e.g., check whether `certHash` is part of the response or check the correctness of the returned status).

The goals of OCSP server testing are presented in three subsets. The first strategy employed is to test basic requests, and by doing so guarantee interoperability on the lowest complexity level. Basic requests consist of the smallest possible set of required fields to receive a response from the OCSP responder by leaving out all optional parts.

For all possible kinds of certificates in the PKI (and therefore types of clients that use OCSP as part of the verification process), we execute tests with basic requests to ensure that all types of certificates are handled by the OCSP responders. Different types of certificates in the tested infrastructure are specified. Certificates are used for authentication, signing and encrypting by different roles like persons, organizations and services (e.g., SSL certificates). These certificates had different specifications for being handled by the OCSP responders, so test cases for each certificate type had to be employed. This also should ensure, that communication between the certificate authority management application and the OCSP responder database is functioning.

After communication on the most basic level is established, we employ additional test cases, to see if the OCSP responder is able to handle all positive variations of an OCSP request using allowed extensions and does respond with valid responses. They are referred to as complex requests for this chapter. An OCSP responder might interpret extensions, although the OCSP responder might choose to ignore certain optional facets of the request to improve performance - yet standard conformity still has to be guaranteed and therefore additional test cases for this circumstance are required.

A special case of a complex request is an OCSP request that has been signed by the requesting party. This will be referred to as a signed request. Signature checking for OCSP responders in the German Health Telematics Infrastructure was ruled out by the specification, so signatures of the request, whether valid,

---

[1] http://www.bouncycastle.org

bad, or signed with different algorithms, should be ignored by the OCSP responders. The test cases have to validate this behavior.

5.1 Generation of OCSP Test Requests

The tests address semantical, syntactical and technical aspects of interoperability testing. A test case for semantical aspects would be sending an OCSP request that is answered in the expected manner with `successful` and `good` (for a certificate with status good). A test case concerning a syntactical aspect would be sending an OCSP request with a corrupted structure that is answered by `malformedRequest` and no certificate status information is given. The technical aspect is considered by using HTTP as transport protocol and constructing valid HTTP requests.

The first set of test cases aims to check if the OCSP responder is answering correctly to a simple request for thorough positive testing of all types of certificates handled by an OCSP responder:

Simple requests: To test if the OCSP responder can handle basic requests

Availability of responder: Testing availability from all required locations, e.g., if the domain name is available and routing in the infrastructure is configured

Certificate verification: Verification of responder certificate (e.g., the certificate is in the list of trusted certificates)

Unknown status response: Requests for certificates with status `unknown` for each OCSP responder to see whether the OCSP responder answers with `unknown` for non-existing certificates

Validating the certificate activation: Requesting status for not yet activated certificates to see whether the OCSP responder answers with `unknown`

Revoked status response: Testing requests for certificates with status `revoked`

The second set of test cases test complex request which includes the handling of multiple certificate-status inquiries in one request and usage of allowed critical and non-critical extensions:

Requests with two inquiries: The OCSP responder is specified to answer only to the first inquiry of the request. It is necessary that the OCSP responder is predictable and consistent in its answering behavior. Therefore variations of two certificates were tested (e.g., test cases for combined status good and `unknown` certificates)

Requests with three inquiries: All variations of states of three certificates were tested (e.g., list of single requests combined for certificates with status good, `revoked` and `unknown`)

Requests with erroneous requests: The OCSP responder was tested with one, two and three out of three inquiries corrupt, with extensions and other variations

Using valid special characters in the request: Including possible variations of valid requests using special characters for fields and extensions

Signed requests as special form of complex requests build another set of test cases. For the German Health Telematics Infrastructure verification of request signatures can be left out due to performance issues. The tests check if implemented signature verification is working correctly. If the OCSP responder ignores the signature, it should not have impact on the functionality of the responder:

Valid signature: Usage of a valid signature should check if the OCSP responder accepts the signature

Invalid signature: Usage of an invalid signature should check if the OCSP responder detects the manipulation

Bad signature algorithms: The request is signed with algorithms that are not allowed in the specified environment (e.g., MD5 with RSA)

Signature certificates: Usage of different certificates for creating the signature should evaluate if the responder accepts signatures only from trusted certificates.

Another set of test cases includes using prohibited and unspecified values and requests with manipulated ASN.1 structure. This tests the robustness of the OCSP responders against bad requests:

Bad serial number: the values for serial number are manipulated (e.g., overlong serial number, serial number is not an integer)

Bad hash algorithm: testing the correct validation of the used hash algorithms for the request, e.g., `issuerNameHash`

Bad issuer key hash or issuer name hash: the values for both fields are manipulated (e.g., overlong, not an octet string, left blank)

Bad structure of the request: the request structure is manipulated (e.g., order of elements is mixed, no request element in the request list, corrupt extensions, standard conformant request with not allowed extensions)

Variations on issuer key hash, issuer name hash and serial number: this test cases aim to verify that the OCSP responder uses all information from the request. Variations include existing issuer key hash, non-existing issuer name hash, and existing serial number

5.2 Validation of OCSP Responses

To validate the success or failure of a test case, we examine whether the response given by the OCSP responder is conformant or not. This includes checking the response structure against the specification (syntactical), comparing the returned values with the expected values (semantical) and analyzing the HTTP response for standard conformance (technical). Different validation methods are implemented by the test driver. By using the configuration files the validation tasks can be added for each test case.

Basic checks: For each response validate the structure of the response and check consistency of the response, e.g., validate if contained signature algorithm was used for the signature, version of the response

Protocol status: Validate returned protocol status, e.g., `successful`

Revocation status: Check certificate revocation status for each contained single response

Revocation reason: If revoked check the `revocationReason`

Responder certificate: Validation of the responder certificate, e.g., is it in the list of trusted certificates, signature verification, and validity

Algorithms: Check if used algorithms for hash values and signature generation are allowed

Time components of response: Validation of time components of the response, e.g., `producedAt`, `nextUpdate`, `thisUpdate`, `revocationTime`

The tests uncovered problems of the implementations as also specification weaknesses which lead to adaptions of the specification. An issue during testing was identified with the handling of single or multiple requests. The issue occurred due to restrictions on the number of inquiries in a request. To avoid interoperability issues, like a client sending multiple requests and expecting multiple responses, behavior of the OCSP responders for multiple requests needs to be specified to guarantee interoperability. In our case multiple requests were allowed but only a single request and response was processed by the OCSP responders (specified behavior), it needs to be specified as well which request in the request list will be accepted and answered.

The negative test cases are mainly used to find any weaknesses in the handling of the requests examined by unexpected responses from the OCSP responder. For ensuring interoperability it is important that OCSP responders within the infrastructure use common failure handling so that client components can generate meaningful error messages. Also the robustness using invalid requests is important, because this can influence the availability of responders which has impact on the interoperation with other components, for example, crashes of responders due to the processing of invalid requests.

An issue that surfaced during test execution concerned the handling of incorrect extensions - the OCSP responder was answering with `malformedRequest` to some optional extensions, while ignoring and therefore answering with `successful` to others. By using all possible variations of extensions during test, this issue was identified - a simple solution is to specify expected behavior when an unexpected extension arrives and answer with `malformedRequest` or `successful` for ALL extensions. Answering with `malformedRequest` to an unexpected extension might cause issues with standard-conform client implementations (e.g., that send the nonce-extension), so ignoring unexpected extensions and handle them gracefully seems the better solution. To flag important extensions, it is always possible to flag them with critical, forcing the responder to process the extension.

Another issue identified during tests was the importance of uniform handling of error messages - the OCSP responder under test was using different error messages when malformed requests were sent. The issue identified was an `internalError` response when a `malformedRequest` message was expected. Giving different answers to the (conceptually) identical test case gives out information about the OCSP responder that an attacker can use, e.g., finger-printing of the used implementation.

The tests also uncovered a security vulnerability of one implementation, which missed correct validation of the input. Therefore with special input a successful denial of service attack could be established. This showed the importance of security tests to find such vulnerabilities.

If signed requests are used, variations of signatures (including invalid signatures, untrusted certificates and prohibited algorithms/key lengths) aim to verify that the OCSP responder correctly verifies the signature. Processing signed requests can cause a considerable performance decrease as signature verification is a resource intensive procedure. Furthermore a signed request is bigger than a normal basic request, so data load implications arise as well.

By using a cluster of responders for load balancing, it showed that not all problems could be identified during the used black box test execution. For example was one problem, that one responder certificate of the cluster was not in the list of trusted certificates. During OCSP responder tests this was not identified but after integration with the client components unpredictable behavior occurred that sometimes the response was rejected by the component because the certificate was not in the list of trusted certificates.

6   Client-Side: Using a Simulator

Components usually have to fulfill several different functions and therefore they undergo an extensive testing cycle until their final accreditation. A component which performs certificate validation on behalf of the Online Certificate Status Protocol is called an OCSP client. Due to extensive usage of PKI within the German Health Telematics Infrastructure, e.g., Secure Socket Layer (SSL), many components are OCSP clients. The OCSP functionality itself - which we are going to validate - is only one small but critical part of these components.

To accomplish the certificate verification process components have to be able to send correct requests and interpret responses received from the OCSP responder. Syntactical, semantical and technical aspects will be considered for each request generation and response processing attempt. It is important to ensure that incorrect responses do not cause system crashes or misinterpretations. That could lead to inconsistent system states, to a compromised behavior or to situations where certificates are stated as valid by the component, even if they are not.

Testing OCSP client implementations turns out to be challenging because one must test a black box library inside of a black box. This circumstance constrains the way we can trigger test cases and evaluate test results to discover, if a component under test (CUT) [18] does not match its external specifications. Moreover the German Health Telematics Infrastructure specifies components which provide interfaces to establish SSL connections to several different services or check various XML signatures. Since a black box approach was chosen, one cannot rely on the CUT to use the same OCSP client implementation for each task and must run the OCSP test cases for each use case implicating an OCSP request. Hence the process of testing OCSP client implementations is somewhat different from testing OCSP responders.

Due to the fact that the OCSP functionality is placed inside of a component, one cannot trigger an OCSP request directly, but instead has to trigger a use case. Components often implement use cases like establishing a SSL connection to another component or sending a signed SOAP message. These tasks imply the initiation of a certificate verification process and during that process the desired OCSP request is sent by the CUT. To initiate these use cases we utilize a functional test driver. That test driver is a general test tool to trigger all specified use cases of a component and should not be confused with the one used during the OCSP server testing process. On the other side of the test track we use an OCSP responder simulator, which grants us the ability to react to any request generated by the component's OCSP module and produce correct but also incorrect OCSP responses based on simulator configurations. Figure 2 illustrates this approach.

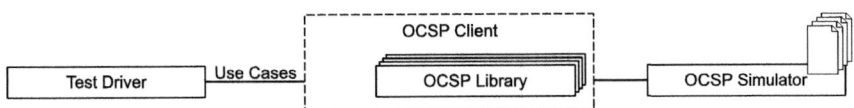

Fig. 2. Test Setup for Client Side OCSP Tests

6.1 Simulation of OCSP Responses

As proposed by Robert V. Binder [2] in his chapter about Testing Theory we created a set of test cases based upon a conformance testing approach. Therefore we make sure that every after condition and data condition of the protocol is true at least once. Additionally we ensure that the CUT has to process every specified element found in OCSP requests and responses at least once. This is done to test the syntactical conformance, namely the protocol conformance of the component.

The OCSP responder simulator plays an important role in this concept, because only with its help are we able to produce different OCSP responses, no matter which request actually is received by the simulator. Special configuration files are used to set up the simulator. They allow us to specify every parameter of an OCSP response. Further the configuration files enable us to answer a certain request from a specific client (based on IP address) about a specific certificate (based on serial number) with our preconfigured response. That distinction between different sources is very helpful because it facilitates the testing of many different CUTs at the same time. To configure the CUT to send OCSP requests to the responder simulator we use a special set of test certificates which refer to the simulator. Those certificates are imported into the component prior to triggering one of the appropriate use cases. The underlying infrastructure uses Trusted-service Status Lists (TSL) [4] to form the trust anchor. Inside of those lists trusted OCSP responder certificates have to be present.

The following paragraphs describe groups of test cases we developed and give some information about found errors and suggestions about how to deal with them. Corresponding to our test strategy we composed test cases to cover semantical, syntactical and technical aspects of the CUT:

Structure of OCSP requests: Within this test group standard conformance of OCSP requests produced by the component is checked. Moreover data fields are tested for their standard conformance, e.g., the OCSP Version or if the ASN.1 structure is valid. The OCSP responder simulator is able to verify the validity of the request structure created by the CUT. The simulator provides extensive log-output which is automatically interpreted by the test driver. It also checks whether the HTTP header of the request is correct. One problem was the wrong usage of header fields of one client which sent the wrong Content-Type header and therefore the OCSP responder does not send a response.

Processing of the certificate status: The basic functionality of the OCSP is to provide certificate status information. We designed test cases for each possible case (good, revoked and unknown) to make sure each CUT is able to handle them.

Processing of exception cases: It is also important to check how and if clients react on error messages. The messages specified in the RFC are tryLater, malformedRequest, internalError, sigRequired and unauthorized. We configured the simulator to respond to flawless requests with the error messages stated above. Again, it is vital to specify the desired reaction to each of these answers to ensure that both sides can interoperate to a maximum extend.

Signature: Furthermore we tested if the client checks the signature and validates the OCSP responder certificate by sending responses with manipulated signatures (randomly changed bytes of the signature) or by sending responses signed with not trusted certificates. We found that no problems occurred when certificate paths were validated.

Algorithms: A major concern here was to ensure that only specified algorithms are accepted by the client. The OCSP responder simulator enables us to sign the response with different algorithms and to use different trusted certificates with not allowed algorithms to sign the response. During test phase it turned out that many CUTs did not check the algorithms used or weren't configured to reject unspecified algorithms. This can be a major security risk because weak algorithms may be abused to create manipulated responses, e.g., MD5 collision attacks [22], which can lead to acceptance of already revoked certificates.

Certificate ID: We created malformed responses which included wrong values for the elements of CertID which differ from those given within the client's request. Throughout the testing process we found that even some standard implementations did not check those fields accordingly. In the case of CertID an attacker can perform a replay attack by sending a valid response with status good for a revoked certificate.

Structure of OCSP responses: This group of test cases concentrates on different OCSP responses and the way clients react to it. This included the usage of extensions (critical and not critical) and manipulation of the response structure (e.g., without signature element for definitive responses). Also wrong values of `ResponderID` were returned and it turned out that many components did not check this value, instead they ignored it completely. We strongly suggest specifying very clearly how each component has to react when it faces wrong `ResponderID` values and how this field has to be processed by the client.

Processing of time based values: Test cases in this group are focused on the three time values within OCSP responses, namely `thisUpdate`, `nextUpdate` and `producedAt`. Once more, the OSCP responder simulator helped us to manipulate those fields at will. The Common-PKI specification [1] states that `thisUpdate` and `nextUpate` times build a validity interval in which the response should be considered reliable. This interval was not checked by some components while others implemented too strict conditions which did not consider the propagation delay and therefore rejected a valid response.

6.2   Validation of Tests

Validation of expected test case results turn out to be difficult as well, since the only information available is the outcome of previously initiated use cases (see Figure 2). Hence it all comes down to one question, "did the use case run successfully or did it fail?". This makes it very difficult to identify, if the reason for a failed use case was really a misinterpretation of the OCSP. Even some tiny configuration parameter set to a wrong value can cause the use case to fail. At this point the human tester is important because all side-effects have to be excluded before an error can be claimed. To find possible side-effects one has to read the component's log file or perform a retest under changed conditions. For example, first use the simulator to return a valid response which should yield to a positive finish of the use case, and afterwards reconfigure the simulator to execute the negative test case. Because of the complexity of this task only a balanced set of test cases, that is a set of test cases, where each one only validates one aspect, can ensure that all aspects are realized in conformance to protocol standards.

The log of the OCSP responder simulator provides specific details about received requests and responses created. Further, the simulator automatically checks the structure of requests that are sent to the OCSP responder simulator.

7   Conclusion

In the previous sections we proposed a solution for the interoperability issues arising out of legal restrictions and different locations of developer teams for a concrete scenario, the OCSP responder and OCSP client interoperation. We showed how this problem was solved for a concrete nationwide IT infrastructure, namely the German Health Telematics Infrastructure. The solution proposed in this paper involved a client/server test driver stub methodology that allows for each individual component to simulate integration into the large-scale system, and therefore decreasing the risk of interoperability issues at the integration stage. The test method that is presented in this paper is based on black box testing, which lowers locality issues and law restrictions, as only certain interfaces have to be exposed.

The executed tests during component tests in the nationwide IT infrastructure showed problems of the implementations. Ignored restrictions in specifications like optional extensions can lead to a significantly higher effort in interoperability testing, asides from any implications toward performance and load of the OCSP responders.

The given method for testing interoperability aspects during component test stage reduces required resources for further stages. This test method can not eliminate required interoperability testing during system tests, because in test environments only some protocol layers are examinable and not additional aspects like firewall rules, network routes, domain name setups and so on.

References

1. Bickenbach, H.-J., Brauckmann, J., Giessler, A., Horváth, T., Knobloch, H.-J.: Common PKI specifications for interoperable applications (2009)
2. Binder, R.V.: Testing object-oriented software: a survey. Software Testing, Verification and Reliability 6(3-4), 125–252 (1996)
3. Brauckmann, J., Alfred, G., Horváth, T., Knobloch, H.-J.: Common PKI specifications for interoperable applications - test specification (2004)
4. European Telecommunications Standards Institute. ETSI technical specification TS 102 231 - provision of harmonized trust service provider TSP status information (2006)
5. Freeman, T., Housley, R., Malpani, A., Cooper, D., Polk, W.: Server-Based Certificate Validation Protocol (SCVP) (2007)
6. gematik - Gesellschaft für Telematikanwendungen der Gesundheitskarte mbH. Einführung der Gesundheitskarte – Verzeichnisdienstkonzept der gematik-Bridge-CA (2008)
7. Housley, R., Polk, W., Ford, W., Solo, D.: Internet X.509 Public Key Infrastructure Certificate and Certificate Revocation List (CRL) Profile (2002)
8. Iliadis, J., Spinellis, D., Gritzalis, D., Preneel, B., Katsikas, S.: Evaluating certificate status information mechanisms. In: CCS 2000: Proceedings of the 7th ACM Conference on Computer and Communications Security, pp. 1–8. ACM, New York (2000)
9. ISO/IEC 9646-1:1994. Part 1: General concepts: Information technology – Open Systems Interconnection – Conformance testing methodology and framework. International Organization for Standardization, Geneva, Switzerland
10. Janssen, M., Scholl, H.J.J.: Interoperability for electronic governance. In: ICEGOV 2007: Proceedings of the 1st International Conference on Theory and Practice of Electronic Governance, pp. 45–48. ACM, New York (2007)
11. Japan Network Security Association. Challenge PKI project - the multidomain PKI interoperability framework

12. Kang, S.: Relating interoperability testing with conformance testing. In: The Bridge to Global Integration Global Telecommunications Conference, 1998. GLOBECOM 1998, vol. 6, pp. 3768–3773. IEEE, Los Alamitos (1998)
13. Kocher, P.C.: On Certificate Revocation and Validation. In: Hirschfeld, R. (ed.) FC 1998. LNCS, vol. 1465, pp. 172–177. Springer, Heidelberg (1998)
14. Lioy, A., Marian, M., Moltchanova, N., Pala, M.: The EuroPKI experience. In: Katsikas, S.K., Gritzalis, S., López, J. (eds.) EuroPKI 2004. LNCS, vol. 3093, pp. 14–27. Springer, Heidelberg (2004)
15. Moseley, S., Randall, S., Wiles, A.: In pursuit of interoperability. International Journal IT Standards and Standardization Research 2(2), 34–48 (2004)
16. Munoz, J.L., Forne, J., Castro, J.C.: Evaluation of certificate revocation policies: OCSP vs. Overissued-CRL. In: Proceedings of 13th International Workshop on Database and Expert Systems Applications, pp. 511–515 (2002)
17. Myers, M., Ankney, R., Malpani, A., Galperin, S., Adams, C.: X.509 Internet Public Key Infrastructure Online Certificate Status Protocol - OCSP (1999)
18. Radatz, J.: IEEE standard glossary of software engineering terminology. Technical report (1990)
19. Sengupta, B., Chandra, S., Sinha, V.: A research agenda for distributed software development. In: ICSE 2006: Proceedings of the 28th International Conference on Software Engineering, pp. 731–740. ACM, New York (2006)
20. Seol, S., Kim, M., Chanson, S., Kang, S.: Interoperability test generation and minimization for communication protocols based on the multiple stimuli principle. IEEE Journal on Selected Areas in Communications 22(10), 2062–2074 (2004)
21. Slagell, A.J., Bonilla, R.: PKI scalability issues. CoRR, cs.CR/0409018 (2004)
22. Stevens, M., Lenstra, A., Weger, B.: Chosen-prefix collisions for md5 and colliding x.509 certificates for different identities. In: Naor, M. (ed.) EUROCRYPT 2007. LNCS, vol. 4515, pp. 1–22. Springer, Heidelberg (2007)
23. Wohlmacher, P.: Digital certificates: a survey of revocation methods. In: MULTIMEDIA 2000: Proceedings of the 2000 ACM Workshops on Multimedia, pp. 111–114. ACM, New York (2000)
24. Zhong, N., He, Z.-w., Kuang, J.-m.: A generic formal framework for protocol interoperability test and test cases minimization. In: AST 2008: Proceedings of the 3rd International Workshop on Automation of Software Test, pp. 57–61. ACM, New York (2008)

On Device Identity Establishment and Verification

Roberto Gallo[1,2], Henrique Kawakami[2], and Ricardo Dahab[1,*]

[1] University of Campinas, Campinas, SP, Brazil
{gallo,dahab}@ic.unicamp.br
[2] KRYPTUS Information Security, Campinas, SP, Brazil
{gallo,kawakami}@kryptus.com

Abstract. Many high security applications rely ultimately on the security of hardware-based solutions in order to protect both data and code against tampering. For these applications, assuring the device's identity and integrity is paramount. In our work, we explore a number of factors that help to improve on device accreditation, by devising and defining both architectural and procedural requirements related to device construction, shipping and usage. Based on that, we proposed two integrity *shared verification schemes* which enable regular and auditing users of such applications to promptly and easily verify whether their interfacing hardware is trustworthy. We implemented our solutions in a key application, namely a hardware security module (HSM) suitable for use in supporting PKIs and also showed how it performs equally well in *Direct Recording Electronic* (DRE) voting machines.

1 Introduction

1.1 Motivation

Secure processors, such as those found in smartcards, and *hardware security modules* are key components of any production-grade PKI. With a minimal set of functionalities, these devices may offer an appropriate *root of trust*, from which a *trust chain* can be constructed, extending all the way to users' applications.

However, while secure processors and HSMs have been around for more than 20 years [1], little has been said about the necessary conditions for accreditation of a device's *root of trust* itself [2].

We believe that this gap poses a real threat to the goal of PKI application- and enterprise-wide trust establishment, as any kind of *root of trust* compromise may render the entire system and its applications insecure.

1.2 Our Contribution

In this paper we explore a set of issues that have a strong influence on the level of device trust, encompassing conceptual, architectural and procedural aspects

---

* Partially funded by Fapesp and CNPq research grants.

F. Martinelli and B. Preneel (Eds.): EuroPKI 2009, LNCS 6391, pp. 130–145, 2010.

related to device construction, shipping and usage. For each of these, we propose refined and novel solutions drawn from our experience in developing and building a commercially available hardware security module designed for PKI use.

In order to provide the necessary background required for device trust establishment, we propose in this paper the concept of *cryptographic device identity* (CID), which extends the concept of a root of trust by adding stronger and more precise existence requirements than those found in other previous works. The CID and the proposed concept of *secure device epoch* (SDE), are then used to construct *shared verification schemes* (SVSs) with trust amplifying capabilities.

In this paper we also propose two such schemes, the Simple SVS and the (Byzantine) Traitor Evidencing SVS. We then implement the Simple SVS in a PKI-enabled HSM and show it performs equally well in such applications and in *Direct Recording Electronic* (DRE) voting machines.

1.3   Paper Organization

This paper is organized as follows: in Section 2 we describe the problem in greater detail and discuss some proposed solutions. In Section 3 we detail our proposals followed, in Section 4, by implementation results. Sections 5 and 6 conclude the paper, giving some ideas for future work.

2   The Problem and Related Work

Many security applications, such as PKIs, make use of hardware security modules in order to protect *critical security parameters* (CSPs) from non-authorized use, disclosure, and modification, and to enforce usage control. The most common CSPs include key material in the form of (possibly many) secret and private keys.

However, CSPs are not restricted to cryptographic keys; for example, the key management algorithm implementations themselves must also be modification-protected, as tampering with them can lead to leakage of key material.

Another typical application that requires both data and code protection is *digital rights management* (DRM) of media contents. In this context, media (data) must be protected from both direct reading and subverted players (code). For this class of applications, specially at end user devices, trusted computing, TPM-based, solutions have been employed with reasonable, although sometimes limited, success, with many improvements being proposed [3, 4].

Threat models for DRM applications are peculiar. For example, whereas the leakage of a first-run movie can cause great losses to the producers, the adversaries' gains are much less obvious. For typical end user DRM applications, the gains an adversary can obtain are limited to its ability to redistribute and charge for the stolen media. The majority of TPM-based solutions targets the end user market and provides only limited protection. The weaknesses of TPM-based solutions stem from the fact that they are used both as passive root of trust and a single-chip, standalone device, not protecting main CPU bus memory.

Only a few commercially available single-chip solutions, designed from scratch, such as the IBM Cell Processor [5], are strong against adversaries trying to abuse the *security API* and launch system-level physical bus attacks (non-invasive local attacks).

The Cerium secure computing architecture [6] enables certified (signed) program execution, protecting against physical and logical attacks by using a tamper-resistant CPU and a special secure kernel, along with a per-device secret key. The AEGIS single chip secure processor architecture proposal [7] is a notable advance, by providing a full encryption/authentication trusted computing base. The AEGIS proposal also provides, through Physical Unclonable Functions (PUFs), a statistically unique quantity that can be used as the per-device unique key expected by Cerium.

For applications with higher attack rewards, the co-processor provided protection is naturally expected to be higher than single-chip solutions can provide [1, 8,9]. The IBM 4758 [2] secure co-processor is a preeminent example of a device that poses a challenge to well funded adversaries. In order to protect against impersonation attacks, the 4758 is personalized with a private/public key pair at the factory, which developers can use to identify a given device and protect their CSPs. A similar key pair was also latterly used by the Safekeyper [10].

Two key examples of high stake applications that may rely on device integrity for security are large government PKIs, (especially their CAs and RAs), and Direct Record Electronic (DRE) Voting Machines. Government PKIs tend to be very attractive targets for adversaries; for instance, in some countries, banking payment systems must use government issued digital certificates. In this context, strong subverting powers may act upon operational and auditing personal, posing a real threat to system reliability and, thus, their CSPs.

DRE voting machines are also under a strong, and quite interesting, adversary model. Protocol-based ingenious solutions have been proposed, including Neff's [11] and Chaum's [12], which try to avoid reliance on DRE physical and logical security by giving voters means to verify vote accountability. Despite these solutions, many attacks are still possible through DRE tampering [13].

Clearly, PKI and DRE have a common security requirement, namely platform/device accreditation. For these applications, very high levels of confidence on the device's integrity and identity are central in the effective protection of CSPs.

For the sake of the establishment of *trust* and *confidence* in a given device and, ultimately, on the entire application, security guarantees must focus on a number of issues, and not only on the device itself. These are: (i) system specification; (ii) system design; (iii) system implementation; (iv) device manufacturing; (v) in-factory device initialization; (vi) device shipping; (vii) device reception; (viii) device user setup; (ix) device use and operation; and (x) device disposal.

Ever since the early 1990s, concerns about trustworthy design and production of hardware security modules have been expressed, a fact reflected in the National Institute of Standards and Technology (NIST) publication FIPS 140 standard series [14]. The current version of this standard, NIST FIPS PUB 140-2, covers in considerable relatively depth items (i) to (v) above, specifying clear requirements and recommendations for achieving device security. However, a large formal and methodological assurance gap exists between device shipping and user configuration, enabling severe security breaches such as hardware Trojans and device cloning.

There are other relevant standards that also apply to HSMs, such as the Common Criteria (ISO/IEC 15408) Protection Profiles (PPs). Some of the most common PPs are the Secure Signatured Creation Devices (SSCD) (European standard CWA 14169) PP, and the BSI Cryptographic Modules Security Level Enhanced PP (BSI-CC-PP-0036). Our proposed schemes are directly related to the Delivery and Operation (ADO) Security Assurance class of these PPs, as they allow the detection of modifications of the TOE (i.e. the HSM) between the manufacturer's and the user's site, and also provide procedures for secure installation, generation and start-up of the TOE.

2.1 Attacks: Device Cloning, Trojans, and Reverse Engineering

Although one can implement security controls for the design and manufacturing phases of an HSM, little can be done to ensure what happens after the device is shipped from the manufacturer without proper care.

Even a device with advanced tamper protection mechanisms can be easily defeated by replacing it with a clone device containing a hardware- or firmware-based Trojan, if no reliable identity and integrity tests can be conducted by the final user during ceremonial procedures.

Device cloning consists of building a device with the same physical appearance and features of the original device. In addition to the original features, the clone might incorporate malicious code/hardware, and must not possess effective tamper detection mechanisms in order to allow for the later extraction of sensitive information.

In our experience, typical rack mounted Ethernet HSMs, for example, could be cloned from an authentic device by replacing its internal electronics with a standard computing platform (e.g. an x86). For such devices, the only way for the end user to detect such attacks would be by inspecting security seals on the outside of the device's enclosure. Nevertheless, these seals [8] have a much lower security level than that expected from the device. Besides, the user will probably not be able to distinguish an authentic label from a fake one.

The clone device would probably be uncovered at some point in the device lifespan (due to firmware update procedures or maintenance), but by that time an adversary might already have performed an attack, and the system will be discredited.

2.2 Device Verification and PKI Operations

Even in critical PKIs, typical ceremonial operations surprisingly do not consider checking device identities. Figure 1 presents a real scenario, where concerns about the integrity of the CA HSM are not even mentioned.

1. The ceremony's participants are identified and invited to enter the safe room. The scripts steps are explained to every participant. Auditors and operators are introduced to the participants.
2. Certificate management servers and the HSM containing the CA key are powered on. Any basic setup is performed (e.g. clock adjustments)
3. The CA private key inside the HSM is reconstructed and enabled for usage through operators smartcards authorization.
4. CSRs are imported, verified and signed by the HSM using the CA private key. Newly signed certificates are exported.
5. HSM unloads the CA private key.
6. Backups are made and logs are generated for the HSM and for the certificate management servers.
7. Certificates are exhibited and published. The ceremony's minutes are printed and hand-signed by all participants.

Fig. 1. Abridged script for certificate issuance by an offline CA drawn from the Brazilian National Academic PKI website [15] (ICP-EDU)

The lack of ceremonial procedures to ensure the integrity of secure hardware modules is present at every level of the typical PKI hierarchy, from HSMs used by the Registration Authorities to those used by the root Certification Authority.

In addition to the tampered device threat, it is possible that one or more traitors exist and in collusion (or not) might try to subvert the applications root of trust. Obviously, not identifying those threats could lead to heavy and irreversible losses, especially in applications such as PKI and e-voting.

On occasions where a reliable third-party may not exist or is unavailable, deciding whether to trust the application is even more difficult. This may be the case when the deployment of private keys is necessary in emergency circumstances (e.g. an online delegated CA key disclosure, or encrypted military messages).

Election days are a typical situation where the three mentioned conditions may apply: there is no clear (reachable) trusted third-party, political party interests are in conflict, and DRE integrity may be in dispute. It is clear that practical tools are necessary to assist in diminishing the risks posed by device tampering and user betrayal.

3   Our Proposals

3.1   Trust Establishment Rationale

Establishing trust in a device has two dimensions: **procedural** and **computational**.

The first, which consists of **device accreditation**, is where auditing takes place, encompassing every stage related to the device's (and the application that makes use of it) life cycle, from system specification to system disposal.

Accreditation is heavily human bounded, as it is related to the confidence the user (or the enterprise) using a given application has on it. Ultimately, it can be expressed in *the trust one has in the device's root of trust*. In this dimension, trust (as security) is seen as process, that must be evaluated [16] from time to time, and that uses auditing as one if its key tools.

The computational dimension is built around the *accredited root of trust*, by cryptographic means, in the form of a *trust chain*. Usually, this chain is built through the use of asymmetric-key techniques, but not necessarily. Binding the computational and procedural dimensions is thus fundamental for the trust establishment of a device and applications dependent on it, as HSMs and PKIs. In order to facilitate this binding, we propose and formalize the concept of device cryptographic identity - CID - and show how to use it to improve on a number of issues regarding hardware security modules, such as:

- assurance of the manufacturing process;
- securing the device's life cycle;
- prevention of important online and offline attacks.

3.2   Cryptographic Identity - CID

The cryptographic identity extends the trusted computing root of trust concept by attaching accreditation meaning and by imposing certain restrictive properties on it. Before continuing, we need to define the concepts of sealing and secure device epoch.

Definition: The sealing is the latest phase of the device manufacturing process where non-cryptographic verification (auditing) must be conducted, in order to decide whether a device can be accredited. The end of the sealing process defines the beginning of the secure device epoch (SDE).

Typically, secure hardware devices are manufactured either by the assembly of electronic components on a PCB (multi-chip modules) or by the masking and encapsulation of silicon wafers (single-chip modules).

In either case, the security of the end device arises from a series of physical and logical features, which are embedded in the system during one or more phases of the manufacturing process.

The early manufacturing phases may allow the auditing of the system. During these phases, the firmware, components, or layout of the system can be freely scanned for integrity.

However, during a specific manufacturing phase, the device is physically or logically sealed, so that any further attempt to audit the system will be recognized as a tampering attempt, causing eventual destruction of keys and other CSPs within the device.

A secure co-processor or HSM, CID enabled, shall have a unique challengeable identity with the following properties:

- **Establishment:** the CID must be automatically created at the hardware's final (human or automated) physical inspection, at the start of the secure device epoch.

- **Uniqueness:** the CID must be statistically unique, per device, bound to a security parameter k.
- **Protection:** at device epoch, the CID shall be protected inside a cryptographic boundary, with physical protections so that: (i) it must be improbable that an adversary could clone or copy a CID from a device without breaking through the device's cryptographic boundary, (ii) the CID must be destroyed with high probability whenever any attempt to violate the device's cryptographic boundary is made.
- **Verification:** the CID must be verifiable with negligible statistical "false positive" probability (key-size dependent)
- **Integrity:** device operation, and related CSPs protected by the secure device, should be possible if and only if the CID is preserved.

3.3   Considerations about Building a CID-enabled Device

In a typical tamper-responsive HSM, there are at least two conceptually distinct components enclosed inside the cryptographic boundary: the Sensing Unit (SU) and the Processing Unit (PU).

The PU has more processing power and less storage constrains. This unit effectively implements the various cryptographic primitives, key storage, key management, and other functions. Although its persistent memory cannot be easily erased, its contents can be encrypted with a key stored in the SU non-volatile SRAM.

The SU is capable of storing sensitive information in a non-volatile memory, and destroying it upon detection of a tamper attempt.

In a multi-chip module, the SU may consist of a low-power microcontroller with built-in or external sensors, and SRAM (Static RAM) or FRAM (Ferroelectric RAM) to store sensitive information. A single-chip module may contain an on-chip, low-power, non-volatile SRAM. It may also contain tamper sensors, and also external inputs pins that directly trigger SRAM wiping.

Typically, the SU is battery powered when there is no available external power source, in order to provide the continuous monitoring of the device's cryptographic boundaries, and the storage of sensitive information.

In the described scenario, the device CID can consist of keys generated after the device enters the secure device epoch, using a secure random number generator as entropy source, and stored inside the SU or PU.

In the latter case, it would be also necessary to protect the CID keys with a master key stored in the SU, allowing for easy CID destruction in case of a tamper attempt. As an added bonus, this master key can also be used to encrypt and to authenticate CSPs and firmware inside the cryptographic perimeter.

The solution that comprises a master key stored in the SU and a larger asymmetric key pair stored in the PU is usually preferable, as multi-chip SU modules may have very limited processing and storage capacity. In single-chip modules, the SU may not have any processing power at all.

It would also be possible to build the CID upon the evaluation of PUFs, generating keys that encrypt sensitive, non-volatile information. A single-chip scheme was presented by the AEGIS architecture proposal [7], and multi-chip schemes would also be possible, although there are no known commercial products using this technology.

3.4   Verifying the Device's CID

The properties of a CID-enabled device allow strong device integrity and trust accreditation. Accreditation is done by auditing means at the beginning of the *secure device epoch*, satisfying the **establishment** property. That is the last instant in which specialized auditing personnel would be required to unambiguously attest a hardware security module's identity.

From that moment on, only logical (cryptographic) challenges are required to attest a device's integrity, by the **verification** property. This is true because any attempt to gain unauthorized access to the CID material would destroy the device's identity as required by the **protection** property.

Generally speaking, challenging the device can be achieved by using a composition of classical cryptographic primitives. The most immediate approach is to have a user client to send a nonce to be signed by the hardware security module using a key protected by the trust chain rooted at the CID.

At first, verifying the nonce signature would be enough to attest the CID enabled device's integrity and identity. However, this is not as simple as it seems. In fact, this verification process *only moves* the security and trust requirements from the verified entity (VDE) to the verifier entity (VRE).

Therefore, if the verifier entity is not trusted at a trust level similar to that expected from the verified entity, we have, in fact, degradation of the global trust level.

To solve this problem we propose *shared verification schemes* which, by using multiple (possibly less trustworthy) VREs, *amplify* the total verifier trust level, possibly beyond that required for the VDE.

All verification schemes are comprised by a set of common items:

i) N, a set of trust weighted nodes, that encompass VREs and the VDE;
ii) T, a set of trust directed edges between nodes in N, that express the trust relationships among nodes, forming a graph G with set of nodes N, and set of edges T;
iii) M, a trust metric that evaluates G and a security parameter P used to decide whether the VDE is trustworthy [17].

It is also assumed that the verifier device presents the result of the verification process directly to the HSM user (e.g. by means of a visual indicator). In other words, the verifier shall not rely on a communication channel that is controlled by the device that is being verified.

In the following, let E_p be the probability that the VDE has been tampered with in a given time frame, in such a way that the attacker has gained total control over it *without* destroying the respective CID; i.e., a **CID-preserving attack**. Note that the more protections a device employs, the closest E_p is to zero, as there is a high chance that the tamper attempt will be detected by a tamper detection mechanism. E_p is also different from the probability of the VDE being tampered with but losing the original CID (a CID non-preserving attack), due to the activity of tamper response mechanisms. The clone attack is an example of a CID non-preserving attack. We call this second probability E_d, and assume it to be significantly greater than zero.

Although E_d is typically much larger than E_p, CID non-preserving attacks will have the same efficacy of CID preserving attacks in the cases where the HSM end user cannot check the authenticity of the CID. As attackers follow the path of least resistance, CID non-preserving attacks would thus be the chosen ones, and all the efforts of physical tamper detection would be foiled. Thus, our objective is to thwart these **CID non-preserving attacks** through detection, bringing E_d as close to E_p (and consequently close to zero) as possible. In this way, HSM tamper detection and reaction mechanisms can really deliver the security level that they were designed to.

Simple SVS (S-SVS): our simple shared verification scheme employs multiple, independent verifiers that, in consensus, must vouch for VDE accreditation.

Let P_i be the probability that the ith VRE has been tampered with. Let n be number of distinct verifiers. Then, if our trust metrics accepts a single CID identity challenge mismatch as a signal that the verified identity is not authentic, then E gives us the VRE-set *composed tampering probability*:

$$E = \prod_{i=1}^{n} P_i \text{ , where } P_i \in (0..1).$$

Although simple, this expression is elucidating, as it tells us that tampering with the shared verification can be made very difficult, if not negligible, just by increasing the number of VREs. That is true because an attacker would need to tamper simultaneously with all the VREs in order to produce a fake result.

Of course, this expression assumes that compromise probabilities are independent, reinforcing the need for the special procedures for VREs production and deployment that will be described in Section 4. These procedures reduce the probability of simultaneously cloning all devices (a "parallel clone" attack) to a level much lower than that of a standard clone attack, even if all VREs share the same hardware design. The S-SVS successfully amplifies verifiers' trust level even with very simple assumptions; this will be especially useful in the DRE voting machine context. Figure 2- "S-SVS Graph" presents the simple scheme, with G an n-degree directed tree.

While simple and powerful, the chosen trust metrics also makes it possible for an attacker, a traitor (a legitimate user that acts as an attacker), to cause denial of service attacks, by denying a single authentic signature.

Traitor Evidencing SVS (TE-SVS): our traitor-evidencing shared verification scheme employs n multiple, cross-verified, verifiers that in consensus either vouch   for   VDE   accreditation   or   point   up   to t possible   traitors.

The key idea is that every VRE and the VDE itself cross-checks every other device, creating a complete graph G, with $n(n-1)$ edges. Thus, each device would challenge and be challenged by every other device. The implementation of such scheme could be done using special USB OTG(On-The-Go) tokens that connect to each other by a special powering hub.

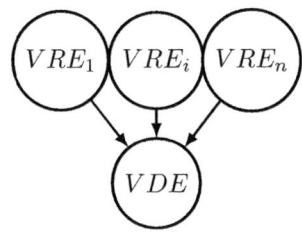

Fig. 2. S-SVS Graph

The problem of identifying traitors on the TE-SVS is similar to the classical Byzantine Generals problem [18] as our model assumes no reliable third-party beyond the VDE and the VREs and only direct communication between "generals". As we have n "generals" deciding whether to accredit or not the VDE, it follows that it can evidence up to t traitors, where t is given by $n \geq 3t + 1$. For larger values of t, it is impossible to decide who is a traitor.

The TE-SVS graph has a clear advantage over the S-SVS one, as it could be made robust against treason by allowing VDE accreditation with a least $n - t$ vouching VREs. However, the composed tampering probability function would suffer a small degradation because tampering with $n - t$ VREs would suffice for a successful attack.

For the sake of simplicity, we will assume for TE-SVS the same trust metric as for S-SVS, even though the TE-SVS graph now allows for much more robust metrics such as group trust [19]. Fortunately, this scheme can promptly make evident a traitor as its identity is checked by every other device on the graph; the possibility of being caught is now the main inhibitor to treason.

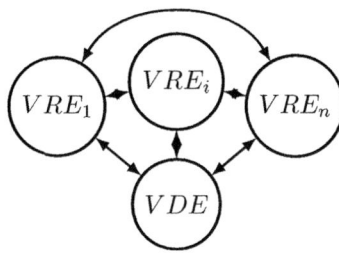

Fig. 3. TE-SVS Graph

4   SVS Architectures, Implementation, and Results

Any SVS architecture must provide components for easy trust verification in a measurable fashion, composing the elements required by the shared verification scheme.

Essentially, the CID verification challenge is the action that builds single edges on the trust graph G. The trust representation, however, do not pose any strong restriction on the nature of the challenge behind the edge. Thus, there is more than one way to prove device integrity by using the CID-rooted trust chain.

4.1 S-SVS Architecture for Cryptographically-Enabled VREs (Cryptographic Tokens)

The most direct form of CID challenge is through the use of an asymmetric cryptographic signing scheme, with a public key pk, a private key sk, a statistically unique *nonce*, a signing function $signature = sf(key, data)$, and a verification function $response = vf(key, data, signature)$, where $response \in \{checkok, checkfailed\}$. A given VRE chooses randomly a nonce, sends it to the previously known challenged entity, which applies sf to it, and returns the signature which is checked by using vf .

The main advantage of this method is that the verification primitives can easily be made computationally intractable, by using suitable mechanisms and appropriate key sizes in relatively constrained devices, as cryptographic tokens.

The system requirements for the VDE and the VRE are not unusual: (i) both must have a (possible unsafe) local communication channel, and (ii) they must have a human interface device that exports the security API function vf.

The VRE and VDE production, the verification procedure, and the interstice between them are described as follows:

VRE and VDE Production: Before the secure device epoch starts, a parameter n is chosen by the device manufacturer, depending on the final application of the secure device. Parameter n defines the maximum number of VREs to be used to verify a given VDE. As the idea is not to depend on any reliable third-party (external trust source, as a CA), VDEs and VREs are *paired* at device production.

During the manufacturing process, the HSM and each of the tokens generate a key pair. The HSM public key is stored inside each token, and all token public keys are stored inside the HSM. The keys inside the HSM are protected against modifications by the CID key material, so they will became invalid if any tamper attempt is detected. The HSM and tokens are then logically sealed (entering the SDE), and no more key exports can be made, nor regeneration of key pairs.

In order to maximize the independence of compromise probabilities for the VREs, thus minimizing the E probability, some basic rules shall be enforced:

Interstice: After manufacture, the two device sets (VDE and VREs) follow distinct logistical paths, and are stored at distinct physical locations. They will only meet again at the end user facilities. The auditing tokens can be kept inside a vault or in possession of mutually conflicting interests.

VDE Ceremonial Verification: The ceremonial-time device verification can be easily achieved. It requires that $1 \leq j \leq n$ randomly chosen auditors, each possessing a VRE, connect their devices to the VDE. For each verification device, one cryptographic challenge is launched by the device itself and other is initiated by the VDE. The challenge response is then output through the human interface device (*hid*) as a single bit message. The VDE challenge is used to indicate whether a given VRE has been replaced, maliciously or not.

4.2 Token Based Implementation

The token-based architecture was employed to implement a variant of the Simple Scheme (S-SVS) in our PKI-enabled HSM. This variant adds the authentication of the VRE (token) by the VDE (HSM), allowing the detection of an invalid VRE.

A special USB token was developed using an AVR microcontroller platform and ECC (Elliptic-curve Cryptography) primitives. Besides the MCU, this device contains a status LED that presents the result of the verification process directly to the HSM user. This effectively exports the security API to the end user. The HSM presents the result of the VRE authentication on its built-in LCD display.

The HSM booting process was also modified so that it now only allows user initialization after the successful authentication of a minimum number of VRE tokens, during a CID verification procedure by the user. This not only avoids unauthorized HSM initialization, but also enforces CID verification by the user. The aforementioned verification procedures were applied to the CA ceremonial script presented in 1, which resulted in the updated step 2 in 4.

2.1 Certificate management servers and HSM containing the CA key are powered on.
2.2 VDE integrity verification is performed by successive VRE interactions
2.3 Any basic setup is performed (e.g. clock adjustments)

Fig. 4. Update step 2 of CA script presented in figure 1

One of the benefits of this solution is that the security risks associated with storage and shipment procedures are greatly diminished. The developed VREs could be manufactured for very low prices, as their required computational power and tamper-resistance are minimal. As each VRE is inexpensive, the added cost of the USB token solution is quite low, even for a relatively large number of devices.

4.3 SVS Architecture for Highly Constrained VREs

For severely cost-restricted verifier entities, the token-based solution presented may be unsuitable. That may be the case in elections, where a large number (hundreds of thousands) of DREs must have their identity checked by an even larger number (millions) of candidates' representatives. In these cases, the computational power of the VREs is restricted to be very low or even near to null.

However, in spite of these strong restrictions, the trust edges of the trust graph G can still be constructed, as long as the verified entity provides specific functionalities, namely: (i) an output human interface device (hid), and (ii) a high stability secure real time clock.

The output hid has no security requirements; it may only allow a user to acquire information from the VDE without further devices. The high stability secure real time clock (HSSRTC) is an extended version of the secure clock required found in [20]. Further than the requirements that it shall be (i) non-resettable, and (ii) monotonic, we demand that it shall be (iii) highly accurate, and (iv) linear with respect of time.

In this context, we explored the VREs and VDEs asymmetry allowed by the simple trust graph to construct a Time-Based One Time Verification Code (TOTV), similar to existing Time-Based One Time Password [21, 22]. Like the One-Time Password, the security of the TOTV relies on the security of a symmetric key. The VREs and VDE production, the verification procedure, and the interstice between them are described as follows:

VREs and VDE Production: Before the secure device epoch, four parameters (n, s, t, d) are chosen by the device manufacturer, depending on the final application of the secure device. Parameter n defines the maximum number of VREs paired to this VDE, t delimits the time frame in which the VDE will be verifiable (usually related to the device's operational life-time), s defines a time step, i.e. the minimum time between two consecutives checks, and d the number of OTP digits. Moreover, at the SDE, at the secure manufacturing location, after the CID is generated, n verification symmetric keys are randomly chosen by the VDE and protected through encryption by the CID key material. Then, for each of these keys, $\frac{t}{s}$ OTP values are output by the VDE, forming an independent verification sheet (IVS), totalizing $n \times \frac{t}{s} \times d$ OTP digits. Each IVS is then isolated and reserved for later delivery and use by the ceremonial auditing personnel.

Interstice: during the interstice, each IVS and the VDE must be kept away, preferably under conflicting interest control, so that an adversary, possibly a traitor, cannot gain access to more than one IVS. The IVSs must be stored safely to prevent forward attacks. The VDE has no further security requirements, as any attempt to attack the VDE device would destroy the device's trust chain, and, thus the TOTV symmetric keys.

VDE Ceremonial Verification: The ceremonial-time device verification is straightforward. It requires only very little memory (to store d-character OTP values) and only enough power from the VRE to perfome comparisons, thus very suitable for human beings. If we use the simple trust metrics, each auditing user memorizes (or copies) from her IVS one or two expected OTP values prior to the device's deployment. Then, at ceremonial time, the VDE device outputs through its hid the calculated OTP values; the VRE sole action is to compare these values, trusting or not the device. If every VRE vouches positively, the device is accredited.

4.4   TOTV Implementation

We implemented the TOTV solution in our PKI-enabled HSM. In our implementation, the VDE hid was the same two line, twenty digit LCD display that was already available on the hardware secure device we built.

In our HSM design, the requirement for a HSSRTC was translated as a temperature-compensated, battery-backed RTC enclosed inside the crypto-graphic perimeter, yielding a tamper-resistant clock. The employed HSSRT has a 5 ppm time drift, not deviating more than 2 minutes per year.

The TOTV algorithm used was similar to the TOTP algorithm for user authentication in web services proposed by the OATH initiative [21, 22]; the sole differences are concentrated on how we use the produced OTP values. In our implementation, we consider the human user as the verifier of the OTP values produced by the secure co-processor (in contrast to the authentication server). The prover, instead of being a token with a single symmetric key, is the HSM itself, that holds not one symmetric key, but n distinct symmetric keys protected by the trust chain rooted at the CID.

In our implementation, oriented to HSMs, we used values 5, $\frac{1}{2}$ day, 10 year, 6 digits as n, s, t, and d parameters, yielding 5 IVS with 43K char each. The 43K chars were printed on A4 paper with font size 8, resulting in a four page IVS, perfectly suitable for almost any ceremonial use.

The generation of the OTP value was done by the 533MHz x86 main processor of the HSM by using the SHA256 based OTH HMAC [21], in negligible time. It is important to note that even low processing power CID-enabled devices would generate the IVS quite quickly.

For the parameters we chose, typical ceremonies require only a 12 character memory, as the 10 year accumulated deviation is only 20 minutes, significantly smaller than step s.

As we could see, the use of the TOTV verification is very convenient as it is very cheap to implement for multiple VREs and enables off-line use, typical of root CA operational environments and massive elections.

General-Purpose HSM Considerations: Clearly both the token based and the TOTV SVS implementations can be employed by general-purpose HSMs successfully. However, for certain applications such as SSL acceleration, the additional VRE ceremonial verification steps, if not automated, may represent some operational burden.

Voting Machine Considerations: For CID-enabled DRE voting machines, the use of the TOTV solution would not dramatically change the parameters presented by the HSM implementation. As long as simple modifications are made, typical IVS will have $1 \sim 2$K chars. The trick is to print only the IVS of the electoral days, as they are usually pre-defined by law.

Suppose that for large countries we have at most 20 political parties; then checks would be made at 30 minutes intervals, the DRE would be used for 10 electoral days (one election per year with 10 hour duration, over ten years), and a 6 char OTP. For that setup we will have 20 IVS with some 1200 char.

5   Conclusion

In this paper we analyzed the importance of device identity establishment and verification in PKI and voting applications.

We presented two specific solutions that enable regular and auditing users to promptly and easily verify whether their interfacing hardware is trustworthy with high levels of confidence at ceremonial time, as the employment of multiple verification devices greatly increases the required effort to clone or subvert the hardware.

The first solution is token based, in which we implemented very low priced verification devices to be used in amplified trust verification schemes.

The second solution relies on a Time-Based One Time Verification Code, and can be used at extremely cost-sensitive applications, but it requires more control over the VREs in the interstice phase and a secure clock inside the VDE. It was shown how this solution could be easily implemented in HSMs and DRE voting machines. We also presented details of our implementation of the first solution on our hardware security module (HSM), and how it prevents unauthorized HSM initialization and diminishes the security risks present during equipment shipment and storage.

6   Future Work

"If you cannot measure, you cannot improve" - Lord Kelvin's quote. Our future work is concentrated in developing a *trust metric framework* which encompasses device trust, ranging from device production, device epoch to device disposal, allowing for better integration with other analytical metric tools already applied to entire applications or enterprises.

We are also working on how to better estimate the E_d and E_p tamper probabilities in real world devices.

Acknowledgements. We would like to thank the referees for their valuable comments.

References

1. Anderson, R., Bond, M., Clulow, J., Skorobogatov, S.: Cryptographic processors—a survey. Proceedings of the IEEE 94(2), 357–369 (2006)
2. Dyer, J.G., Lindemann, M., Perez, R., Sailer, R., van Doorn, L., Smith, S.W., Weingart, S.: Building the IBM 4758 secure coprocessor. Computer 34(10), 57–66 (2001)
3. Costan, V., Sarmenta, L.F., van Dijk, M., Devadas, S.: The Trusted Execution Module: Commodity General-Purpose Trusted Computing. In: Grimaud, G., Standaert, F.-X. (eds.) CARDIS 2008. LNCS, vol. 5189, pp. 133–148. Springer, Heidelberg (2008)
4. Zheng, Y., He, D., Wang, H., Tang, X.: Secure drm scheme for future mobile networks based on trusted mobile platform. In: Proceedings of the IEEE International Conference on Wireless Communications, Networking and Mobile Computing 2005 (WCNM 2005). IEEE Press, Elsevier (2005)
5. Shimizu, K., Hofstee, H.P., Liberty, J.S.: Cell broadband engine processor vault security architecture. IBM J. Res. Dev. 51(5), 521–528 (2007)
6. Chen, B., Morris, R.: Certifying program execution with secure processors. In: HOTOS 2003: Proceedings of the 9th conference on Hot Topics in Operating Systems, p. 23. USENIX Association, Berkeley (2003)

7. Suh, G.E., O'Donnell, C.W., Devadas, S.: Aegis: A single-chip secure processor. IEEE Design and Test of Computers 24(6), 570–580 (2007)
8. Anderson, R.J.: Security Engineering: A Guide to Building Dependable Distributed Systems, 2nd edn. Wiley, Chichester (April 2008)
9. Anderson, R., Kuhn, M.: Tamper resistance—a cautionary note, USENIX (November 1996)
10. Kent, S.: Evaluating certification authority security, vol. 4, pp. 319–327. IEEE, Los Alamitos
11. Neff, C.A.: Practical high certainty intent verification for encrypted votes (October 2004)
12. Chaum, D.: Secret-ballot receipts: True voter-verifiable elections. IEEE Security & Privacy 2(1), 38–47 (2004)
13. Sastry, N.K.: Verifying security properties in electronic voting machines. PhD thesis, Berkeley, CA, USA, Adviser-Wagner, David (2007)
14. NIST: Security requirements for cryptographic modules. Federal Information Processing Standards Publication (FIPS PUB) 140-2 (2002)
15. ICP-EDU: Emissão de certificados pela AC raiz (August 2009), http://www.icp.edu.br/svn/docs/template-emissao-cert-ac-credenciada.pdf
16. ISO/IEC: ISO/IEC 27002 Information technology — Security techniques — Code of practice for information security management (July 2005)
17. Levien, R., Aiken, A.: Attack-resistant trust metrics for public key certification. In: 7th USENIX Security Symposium, pp. 229–242 (1998)
18. Lamport, L., Shostak, R., Pease, M.: The byzantine generals problem. ACM Transactions on Programming Languages and Systems 4, 382–401 (1982)
19. Levien, R.: Attack-Resistant Trust Metrics. In: Computing with Social Trust, pp. 121–132. Springer, London (November 2008)
20. van Dijk, M., Rhodes, J., Sarmenta, L.F.G., Devadas, S.: Offline untrusted storage with immediate detection of forking and replay attacks. In: STC 2007: Proceedings of the 2007 ACM workshop on Scalable trusted computing, pp. 41–48. ACM, New York (2007)
21. M'Raihi, D., Bellare, M., Hoornaert, F., Naccache, D., Ranen, O.: RFC 4226: HOTP: An HMAC-based one-time password algorithm (December 2005)
22. M'Raihi, D., Machani, S., Pei, M., Rydell, J.: RFC draft: TOTP: Time-based one-time password algorithm (January 2009)

ABUSE: PKI for Real-World Email Trust*

Chris Masone and Sean W. Smith

Dartmouth College, Hanover NH 03755 USA

Abstract. Current PKI-based email systems (such as X.509 S/MIME and PGP/ MIME) potentially enable a recipient to determine a name and organizational affiliation of the sender. This information can suffice for a trust decision when the recipient already knows the sender—but how can a recipient decide whether or not trust email from a *new* correspondent? Current systems are not expressive enough to capture the real ways that trust flows in these sorts of scenarios. To solve this problem, we begin by applying concepts from social science research to a variety of such cases from interesting application domains; primarily, crisis management in the North American power grid. We have examined transcripts of telephone calls made between grid management personnel during the August 2003 North American blackout and extracted several different classes of *trust flows* from these real-world scenarios. Combining this knowledge with some design patterns from HCISEC, we develop criteria for a system that will enable humans apply these same methods of trust-building in the digital world. We then present the design and prototype of *Attribute-Based, Usefully Secure Email* (ABUSE)—and present experimental evaluation showing that it solves the problem.

1 Introduction

Problem. Why should Alice trust an email message allegedly sent by Bob? A natural answer is to use digital signatures. PKIs work to establish a binding between identity and a key pair, and in a small organization, most users probably know each other and this will be enough to establish trust. However, in large organizations or in federations of organizations, it becomes less likely that a sender and recipient knew each other prior to contact. Thus, assurance of only the sender's name and/or email address would not be enough to help the recipient make a good decision. *Digital signatures no longer automatically imply trustworthiness.* Systems that focus only on identity are not expressive enough to allow users to specify the right properties for conclusions in human trust settings.

Example Application Domain. The electrical power grid (particularly the North American blackout of August 2003) provides wonderful examples of users needing to be able to make quick trust decisions about communication from other humans – often from other enterprises – they haven't met. *In such scenarios, knowing the name and organization of the sender is not sufficient for trustworthiness.* The sender's job, standing

---

* This paper is based on the first author's Ph.D. dissertation [1]; a preliminary design report appeared as [2]. This research was supported in part by the NSF under grants CNS-0448499 and CNS-0524695; views and conclusions do not represent those of the sponsors.

F. Martinelli and B. Preneel (Eds.): EuroPKI 2009, LNCS 6391, pp. 146–162, 2010.
© Springer-Verlag Berlin Heidelberg 2010

within the relying party's professional or social network, and even characteristics that the sender used to possess can all play a role in this trust calculation [2,3].

Even within the same power company, operational decision makers sit in centralized control facilities that are geographically separated from the power generation and transmission stations. Furthermore, many different companies and management organizations need to collaborate in the event of a crisis. Thus, there is nearly always a requirement for some kind of technologically mediated communication, and a reduced likelihood that the people who run the actual equipment are personally familiar with all the people authorized to request operational changes. Additionally, we have seen these centralized control facilities, and observed their control panels annotated here and there with handwritten notes indicating the myriad of small ways in which standard procedure needs to be worked around in the cases of various facilities and pieces of equipment. Operators may need to take the central controllers at their word in situations that involve these exceptions. Moreover, deregulation has created a greater number of organizational boundaries within the industry than ever before [4], decreasing the probability that communicants share pre-existing trust relationships even further. Currently, this communication is primarily done via telephone.

As was observed during the 2003 blackout, relying on control room phones for communication during emergencies can be problematic; a given individual can only be handling one call at a time, and a lack of available phones can cause a bottleneck. Migrating communication in the grid to some form of digital messaging system could alleviate these issues, but current technologies do not provide support for the kinds of trust building we saw during the blackout.

Our Solution. To solve this problem, we begin by applying concepts from social science research to a variety of such cases from interesting application domains; primarily, crisis management in the North American power grid. We have examined transcripts of telephone calls [5] made between grid management personnel during the August 2003 North American blackout and extracted several different classes of *trust flows* from these real-world scenarios. Combining this knowledge with some design patterns from HCISEC, we develop criteria for a system that will enable humans apply these same methods in the digital world. We then built *Attribute-Based, Usefully Secure Email* (ABUSE), a PKI-based system to solve this problem. (Our use of "attribute" here refers to special chains of assertions, and should not be confused with X.509 Attribute Certificates.) Our design explicitly allows scalability; ABUSE users distributed across a set of organizations can use these enhanced features for trust judgment, but can these messages are still compatible with mail clients that are not ABUSE-aware.

This Paper. This paper discusses the building blocks (Sect. 2), design and implementation of our prototype (Sect. 3). Sect. 4 and Sect. 5 then present the experiments we did to determine whether our system in fact solved this problem. Sect. 6 concludes.

2   Related Work and Building Blocks

S/MIME. To address email security and privacy concerns, many organizations in the commercial, federal and educational sectors have deployed S/MIME [6,7], a secure email standard that leverages an X.509 PKI [8] to provide message integrity and non-repudiation via digital signatures [9,10]. An S/MIME signature block contains, in addition to the actual digital signature over the message body, the identity certificate of the sender. In this way, the system also provides sender authenticity and assurance of sender identity—in addition to the sender's public key. (Note that S/MIME does not cover the headers of a message, which could leave some issues.)

Even in cases in which the sender is familiar to the recipient, usability issues exist. One interesting problem arises from the fact that standard S/MIME clients treat all installed trust roots as equal. S/MIME can do one of two things for the recipient, depending on whether she has experience with the sender. If she knows the sender a priori, S/MIME can enable the recipient to leverage her trust in an institution to assure herself of the sender's identity and thus apply her process-based trust[1] to the incoming message. If she has little or no prior experience with the sender, then S/MIME allows the recipient to extend some measure of institutionally-based trust to the sender. This is not enough for our scenarios.

S/MIME *has* provided both message integrity and sender authenticity, as well as the sender's public key—provided that the recipient trusts the sender's CA and that the sender's private key has remained private. S/MIME, therefore, is a good starting point for our trustworthy email system, and the public key in particular could provide a way to hook further contextual information about the sender into the message.

Other Approaches. X.509 Attribute-Based Messaging (ABM) [12] does not work on the behalf of message recipients. Instead, it focuses on allowing sender to address messages using attributes instead of identities. The problems considered in ABM are orthogonal to our work. Both Lotus Notes [13] and Groove Virtual Office [14] provide some measure of context for their users. However, none focus on the problem of providing for users adequate context for deciding whether to trust unfamiliar correspondents. *Trust Management (TM)* deals with automatically deciding a form of trust based on attributes and policies. TM systems use many different methods of representing credentials, varying across systems [15,16,17,18,19,20,21,22,23].

TM systems, with their focus on deciding trust based on policies, would dictate an algorithmic approach to the email trust problem we have laid out. This approach cannot solve our problem: it would require the automated comprehension of arbitrary text from arbitrary senders; users are incapable of effectively enumerating their personal trust policies (a priori) in a machine comprehensible format; administrator-defined domain policies are difficult (and expensive) to get right; domain policies are even harder and more expensive to maintain over time; and it is unclear that domain policies useful for the average case are still applicable in exceptional circumstances.

Non-identity X.509 PKI. Both *X.509 Attribute Certificates (ACs)* [24] and *X.509 Proxy Certificates (PCs)* [25,26] are expressed in ASN.1, a binary format, just like regular X.509 ID certificates. Both ACs and PCs allow for arbitrary assertions to be built into X.509 certificates, and signed by users. Attribute Certificates are designed to, as the name suggests, use a hierarchy of Attribute Authorities (analogous to Certificate Authorities) to issue X.509 credentials binding arbitrary assertions to identities. Trust would be institutional in such a deployment; users trust that these assertions are granted

---

[1] *Process-based trust* leverages reputation and prior experience; *institutional* uses formal social constructs [11].

to individuals based on some policy implemented by the issuing organization, and so they are willing to believe the bindings provided.

PCs are designed to be issued by users who wish to delegate a subset of their permissions to processes running on their behalf in grid computing environments. As PCs are not meant for human consumption, it does not make sense to apply our model of human trust to a system that deploys them.

Choosing the right technology. ABUSE requires signed assertions. As there are a plethora of formats available for this, it seems unnecessary to define our own. SDSI/SPKI has not seen much use outside of academic prototypes, though there is a C library for manipulating SDSI/SPKI certificates. Prior experience [27] has shown that trying to shoehorn SDSI/SPKI into an X.509-centric world can be frustrating, however. This leaves us with ACs and PCs. OpenSSL [28], a widely used cryptographic library, and NSS [29], the Mozilla cryptography infrastructure, support X.509 well. OpenSSL supports PCs off the shelf. AC support, on the other hand, requires some extra code to be patched into OpenSSL. Thus, Proxy Certificates are our signed assertion format of choice. They have the best support among commodity tools and, moreover, the special features provided by them (allowing new key pairs and novel assertions to be combined in one data structure) are beneficial in our system.

3   ABUSE Design and Prototype

ABUSE was introduced in [2], and the first author's dissertation [1] discusses the prototype at length. The system is designed to rely upon two pieces of existing infrastructure: an email system and an X.509 identity PKI. In addition to these, ABUSE requires two component pieces: an ABUSE-savvy email client and, in the initial prototype, an organization-level centralized store for ABUSE attributes. The ABUSE client participates in a number of different facets of the system: attribute *presentation*, *issuance*, *distribution* and *validation*. A decentralized design for ABUSE [1] would be used in a real deployment, but for expediency and ease of user testing, the centralized design was implemented for this research.

When humans decide trust, the providence of a statement is often as important as the content; thus each ABUSE attribute is a chain of digitally signed assertions Fig. 1 (a). As is the case with a vast number of enterprise X.509 identity CAs, we expect the root of these chains to be a local entity at an organization, perhaps with a sub-CA certificate from a higher root or a cross-certificate from a bridge. Each assertion is an X.509 Proxy Certificate (PC). The two aspects of the PC specification that we bend relate to *naming* and certificate *validity period*. We use both *distinguished names* and public keys as identifiers in ABUSE; the identity PKI on which we rely uses distinguished names to bind human users to public keys (which is how real-world deployments work, for good or ill), and we use the public keys from this PKI to identify issuers and subjects within ABUSE. This is the first way in which we depart from the PC specification [25], which calls for distinguished names to be used as identifiers. As with standard PCs, ABUSE does not mandate a maximum validity period. Our approach to representing the content of an assertion stays within the PC specification; Proxy Certificates contain a *policy* field that can contain arbitrary text. Lastly, PCs bind an assertion and a subject identifier to a key pair. The private half of this pair can be used to issue new PCs. Thus, given a chain of assertions representing an attribute, Alice can use the private key associated with the final PC to append a new assertion to the chain, creating a new attribute for her associate Bob. In this manner Alice can make a signed statement about Bob, and provenance information is built right into the data format.

In a true PKI, individual entities generate and control their own private keys. However, to simplify the implementation of our prototype, we did not implement ABUSE attribute issuance in a distributed fashion; instead, the centralized store plays a key role in the process.

In ABUSE, attribute issuance is really just creating a new signed assertion bound to an existing attribute (which is represented by a chain of PCs). In the current prototype, when Alice wishes to grant a new ABUSE attribute to Bob, she first decides what she wants to say about him. This is a string of arbitrary text, of Alice's choice. Then, she authenticates to the ABUSE attribute store with her identity certificate, downloads her current ABUSE attributes from the centralized store and selects one whose authority she feels allows her to make the desired statement. After inputting the assertion content, Alice indicates for how long she would like this assertion to be considered valid. Her client then sends this data, along with Bob's public key, over the authenticated channel to the store. The store mints a proxy certificate containing the hash of Bob's public key in the subject field, the assertion content in the policy field, the validity period specified by Alice, and the public half of the key pair that has been generated for this PC, signing it with the private key associated with the final assertion in the chain indicated by Alice.

All of Alice's ABUSE attributes are available to her in the centralized store after she correctly authenticates using her credentials from the organizational identity PKI. This store is an LDAP directory, which Alice's client can search by public key on her behalf. Alice cannot get the private keys associated with her attributes; those never leave the

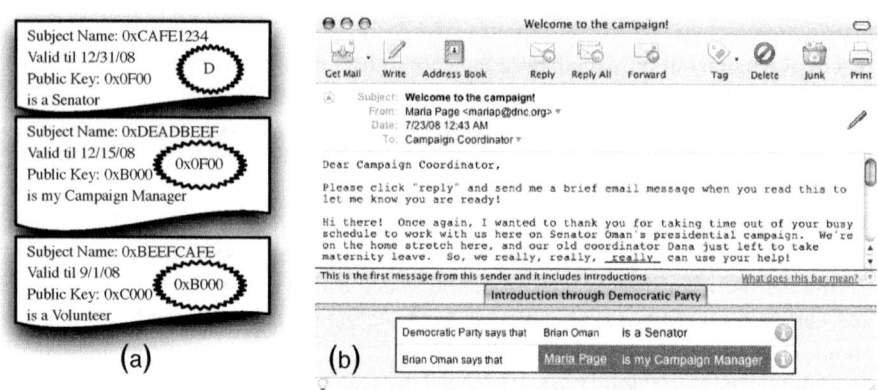

Fig. 1. (a) A chain of signed assertions, part of which is shown in (b). We use X.509 Proxy Certificates as our assertion format. The ordering of the elements of this chain is unambiguously determined by the signatures on the certificates. Note the use of public keys in the place of human names; we rely on the organizational identity PKI to connect public keys to individuals. (b) An example ABUSE message.

store. Again, a design that obviates the need for this central store is discussed in the final chapter of [1].

PCs are natively formatted as binary data, which must be encoded as printable text in order to be sent along with email. Fortunately, there are standardized ways to do this encoding, which we use to prepare our assertion chains for transmission with an email message. Delineators are inserted between individual assertions and also between chains, so that the client on the receiving end can appropriately parse the ABUSE content for verification and display. By sending information in headers, we prevent graphical email clients that do not recognize the headers from displaying the content; this is in contrast to schemes that enclose extra information as email attachments, like S/MIME and PGP/MIME. Before widespread client support for the format existed, users of PGP would experience push-back from the non-users to whom they sent mail, as the signature would be presented as a mysteriously named attachment by the recipient's email software [30, p. 322].

Standard digital signatures on email cover only the body of the message. As our assertions are contained in headers, it is possible that they might be vulnerable. However, each assertion is packaged as an X.509 Proxy Certificate, digitally signed by the private key associated with the previous certificate in the chain. Thus, none of the assertions can be removed or modified without the system detecting it during the validation process. The signatures on the certificates also allow us to determine the appropriate order of the assertions in an ABUSE attribute, so attackers cannot insert single assertions or re-order the existing ones without detection. An attacker could *add* an entire attribute, though he would have to possess or create one that has been appropriately issued to the sender. He could also remove one or more chains without detection, as long as he deletes them in their entirety. In order to detect such an attack, we generate a hash of all the attributes that the sender has chosen to bind to the message, append the hash to the message text, and then allow the client to generate a signature over the entirety of the message body as usual; this preserves compatibility with current S/MIME clients (again, making it possible for ABUSE to gradually role out among a subset of distributed users).

When a message is received, the email client does its standard S/MIME signature validation. Assuming the signing certificate is not revoked, the assertions are parsed out of the header and individually validated using OpenSSL.

In ABUSE, our goal is to enable the relying party to make a decision at the time the message is received; whether the accompanying chains are still valid a year after the decision is not relevant. Consequently, the problem of rolling over public keys is not an issue for assertions in ABUSE attributes. Similarly, we felt revocation of individual assertions or whole ABUSE attributes would introduce a raft of usability problems without adding significant utility, so we chose not to explore that. (Section 5.5.1 in [1] discusses this tradeoff further.)

Presenting an assertion chain to the user is primarily a GUI issue (Fig. 1 (b)). We wish to support the use of process-based trust in ABUSE by calling users' attention to assertions made by people with whom they are familiar. We also wish to downplay information that users have seen frequently in order to avoid *habituation*. Intuitively, the visual impact of our GUI will scale with the novelty of the information ABUSE has to display. Familiar assertions from familiar senders are of the least import; the message recipient already shares some trust relationship with the sender, and so ABUSE is not particularly helpful. Messages from unfamiliar senders, the case in which ABUSE is designed to be most useful, have attributes displayed prominently. Consequently, our system includes techniques to track familiarity heuristically and to use it to guide presentation; a full discussion is beyond the scope of this paper (but see [1]).

4   Evaluation in Power Grid Scenarios

Our first user study, which used task setups drawn directly from the August 2003 blackout [5], was designed to compare users' ability to make trust judgments when equipped with ABUSE-enhanced email versus their ability to do so when equipped only with current email technologies. We hoped to verify two hypotheses during this comparison: ABUSE enables users to identify trustworthy messages from unfamiliar third parties, and ABUSE users do not exhibit a significantly higher rate of false positives during identification of "trustworthy messages" (those whose assertion chains indicate that it is reasonable to believe that the sender has the authority to request the stated course of action).

ABUSE seeks to provide users with better context for making risky decisions than S/MIME and plaintext email. Setting plaintext against S/MIME against ABUSE, however, is not an entirely fair comparison. ABUSE includes extra contextual information that the others do not. Currently, users may resort to out-of-band channels to get this extra context. To more fairly compare these pre-existing technologies to ABUSE, it is necessary to simulate for subjects the ability to consult those extra sources of information.

Consulting out-of-band channels causes delay, which users in time-sensitive situations (like crises in the grid) may not be able to afford. Indeed there may be cases in which these channels are not even available. To answer the questions posed above, we needed to put subjects in situations in which they needed to trust messages from unfamiliar third parties in order to complete a task, and also had reason to worry about getting fooled by untrustworthy messages—but were not so afraid of getting tricked that they would invariably seek the reassurance of traditional trust-building methods (i.e. contacting some trusted individual with knowledge of the situation).

We used scenarios inspired by the August 2003 blackout for this study. An emergency in the power grid (a *contingency* in the parlance of the industry) is clearly a high-stakes situation and the people working to keep the system under control frequently have to trust people that they have not encountered before. Furthermore, they use informal methods to build that trust. They currently either leverage human connections by making phone calls to people they *do* know [5, pp. 56–58], or they assume that anyone who knows the right phone numbers to call and can "talk the talk" is worthy of at least a measure of trust [31]. These operators know that, when a contingency arises, the more quickly it can be mitigated the better—and that doing nothing can sometimes be just as bad as doing the wrong thing [5, pp. 480–484]. However, the conversations in the phone transcripts indicated that the operators were simultaneously hesitant to act unless they felt confident in the decision they were making—or, at least, confident that someone with the appropriate authority was ordering the action they were about to take

Table 1. Scores for trustworthy message and attack message (resp.), depending on out-of-band channel used. Subjects are rewarded for making correct choices, penalized for delaying in proportion with how problematic the delay might be, and strongly penalized for making the wrong choices.

	None	Phoned someone	Checked chart	Both
Reject	$(-20, +10)$	$(-20, +8)$	$(-20, +8)$	$(-20, +6)$
Accept	$(+10, -20)$	$(+5, -20)$	$(+7, -20)$	$(+2, -20)$

[5, pp. 236–238]. So, in these power grid scenarios, operators need to trust third parties they do not know in order to do their jobs, but concern over a variety of factors gives them pause.

Subjects. A total of 34 subjects took part in the study, 12 in the ABUSE group and 11 in each of the others. Ideally, we would have been able to perform the study on actual grid operators, provide as much realism as possible, and report the results. However, this was infeasible; like most academic researchers performing these kinds of experiments, our pool of subjects is mostly limited to college students. Choosing this scenario, therefore, required us to devise an incentive structure that adequately mirrored the tradeoffs faced by real grid operators while remaining comprehensible to the subjects.

Incentives. We determined that the disincentive for making the wrong decision about a message had to be more highly negative than the reward for making the right choice was positive. Breaking-even after one correct choice and one incorrect choice would be unrealistic. A subject who makes a wrong decision should still have the opportunity to be above the break-even point. Furthermore, a subject should not be able to simply make the same choice every time and come out ahead.

As a secondary concern, though, we also wanted to provide a disincentive against delaying a trust decision by consulting out-of-band sources. In real situations, doing so delays operator action, exposing the grid to more risk. Leaving such a disincentive out of the study would likely cause subjects to go for the potential extra certainty every time. We provided two simulated out-of-band channels for the subject to get extra context: calling an acquaintance for more information and using the company organizational chart to check for someone's presence or position. As the former would take more time than the latter in the real world, it was assigned a stronger disincentive. Pre-tests indicated that the stronger of the two needed to be half of the potential gain; subjects were never disinclined to "phone a friend" otherwise.

Finally, we wanted to moderate the disincentive for delaying a decision in the event that a message turned out to be untrustworthy. Logically, the right thing to do with an attack message in real life is to ignore it; while the subject is still wasting time, he should not be penalized as much for delaying a choice to do nothing as for delaying a choice to act. Taking all this into account, the final structure is presented in Table 1.

The Study. The study employed a between-subjects design to examine whether ABUSE users are better able to identify trustworthy messages compared to users of other email clients. Subjects were randomly assigned to one of three groups defined by the type of simulated email client used during the study: (1) Plaintext, (2) S/MIME (with validly signed messages), and (3) ABUSE (with cryptographically valid signed assertions). The pre-study instructions, the simulated email headers displayed, the bodies of the messages, the task scenarios and the post-study debriefing were identical across the three groups. We randomized the order of tasks within each email group to control for order effects; the results could be muddied if our chosen ordering predisposed users in a given group to make certain types of decisions.

The study was constructed as a game that consisted of a set of five tasks. Having five tasks allowed us to test each of three interesting attack scenarios while also having a pair of trustworthy scenarios to help verify that the subjects who correctly identified the trustworthy messages didn't just get lucky. In each scenario, the subject was given a new persona with a name, email address, social network, and position at some power grid organization unique to that task scenario. The subject was also presented with a summary of the status of the portion of the grid over which she exercised control, and told of a problem that had arisen. Her goal was to help return the grid to stability as soon as possible, but she was incapable of doing this on her own. The study infrastructure then presented her with a message that provided her with a strategy that the sender claimed would help mitigate the contingency. The subject had to decide whether to heed the message right away, reject it out of hand, or consult out-of-band channels to attempt to get more context for her decision. These out-of-band channels (the ability to query an acquaintance or consult a company organizational chart) are provided for two reasons: first, to provide greater verisimilitude; and second, to enable subjects without the benefit of ABUSE to have a chance to make the correct trust decisions in all cases.

Scenarios. Each task scenario was based on an actual event that occurred during the North American August 2003 blackout. In each scenario, we identified the relying party, the trust source, the trust sink, the authorizer and any intermediaries. The experimental subject was put in the position of the relying party. The scenarios in which the subjects received trustworthy messages are actual contingencies that actually occurred, and the action requested by the sender is the strategy that was actually used to mitigate the real problem. The assertions bound to the message express the same flows of trust that we distilled from the phone transcripts. The scenarios in which the subjects received attack messages were designed to closely ape the trustworthy cases, with contingencies that were analogous to real problems that arose in the grid. The "mitigation strategy" recommended by each attack message was designed to seem plausible when evaluated in the context of its accompanying scenario. There were three different kinds of attackers: a completely external attacker, an *internal-insider*, employed at the same company, and an *external-insider*. The subjects took the study through a web browser (Mozilla Firefox 2). Once the subject inputs his randomly-assigned ID number, the system generates a random ordering of the five scenarios and presents them one-by-one, populating a standard GUI each time. After the subject makes his decision, the system moves to the next scenario in its random ordering.

The Tests. After having some time to digest the initial setup information, the subject "receives" the message for this scenario. The links to access out-of-band information are also presented at this time, as well as the buttons that allow the user to indicate whether they wish to act upon or disregard the message. If the subject is in the S/MIME or ABUSE groups, the simulated message will have the standard Thunderbird signature indicator present, and mousing over it will provide explanatory text pulled from the real email client software. Subjects in the ABUSE group also, obviously, see ABUSE assertion chains in the simulated message window.

At the beginning of the debriefing phase, subjects were informed that they had completed the tasks and told that they would now be asked to review their answers. They were also reminded that they would not be able to change them; they would only be allowed to indicate whether or not they, in retrospect, would change the decision they made. In addition, the subjects were allowed to provide free-form comments about why they were comfortable with their initial trust decision or not. These comments allowed us to not only see some very encouraging signs that people were actually reading and using ABUSE assertions in their decision-making process, but also allowed for us to find cases in which a subject had become confused by the study interface or by some of the power-grid trappings of the setup.

Results. Overall success rates are shown in Table 2. Success is measured as the percent of all tasks ($n = 5$ per subject) that were correctly completed, i.e. the subject acted on trustworthy messages and chose to ignore untrustworthy messages. In Table 2a, we look at the performance of subjects in all scenarios across the three email groups. Subjects using ABUSE were correct 75% of the time, compared to rates of 65% and 60% among plaintext users and S/MIME users respectively. Statistically comparing the mean percent correct in each group using an analysis of variance (ANOVA) test indicates that there is no statistically significant difference between the three email groups ($F = 1.5, P = .224$). Table 2b compares overall success for ABUSE (again, 75%) to success in all non-ABUSE user-rounds, showing a nearly statistically significant difference considering a p-value of .10 ($F = .266, P = .105$). This is nice to see, but it really isn't actually what we want to know. We wish to see whether users armed with ABUSE can identify trustworthy messages without requiring out-of-band help more frequently than users with existing technologies.

Next, we examine whether subjects in each email type were correct more or less often depending on scenario type—trustworthy vs. untrustworthy. Table 3 shows this analysis. In trustworthy scenarios, a significantly higher percentage of ABUSE users were correct overall ($F = 4.24, P = .019$), though additional analysis (a Bonferroni test) shows that there is no statistical difference between the plaintext and ABUSE email groups. Both, however, are significantly higher than S/MIME. More importantly, a significantly higher percentage of ABUSE users were correct without help in trustworthy scenarios (column in bold) compared to plaintext and S/MIME users. These results support the hypothesis that ABUSE subjects can correctly identify trustworthy messages without getting help significantly more often than either the S/MIME or plaintext subjects.

To examine the relationship between email type and success level in more depth, we performed a logistic regression analysis of the likelihood of success in trustworthy scenarios, controlling for any positive correlation between subjects seeking help and having success. We found a significant correlation ($p = .033$) between using ABUSE and the correct identification of trustworthy messages without seeking help.

One might find it surprising, looking back at Table 3, that ABUSE users were no more successful than others in untrustworthy scenarios, with or without help. In these scenarios, use of ABUSE does not significantly correlate with willingness to forego

Table 2. a: the mean overall level of success rates for each email type; b: overall success, ABUSE vs. all non-ABUSE user-rounds

Email type	n	% correct overall	
ABUSE	60	75%	$F = 1.5$,
Plaintext	55	65%	$p = .224$
S/MIME	55	60%	

Email type	n	% correct overall	
ABUSE	60	75%	$F = 2.66$,
Non-ABUSE	110	63%	$p = .105$

Table 3. Success rates by type of scenario and whether subjects resorted to out-of-band channels before making a decision. In trustworthy scenarios, a significantly higher percentage of ABUSE users were correct overall, and correct without help (column in bold). In untrustworthy scenarios, we see no significant difference in percentage correct across email types, with or without help.

		Trustworthy scenarios			Untrustworthy scenarios	
Email type	n	% right overall	% right, no help	n	% right overall	% right, no help
ABUSE	24	92%	**67%**	36	64%	14%
Plaintext	22	91%	**14%**	33	48%	18%
S/MIME	22	64%	**27%**	33	58%	18%
		$F = 4.24, p = .9186$	$F = 9.31, p = 0003$		$F = 0.83, p = .4405$	$F = 0.15, p = .8605$

help ($p = .193$). This implies that subjects in all three groups, when faced with an untrustworthy message, were similarly likely to resort to out-of-band channels before making their decision. We believe this can be explained by looking back at the incentive structure shown in Table 1. Recall that the penalty for going out-of-band in situations where the subject suspected that the message was an attack was quite low. We designed the study to attempt to mimic real world costs and benefits; when the subject believes he is being attacked, and the correct response to an attack is to do nothing, there is little harm in taking extra time to be certain.

In addition to commenting on their decisions at the conclusion of the study, the subjects were asked which choices they would change, given the chance. In rounds in which subjects did not seek help, subjects in the ABUSE group who felt confident were more likely to have made the right choice.

Looking at the observations in trustworthy scenarios within Table 3 again, it is interesting to note that the S/MIME group performed significantly worse when compared to the plaintext group. This is counterintuitive; S/MIME, when compared to plaintext email, is supposed to help users better identify messages that are trustworthy! Subjects in these power grid scenarios seemed to miss trustworthy messages more often when equipped with S/MIME than with even just plaintext email. This correlated with the increase in penalty for resorting to out-of-band channels in trustworthy scenarios; when subjects had something to lose, S/MIME made them more willing to go out on a limb. They wound up losing more frequently than the plaintext users who, because they really did not have much to go on, played it safe, took the help, and took the smaller number of more certain points.

5   Evaluation of User Understanding

The second user study that we performed to evaluate ABUSE focused on finding qualitative evidence that users could understand the information conveyed by the ABUSE assertion presentation GUI.

This time, we provided a *series* of related tasks; in this fashion, we could allow subjects to build at least some semblance of a trust relationship with the characters in the study and investigate the ability of ABUSE to express trust flows that involve process-based relationships in some way.

Following in the footsteps of previous research into secure email usability [32,30], we based our study on the trappings used by Whitten and Tygar in their seminal study of PGP usability "Why Johnny Can't Encrypt" [33]. In our work, the subject is placed in the role of a political campaign volunteer who is charged with maintaining his candidate's schedule for the next week. The subject is to update the schedule in response to authorized requests and to distribute it to other individuals working on the campaign upon request—but no one else. Previous work by other researchers did not concern itself with attackers adding events to or removing events from the schedule—but we do. This gives us the opportunity to create a wider range of interesting trustworthy and untrustworthy messages. In addition to modifying the subject's task from the original study and Garfinkel's follow-on "Johnny 2" [32,30], we have expanded the campaign scenario used in previous experiments by adding a wider range of characters with a more diverse set of characteristics.

Like our first experiment, this study employed a between-subjects design. The subjects were randomly assigned to one of three groups. All three groups saw the same validly-signed message content sent by the same senders. The first group, who we will call the *control* group, saw no ABUSE content. The other two groups, *ABUSE-one* and *ABUSE-two*, saw different sets of ABUSE assertions over the course of the study. For a given message, subjects would see the same text, signed by the same sender, but in some cases subjects in ABUSE-one would see different assertions bound to the message than subjects in ABUSE-two. For one group, the presented assertions would justify taking action on the message; the other group would see a different set of assertions, which should not lead them to trust the accompanying message. The exact same message, received under the exact same circumstances, should be heeded when accompanied by one set of assertions and a ignored when accompanied by another.

Our Abusing Johnny study consisted of ten email messages sent to the subject, who was playing the role of a Campaign Coordinator on fictional Democratic Senator Oman's presidential primary campaign. In the scenario presented, the campaign was ramping up for the Pennsylvania primary election when their former Coordinator had a baby and went on maternity leave; the subject stepped in for her in the middle of a very busy time. Over the course of the first three messages, which the subject always received in order, he was introduced to the campaign, informed of the details of his task, provided with the campaign schedule, and asked to update the schedule.

After the three setup messages, subjects began the meat of the task. They received messages requesting urgent action; the order these messages was randomized across subjects to control for order effects as in our previous study. Some messages have the same assertions in both groups; some differ.

Table 4. The kinds of attacks we explored

Expired ABUSE attribute: The attacker leverages an expired attribute to earn trust he does not deserve.
Nonsense chain: The attacker binds an attribute whose assertions do not logically follow from one another. Requires collusion on the part of some issuer in the attribute chain.
No attribute: The attacker tries to convince the subject to trust him using the message body alone.
Vague attribute: The attacker binds a valid assertion chain to his message, but not one that confers authority for the accompanying request.
"John Wilson": The attacker's name is similar to someone in a position of authority. He tries to leverage this to get the subject to trust him.

Among the seven trustworthy messages, each kind of trust flow we identified from our analysis of the blackout transcripts is expressed at least once. Thus, showing that users can understand the assertions on these messages shows that ABUSE is sufficiently expressive. The other five messages exhibit a selection of possible social engineering attacks that remain possible in ABUSE–see Table 4.

The Study. After arriving in the study location, all subjects received a study procedure information sheet. The subjects were asked to "think aloud", as we needed to keep track of not only what they were doing, but also get insight into their thought process during the study. All subjects also received a short pre-study briefing. The briefing received by the ABUSE groups had added content providing a short (less than one page) introduction to "digital introductions." This is in line with Garfinkel's approach in his revision [32] of Whitten's original study [33]. The idea is that, in an environment in which ABUSE would be deployed, users would not be asked to figure everything out on their own. They would have at least *some* help. However, the experimenter would not answer any questions during the study beyond those about basic Thunderbird functionality (sending mail, opening new mail, etc.).

Subjects were allowed to ask for a "phone" at any time, though upon doing so they would discover that the land lines were jammed (as per [34]) and that they had forgotten to charge their cell phone. If the subjects became quiet for any period of time, they were gently reminded to think out loud. Upon completion of the task, subjects were given a debriefing questionnaire.

Results. The data we collected in this study provides qualitative evidence that users are able to understand the communication coming from the ABUSE assertion presentation GUI. Subjects exhibited an understanding of the six different kinds of trust flows we enumerated; In addition, subjects using ABUSE showed that they had not become any more vulnerable than the control group when attacked in any of the five ways we detailed in Table 4.

In the ABUSE-one group, we used one message to test role-sourced arbitrary delegation and role-based delegation. In the ABUSE-two group, the same message was paired with different assertions to test resistance to the no-assertions attack. In the latter case, no subjects were fooled; conditioning the subjects to expect assertions on legitimate messages made them reject this attack out of hand.

We used another message to test both the nonsense-chain attack and friend-sourced arbitrary delegation. In the ABUSE-one group, subjects saw the message with an assertion chained off of a generic "employee" attribute. Compared to the control, in which 33% of the subjects acted on this message, 46% of the subjects in this group chose to respond to the sender, despite his meaningless assertion chain. These rates are comparable, especially when placed against the 93% in ABUSE-two who acted on the message when it was accompanied by an assertion chain from the campaign manager that expressed friend-sourced arbitrary delegation.

We crafter another "coopetition" message, which was inherently suspicious. We expected subjects to be pre-disposed against trusting it, and we were correct. 17% of subjects in the control group acted on this message, with that number dropping to 15% in the ABUSE-two group, who saw the message paired with the vague-attribute attack. 6/13(46%) ABUSE-one subjects acted on the coopetition message; for them, it was accompanied by a coopetition trust flow. There were also three more ABUSE-onw users who clearly indicated that they understood what was being expressed by the assertions on the message; they simply remained leery of responding with sensitive information.

In the real world, we often see situations where relying parties make trust judgments based on a *former* affiliation a sender had; e.g., in the blackout transcripts, Alice would indicate trust of Bob because of whom he used to work with at a previous job. Thus, we wanted to test how ABUSE users handled valid, unexpired messages supported by assertions that had expired. We crafted a set of messages to cover the necessary cases: the first was trustworthy in the control group, and remained so when bound to an expired assertion chain; the second was *untrustworthy* in the control group, and became trustworthy when a chain of useful, unexpired assertions were sent with the message; the last, essentially the same as the second, was deemed untrustworthy by both the control subjects as well as those who saw a version of the message bound to an expired assertion chain. The numbers we see confirm that users pay attention to expiration status. The first was acted upon in 78% of cases across both ABUSE groups, the last in only 15%. The second message was trusted by 25% of control subjects, mistrusted by 100% of users who saw it with no assertions, and trusted by 83% of those who saw it bound to a chain of useful, valid assertions.

We also tried a "John Wilson" attack, difficult to defend against, especially when the user is not personally familiar with the "John Wilson" being impersonated. The numbers were consistent across the groups; six of twelve fell for the attack in the control group as opposed to 13/27 in the ABUSE groups. However, the subjects who avoided this attack in the control group were mostly those who generally refused to trust messages in the study at all. The ABUSE subjects who rejected the message did not show any such pattern, and many verbally indicated that it was odd that this message "doesn't say he's part of the campaign." (S 32)

6 Conclusions

In this work, we applied tools from the social sciences (economics, sociology, psychology, etc.) to real-world scenarios in order to understand the ways in which humans decide to trust people that they have never encountered before. Phone transcripts from the August 2003 North American blackout provided a rich set of example cases.

We contribute the design and implementation of ABUSE, a usably and usefully secure email system. By starting with the appropriate tools to understand the issues underlying the extension of human calculus-based trust and then designing with usability goals in mind from the start, we were able to create a system capable of expressing and reliably conveying to users the kinds of information they need to decide trust.

We evaluate ABUSE through user studies. The first is based directly on scenarios drawn from the power grid. ABUSE is compared to plaintext email and S/MIME, and determined to enable users to better identify trustworthy messages from senders that they do not know without needing to resort to out-of-band channels for assistance. This information, while useful, does not necessarily confirm that users are really understanding assertion chain content. To investigate this issue, we performed a second user study, based on a venerable scenario in secure email usability research. Subjects indicated by thinking aloud during the study, and through the answers on their debriefing questionnaires, that the information communicated by ABUSE was comprehensible and contributed to their ability to succeed at the task set before them. (Future work should also examine the usability of assertion creation and selection.)

Our system thus provides a usable, scalable way for users in such distributed organizations to make meaningful but speedy trust judgments about messages from senders they do not know a priori; previous PKI systems did not.

The problem of human trust requires large amounts of human context to decide, and computers are ill-suited for these kinds of tasks. Our approach has been to build a system that gets the right information from one human to another, and then lets the relying party decide what she wants to do. Applying tools from the social science was a key part of exploring what that "right information" is, and we hope that more computer science researchers will take these tools into account when studying problems that involve users.

References

1. Masone, C.: Attribute-Based, Usefully Secure Email. PhD thesis, Dartmouth College (August 2008)
2. Masone, C., Smith, S.: Towards usefully secure email. IEEE Technology and Society Magazine, Special Issue on Security and Usability (March 2007)
3. Smith, S.W., Masone, C., Sinclair, S.: Expressing trust in distributed systems: the mismatch between tools and reality. In: Forty-Second Annual Allerton Conference on Privacy, Security and Trust, September 2004, pp. 29–39 (2004)
4. Ilic, M., Galiana, F., Fink, L. (eds.): Power Systems Restructuring: Engineering and Economics. Power Electronics and Power Systems Series, vol. 11. Kluwer Academic Publishers, Massachusettes (1998)
5. U.S. House Committee on Energy and Commerce: Blackout 2003: How did it happen and why, Telephone transcripts from MISO (September 2003), http://energycommerce.house.gov/108/hearings/09032003Hearing1061/hearing.htm#docs
6. Ramsdell, B.: Secure/Multipurpose Internet Mail Extensions (S/MIME) version 3.1 message specification. RFC 3851 (July 2004)
7. Ramsdell, B.: Secure/Multipurpose Internet Mail Extensions (S/MIME) version 3.1 certificate handling. RFC 3850 (July 2004)

8. Cooper, D., Santesson, S., Farrell, S., Boeyan, S., Housley, R., Polk, W.: Internet X.509 Public Key Infrastructure Certificate and CRL Profile. RFC 5280 (2008)
9. Kuhn, D.R., Hu, V.C., Polk, W.T., Chang, S.J.: Introduction to public key technology and the federal PKI infrastructure (February 2001), http://www.csrc.nist.gov/publications/nistpubs/800-32/sp800-32.pdf
10. Nielsen, R.: Observations from the deployment of a large scale PKI. In: Neuman, C., Hastings, N.E., Polk, W.T. (eds.) 4th Annual PKI R&D Workshop, NIST, August 2005, pp. 159–165 (2005)
11. Zucker, L.G.: Production of trust: Institutional sources of economic structure, 1840–1920. In: Research in Organizational Behavior, vol. 8, pp. 53–111. JAI Press Inc. (1986)
12. Bobba, R., Fatemieh, O., Khan, F., Gunter, C.A., Khurana, H.: Using attribute-based access control to enable attribute-based messaging. In: ACSAC 2006, pp. 403–413. IEEE Computer Society, Washington (2006)
13. Zurko, M.E.: Lotus notes/domino: Embedding security in collaborative applications. In: Cranor, L., Garfinkel, S. (eds.) Usability & Security. O'Reilly, Sebastopol (2005)
14. Moromisato, G., Boyd, P., Asthagiri, N.: Achieving usable security in Groove Virtual Office. In: Cranor, L., Garfinkel, S. (eds.) Usability & Security. O'Reilly, Sebastopol (2005)
15. Li, N., Grosof, B.N., Figenbaum, J.: Delegation logic: A logic-based approach to distributed authorization. ACM Transactions on Information and System Security (TISSEC) 6(1), 128–171 (2003)
16. Li, N., Mitchell, J.C., Winsborough, W.H.: Design of a role-based trust management framework. In: Proceedings of the 2002 IEEE Symposium on Security and Privacy, May 2002, IEEE Computer Society Press, Los Alamitos (2002)
17. Li, N., Mitchell, J.C.: RT: A role-based trust-management framework. In: Proceedings of The Third DARPA Information Survivability Conference and Exposition (DISCEX III), April 2003, pp. 201–212. IEEE Computer Society Press, Los Alamitos (2003)
18. Li, N., Mitchell, J.C., Winsborough, W.H.: Beyond proof-of-compliance: Security analysis in trust management. Journal of the ACM 52(3) (May 2005)
19. Jim, T.: Sd3: A trust management system with certified evaluation. In: SP 2001: Proceedings of the 2001 IEEE Symposium on Security and Privacy, Washington, DC, USA, p. 106. IEEE Computer Society Press, Los Alamitos (2001)
20. Herzberg, A., Mass, Y., Michaeli, J., Naor, D., Ravid, Y.: Access control meets public key infrastructure, or: Assigning roles to strangers. In: Proceedings of IEEE Symposium on Security and Privacy, May 2000, pp. 2–14 (2000)
21. Blaze, M., Figenbaum, J., Ioannidis, J., Keromytis, A.D.: The KeyNote trust-management system version 2. RFC 2704 (September 1999)
22. Blaze, M., Feigenbaum, J., Lacy, J.: Decentralized trust management. In: Proceedings of IEEE Symposium on Security and Privacy, May 1996, pp. 164–173 (1996)
23. Chu, Y.H., Feigenbaum, J., LaMacchia, B., Resnick, P., Strauss, M.: REFEREE: Trust management for Web applications. Computer Networks and ISDN Systems 29(8–13), 953–964 (1997)
24. Farrell, S., Housley, R.: An Internet Attribute Certificate Profile for Authorization. RFC 3281 (2002)
25. Tuecke, S., Welch, V., Engert, D., Pearlman, L., Thompson, M.: Internet X.509 Public Key Infrastructure (PKI) Proxy Certificate Profile. RFC 3820 (2004)
26. Welch, V., Foster, I., Kesselman, C., Mulmo, O., Pearlman, L., Tuecke, S., Gawor, J., Meder, S., Siebenlist, F.: X.509 Proxy Certificates for Dynamic Delegation. In: Proceedings of 3rd Annual PKI R&D Workshop, NIST/Internet2/NIH, pp. 31–47 (2004)
27. Goffee, N., Kim, S., Smith, S., Taylor, W., Zhao, M., Marchesini, J.: Greenpass: Decentralized, PKI-based Authorization for Wireless LANs. In: Proceedings of 3rd Annual PKI R&D Workshop, NIST/NIH/Internet2 (April 2004)

28. OpenSSL: The Open Source toolkit for SSL/TLS, http://www.openssl.org
29. NSS: Network Security Services,
    http://www.mozilla.org/projects/security/pki/nss/
30. Garfinkel, S.: Design Principles and Patterns for Computer Systems That Are Simultaneously Secure and Usable. PhD thesis, Massachusetts Institute of Technology (2005)
31. Dodd, B.: Ameren. personal communication (October 15, 2007)
32. Garfinkel, S.L., Miller, R.C.: Johnny 2: a user test of key continuity management with s/mime and outlook express. In: SOUPS 2005: Proceedings of the 2005 symposium on Usable privacy and security, pp. 13–24. ACM, New York (2005)
33. Whitten, A., Tygar, J.: Why Johnny Can't Encrypt: A Usability Evaluation of PGP 5.0. In: 8th USENIX Security Symposium, pp. 169–184 (1999)
34. Schweitzer, S.: Parties call foul over N. H. phone-jamming suit. The Boston Globe (October 23, 2004)

Public-Key Encryption
with Registered Keyword Search

Qiang Tang[1] and Liqun Chen[2]

[1] DIES, Faculty of EEMCS, University of Twente, The Netherlands
q.tang@utwente.nl
[2] Hewlett-Packard Laboratories, Bristol, UK
liqun.chen@hp.com

Abstract. Public-key Encryption with Keyword Search (PEKS) enables a server to test whether a tag from a sender and a trapdoor from
a receiver contain the same keyword. In this paper, we highlight some
potential security concern, i.e. a curious server is able to answer whether
any selected keyword is corresponding to a given trapdoor or not (called
an offline keyword guessing attack). The existing semantic security definition for PEKS does not capture this vulnerability. We propose a new
concept, namely Public-key Encryption with Registered Keyword Search
(PERKS), which requires a sender to register a keyword with a receiver
before the sender can generate a tag for this keyword. Clearly the keyword preregistration is a disadvantage. The payback is that the semantic security definition for PERKS proposed in this paper is immune to
the offline keyword guessing attack. We also propose a construction of
PERKS and prove its security. The construction supports testing multiple tags in batch mode, which can significantly reduce the computational
complexity in some situations.

1 Introduction

Public-key Encryption with Keyword Search (PEKS), proposed by Boneh *et al.*
[5], allows senders to store encrypted messages at a server; to each message one
or more tags are attached that are keywords encrypted with the receiver's public
key. Later on, the receiver may send a trapdoor, generated based on the receiver's
private key, to the server so that the latter can search the tags attached to each
encrypted message. In [5], PEKS is also referred to as searchable encryption. As
a motivation example, Boneh *et al.* [5] show that PEKS can be used for routing
emails. Besides this, Waters *et al.* [22] show that PEKS can be used to build an
encrypted and searchable audit log.

Related Work. Abdalla *et al.* [1] provide a transform of an anonymous Identity-
Based Encryption (IBE) scheme to a secure PEKS scheme, and propose three
extensions, namely anonymous Hierarchical IBE (HIBE), public-key encryption
with temporary keyword search, and identity-based encryption with keyword
search. Di Crescenzo and Saraswat [11] propose a PEKS construction based on

F. Martinelli and B. Preneel (Eds.): EuroPKI 2009, LNCS 6391, pp. 163–178, 2010.
© Springer-Verlag Berlin Heidelberg 2010

Jacobi symbols. Khader [17] shows how to construct PEKS based on K-Resilient IBE. Baek, Safavi-Naini, and Susilo [3] discuss refreshing keywords, avoiding the secure channel for protecting trapdoors, and searching on multiple keywords. Offline keyword guessing attacks against PEKS have been discussed in [8,23]. In fact, all the schemes in [1,2,3,11,17,16,24] are vulnerable to this attack.

There are a number of extensions to the concept of PEKS. Hwang and Lee [16] investigate PEKS in multi-user setting, where there are m receivers in the scheme and the m public keys are used to encrypt the keywords. Implicitly assumed in [5], the public-key encryption scheme and the PEKS scheme share the same key pair but none of the security definitions for these primitives has taken this into account. The authors in [2,24] investigate hybrid models for combining public-key encryption and PEKS, where both primitives share the same public/private key pair.

Generally speaking, PEKS is related to the information retrieval problem in the private database setting and the public database setting. In the private database setting, a user wishes to upload its private data to a remote database and wishes to keep the data private from the database. Later, the user must be able to retrieve from the remote database all records that contain a particular keyword. Goldreich and Ostrovsky [15] first propose solutions to this problem, and many follow-ups exist (e.g. [4,9,12,14,20]). In this setting, the user stores the encrypted data at the server, hence, it is different from the case of PEKS. In the public database setting, a user retrieves data stored in plaintext from a database and wants to keep the index of the retrieved data private from the database. Public Information Retrieval (PIR) protocols, proposed by Chor *et al.* [10], are solutions to this problem. Gasarch [13] provides a very detailed summary of PIR protocols and lower/upper bounds on communication complexity, and Ostrovsky and Skeith III [19] also provides a summary. In this setting, the database stores data in plaintext, hence, it is also different from the case of PEKS.

Based on PEKS and PIR, Boneh *et al.* [7] formalize a hybrid primitive, namely Public Key Encryption that allows PIR queries. Two security properties, namely sender privacy and receiver privacy, are defined for this hybrid primitive.

- Sender privacy implies that a curious server learns nothing about the message and keyword in any ciphertext generated by senders.
- Receiver privacy implies that a curious server learns nothing about the involved keyword from any retrieval query performed by the receiver.

Note that, in the definition of receiver privacy in [7], the adversary is assumed to be curious-but-honest, which means that the adversary is not allowed to manipulate the database (or, the server is not allowed to collude with any sender).

Problem Statement. The semantic security definition for PEKS does not capture the vulnerability of a (partial) offline keyword guessing attack by a curious server, which is not only able to generate tags for every keyword but also able to access the trapdoors of every keyword. As shown in Section 2, an offline keyword guessing attack enables the adversary to fully recover the keyword, while a partial offline keyword guessing attack enables the adversary to determine only some partial information on the keyword. Some provably secure PEKS schemes have been shown vulnerable to the offline keyword guessing attack [8,23]. In fact, all the schemes in [1,2,3,11,17,16,24] are vulnerable to this attack. Nevertheless, we should note that this attack is beyond the given theoretical security models, although it is a serious concern for a primitive like PEKS to be used in practice.

Our Contribution. In this paper, we propose a new concept, namely Public-key Encryption with Registered Keyword Search (PERKS), which requires a sender to register a keyword with a receiver first before it is able to generate a tag for it. In other words, in this new primitive, the receiver must define the keyword subset that a sender can generate tags for. We note that the keyword preregistration is a disadvantage, since the receiver has to get involved to send the registered keywords to the sender, and the sender cannot freely choose keywords without prior interaction with the receiver. However, if an application needs to be resistant to an offline keyword guessing attack, then PERKS could be an alternative to PEKS.

The semantic security definition for PERKS has covered all the potential adversaries (including a curious server) by faithfully considering their abilities in generating tags and accessing trapdoors. More specifically, PERKS has the following advantages while detailed discussions are presented in Section 3.3.

1. In contrast to PEKS, if a PERKS protocol achieves semantic security, then it is immune to the (partial) offline keyword guessing attack.
2. In contrast to the hybrid primitive in [7], our security definition considers curious and adaptive adversaries. In the semantic security attack game, the adversary is implicitly allowed to manipulate the database adaptively.
3. PERKS provides additional features for the underlying applications. In Section 3.3, we show that, in the email routing scenario proposed by Boneh *et al.* [5], PERKS can also play an important role in fighting against junk emails.

We propose a construction for PERKS based on the first scheme presented in [5]. Our construction supports testing multiple tags in batch mode to determine whether these tags contain the same keyword. In more detail, any number of tags can be aggregated into a single value of the same size as a single tag, while the testing can be done in one step as in the normal case. This new feature can significantly reduce the computational complexity in some situations. In addition, we also present an extension of the proposed construction in order to enhance the privacy of keywords.

Organization. Section 2 reviews the concept of PEKS and shows the security concerns. Section 3 introduces the concept of PERKS and provides corresponding security definitions. Section 4 proposes a construction for PERKS and proves its security. Section 5 provides some further remarks on our construction of PERKS. Section 6 concludes the paper.

2 Review the Concept of PEKS

As defined in [5], a PEKS scheme involves the following entities: senders, a receiver, and a server. Formally, a PEKS scheme consists of the following polynomial time algorithms:

- KeyGen(k): Run by the receiver, this algorithm takes a security parameter k as input and generates a public/private key pair (A_{pub}, A_{priv}). In addition, the receiver generates the public keyword set $\mathcal{W}$.
- Tag(A_{pub}, W): Run by a sender, this algorithm takes A_{pub} and a keyword W as input and outputs a tag S_W.
- Trapdoor(A_{priv}, W): Run by the receiver, this algorithm takes A_{priv} and a keyword W as input and outputs a trapdoor T_W.
- Test($A_{pub}, S_W, T_{W'}$): Run by the server, this algorithm takes A_{pub}, S_W, and $T_{W'}$ as input, and outputs 1 if $W = W'$ and 0 otherwise.

In the setting of PEKS, the server plays the role of data warehouse for the receiver. With a PEKS scheme, the workflow of the underlying application consists of two phases.

1. In the first phase, a sender encrypts her message, runs Tag to generate some tags for the message, and stores the ciphertext and the tags at the server.
2. In the second phase, the receiver runs Trapdoor to generate a trapdoor for each selected keyword, sends the trapdoors to the server which will run Test to search over the tags attached to each encrypted message.

For PEKS, as the tags attached to encrypted messages are assumed to be public, the main security concern is that these tags should not leak any information about the embedded keywords. According to [5], the semantic security is defined as follows.

Definition 1. *A PEKS scheme is semantically secure if any polynomial time adversary has only a negligible advantage in the attack game shown in Figure 1, where the advantage is defined to be $|\Pr[b' = b] - \frac{1}{2}|$. During the game, the adversary is not allowed to query the* Trapdoor *oracle with W_0 or W_1.*

---

1. $(A_{pub}, A_{priv}) \xleftarrow{\$} \mathsf{KeyGen}(k)$
2. $(W_0, W_1) \xleftarrow{\$} \mathcal{A}^{(\mathsf{Trapdoor})}(A_{pub})$
3. $b \xleftarrow{\$} \{0, 1\}; S_{W_b} \xleftarrow{\$} \mathsf{Tag}(A_{pub}, W_b)$
4. $b' \xleftarrow{\$} \mathcal{A}^{(\mathsf{Trapdoor})}(A_{pub}, S_{W_b})$

Fig. 1. Semantic Security of PEKS

Semantic security under Definition 1 implies that the adversary cannot determine whether or not two tags contain the same keyword without accessing the corresponding trapdoors (through the Trapdoor oracle in the game). In many practical applications of PEKS, it is reasonable to assume that the receiver will only trust the server to be semi-honest (we say that the server is curious). In other words, a curious server will also be regarded as an adversary against the keyword privacy. Unfortunately, the adversary in Definition 1 does not faithfully capture the threats from a curious server towards violating the privacy of embedded keywords in tags.

In more details, in the presence of a curious server, two security concerns arise.

1. *Offline keyword guessing attack.* Contrary to the assumption made on the adversary in the above semantic security definition, a curious server may obtain the trapdoor for any keyword $W \in \mathcal{W}$. In many application scenarios of PEKS, it is reasonable to assume that the keyword set is public and has polynomial size in the security parameter. For example, in the email routing case, we could expect the size of the keyword set {Urgent, Normal, $\cdots$} to be very small. For a PEKS scheme, since the server can generate tags for every keyword, therefore, it may sort out the relationships between keywords and the trapdoors that it has received. To do this, the server can generate a tag for each keyword and test it with the trapdoors at hand. With the knowledge of the relationships between keywords and the trapdoors, given a tag, the server can straightforwardly determine the embedded keyword and therefore violate the privacy. This type of attack, referred as offline keyword guessing attack, has been mentioned in [8,23], and it can be applied to all the schemes in [1,2,3,11,16,17,24].

2. *Partial offline keyword guessing attack.* In this case, we do not need to assume the keyword set to be polynomial size. Suppose the server has received a trapdoor T_W, then it can determine whether or not the embedded W is equal to a keyword $W' \in \mathcal{W}$. To do this, the server can generate a tag for W' and test it with the trapdoor T_W at hand[1]. As a result, given a tag S_W, the server can determine whether or not $W = W'$ for any given W'. By mounting such an attack, a curious server can determine some information on the embedded keywords in tags, although it may not be able to definitely recover the keywords (as $\mathcal{W}$ is not polynomial size). To be more precise, if the server has accumulated the trapdoors $T_{W^{(i)}}$ ($1 \leq i \leq n$), then, given $S_{W^{(i)}}$, the server can tell whether or not $W^{(i)} = W'$ for any given $W' \in \mathcal{W}$.

When taking into account the potential applications of PEKS, such as the email routing scenario described in [5], there exist (at least) the following additional security concerns.

The issue of inference attack. Suppose a malicious sender Eve has sent

$$\mathsf{Encrypt}(A_{pub}, M), \mathsf{Tag}(A_{pub}, W)$$

to the server. If Eve notices the receiver has retrieved her message and another encrypted message from Bob, then Eve can determine that Bob has sent a

---

[1] Take the first PEKS scheme in [5] as an example, given a trapdoor T_W, the server can test a keyword W' by evaluating $\hat{e}(\mathsf{H}(W'), g^{\alpha}) \stackrel{?}{=} \hat{e}(T_W, g)$.

message containing the same keyword W. Note that the protection of the trapdoor is not enough here, which means that the proposal of Baek, Safavi-Naini, and Susilo [3] may also be vulnerable to this attack.

The issue of private key usage. With a PEKS scheme, a sender could send

$$\mathsf{Encrypt}(A_{pub}, M), \mathsf{Tag}(A_{pub}, W^{(1)}), \mathsf{Tag}(A_{pub}, W^{(2)}), \cdots, \mathsf{Tag}(A_{pub}, W^{(n)})$$

to the server. In this case, it is unclear whether or not the privacy of message M is achieved even if the public-key encryption scheme is secure. The reason is that both primitives, namely the public-key encryption scheme and the PEKS scheme, share the same key pair but none of the security definitions for these primitives has taken this into account. In fact, this problem has motivated the formulation of hybrid models in [2,24]. Generally, we can require that different key pairs should be generated to encrypt messages and keywords when a PEKS scheme is used.

3   The Concept of PERKS

In this section, we first introduce the concept of PERKS and then present the formal security definitions.

3.1   Formal Definition of PERKS

In the definition of PEKS [5], a PERKS scheme also involves the following entities: senders, a receiver, and a server. For the simplicity of description, the server is assumed not to act as a sender. Nevertheless, our security model will consider the adversary which acts as a curious server colluding with a sender.

Formally, a PERKS scheme consists of the following polynomial time algorithms:

- KeyGen(k): Run by the receiver, this algorithm takes a security parameter k as input and generates a public/private key pair (A_{pub}, A_{priv}). The receiver also generates the public keyword set $\mathcal{W}$ of cardinality N, where $N \geq 2$ is an integer and every keyword is a binary string. Note that we do not make any assumption on the size of N, which could be either polynomial or exponential in the security parameter.

- KeywordReg(A_{priv}, W): Run by the receiver, this algorithm takes A_{priv} and a keyword W as input, and outputs a pre-tag s_W.

- Tag(A_{pub}, W, s_W): Run by a sender, this algorithm takes A_{pub}, a keyword W, and a pre-tag s_W as input, and outputs a tag S_W.

- Trapdoor(A_{priv}, W): Run by the receiver, this algorithm takes A_{priv} and a keyword W as input, and outputs a trapdoor T_W.

- Test($A_{pub}, S_W, T_{W'}$): Run by the server, this algorithm takes A_{pub}, S_W, and $T_{W'}$ as input, and outputs 1 if $W = W'$ and 0 otherwise.

Remark 1. In the algorithm definitions, besides the explicitly specified parameters, other public parameters such as the keyword set $\mathcal{W}$ could also be implicitly part of the input. We omit those parameters for the simplicity of description.

Compared with PEKS, with a PERKS scheme, the workflow of the underlying application requires an *initialization phase* for every potential sender. In the initialization phase, if the receiver wants to grant a sender the privilege of generating tags for the keywords $W^{(j)}$ $(1 \leq j \leq n)$, then it should run KeywordReg to generate pre-tags $s_{W^{(j)}}$ $(1 \leq j \leq n)$ for this sender. It is worth stressing that, for an individual keyword, the sender only needs to request the pre-tag once and can run Tag to generate tags for as many times as possible. After the initialization phase, the workflow is the same as that of PEKS.

3.2   Property Definitions for PERKS

We firstly describe the communication model, and then define the following properties: soundness, consistency, and semantic security.

Communication Model. We make the following assumptions on the communication channels among senders, the server, and the receiver.

– The communication channel between the receiver and the server is private.
– The communication channel between a sender and the receiver is private (only) in the initialization phase.

The first assumption is essential to prevent the inference attack, which is described in Section 2.

Soundness and Consistency. Generally speaking, the soundness and consistency properties are not security relevant. Informally, the soundness property guarantees that if the receiver sends a trapdoor T_W, then the server will be able to match all the tags containing the keyword W. Formally,

Definition 2. *A PERKS scheme is sound if the probability $\mathcal{P}$ is negligible, where*

$$\mathcal{P} = \max_{W \in \mathcal{W}, S_W, T_W} \Pr[\text{Test}(A_{pub}, S_W, T_W) = 0].$$

Remark 2. In this definition, the max operation considers all the values of S_W and T_W because the algorithms Tag and Trapdoor may be probabilistic.

If a PERKS scheme does not achieve soundness, then it is useless in practice because, with such a protocol, the receiver cannot retrieve all the messages it wants.

Informally, the consistency attribute guarantees that if the receiver sends a trapdoor T_W for any $W \in \mathcal{W}$, the server will match only the tags containing the keyword W. We wish to eliminate the following two possibilities:

1. The trapdoor T_W matches a tag $S_{W'}$ (or, equivalently $\mathsf{Test}(A_{pub}, S_{W'}, T_W) = 1$), where $W' \neq W$. An extreme situation of this case is that $\mathsf{Test}(A_{pub}, S_{W'}, T_W) = 1$ for any $W, W' \neq W \in \mathcal{W}$.
2. The trapdoor T_W matches a string X (or, equivalently $\mathsf{Test}(A_{pub}, X, T_W) = 1$), where X is not a tag of any keyword (or, equivalently $X \notin \mathcal{S}$).

$$\mathcal{S} = \{\mathsf{Tag}(A_{pub}, W', \mathsf{KeywordReg}(A_{priv}, W')) \text{ where } W' \in \mathcal{W}\}$$

Formally, the consistency property is defined as follows.

Definition 3. *A PERKS scheme is consistent if the probability $\mathcal{P}$ is negligible, where*

$$\mathcal{P} = \max\{\max_{W \neq W' \in \mathcal{W}, S_{W'}, T_W} \Pr[\mathsf{Test}(A_{pub}, S_{W'}, T_W) = 1], \max_{W \in \mathcal{W}, X \notin \mathcal{S}, T_W} \Pr[\mathsf{Test}(A_{pub}, X, T_W) = 1]\}.$$

Remark 3. In this definition, the max operation considers all the values of $S_{W'}$ and T_W because the algorithms Tag and Trapdoor may be probabilistic.

If a PERKS scheme does not achieve consistency, by sending T_W, the receiver may still be able to retrieve all the messages it wants as long as the soundness property is achieved. However, the receiver may need to discard some unwanted messages which are not tagged with S_W. As such, it will result in unnecessary communication and computation complexities.

Semantic Security. As in the case of PEKS, the privacy of embedded keywords in tags is the main security concern for PERKS. We will consider three types of adversaries.

1. A curious sender, which can potentially access all pre-tags and tags of any keyword. This coincides with the assumption we made at the beginning of Section 3.2, i.e. the communication link between the server and the receiver is secure in confidentiality.
2. A curious server, which can potentially access all trapdoors and tags in an oblivious way. This coincides with the practical situation: on one hand, the server will receive encrypted messages and tags from senders; on the other hand, the server will receive trapdoors from the receiver to retrieve messages.
3. A sender colluding with a curious server (or, the server is also a sender at the same time), which may potentially obtain the pre-tags, tags, and trapdoors for any keyword $W \in \mathcal{W}$.

Definition 4. *A PERKS scheme achieves semantic security if any polynomial time adversary has only a negligible advantage in the semantic security game (defined below), where the advantage is defined to be $|\Pr[b' = b] - \frac{1}{2}|$.*

In the attack game, the challenger and an adversary $\mathcal{A}$ perform the following steps.

1. The challenger runs KeyGen to generate A_{pub} and A_{priv}. It gives A_{pub} to the adversary.

2. The adversary can adaptively query the following types of oracles.
   - KeywordReg with $W \in \mathcal{W}$: the challenger returns KeywordReg(A_{priv}, W).
   - Trapdoor: the challenger chooses $W \in_R \mathcal{W}$ and returns Trapdoor (A_{priv}, W).
   - Tag: the challenger chooses $W \in_R \mathcal{W}$ and returns

$$\text{Tag}(A_{pub}, W, \text{KeywordReg}(A_{priv}, W)).$$

At some point, the adversary $\mathcal{A}$ sends the challenger two keywords W_0, W_1 on which it wishes to be challenged. The only restriction is that, with respect to W_0 and W_1, (at most) one of the following could have occurred.
(a) The KeywordReg oracle has been queried with W_0 or W_1.
(b) The Trapdoor oracle has returned Trapdoor(A_{priv}, W_0) or Trapdoor (A_{priv}, W_1).

3. The challenger picks a random bit $b \in \{0, 1\}$ and gives the adversary S_{W_b} as the challenge, where

$$S_{W_b} = \text{Tag}(A_{pub}, W_b, \text{KeywordReg}(A_{priv}, W_b)).$$

4. The adversary can continue to query the same types of oracles with the same restriction as in Step 2.
5. Eventually, the adversary $\mathcal{A}$ outputs b'.

Remark 4. The presence of Tag oracle queries reflects the fact that any adversarial entity (including a curious sender and the curious server) may observe the tags attached to encrypted messages, due to the fact that there is no assumed secure link between senders and the server, and the server is not required to keep its storage private.

The above attack game has modeled the aforementioned three types of adversaries. In more details, we have the following.

1. A curious sender has been modeled because in the attack game the adversary may obtain s_W for any $W \in \mathcal{W}$ through the KeywordReg oracle, if according to the restriction in Steps 2 and 4 of the game (a) has occurred. This is consistent with the definition of a curious sender.
2. A curious server has been modeled because in the attack game the adversary can obtain T_W for any W in an oblivious way, if according to the restriction in Steps 2 and 4 of the game (b) has occurred. This is consistent with the definition of a curious server.
3. If a sender colludes with the server (or, the server is also a sender at the same time), then the adversary may obtain the pre-tag and trapdoor for any keyword $W \in \mathcal{W}$. Such an adversary has been modeled in the attack game, because the adversary can query the KeywordReg and Trapdoor oracles. The only restriction in Steps 2 and 4, namely (a) and (b) could not occur simultaneously, eliminates the situation where such an adversary can trivially win the game. If the adversary has queried the KeywordReg oracle with W_0 or W_1 and also obtained T_{W_e} for any $e \in \{0, 1\}$, then it is able to determine e: Given S_{W_b}, the adversary can determine b by the value of Test($A_{pub}, S_{W_b}, T_{W_e}$).

According to this definition, if a PERKS scheme is proven semantically secure, then it is immune to a (partial) offline keyword guessing attack, which are practical threats against all existing PEKS schemes as shown in Section 2.

3.3   Rationale behind PERKS

In the setting of PERKS, the new algorithm KeywordReg (or, the introduction of the concept of pre-tag) is both theoretically and practically important.

– Theoretically, it enables us to precisely define the semantic security for PERKS through restricting the adversary's access to the KeywordReg and Trapdoor oracles. Especially, it allows us to faithfully model a curious server. As mentioned in Section 1, PERKS has advantages over the hybrid primitive in [7].
– Practically, when a PERKS scheme is used, because the pre-tag is required for constructing a tag, the receiver can restrict a sender's ability to generate tags by only running KeywordReg on selected keywords for this sender. Therefore, PERKS may provide additional features for the underlying applications.

Despite its advantages, compared with PEKS, the new algorithm KeywordReg brings a new requirement of a private channel in the initialization phase incurs additional communication and computation complexities for PERKS. This is a major disadvantage because it requires interaction from the recipient to each sender for those keywords which are required to remain hidden. This seems to remove the main advantage of using public key encryption in the first place. However, if in some applications, a subset of keywords is fixed, then the generation of pre-tags is only required to be carried out only once for each sender. In that case, we argue that these disadvantages will be paid off by the improved security and additional features brought into the applications. Emails might be that kind of applications.

Taking the email routing scenario proposed by Boneh *et al.* as an example, we show that, as an additional feature, PERKS can play an important role in fighting against junk emails.

> **Example.** Suppose that Alice wants her emails to be labeled with tags so that she can retrieve the appropriate ones at a suitable time. For simplicity, suppose that the keyword set is { *Urgent,Normal,Low-priority* }. To implement a PERKS scheme, Alice will act as the receiver and the email gateway will act as the server. Alice can categorize the potential senders into different groups, and runs KeywordReg to generate the corresponding pre-tags for each group. For example, Alice may categorize her boss as *Urgent*, categorize her family as *Normal*, while categorize others as *Low-priority*. To make the solution practical, Alice may just publish the pre-tag for *Low-priority*. If we can assume that the tags would be sent to the email gateway through a confidential link, a spammer cannot forge a tag for *Urgent* or *Normal* based on the semantic security of the PERKS, therefore, it cannot forge Alice to read junk emails with a higher priority than *Low-priority*.

One might solve the above problem by using a key-private public key encryption scheme to encrypt the keyword and by simply sending a "private public" key during the initiating interaction from a receiver to a sender. However, this simple solution cannot efficiently involve a third-party server to test a selected keyword but without revealing the value of keyword. So we believe a PERKS protocol can offer more interesting features than the simple encryption solution, because of the nature of PEKS.

It is worth mentioning that many different approaches, either cryptographic or engineering, have been proposed to solve the junk email problem. Mitigating the junk email problem is only an additional feature if a PERKS scheme is deployed, while the main functionality of PERKS lies in searching tags with preserving the defined properties. Needless to say, PERKS itself does not provide an adequate and perfect solution to combat junk emails. In the contrary, using a PEKS scheme, the junk email problem may become worse. To make the receiver read junk emails with a higher priority, the spammer can generate tags for the keyword *Urgent* and attach them to every junk email it sends. When the receiver retrieves the *Urgent* emails, it would expect most of them are junk ones. In order to achieve the same level of security and efficiency as that of PERKS, additional mechanisms should be implemented together with PEKS.

4   A Construction of PERKS

In this section we propose a pairing-based construction for PERKS and prove its security.

4.1   Preliminary of Pairing

We review the necessary knowledge about pairing and the related assumptions. More detailed information can be found in the seminal paper [6]. A pairing (or, bilinear map) satisfies the following properties:

1. $\mathbb{G}$ and $\mathbb{G}_1$ are two multiplicative groups of prime order p;
2. g is a generator of $\mathbb{G}$;
3. $\hat{e} : \mathbb{G} \times \mathbb{G} \rightarrow \mathbb{G}_1$ is an efficiently-computable bilinear map with the following properties:
    - Bilinear: for all $u, v \in \mathbb{G}$ and $a, b \in \mathbb{Z}_p$, we have $\hat{e}(u^a, v^b) = \hat{e}(u, v)^{ab}$.
    - Non-degenerate: $\hat{e}(g, g) \neq 1$.

Definition 5. *An algorithm $\mathcal{A}$ has advantage ϵ in solving the decision BDH problem in $\mathbb{G}$ if*

$$|\Pr[\mathcal{A}(g, g^a, g^b, g^c, \hat{e}(g, g)^{abc}) = 0] - \Pr[\mathcal{A}(g, g^a, g^b, g^c, T) = 0]| \geq \epsilon,$$

where the probability is over the random choice of $a, b, c \in \mathbb{Z}_p$, the random choice of $T \in \mathbb{G}_1$, and the random bits of $\mathcal{A}$. We say that the decision BDH assumption holds in $\mathbb{G}$ if no polynomial time algorithm has a non-negligible advantage ϵ in solving the decision BDH problem in $\mathbb{G}$.

4.2   The Proposed Construction

We construct a PERKS scheme based on the first PEKS scheme proposed in [5]. The algorithms are defined as follows.

- KeyGen(k): This algorithm generates two cyclic groups $\mathbb{G}$ and $\mathbb{G}_1$ of prime order p, a generator g of $\mathbb{G}$, a bilinear map $\hat{e} : \mathbb{G} \times \mathbb{G} \to \mathbb{G}_1$, $\alpha, \beta \in_R \mathbb{Z}_p^*$, and a hash function $\mathsf{H}_1 : \{0,1\}^* \to \mathbb{G}\backslash 1$, where 1 denotes the identity element of $\mathbb{G}$. The public key is $A_{pub} = (\mathbb{G}, \mathbb{G}_1, p, g, \mathsf{H}_1, \hat{e}, g^\alpha)$ and the private key is $A_{priv} = (\alpha, \beta)$. The algorithm also generates the keyword set $\mathcal{W}$ which is a set of binary strings. Our analysis afterwards are independent of the cardinality of $\mathcal{W}$.
- KeywordReg(A_{priv}, W): This algorithm returns s_W, where $s_W = \mathsf{H}_1(W\|\beta)$.
- Tag(A_{pub}, W, s_W): This algorithm returns $S_W = (S_{W,1}, S_{W,2})$, where

$$r \in_R \mathbb{Z}_p^*, \ S_{W,1} = g^r, \ S_{W,2} = \hat{e}(g^\alpha, s_W)^r.$$

- Trapdoor(A_{priv}, W): This algorithm outputs a trapdoor T_W for W, where $T_W = \mathsf{H}_1(W\|\beta)^\alpha$.
- Test($A_{pub}, S_W, T_{W'}$): With the input $A_{pub}, S_W, T_{W'}$, where $S_W = (S_{W,1}, S_{W,2})$, this algorithm outputs 1 if $S_{W,2} = \hat{e}(S_{W,1}, T_{W'})$ and 0 otherwise.

Compared with the PEKS scheme in [5], the main difference is that we introduce a new private parameter β. As a result, without being given s_W, a curious sender cannot generate a tag S_W even if it has been given the pre-tags for all $W' \neq W$. This helps the protocol to achieve the semantic security.

4.3   Analysis of the Proposed Construction

From the above description, the scheme is sound unconditionally, i.e. the following equation holds for any W:

$$\mathsf{Test}(A_{pub}, \mathsf{Tag}(A_{pub}, W, \mathsf{KeywordReg}(A_{priv}, W)), \mathsf{Trapdoor}(A_{priv}, W)) = 1.$$

The proof details of the following lemmas appear in the full version of this paper [21].

Lemma 1. *The proposed scheme is consistent if* H_1 *is collision resistant.*

Lemma 2. *The proposed scheme achieves semantic security based on the decision BDH assumption in the random oracle model.*

5   Further Remarks on the Proposed Construction

In this section we describe an additional property and an extension to the proposed construction in Section 4.2.

5.1   An Additional Property of the Construction

In some circumstances, a sender may attach only one tag to an encrypted message, such as in the case of encrypting a priority tag for every email in the aforementioned email routing example. In this case, if the receiver wants to retrieve messages containing a selected keyword, a general solution is the following.

The server tests the received trapdoor with the tag of every encrypted message, and returns the encrypted message, the tag of which matches the trapdoor.

Compared with the general solution, the proposed construction in Section 4.2 supports testing multiple tags in batch mode, which may significantly reduce the computation complexity in some situations. We illustrate the idea of batch testing by the following fabricated situation for the email routing example, where

1. The keyword set is $\mathcal{W} = \{W_0, W_1\}$, where only one tag is attached to every encrypted message.
2. The keyword W_0 is rarely used, but this background distribution is a secret.

Recall from the construction definition, for any keyword $W_i \in \mathcal{W}$, the tag S_{W_i} can be denoted as $(S_{W_i,1}, S_{W_i,2})$, where $S_{W_i,1} = g^{r_i}$, $S_{W_i,2} = \hat{e}(g^{\alpha}, \mathsf{H}_1(W_i \| \beta))^{r_i}$. Suppose there are n new emails with tags $S_{W^{(j)}}$ $(1 \le j \le n)$ where $W^{(j)} = W_0$ or $W^{(j)} = W_1$. Based on the above assumptions, the following equation will hold with a very high probability.

$$\prod_{j=1}^{n} S_{W^{(j)},2} = \hat{e}(\prod_{j=1}^{n} S_{W^{(j)},1}, T_{W_1}). \tag{1}$$

The retrieval process may work as follows.

1. The receiver first sends T_{W_1} to the server. Additionally, when the receiver wants to retrieve the emails labeled with W_1 it sends a message "normal operation" to the server, otherwise "exceptional operation" is sent.
2. The server proceeds as follows.
   - If "normal operation" is received, the server first tests whether Equation (1) holds. If so, then the server returns all messages. Otherwise, it can use a similar technique to the binary search algorithm [18] to exclude the emails labeled with W_0 and return others.
   - If "exceptional operation" is received, the server first tests whether Equation (1) holds. If so, then the server returns nothing. Otherwise, it can use a similar technique to the binary search algorithm [18] to find out and return the emails labeled with W_0.

Based on the assumption that W_0 is rarely used, the batch testing technique requires much less pairing computations than the general solution which requires n pairing computations.

It is worth noting that the PEKS scheme in [5] also possesses this property.

5.2   An Extension of the Construction

It is required that the senders should securely store their pre-tags. However, if the pre-tags are compromised, some privacy information about the relevant keywords could be leaked. Taking the proposed construction in Section 4.2 as an example, the pre-tag $s_W = H_1(W\|\beta)$ is indeed a deterministic value. Suppose that Bob and Eve are two senders, that they obtained the pre-tag s_W and $s_{W'}$, respectively, from the receiver. If Eve compromises Bob's storage and obtains s_W, then Eve is able to tell whether or not $W = W'$. This could cause some privacy breach in some application scenarios of PERKS, although it may not be an issue in others.

Intuitively, if we can make the pre-tags indistinguishable from each other, then this privacy breach can be avoid. The proposed construction in Section 4.2 can be enhanced as follows.

- KeyGen(k): This algorithm is the same as that in the original construction except that a public/private key pair (PK, SK) is generated for a public key encryption scheme (Encrypt, Decrypt). The private key SK is given to the server.
- KeywordReg(A_{priv}, W): This algorithm returns $s_W = (s_{W,1}, s_{W,2})$, where

$$x \in \mathbb{Z}_p,\ s_{W,1} = \text{Encrypt}(x, PK),\ s_{W,2} = g^x \cdot H_1(W\|\beta).$$

- Tag(A_{pub}, W, s_W): This algorithm returns $S_W = (S_{W,1}, S_{W,2}, S_{W,3})$, where

$$r \in_R \mathbb{Z}_p,\ S_{W,1} = g^r,\ S_{W,2} = \hat{e}(g^\alpha, s_{W,2})^r,\ S_{W,3} = s_{W,1}.$$

- Trapdoor(A_{priv}, W): This algorithm is the same as in the original construction.
- Test($A_{pub}, S_W, T_{W'}$): With the input $A_{pub}, S_W, T_{W'}$, where $S_W = (S_{W,1}, S_{W,2}, S_{W,3})$, this algorithm outputs 1 if $S_{W,2} = \hat{e}(S_{W,1}, T_{W'}) \cdot \hat{e}(S_{W,1}, g^\alpha)^{\text{Decrypt}(S_{W,3}, SK)}$ and 0 otherwise.

In this enhancement, the parameter g^x has been used to randomize the pre-tag, while the secret x is encrypted using the public key of the server. It is straightforward to verify that, if the encryption scheme is IND-CPA secure, then any two tags s_W and $s_{W'}$ are indistinguishable. Detailed analysis would be an interesting future work.

6   Conclusion

In this paper we have highlighted the security concerns associated with PEKS, and proposed the concept of PERKS as an alternative. We have also proposed a construction for PERKS and proven its security in the proposed security model. Along the line, there are a number of interesting future research topics. Similar to the works done for PEKS, it is interesting to investigate PERKS with the capability of searching on multiple keywords, investigate PERKS in the multi-user setting, investigate PERKS in hybrid models, etc. In this paper, we have shown that PERKS can play an important role in fighting junk emails. It is also interesting to investigate more valuable features that PERKS can provide for the underlying applications.

We have also noted that the keyword preregistration is the major technique to protect a keyword searching protocol being vulnerable to the offline keyword guessing attack, but also is the major disadvantage of PERKS since it requires an interaction between the sender and receiver. We leave it as an open problem to provide a new alternative of PEKS, which is offline keyword guessing free but without keyword preregistation.

Acknowledgement. The authors would like to express their deep appreciation for the valuable comments provided by Prof. Bart Preneel and the anonymous reviewers from EUROPKI 2009.

References

1. Abdalla, M., Bellare, M., Catalano, D., Kiltz, E., Kohno, T., Lange, T., Malone-Lee, J., Neven, G., Paillier, P., Shi, H.: Searchable Encryption Revisited: Consistency Properties, Relation to Anonymous IBE, and Extensions. In: Shoup, V. (ed.) CRYPTO 2005. LNCS, vol. 3621, pp. 205–222. Springer, Heidelberg (2005)
2. Baek, J., Safavi-Naini, R., Susilo, W.: On the Integration of Public Key Data Encryption and Public Key Encryption with Keyword Search. In: Katsikas, S.K., López, J., Backes, M., Gritzalis, S., Preneel, B. (eds.) ISC 2006. LNCS, vol. 4176, pp. 217–232. Springer, Heidelberg (2006)
3. Baek, J., Safavi-Naini, R., Susilo, W.: Public Key Encryption with Keyword Search Revisited. In: Gervasi, O., Murgante, B., Laganà, A., Taniar, D., Mun, Y., Gavrilova, M.L. (eds.) ICCSA 2008, Part I. LNCS, vol. 5072, pp. 1249–1259. Springer, Heidelberg (2008)
4. Bao, F., Deng, R.H., Ding, X., Yang, Y.: Private Query on Encrypted Data in Multi-user Settings. In: Chen, L., Mu, Y., Susilo, W. (eds.) ISPEC 2008. LNCS, vol. 4991, pp. 71–85. Springer, Heidelberg (2008)
5. Boneh, D., Di Crescenzo, G., Ostrovsky, R., Persiano, G.: Public Key Encryption with Keyword Search. In: Cachin, C., Camenisch, J.L. (eds.) EUROCRYPT 2004. LNCS, vol. 3027, pp. 506–522. Springer, Heidelberg (2004)
6. Boneh, D., Franklin, M.K.: Identity-Based Encryption from the Weil Pairing. In: Kilian, J. (ed.) CRYPTO 2001. LNCS, vol. 2139, pp. 213–229. Springer, Heidelberg (2001)
7. Boneh, D., Kushilevitz, E., Ostrovsky, R., Skeith III., W.E.: Public Key Encryption That Allows PIR Queries. In: Menezes, A. (ed.) CRYPTO 2007. LNCS, vol. 4622, pp. 50–67. Springer, Heidelberg (2007)
8. Byun, J.W., Rhee, H.S., Park, H., Lee, D.H.: Off-Line Keyword Guessing Attacks on Recent Keyword Search Schemes over Encrypted Data. In: Jonker, W., Petković, M. (eds.) SDM 2006. LNCS, vol. 4165, pp. 75–83. Springer, Heidelberg (2006)
9. Chang, Y., Mitzenmacher, M.: Privacy Preserving Keyword Searches on Remote Encrypted Data. In: Ioannidis, J., Keromytis, A.D., Yung, M. (eds.) ACNS 2005. LNCS, vol. 3531, pp. 442–455. Springer, Heidelberg (2005)

10. Chor, B., Kushilevitz, E., Goldreich, O., Sudan, M.: Private information retrieval. J. ACM 45(6), 965–981 (1998)
11. Di Crescenzo, G., Saraswat, V.: Public Key Encryption with Searchable Keywords Based on Jacobi Symbols. In: Srinathan, K., Rangan, C.P., Yung, M. (eds.) INDOCRYPT 2007. LNCS, vol. 4859, pp. 282–296. Springer, Heidelberg (2007)
12. Curtmola, R., Garay, J.A., Kamara, S., Ostrovsky, R.: Searchable symmetric encryption: improved definitions and efficient constructions. In: Juels, A., Wright, R.N., De Capitani di Vimercati, S. (eds.) ACM Conference on Computer and Communications Security, pp. 79–88. ACM, New York (2006)
13. Gasarch, W.: A Survey on Private Information Retrieval, http://www.cs.umd.edu/~gasarch/pir/pir.html
14. Goh, E.: Secure Indexes. Cryptology ePrint Archive, Report 2003/216 (2003), http://eprint.iacr.org/2003/216/
15. Goldreich, O., Ostrovsky, R.: Software protection and simulation on oblivious RAMs. J. ACM 43(3), 431–473 (1996)
16. Hwang, Y.H., Lee, P.J.: Public Key Encryption with Conjunctive Keyword Search and Its Extension to a Multi-user System. In: Takagi, T., Okamoto, T., Okamoto, E., Okamoto, T. (eds.) Pairing 2007. LNCS, vol. 4575, pp. 2–22. Springer, Heidelberg (2007)
17. Khader, D.: Public Key Encryption with Keyword Search Based on K-Resilient IBE. In: Gervasi, O., Gavrilova, M.L. (eds.) ICCSA 2007, Part III. LNCS, vol. 4707, pp. 1086–1095. Springer, Heidelberg (2007)
18. Knuth, D.E.: The Art of Computer Programming, 3rd edn. Sorting and Searching. Addison-Wesley, Reading (1997)
19. Ostrovsky, R., Skeith III, W.E.: A Survey of Single Database PIR: Techniques and Applications. Cryptology ePrint Archive: Report 2007/059 (2007)
20. Song, D.X., Wagner, D., Perrig, A.: Practical Techniques for Searches on Encrypted Data. In: IEEE Symposium on Security and Privacy, pp. 44–55 (2000)
21. Tang, Q., Chen, L.: Public-key encryption with registered keyword search. Technical report, Centre for Telematics and Information Technology, University of Twente (2009), http://eprints.eemcs.utwente.nl/15836/
22. Waters, B.R., Balfanz, D., Durfee, G., Smetters, D.K.: Building an Encrypted and Searchable Audit Log. In: Proceedings of the Network and Distributed System Security Symposium (NDSS 2004). The Internet Society (2004)
23. Yau, W.-C., Heng, S.-H., Goi, B.-M.: Off-Line Keyword Guessing Attacks on Recent Public Key Encryption with Keyword Search Schemes. In: Rong, C., Jaatun, M.G., Sandnes, F.E., Yang, L.T., Ma, J. (eds.) ATC 2008. LNCS, vol. 5060, pp. 100–105. Springer, Heidelberg (2008)
24. Zhang, R., Imai, H.: Generic Combination of Public Key Encryption with Keyword Search and Public Key Encryption. In: Bao, F., Ling, S., Okamoto, T., Wang, H., Xing, C. (eds.) CANS 2007. LNCS, vol. 4856, pp. 159–174. Springer, Heidelberg (2007)

Practicalization of a Range Test and Its Application to E-Auction

Kun Peng and Feng Bao

Institute for Infocomm Research, Singapore
dr.kun.peng@gmail.com

Abstract. A range test scheme proposed by Peng *et al.* presents a new method to test whether a secret integer is in a certain interval range. However, several limitations affect its applicability and make its suggested applications difficult. In this paper, the range test technique is practicalized to overcome the limitations. The practicalized range test technique is employed to design a secure e-auction scheme, which has advantages over the existing secure e-auction schemes and demonstrates practicality of the optimised range test technique.

1 Introduction

Peng *et al.* [20,21,22] propose a novel method to test whether an encrypted integer is in a certain interval range. The new method is very efficient and no matter how large the integer or the range is it only needs a constant cost. However, the trust-sharing model and communication pattern in [20,21,22] are impractical for most applications. It assumes that one party holds the ciphertext of the integer while another party holds the decryption key. They cooperate to implement the range test through a query-and-reply communication pattern where the ciphertext must be kept secret. As most secure multiparty computation schemes adopt a private-key-sharing mechanism and publish the input ciphertexts, it is difficult to apply the range test technique in [20,21,22] to popular cryptographic applications although its low cost may improve their efficiency.

In this paper, the range test technique in [20,21,22] is practicalized. A new range test technique overcoming its limitations and improving its practicality is proposed. The new technique adopts the common two-party trust-sharing model, where the two parties share the decryption key and the input ciphertexts are public. Like in the range test technique in [20,21,22], it is not easy to achieve security in the new technique in the active-malicious model, where the participants in a protocol may deviate from the protocol. So at first a new range test protocol overcoming the impractical limitations but only secure in the negative-malicious model (where the participants in a protocol may be curious and try to obtain more information than permitted but do not deviate from the protocol) is proposed. To make it secure in the active-malicious model, we do not employ the complex cut-and-choose mechanism in [21,22]. Instead a more efficient public verification mechanism is designed to optimise the new range test protocol and

F. Martinelli and B. Preneel (Eds.): EuroPKI 2009, LNCS 6391, pp. 179–194, 2010.
© Springer-Verlag Berlin Heidelberg 2010

achieve security in the active-malicious model. So in the active-malicious model, our new range test technique is even more efficient than that in [22].

To convincingly demonstrate practicality and high efficiency of the new range test technique, it is employed to design a new secure e-auction scheme, which achieves provable security and has advantages in efficiency and precision over the existing secure e-auction schemes.

2 The Range Test Technique by Peng *et al.* and Its Limitations and Impracticality

In [20,21,22], a novel range test technique is proposed. Suppose a party A_1 holds a ciphertext c and want to test whether the integer encrypted in it is in a range Z_q, while he does not know the private key to decrypt c. If the encryption algorithm used in c is additive homomorphic[1], the test can be implemented by querying another party A_2, who holds the private key but does not know c. Firstly, a basic range test protocol denoted as $BR\ (\ A_1,\ A_2\ |\ c\ )$ is proposed in [20,22] as in Figure 1, such that

$$BR\ (\ A_1,\ A_2\ |\ c\ ) = \begin{cases} \text{TRUE} & \text{if } (2) = \text{TRUE} \\ \text{FALSE} & \text{if } (2) = \text{FALSE} \end{cases}$$

where the following denotations are used.

- $E_1()$ stands for the encryption algorithm used in c, while $E_2()$ stands for another encryption algorithm. $D_1()$ and $D_2()$ stand for their corresponding decryption algorithm respectively. Both of them must be additive homomorphic. They are called the first encryption system and the second encryption system respectively.
- Like the private key of the first encryption system, the private key of the second encryption system is held by A_2 as well.
- The message spaces of the two encryption systems are Z_{p_1} and Z_{p_2} respectively. It is required that $p_2 \geq 3p_1$ and p_2 is a prime.
- It is required that $5q \leq p_1$. As p_1 is usually very large (e.g. 1024 bits long), $p_1/5$ is large enough for any known cryptographic applications.
- Although any additive homomorphic semantically-secure encryption algorithm like Paillier encryption [19] can be employed in the first encryption system, it is suggested to employ modified ElGamal encryption [15] in the second encryption system so that p_2 is a prime.
- $ZM\ (\ A_1,\ A_2\ |\ c_1, c_2, \ldots, c_n\ )$ stands for a cryptographic primitive called specialized zero test. A_1 holds ciphertexts $c_1, c_2, \ldots, c_n$, which are either all non-zero integers or one zero and $n-1$ non-zero integers. A_2 holds the private key and helps A_1 to test whether all the ciphertexts are non-zero integers or there is a zero in them. Except the test result, no other information is revealed in the specialized zero test. Detailed implementation of specialized zero test and formal proof of its security properties can be found in [20,22].

---

[1] An encryption algorithm with decryption function $D()$ is additive homomorphic if $D(c_1) + D(c_2) = D(c_1 c_2)$ for any ciphertexts c_1 and c_2.

1. A_1 randomly chooses m_1 from Z_{p_1}. He calculates $c_1 = E_1(m_1)$ and sends $c_2 = c/c_1$ to A_2.
2. (a) A_2 calculates $m_2 = D_1(c_2)$.
   (b) A_2 calculates $c_2' = E_2(m_2)$ and $e_2 = E_2(m_2 \% q)$ and sends them to A_1.
3. (a) A_1 calculates $c_1' = E_2(m_1)$ and $e_1 = E_2(m_1 \% q)$.
   (b) A_1 needs to perform the following logic test with the help of A_2:

$$D_2(e_1 e_2/(c_1' c_2')) = 0 \ \lor \ D_2(e_1 e_2/(c_1' c_2' E_2(q))) = 0 \ \lor \ D_2(e_1 e_2/(c_1' c_2' E_2(p_1 \% q))) = 0$$
$$\lor \ D_2(e_1 e_2/(c_1' c_2' E_2(p_1 \% q - q))) = 0 \ \lor \ D_2(e_1 e_2/(c_1' c_2' E_2(p_1 \% q + q))) = 0 \quad (1)$$

In logic expression (1), either all the five clauses are false or only one of them is true. So the logic test of (1) can be implemented through a specialized zero test:

$$ZM \ (\ A_1, A_2 \mid e_1 e_2/(c_1' c_2'), \ e_1 e_2/(c_1' c_2' E_2(q)), \ e_1 e_2/(c_1' c_2' E_2(p_1 \% q)),$$
$$e_1 e_2/(c_1' c_2' E_2(p_1 \% q - q)), \ e_1 e_2/(c_1' c_2' E_2(p_1 \% q + q)) \ ) \quad (2)$$

Fig. 1. Basic range test

In [20,22], Theorem 1 and Theorem 2 are formally proved. They illustrate that correctness and partial soundness of basic range test can be achieved in the negatively-malicious model. It is also formally proved in [20,22] that basic range test is private and does not reveal other information than the test result.

Theorem 1. *The basic range test is correct in the negatively-malicious model. More precisely, if nobody deviates from the protocol and $0 \leq D_1(c) < q$, the specialized zero test in Formula (2) outputs* TRUE.

Theorem 2. *The basic range test is partially sound in the negatively-malicious model. More precisely, if nobody deviates from the protocol and the specialized zero test in Formula (2) outputs* TRUE, *then* $0 \leq D_1(c) < 3q$.

To achieve complete soundness, basic range test is upgraded in [20,22] to precise range test, which is absolutely sound in the negatively-malicious model. The precise range test of a ciphertext c in the first encryption system is denoted as $PR \ (\ A_1, \ A_2 \mid c \ )$, such that $PR \ (\ A_1, \ A_2 \mid c \ ) = $ TRUE $\Longleftrightarrow 0 \leq D_1(c) < q$. The precise range test of c is described in Figure 2, in which $PR \ (\ A_1, \ A_2 \mid c \ ) = $ TRUE guarantees $0 \leq D_1(c) < 3q$ while $BR \ (\ A_1, \ A_2 \mid E_1(q-1)/c \ ) = $ TRUE guarantees $D_1(c) \in \{0, 1, \ldots, q-1\} \cup \{p_1 - 2q + 1, p_1 - 2q + 2, \ldots, p_1\}$. The intersection of the two ranges is Z_q.

Correctness and soundness of precise range test are formally proved in the negatively-malicious model in [20,22]. To achieve correctness and soundness in the actively-malicious model, the range test technique is finally upgraded to optimized precise range test in [21,22] by applying the cut-and choose strategy to precise range test. Detailed implementation of optimized precise range test and formal proof of its security properties can be found in [21,22].

The range test in [20,21,22] employs some clever and useful methods like reducing range test to simpler zero test and using cut-and-choose strategy at an acceptable cost. However, it has a drawback. The range test technique by Peng *et al.* has the following limitations, which make it difficult to apply it to practical applications.

1. A_1 prepares two basic range tests BR (A_1, $A_2 \mid c$) and BR (A_1, $A_2 \mid E_1(q - 1)/c$).
2. A_1 presents the two basic range tests to A_2 in a random order.
3. A_2 finishes the two basic range tests and tells A_1 whether both basic range tests output TRUE and no more information.
4.

$$PR \ (\ A_1, \ A_2 \mid c \ ) = \begin{cases} \text{TRUE} & \text{if } BR \ (\ A_1, \ A_2 \mid c \ ) = \text{TRUE and} \\ & BR \ (\ A_1, \ A_2 \mid E_1(q-1)/c \ ) = \text{TRUE} \\ \text{FALSE} & \text{otherwise} \end{cases} \tag{3}$$

Fig. 2. Precise range test

- It assumes that c is not public and only known to A_1. However, in practical applications like e-auction and e-voting, it is unusual to assume that encryption of any integer is secret.
- It assumes that the private key is held by A_2, which is contradictory to a requirement of most practical applications: the private key should be shared by multiple parties to enhance privacy.
- The query-and-reply communication pattern in [20,21,22] is seldom employed in most cryptographic applications.
- Its security in the active-malicious model depends on an assumption: A_1 is honest as he wants to know the true test result. So it only attempts to prevent dishonest operations by A_2. In practical applications, this assumption is not reliable and each party must be prevented from deviating from the protocol.

3   A More Practical Range Test in the Negative-Malicious Model and Its Application to E-Auction

Basic range test in [20,22] is upgraded into a new range test protocol called *practical range test*, which is then further upgraded into precise practical range test. The two new protocols test an integer with public encryption, while the private key of the second encryption system (which is actually used in the test) is shared by A_1 and A_2. Moreover, they have no limitation to the first encryption system, which can even be a highly efficient symmetric encryption algorithm. Their difference lie in that the former is only partially sound and the latter is completely sound. Practical range test mechanism is described as follows.

1. An additive homomorphic encryption algorithm with encryption function $E_2()$, decryption function $D_2()$ and message space Z_p is set up such that $5q \leq p$. The private key is shared by A_1 and A_2. Possible choices for the encryption algorithm includes modified ElGamal encryption [15] and Paillier encryption [19].
2. An application needs to test whether a secret integer m is in a range Z_q. The secret integer may be generated or held by a single party (e.g. a secret bid by a bidder or a secret vote by a voter) or by multiple parties (e.g. the

distance between two bids from two different bidders or the sum of multiple votes from different voters). The party or parties share the secret integer among A_1 and A_2 such that they respectively holds shares m_1 and m_2 and $m_1 + m_2 = m \bmod p$. Sharing of the secret integer can be implemented in various ways on the condition that there is a secure communication channel (e.g. implemented through any encryption algorithm) between the sharing dealer and the share holders. The communication channel does not have to be untappable, so encryption of the secret integer (which is in the form of encrypted shares) is public. An concrete example of such sharing will be given in the e-auction scheme presented later in this section, which demonstrates that such sharing can be simple and efficient.

3. A_1 and A_2 implement the range test as in Figure 3 where ZM' (A_1, A_2 | $c_1, c_2, \ldots, c_n$) is a modification of the specialized zero test ZM (A_1, A_2 | $c_1, c_2, \ldots, c_n$) in [20,22] and is described in Figure 4.

---

1. A_1 calculates and publishes $c_1' = E_2(m_1)$ and $e_1 = E_2(m_1\%q)$.
2. A_2 calculates and publishes $c_2' = E_2(m_2)$ and $e_2 = E_2(m_2\%q)$.
3. A_1 and A_2 cooperate to perform the following logic test:

$$D_2(e_1e_2/(c_1'c_2')) = 0 \ \lor \ D_2(e_1e_2/(c_1'c_2'E_2(q))) = 0 \ \lor \ D_2(e_1e_2/(c_1'c_2'E_2(p\%q))) = 0$$
$$\lor \ D_2(e_1e_2/(c_1'c_2'E_2(p\%q - q))) = 0 \ \lor \ D_2(e_1e_2/(c_1'c_2'E_2(p\%q + q))) = 0 \qquad (4)$$

In logic expression (4), either all the five clauses are false or only one of them is true. So the logic test of (4) can be implemented through a modified zero test:

$$ZM' \ (\ A_1, A_2 \mid e_1e_2/(c_1'c_2'), \ e_1e_2/(c_1'c_2'E_2(q)), \ e_1e_2/(c_1'c_2'E_2(p\%q)),$$
$$e_1e_2/(c_1'c_2'E_2(p\%q - q)), \ e_1e_2/(c_1'c_2'E_2(p\%q + q)) \ ) \qquad (5)$$

Fig. 3. Practical range test

Although some modifications are made and practical range test has some difference from basic range test in [20,21,22], they employ the same main idea. Firstly, in both of them the message encrypted in c is randomly shared between A_1 and A_2. Namely, A_1 holds random integer m_1 and A_2 holds random integer m_2 such that $m = m_1 + m_2 \bmod p$. Then in both of them $c_1' = E_2(m_1)$, $e_1 = E_2(m_1\%q)$, $c_2' = E_2(m_2)$ and $e_2 = E_2(m_2\%q)$ are calculated. Finally, both of them test whether there is a zero among $e_1e_2/(c_1'c_2')$, $e_1e_2/(c_1'c_2'E_2(q))$, $e_1e_2/(c_1'c_2'E_2(p\%q))$, $e_1e_2/(c_1'c_2'E_2(p\%q - q))$ and $e_1e_2/(c_1'c_2'E_2(p\%q + q))$. Both of them returns TRUE if and only if the zero test resturns TRUE. Their difference only lies in how some of the operations are performed and who performs them. So Theorem 1 and Theorem 2 guarantee correctness and partial soundness of practical range test like basic range test in [20,22]. Namely, practical range test guarantees that $0 \le m < 3q$ in the negative-malicious model. As no more information about the secret integer either in the form of plaintext or in the form of ciphertext is revealed in practical range test than in basic range test, privacy of practical range test is not compromised and the formal

It is known that either one zero is encrypted in one of the ciphertexts $c_1, c_2, \ldots, c_n$ or none of the ciphertexts encrypts zero. It is desired to test which case is true.

1. A_1 chooses $\pi()$, a permutation on $\{1, 2, \ldots, n\}$, and random integers r_i from $Z_p - \{0\}$ for $i = 1, 2, \ldots, n$. Then he calculates $c_i' = c_{\pi(i)}^{r_i}$ for $i = 1, 2, \ldots, n$. He sends $c_1', c_2', \ldots, c_n'$ to A_2.
2. A_2 chooses $\pi'()$, a permutation on $\{1, 2, \ldots, n\}$, and random integers r_i' from $Z_p - \{0\}$ for $i = 1, 2, \ldots, n$. Then he calculates $c_i'' = c'_{\pi'(i)}^{r_i'}$ for $i = 1, 2, \ldots, n$. He sends $c_1'', c_2'', \ldots, c_n''$ to A_2.
3. A_1 and A_2 cooperate to calculate $d_i = D_2(c_i'')$ for $i = 1, 2, \ldots, n$ one by one until one d_i is found to be zero or all the n ciphertexts are decrypted. The output of the modified zero test is as follows.

$$ZM'\ (\ A_1,\ A_2 \mid c_1, c_2, \ldots, c_n\ ) = \begin{cases} \text{TRUE} & \text{if a zero is found in } d_i \text{ for } i = 1, 2, \ldots, n \\ \text{FALSE} & \text{if no zero in } d_i \text{ for } i = 1, 2, \ldots, n \end{cases}$$
(6)

Fig. 4. Modified zero test

proof of privacy of basic range test in [20,22] guarantees privacy of practical range test as well. Practical range test of secret integer m through a modified zero test using c_1', c_2', e_1, e_2 such that $D_2(c_1') + D_2(c_2') = m$, $e_1 = E_2(D_2(c_1)\%q)$ and $e_2 = E_2(D_2(c_2)\%q)$ is denoted as $NPR\ (\ A_1, A_2 \mid c_1', c_2', e_1, e_2\ )$, which is upgraded to precise practical range test in Figure 5, which returns TRUE iff $m \in Z_q$ as the two $NPR()$ respectively guarantees that $0 \leq m < 3q$ and $m \in \{0, 1, \ldots, q - 1\} \cup \{p - 2q + 1, p - 2q + 2, \ldots, p\}$.

1. To implement precise and practical range test of m, A_1 and A_2 perform two practical range tests $NPR\ (\ A_1, A_2 \mid c_1', c_2', e_1, e_2\ )$ and $NPR\ (\ A_1, A_2 \mid 1/c_1', E_2(q-1)/c_2', E_2(q)/e_1, E_2(q-1)/e_2\ )$ such that $D_2(c_1') + D_2(c_2') = m$, $e_1 = E_2(D_2(c_1)\%q)$ and $e_2 = E_2(D_2(c_2)\%q)$ and $D_2(c_1)\%q \neq 0$. The two instances of $NPR()$ respectively guarantee that $0 \leq m < 3q$ and $0 \leq (q - 1 - m)\%p < 3q$. The precise practical range test protocol is denoted as $PPR\ (\ A_1, A_2 \mid c_1', c_2', e_1, e_2\ )$.
2.

$$PPR\ (\ A_1, A_2 \mid c_1', c_2', e_1, e_2\ ) = \begin{cases} \text{TRUE} & \text{if } NPR\ (\ A_1, A_2 \mid c_1', c_2', e_1, e_2\ ) = \text{TRUE} \\ & \text{and } NPR\ (\ A_1, A_2 \mid 1/c_1', E_2(q-1)/c_2', \\ & E_2(q)/e_1, E_2(q-1)/e_2\ ) = \text{TRUE} \\ \text{FALSE} & \text{otherwise} \end{cases}$$
(7)

Fig. 5. Precise practical range test

Theorem 3. $NPR\ (\ A_1, A_2 \mid 1/c_1', E_2(q - 1)/c_2', E_2(q)/e_1, E_2(q - 1)/e_2\ ) = $ TRUE *guarantees that* $0 \leq (q - 1 - m)\%p < 3q$.

Proof: Suppose $c_1 = E_2(m_1)$ and $c_2 = E_2(m_2)$. In $NPR\ (\ A_1, A_2 \mid 1/c_1', E_2(q - 1)/c_2', E_2(q)/e_1, E_2(q - 1)/e_2\ )$, as $D_2(c_1') + D_2(c_2') = E_1(m)$, $e_1 = E_2(m_1\%q)$, $e_2 = E_2(m_2\%q)$,

- firstly,
$$D_2(1/c_1') + D_2(E_2(q-1)/c_2') = q - 1 - m,$$
namely the sum of the integers encrypted in the first two ciphertexts is $q - 1 - m$;
- secondly, as $m_1\%q \neq 0$,
$$E_2(q)/e_1 = E_2(q)/E_2(m_1\%q) = E_2(q - (m_1\%q)) = E_2((q - (m_1\%q))\%q)$$
$$= E_2((q\%q - (m_1\%q))\%q) = E_2(-m_1\%q),$$

namely the third ciphertext is an encryption of the remainder mod q of the message in the first ciphertext;
- thirdly,
$$E_2(q-1)/e_2 = E_2(q-1)/E_2(m_2\%q) = E_2(q - 1 - (m_2\%q))$$
$$= E_2((q - 1 - (m_2\%q))\%q)$$
$$= E_2(((q-1)\%q - (m_2\%q))\%q) = E_2((q - 1 - m_2)\%q),$$

namely the fourth ciphertext is an encryption of the remainder mod q of the message in the second ciphertext.

Therefore, NPR ($A_1, A_2 \mid 1/c_1', E_2(q-1)/c_2', E_2(q)/e_1, E_2(q-1)/e_2$) is a practical range test of $q - 1 - m$, which returns TRUE if and only if $q - 1 - m$ is in Z_q. □

An e-auction scheme based on precise practical range test is designed as follows. It is only secure in the negative-malicious model.

1. A_1 and A_2 act as auctioneers and n bidders $B_1, B_2, \ldots, B_n$ take part in the auction. The auction rule is published and each bidder is asked to submit one ciphertext encrypting his vote. Suppose any reasonable bid is smaller than q. For example, the item on auction is estimated to be worth one million and q is no smaller than one hundred million such that any bidder can always find a valid bid for himself. A bid can be any integer in Z_q. A public large integer p is set up such that $5q \leq p$.
2. Each bidder B_i chooses his bid b_i and randomly divides it into two shares $b_{i,1}$ and $b_{i,2}$ such that $b_i = b_{i,1} + b_{i,2} \mod p$ and $b_{i,1}\%q \neq 0$. Suppose B_i has a session key $k_{i,1}$ to communicate with A_1 and a session key $k_{i,2}$ to communicate with A_2. B_i sends $c_{i,1} = E_{k_{i,1}}(b_{i,1})$ to A_1 and $c_{i,2} = E_{k_{i,2}}(b_{i,2})$ to A_2 where $E_{k_{i,j}}()$ stands for encryption using key $k_{i,j}$. There is no limitation on the encryption algorithm $E_{k_{i,j}}$, which can be any encryption algorithm suitable for session encryption. For the sake of high efficiency, we suppose symmetric encryption like AES is employed to implement $E_{k_{i,j}}$.
3. The auctioneers cooperate to compare the bids to decide the winning bid. The concrete implementation of the comparison depends on the concrete auction rules. For example, in first bid auction[2] the auctioneers cooperate to compare the bids in pairs as follows.

---

[2] The bidder with the highest bid wins and winning price is his bid, which is the most common auction rule.

(a) A_1 obtains $b_{1,1}$ and $b_{2,1}$ by decrypting the shares from B_1 and B_2. He calculates $c_1 = E_2(b_{1,1} - b_{2,1})$ and $e_1 = E_2((b_{1,1} - b_{2,1})\%q)$.

(b) A_2 obtains $b_{1,2}$ and $b_{2,2}$ by decrypting the shares from B_1 and B_2. He calculates $c_2 = E_2(b_{1,2} - b_{2,2})$ and $e_1 = E_2((b_{1,2} - b_{2,2})\%q)$.

(c) A_1 and A_2 compare the first two bids using PPR (A_1, $A_2 \mid c_1, c_2, e_1, e_2$). If the precise practical range test returns TRUE, they know that $b_1 \geq b_2$; otherwise they know that $b_1 < b_2$.

(d) They compare b_3 with the larger bid in the previous step. The implementation of comparison is the same: decrypting and obtaining the shares of the two bids and then comparing them using $PPR()$.

(e) A_1 and A_2 cooperate to continue the comparison until the highest bid is found after $n - 1$ comparisons and declared as the winning bid.

Other auction rules are supported as well and can be implemented similarly. For example, in second bid auction[3], a little more comparisons are needed to find the highest encrypted bid and the second highest bid, belonging to the winner and being the winning price respectively. Other auctions with different rules can be implemented by fewer or more comparisons.

4. A_1 and A_2 cooperate to decrypt the winning bid by putting their shares of it together.

This auction scheme does not reveal any information about any single bid except the winning price, which is a part of the auction result. However, it may reveal that a certain bid is no lower than another bid as it employs multiple comparisons of the bids. It is easy to prevent this revealing from compromising privacy of the auction: making the bidders anonymous like in many other e-auction schemes. The anonymity mechanisms in existing e-auction schemes like [7,28] (e.g. blind signature) can be employed (although we are designing more secure e-auction than them) and are not further detailed in this paper due to space limitation.

4   Practical Range Test in the Active-Malicious Model and Its Application to Publicly Verifiable E-Auction

The range test protocol in Section 3 is not publicly verifiable and thus its application is only secure in the negative-malicious model. However, many cryptographic applications including secure e-auction require security in the active-malicious model. To make the applications secure in the active-malicious model, practical range test and the way it is employed must be further optimised such that every detail is publicly verifiable. More precisely, the following verification operations are needed to check that the inputs are valid and the calculations are correct.

1. It must be publicly verified that the applications submit valid inputs to practical range test. In the example of e-auction, it must be publicly verified that each bidder submits a valid bid so that bid comparison can be reduced to range tests and zero tests.

---

[3] The bidder with the highest bid wins but pays the second highest bid.

2. It must be publicly verified that correct inputs are submitted to the multiple instances of modified zero tests employed in each practical range test.
3. The multiple instances of modified zero tests should be publicly verifiable.

A publicly verifiable practical range test secure in the active-malicious model and its application to publicly verifiable e-auction are designed in Section 4.1, where the three required public verifications are implemented. Some implementation details are supplemented in Section 4.2 and Section 4.3 and further analysis is provided in Section 4.4.

4.1   Description of the Protocol

Firstly, the bidders submit their sealed bids and prove that they are in Z_q. The auctioneers employ a range test to check validity of each vote. In the range test, validity of the inputs are publicly verified by asking each bidder to publish remainders modulo q of two shares of his bid. It is illustrated in Section 4.4 that although the two shares sum up the bid modulo p, the two remainders do not reveal any information about the bid. Secondly, the auctioneers compare the bids in pairs using range test. In each range test, validity of the first two inputs are obvious, while validity of the last two inputs are publicly proved in a special way as detailed in Section 4.3.

1. Like in the e-auction protocol in the negative-malicious model A_1 and A_2 are auctioneers, $B_1, B_2, \ldots, B_n$ are bidders, a bid can be any integer in Z_q and $5q \leq p$. An extra requirement is that $GCD(q, p) = 1$.
2. Unlike in the e-auction protocol in the negative-malicious model, additive homomorphic encryption algorithm $E_2()$ is used by the bidders to seal their bid shares where the private key is shared by A_1 and A_2. Re-encryption is denoted as $RE()$. The bidders seal their bids, submit them and prove their validity. Submission and public check of validity of B_i's bid is as follows.
   (a) B_i chooses his bid b_i, randomly chooses $b_{i,1}$ such that $b_{i,1}\%q \neq 0$ and randomly generates $b_{i,2} = b_i - b_{i,1} \bmod p$.
   (b) B_i publishes $c_{i,1} = E_2(b_{i,1})$ and $c_{i,2} = E_2(b_{i,2})$.
   (c) B_i publishes $e_{i,1} = E_2(b_{i,1}\%q)$ and $e_{i,2} = E_2(b_{i,2}\%q)$.
   (d) B_i publishes $d_{i,1} = b_{i,1}\%q$ and $d_{i,2} = b_{i,2}\%q$. He publicly proves that $d_{i,1}$ is encrypted in $e_{i,1}$ and $d_{i,2}$ is encrypted in $e_{i,2}$ by publising the encryption details (the random secret integers used in the probabilstic encryption function). Anyone can verify that $d_{i,1} \neq 0$, $d_{i,1}$ is encrypted in $e_{i,1}$, $d_{i,2}$ is encrypted in $e_{i,2}$ and they are in Z_q. If the verification fails, B_i is dishonest and expelled.
   (e) B_i proves knowledge of a secret integer $d_{i,1}$ such that $RE(c_{i,1}/e_{i,1}) = E_2(q)^{d_{i,1}}$ using a standard zero knowledge proof of knowledge of discrete logarithm [30] and a standard zero knowledge proof of re-encryption (e.g. zero knowledge of equality of discrete logarithms [3] in the case of ElGamal encryption or zero knowledge of Nth root [9] in the case of Paillier encryption). The proof ensures that $D_2(c_{i,1}) = D_2(e_{i,1}) \bmod q$ and can

be publicly verified by anyone. If the verification fails, B_i is dishonest and expelled. Together with the guarantee that $d_{i,1}$ is encrypted in $e_{i,1}$ and is in Z_q, it is finally guaranteed that $e_{i,1} = E_2(D_2(c_{i,1})\%q)$.

(f) B_i proves knowledge of a secret integer $d_{i,2}$ such that $RE(c_{i,2}/e_{i,2}) = E(q)^{d_{i,2}}$ using a standard zero knowledge proof of knowledge of discrete logarithm [30] and a standard zero knowledge proof of re-encryption. The proof ensures that $D_2(c_{i,2}) = D_2(e_{i,2}) \bmod q$ and can be publicly verified by anyone. If the verification fails, B_i is dishonest and expelled. Together with the guarantee that $d_{i,2}$ is encrypted in $e_{i,2}$ and is in Z_q, it is finally guaranteed that $e_{i,2} = E_2(D_2(c_{i,2})\%q)$.

(g) If the verifications in the last three steps are successful, A_1 and A_2 employ PPR (A_1, $A_2 \mid c_{i,1}, c_{i,2}, e_{i,1}, e_{i,2}$) to test whether b_i is valid and in Z_q. Theorem 4 illustrates that validity of b_i is ensured if and only if the range test returns TRUE. The inputs to the precise practical range test have been publicly verified to be valid. The only left requirement for public verifiability in bid validity check is public verification of the multiple instances of zero test employed in the precise practical range test. A publicly verifiable zero test protocol is implemented in Section 4.2 and can be employed here.

3. A_1 and A_2 cooperate to compare the bids in pairs. Comparison of bids b_i and b_l is implemented through a range test of $b_i - b_l$. If $b_i - b_l$ is in Z_q, $b_i \geq b_l$; otherwise $b_i < b_l$. The range test is publicly implemented as follows.

(a) A_1 does his own part of decryption of $c_{i,1}$ and $c_{l,1}$. Then he asks A_2 to publish the other part of decryption of $c_{i,1}$ and $c_{l,1}$ and to publicly prove correctness of his part of decryption (e.g. using the standard zero knowledge proof of equality of discrete logarithms in the case that $E_2()$ is ElGamal encryption or Paillier encryption with distributed decryption [6]). In this way, A_1 obtains the decryption result $D_2(c_{i,1})$ and $D_2(c_{l,1})$. Using this information, he has to find out $E_2(D_2(c_{i,1}/c_{l,1})\%q)$ so that range test of $b_i - b_l$ can be implemented. According to Theorem 5, there are three possibilities: $E_2(D_2(c_{i,1}/c_{l,1})\%q) = e_{i,1}/e_{l,1}$ or $E_2(D_2(c_{i,1}/c_{l,1})\%q) = E_2(p\%q)/(e_{l,1}/e_{i,1})$ or $E_2(D_2(c_{i,1}/c_{l,1})\%q) = E_2(p\%q + q)/(e_{l,1}/e_{i,1})$.

(b) A_2 does his own part of decryption of $c_{i,2}$ and $c_{l,2}$. Then he asks A_1 to publish the other part of decryption of $c_{i,2}$ and $c_{l,2}$ and to publicly prove correctness of his part of decryption. In this way, A_2 obtains the decryption result $D_2(c_{i,2})$ and $D_2(c_{l,2})$. Using this information, he has to find out $E_2(D_2(c_{i,2}/c_{l,2})\%q)$ so that range test of $b_i - b_l$ can be implemented. For the same reason as explained in Theorem 5, there are three possibilities: $E_2(D_2(c_{i,2}/c_{l,2})\%q) = e_{i,2}/e_{l,2}$ or $E_2(D_2(c_{i,2}/c_{l,2})\%q) = E_2(p\%q)/(e_{l,2}/e_{i,2})$ or $E_2(D_2(c_{i,2}/c_{l,2})\%q) = E_2(p\%q + q)/(e_{l,2}/e_{i,2})$.

(c) A_1 denotes the correct choice for $E_2(D_2(c_{i,1}/c_{l,1})\%q)$ as $e_{i,l,1}$ and A_2 denoted the correct choice for $E_2(D_2(c_{i,2}/c_{l,2})\%q)$ as $e_{i,l,2}$. They have to publicly prove that they make the correctness choice respectively for $e_{i,l,1}$ and $e_{i,l,2}$ as detailed in Section 4.3.

(d) A_1 and A_2 cooperate to perform PPR (A_1, $A_2 \mid c_{i,1}/c_{l,1}, c_{i,2}/c_{l,2}, e_{i,l,1}, e_{i,l,2}$). As $e_{i,l,1} = E_2(D_2(c_{i,1}/c_{l,1})\%q)$ and $e_{i,l,2} = E_2(D_2(c_{i,2}/c_{l,2})\%q)$,

$b_i \geq b_l$ if and only if the range test returns TRUE. The inputs to the precise practical range test have been publicly verified to be valid as illustrated. The only left requirement for public verifiability in bid comparison is public verification of the multiple instances of zero test employed in the precise practical range test. A publicly verifiable zero test protocol is implemented in Section 4.2 and can be employed here.

A_1 and A_2 cooperate to continue the comparison until the winning bid is found. The number of pairs of encrypted bids to compare depends on the concrete auction rules. For example, in the first bid auction, $n-1$ PPR comparisons are needed. Other auctions with different rules can be implemented by fewer or more comparisons.

4. A_1 and A_2 cooperate to decrypt the winning bid by putting their shares of it together. They publicly prove that their decryption operations are valid using standard zero knowledge proof of validity of decryption.

Theorem 4. *In PPR (A_1, A_2 | $c_{i,1}, c_{i,2}, e_{i,1}, e_{i,2}$) to test validity of b_i, the four input ciphertext are publicly verified to be correct.*

Proof: Correctness of $c_{i,1}$, $c_{i,2}$, $e_{i,1}$ and $e_{i,2}$ are demonstrated as follows.

– As $c_{i,1}$, $c_{i,2}$ are generated and submitted by B_i, who understands that the message decrypted from their product is his bid. So $c_{i,1}c_{i,2} = E_2(b_i)$ and thus $D_2(c_{i,1}) + D_2(c_{i,2}) = b_i \bmod p$, namely the sum of the integers encrypted in the first two ciphertexts is the message to be tested.

– As $d_{i,1}$ is encrypted in $e_{i,1}$ and is in Z_q and it is proved that $D_2(c_{i,1}) = D_2(e_{i,1}) \bmod q$, $d_{i,1} = D_2(c_{i,1})\%q$. So

$$e_{i,1} = E_2(d_{i,1}) = E_2(D_2(c_{i,1})\%q),$$

namely the third ciphertext is an encryption of the remainder mod q of the message in the first ciphertext.

– As $d_{i,2}$ is encrypted in $e_{i,2}$ and is in Z_q and it is proved that $D_2(c_{i,2}) = D_2(e_{i,2}) \bmod q$, $d_{i,2} = D_2(c_{i,2})\%q$. So

$$e_{i,2} = E_2(d_{i,2}) = E_2(D_2(c_{i,2})\%q),$$

namely the fourth ciphertext is an encryption of the remainder mod q of the message in the second ciphertext.   □

Theorem 5. *In Step 3(a), $E_2(D_2(c_{i,1}/c_{l,1})\%q)$ is $e_{i,1}/e_{l,1}$ or $E_2(p\%q)/(e_{l,1}/e_{i,1})$ or $E_2(p\%q + q)/(e_{l,1}/e_{i,1})$.*

Proof:

– If $D_2(c_{i,1})\%q \geq D_2(c_{l,1})\%q$, then $0 \leq D_2(e_{i,1}) - D_2(e_{l,1}) < q$ and thus

$$D_2(c_{i,1}/c_{l,1})\%q = (D_2(c_{i,1}) - D_2(c_{l,1}))\%q = (D_2(c_{i,1})\%q - D_2(c_{l,1})\%q)\%q$$
$$= D_2(c_{i,1})\%q - D_2(c_{l,1})\%q = D_2(e_{i,1}) - D_2(e_{l,1}) = D_2(e_{i,1}/e_{l,1}).$$

In this case, $E_2(D_2(c_{i,1}/c_{l,1})\%q) = e_{i,1}/e_{l,1}$.

– If $D_2(c_{i,1})\%q < D_2(c_{l,1})\%q$, then $0 \le D_2(e_{l,1}) - D_2(e_{i,1}) < q$ and thus

$$D_2(c_{i,1}/c_{l,1})\%q = (D_2(c_{i,1}) - D_2(c_{l,1}) + p)\%q$$
$$= (p - (D_2(c_{l,1})\%q - D_2(c_{i,1})\%q))\%q$$
$$= (p - (D_2(e_{l,1}) - D_2(e_{i,1})))\%q = p\%q - (D_2(e_{l,1}) - D_2(e_{i,1}))$$
$$\text{or } p\%q - (D_2(e_{l,1}) - D_2(e_{i,1})) + q$$

In this case, $E_2(D_2(c_{i,1}/c_{l,1})\%q) = E_2(p\%q)/(e_{l,1}/e_{i,1})$ or
$E_2(p\%q + q)/(e_{l,1}/e_{i,1})$ □

4.2   Publicly Verifiable Zero Test

The zero Test protocol in Figure 6 is implemented in a public way by A_1 and A_2, who share the decryption key.

It is known that either one zero is encrypted in one of the ciphertexts $c_1, c_2, \ldots, c_n$ or none of the ciphertexts encrypts zero. It is desired to test which case is true.

1. A_1 chooses $\pi()$, a permutation on $\{1, 2, \ldots, n\}$, and random integers r_i from $Z_p - \{0\}$ for $i = 1, 2, \ldots, n$. Then he calculates $c'_i = c_{\pi(i)}^{r_i}$ for $i = 1, 2, \ldots, n$. He publishes $c'_1, c'_2, \ldots, c'_n$ and proves that he knows $\log_{c_{\pi(i)}} c'_i$ for $i = 1, 2, \ldots, n$ using the standard zero knowledge proof of knowledge of discrete logarithm and one of the the most efficient zero knowledge proofs of permutation [23, 8].
2. A_2 chooses $\pi'()$, a permutation on $\{1, 2, \ldots, n\}$, and random integers r'_i from $Z_p - \{0\}$ for $i = 1, 2, \ldots, n$. Then he calculates $c''_i = c'^{r'_i}_{\pi'(i)}$ for $i = 1, 2, \ldots, n$. He publishes $c''_1, c''_2, \ldots, c''_n$ and proves that he knows $\log_{c'_{\pi'(i)}} c''_i$ for $i = 1, 2, \ldots, n$ using the standard zero knowledge proof of knowledge of discrete logarithm and one of the most efficient zero knowledge proofs of permutation [23, 8].
3. A_1 and A_2 cooperate to calculate $d_i = D_2(c''_i)$ for $i = 1, 2, \ldots, n$ one by one until one d_i is found to be zero or all the n ciphertexts are decrypted. They publicly proves correctness of their decryption using standard zero knowledge proof of decryption. The output of the zero test is as follows.

$$\text{The zero test returns} \begin{cases} \text{TRUE} & \text{if a zero is found in } d_i \text{ for } i = 1, 2, \ldots, n \\ \text{FALSE} & \text{if no zero in } d_i \text{ for } i = 1, 2, \ldots, n \end{cases} \quad (8)$$

Fig. 6. Publicly verifiable zero test

4.3   Public Proof of Correct Choice for the Third and Fourth Ciphertext in the PPT

Suppose there are four ciphertexts c, ϵ_1, ϵ_2 and ϵ_3. There exists $k \in \{1, 2, 3\}$ such that

– $D_2(c)\%q = D_2(\epsilon_k)$;
– $D_2(c) \ne D_2(\epsilon_j) \bmod q$ for $j \ne k$;

A party A_α shares the decryption key with another party A_β and knows k. A_α does not know the encryption details of any ciphertext and has to prove $D_2(c)\%q = D_2(\epsilon_k)$. He cannot reveal any other information about the messages in any ciphertext in the proof. Our proof strategy is that although it is difficult to prove $D_2(c)\%q = D_2(\epsilon_k)$ directly, we can implement the proof indirectly by proving $D_2(c) \neq D_2(\epsilon_j) \bmod q$ for $j \neq k$. For simplicty and without losing generality, suppose $D_2(c)\%q = D_2(\epsilon_1)$, the proof is as follows.

1. A_α randomly chooses integer r_1 such that $r_1 \neq 0 \bmod q$. He publishes $\theta_1 = RE((c/\epsilon_2)^{r_1})$ and proves that $\theta_1 = RE((c/\epsilon_2)^{r_1})$ using standard zero knowledge proof of knowledge of discrete logarithm and standard zero knowledge proof of re-encryption.
2. A_α randomly choose integer r_2 such that $r_2 \neq 0 \bmod q$. He publishes $\theta_2 = RE((c/\epsilon_3)^{r_2})$ and proves that $\theta_1 = RE((c/\epsilon_3)^{r_2})$ using standard zero knowledge proof of knowledge of discrete logarithm and standard zero knowledge proof of re-encryption.
3. A_α and A_β cooperate to decrypt θ_1 and θ_2. They publicly prove correctness of their decryption using standard zero knowledge proof of decryption.
4. Anyone can check neither of the two decryption results has a factor q.

4.4   Analysis and Advantages

Correctness of the optimised range test and its application to e-auction has been proved in the last four theorems in the previous sections. Privacy in application of the range test is explained as follows.

- All the employed proof protocols are standard zero knowledge proofs.
- Semantically secure encryption algorithms like ElGamal encryption and Paillier encryption can be employed, so there is no information revealed from any ciphertext with a reasonable assumption on hardness of the trapdoor problem the encryption algorithm is based on.
- The only left resource for information revealing lies in the plaintexts published in the application. In the example of the e-auction scheme in Section 4, besides the auction result, there are two such resources. Firstly, the number of zeros are revealed in the zero test. Secondly, in proof of validity of bid b_i, $d_{i,1}$ and $d_{i,2}$ are published where $d_{i,1} = b_{i,1}\%q$, $d_{i,2} = b_{i,12}\%q$ and $b_i = b_{i,1} + b_{i,2} \bmod p$. As in the zero tests performed in this paper, the number of zeros encrypted in the tested ciphertexts is either 0 ir 1 and cannot be any other integer, so the results of the zero tests do not reveal additional information. As illustrated in Theorem 6, $d_{i,1}$ and $d_{i,2}$ do not reveal any information about b_i.

Theorem 6. $d_{i,1}$ and $d_{i,2}$ can be simulated without any difference by a polynomial party without any knowledge of b_i.

Proof: As B_i randomly chooses $b_{i,1}$ such that $b_{i,1}\%q \neq 0$, $d_{i,1} = b_{i,1}\%q$ is uniformly distributed in $Z_q - \{0, \}$. $b_{i,2} = b_i - b_{i,1} \bmod p$ implies that

$$b_{i,2} = b_i - b_{i,1} + kp$$

where k is an integer. Note that $b_{i,1}$ is randomly chosen by B_i. The only requirement for B_i is that $b_i = b_{i,1} + b_{i,2}$. So k is a random integer. So

$$d_{i,2} = b_{i,2}\%q = (b_i\%q - b_{i,1}\%q + kp\%q)\%q = (b_i\%q - d_{i,1} + kp\%q)\%q$$

As $GCD(q,p) = 1$, $kp\%q$ is uniformly distributed in Z_q. So given any b_i, $d_{i,2}$ is uniformly distributed in Z_q and its distribution has nothing to do with b_i or $b_{i,1}$. Therefore a polynomial party without any knowledge of b_i can simulate $d_{i,1}$ and $d_{i,2}$ by randomly choosing the former from $Z_q - \{0,\}$ and randomly choosing the latter from Z_q. His simulation has the same distribution as the distribution of $d_{i,1}$ and $d_{i,2}$ published by B_i.   □

The main advantages of the new publicly verifiable e-auction scheme over the existing secure e-auction schemes include high efficiency and complete support to precise bids. E-auction schemes with too strong a trust or too weak bid privacy (e.g. [7,16,28]) are not secure enough, so are not included. In the existing secure e-auction schemes, there are two solutions: multi-party computation and homomorphic bid opening. The former regards bid opening as a multi-party secure computation of the sealed bids (as encrypted inputs). The latter's principle is as follows. In e-auction with homomorphic bid opening (and also some e-auction schemes in the first category), there is a bid space, which contains w biddable prices. Each bidder can only choose one bid from the bid space and has to include w ciphertexts with zero knowledge proof of valid contents in his sealed bid, otherwise privacy of the bids cannot be guaranteed. This mechanism allows the auctioneers to employ efficient homomorphic bid opening after verification of bid validity, but causes high cost in bidding for the bidders and in bid validity verification for the auctioneers. Moreover, to avoid extremely low efficiency, w cannot be too large, so the bids cannot be very precise. In our new e-auction scheme, each bidder only need include four ciphertexts in his bid and his bid can be any integer in Z_q, where q can be hundreds of bits long and is large enough for any precise bid. Comparison of the computational cost of the existing secure e-auction schemes and the new e-auction scheme is in Table 1, where the number of exponentiations are counted. For fairness of comparison, it is assumed that in every auction scheme there are 2 auctioneers and validity of bid (if necessary)

Table 1. Efficiency comparison

Secure e-auction schemes	a bidder's cost	an auctioneer's cost
multi-party computation based [17, 11, 10, 5, 2, 14]	at least $2\log_2 w$ =20	at least $220n\log_2 w$ =22000
homomorphic opening & binary search[a] [4, 13, 12, 18, 27, 1, 24, 25]	at least $6w$ =7144	at least $4wn + 3\log_2 w$ =50030
New scheme	16	averagely $20n$ =200

[a] Some other schemes [29, 26] employ downward search and is less efficient.

and decryption are publicly proved and verified. A concrete example is given in Table 1, where $n = 10$ and $w = 1024$. The new e-auction scheme is the only one to achieve high efficiency for both the bidders and the auctioneers.

5   Conclusion

The range test protocol in [22] is optimised and becomes practical for cryptographic applications. For example, it can be employed to design secure and efficient e-auction.

References

1. Abe, M., Suzuki, K.: $M+1$-st price auction using homomorphic encryption. In: Naccache, D., Paillier, P. (eds.) PKC 2002. LNCS, vol. 2274, pp. 115–124. Springer, Heidelberg (2002)
2. Cachin, C.: Efficient private bidding and auctions with an oblivious third party. In: The ACM CCS, pp. 120–127 (1999)
3. Chaum, D., Pedersen, T.: Wallet databases with observers. In: Brickell, E.F. (ed.) CRYPTO 1992. LNCS, vol. 740, pp. 89–105. Springer, Heidelberg (1993)
4. Chida, K., Kobayashi, K., Morita, H.: Efficient sealed-bid auctions for massive numbers of bidders with lump comparison. In: Davida, G.I., Frankel, Y. (eds.) ISC 2001. LNCS, vol. 2200, pp. 408–419. Springer, Heidelberg (2001)
5. Cramer, R., Damgård, I., Nielsen, J.: Multiparty computation from threshold homomorphic encryption. In: Pfitzmann, B. (ed.) EUROCRYPT 2001. LNCS, vol. 2045, pp. 280–299. Springer, Heidelberg (2001)
6. Fouque, P., Poupard, G., Stern, J.: Sharing decryption in the context of voting or lotteries. In: Frankel, Y. (ed.) FC 2000. LNCS, vol. 1962, pp. 90–104. Springer, Heidelberg (2001)
7. Franklin, M., Reiter, M.: The design and implementation of a secure auction service. IEEE Transactions on Software Engineering 5, 302–312
8. Groth, J., Lu, S.: Verifiable shuffle of large size ciphertexts. In: Okamoto, T., Wang, X. (eds.) PKC 2007. LNCS, vol. 4450, pp. 377–392. Springer, Heidelberg (2007)
9. Guillou, L., Quisquater, J.: A "paradoxical" identity-based signature scheme resulting from zero-knowledge. In: Goldwasser, S. (ed.) CRYPTO 1988. LNCS, vol. 403, pp. 216–231. Springer, Heidelberg (1990)
10. Jakobsson, M., Juels, A.: Mix and match: Secure function evaluation via ciphertexts. In: Okamoto, T. (ed.) ASIACRYPT 2000. LNCS, vol. 1976, pp. 143–161. Springer, Heidelberg (2000)
11. Juels, A., Szydlo, M.: A two-server, sealed-bid auction protocol. In: Blaze, M. (ed.) FC 2002. LNCS, vol. 2357, pp. 72–86. Springer, Heidelberg (2003)
12. Kikuchi, H.: (m+1)st-price auction. In: Syverson, P.F. (ed.) FC 2001. LNCS, vol. 2339, pp. 291–298. Springer, Heidelberg (2002)
13. Kikuchi, H., Hotta, S., Abe, K., Nakanishi, S.: Distributed auction servers resolving winner and winning bid without revealing privacy of bids. In: NGITA 2000, pp. 307–312 (2000)
14. Kurosawa, K., Ogata, W.: Bit-slice auction circuit. In: Gollmann, D., Karjoth, G., Waidner, M. (eds.) ESORICS 2002. LNCS, vol. 2502, pp. 24–38. Springer, Heidelberg (2002)

15. Lee, B., Kim, K.: Receipt-free electronic voting through collaboration of voter and honest verifier. In: JW-ISC 2000, pp. 101–108 (2000)
16. Lipmaa, H., Asokan, N., Niemi, V.: Secure vickrey auctions without thresh-old trust. In: Blaze, M. (ed.) FC 2002. LNCS, vol. 2357, pp. 87–101. Springer, Heidelberg (2003)
17. Naor, M., Pinkas, B., Sumner, R.: Privacy perserving auctions and mechanism design. In: ACM Conference on Electronic Commerce 1999, pp. 129–139 (1999)
18. Omote, K., Miyaji, A.: A second-price sealed-bid auction with the discriminant of the p-th root. In: Blaze, M. (ed.) FC 2002. LNCS, vol. 2357, pp. 57–71. Springer, Heidelberg (2003)
19. Paillier, P.: Public key cryptosystem based on composite degree residuosity classes. In: Stern, J. (ed.) EUROCRYPT 1999. LNCS, vol. 1592, pp. 223–238. Springer, Heidelberg (1999)
20. Peng, K., Boyd, C., Dawson, E., Okamoto, E.: A Novel Range Test. In: Batten, L.M., Safavi-Naini, R. (eds.) ACISP 2006. LNCS, vol. 4058, pp. 247–258. Springer, Heidelberg (2006)
21. Peng, K., Dawson, E.: Range Test Secure in the Active Adversary Model. In: Boyd, C., González Nieto, J.M. (eds.) ACISP 2005. LNCS, vol. 3574, pp. 159–162. Springer, Heidelberg (2005)
22. Peng, K., Bao, F., Dawson, E.: Correct, private, flexible and efficient range test. Journal of Researchand Practice in Information Technology 40(4), 275–291 (2008)
23. Peng, K., Boyd, C., Dawson, E.: Simple And Efficient Shuffling With Provable Correctness and ZK Privacy. In: Jakobsson, M., Yung, M., Zhou, J. (eds.) ACNS 2004. LNCS, vol. 3089, pp. 188–204. Springer, Heidelberg (2004)
24. Peng, K., Boyd, C., Dawson, E.: A multiplicative homomorphic sealed-bid auction based on Goldwasser-Micali encryption. In: Zhou, J., López, J., Deng, R.H., Bao, F. (eds.) ISC 2005. LNCS, vol. 3650, pp. 374–388. Springer, Heidelberg (2005)
25. Peng, K., Boyd, C., Dawson, E.: Optimization of electronic first-bid sealed-bid auction based on homomorphic secret sharing. In: Dawson, E., Vaudenay, S. (eds.) Mycrypt 2005. LNCS, vol. 3715, pp. 84–98. Springer, Heidelberg (2005)
26. Peng, K., Boyd, C., Dawson, E., Viswanathan, K.: Non-interactive auction scheme with strong privacy. In: Lee, P.J., Lim, C.H. (eds.) ICISC 2002. LNCS, vol. 2587, pp. 407–420. Springer, Heidelberg (2003)
27. Peng, K., Boyd, C., Dawson, E., Viswanathan, K.: Robust, privacy protecting and publicly verifiable sealed-bid auction. In: Deng, R.H., Qing, S., Bao, F., Zhou, J. (eds.) ICICS 2002. LNCS, vol. 2513, pp. 147–159. Springer, Heidelberg (2002)
28. Peng, K., Boyd, C., Dawson, E., Viswanathan, K.: Efficient implementation of relative bid privacy in sealed-bid auction. In: Chae, K.-J., Yung, M. (eds.) WISA 2003. LNCS, vol. 2908, pp. 244–256. Springer, Heidelberg (2004)
29. Sakurai, K., Miyazaki, S.: A bulletin-board based digital auction scheme with bidding down strategy -towards anonymous electronic bidding without anonymous channels nor trusted centers. In: International Workshop on Cryptographic Techniques and E-Commerce, pp. 180–187 (1999)
30. Schnorr, C.: Efficient signature generation by smart cards. Journal of Cryptology 4, 161–174 (1991)

Timed-Ephemerizer: Make Assured Data Appear and Disappear

Qiang Tang

DIES, Faculty of EEMCS, University of Twente, The Netherlands
q.tang@utwente.nl

Abstract. The concept of Ephemerizer, proposed by Perlman, is a mechanism for assured data deletion. Ephemerizer provides a useful service that expired data deleted from the persistent storage devices will be unrecoverable, even if later on some of the private keys in the system are compromised. However, no security model has ever been proposed for this primitive and existing protocols have not been studied formally. In practice, a potential shortcoming of existing Ephemerizer protocols is that they are supposed to provide only assured deletion but not assured initial disclosure. In other words, there is no guarantee on when the data will be initially disclosed. In this paper, we formalize the notion of Timed-Ephemerizer which can be regarded as augmented Ephemerizer and can provide both assured initial disclosure and deletion for sensitive data. We propose a new Timed-Ephemerizer protocol and prove its security in the proposed security model.

1 Introduction

Rapid growth of information technology has greatly facilitated individuals and enterprizes to generate and store information (business transaction details, electronic health records, personal profiles, etc.). It is common that backups of the same piece of data will be placed on many different persistent storage devices, such as hard disks, tapes, and USB tokens. To protect the confidentiality, sensitive data are often firstly encrypted then stored on various devices, while the cryptographic keys also need to be stored and backuped on some persistent storage devices. With respect to storing data in persistent storage devices, there are two concerns.

1. It is relatively easy to recover data from persistent storage devices, even when the data has been deleted. As such, the US government specification has suggested to overwrite non-classified information three times [10].
2. Backups of encrypted sensitive data and cryptographic keys often reside in many devices. Consequently, it is difficult to make sure that all relevant backups have been deleted.

The above observations imply that an adversary may simultaneously obtain a copy of encrypted data and relevant cryptographic keys due to the potential

F. Martinelli and B. Preneel (Eds.): EuroPKI 2009, LNCS 6391, pp. 195–208, 2010.

management carelessness. Especially, this may be fairly easy for a malicious insider in organizations. As a result, even with encryption implemented, sensitive data may still be in potential danger.

To protect sensitive data from illegitimate leakage, Ephemerizer, proposed by Perlman [12,13], has shown a promising direction. For an application with Ephemerizer, data is encrypted using the public keys from both the data consumer and the Ephemerizer, and the ciphertext resides in the data consumer's persistent storage devices. If the data consumer wants to recover the data, it can decrypt the ciphertext with the help from the Ephemerizer. If we assume that the plaintext data will only reside in volatile storages[1] and the Ephemerizer will securely delete the expired ephemeral keys periodically, the decryption can only occur before the expiration of the relevant key pair of the Ephemerizer. In other words, a Ephemerizer protocol will provide assured deletion for sensitive data.

Contribution. In the literature, no security model has ever been proposed for Ephemerizer and existing protocols have not been analyzed formally. Some protocols have been shown suffering from security vulnerabilities (as surveyed in Section 2). In addition, we show that the Ephemerizer protocol in [9] suffers from serious security vulnerabilities in the technical report [16]. In practice, a potential shortcoming of existing Ephemerizer protocols is that they are only supposed to provide assured deletion but not assured initial disclosure. In other words, there is no guarantee on when the data will be initially disclosed.

We formalize the notion of Timed-Ephemerizer, aimed to provide an assured disclosure policy enforcement for the lifecycle of sensitive data, where the lifecycle is marked by the initial disclosure and the deletion after expiration. Conceptually, the new primitive can be regarded as augmented Ephemerizer by combining Ephemerizer (for assured deletion)[12,13] and Timed-Release Encryption (for assured initial disclosure)[8]. In other words, Ephemerizer can be seen as a Timed-Ephemerizer without the timed-release property. Furthermore, we propose a new Timed-Ephemerizer protocol and prove its security in our model.

Organization. The rest of the paper is organized as follows. In Section 2 we briefly review the relevant works on Ephemerizer and Timed-Release Encryption. In Section 3 we introduce the concept of Timed-Ephemerizer and formalize the security properties. In Section 4 we propose a new Timed-Ephemerizer protocol and prove its security. In Section 5 we conclude the paper.

2   Related Work

2.1   Ephemerizer Protocols

Perlman [12,13] proposes two Ephemerizer protocols without providing rigorous security proofs. One protocol uses a blind encryption technique, which is a kind

---

[1] In contrast to persistent storage devices, it is more difficult for an adversary to corrupt volatile storage devices (for example, most forms of modern random access memory) because the data in such devices will disappear when the electricity/power is gone. However, it is worth noting that this could be very subtle in the presence of side channel attacks, especially when considering the cold boot attacks [6].

of homomorphic property between two encryption schemes. The other protocol uses a triple encryption technique, where data is encrypted using a symmetric key which is sequentially encrypted using the public key of the data consumer, the public key of the Ephemerizer, and the public key of the data consumer. However, this protocol has been shown suffering from a fatal vulnerability by Nair *et al.* [9]. In addition, Nair *et al.* [9] observe that both protocols proposed by Perlman do not provide support for fine-grained user settings on the lifetime of the data. As a solution, Nair *et al.* propose a protocol using identity-based public-key encryption. However, they have not provided a security analysis in a formal security model. In the technical report [16], we show that their protocol also suffers from fatal vulnerabilities.

2.2 Timed-Release Encryption

The concept of Timed-Release Encryption (TRE), i.e. sending a message which can only be decrypted after a pre-defined release time, is attributed to May [8]. Later on, Rivest, Shamir, and Wagner further elaborate on this concept and gave a number of its applications including electronic auctions, key escrow, chess moves, release of documents over time, payment schedules, press releases [14]. Hwang, Yum, and Lee [7] extend the concept of TRE schemes to include the Pre-Open Capability which allows the message sender to assist the receiver to decrypt the ciphertext before the pre-defined disclosure time. Later on, Dent and Tang [5] propose a refined model and comprehensive analysis for this extended primitive.

There are two approaches to embed a timestamp in a ciphertext. One approach, proposed in [14], is that a secret is transformed in such a way that all kinds of machines (serial or parallel) take at least a certain amount of time to solve the underlying computational problems (puzzle) in order to recover the secret. The release time is equal to the time at which the puzzle is released plus the minimum amount of time that it would take to solve the puzzle. However, this means that not all users are capable of decrypting the ciphertext at the release time as they may have different computing power. The other approach is to use a trusted time server, which, at an appointed time, will assist in releasing a secret to help decrypt the ciphertext (e.g. [3,14]). Using this approach, the underlying schemes require interaction between the server and the users, and should prevent possible malicious behaviour of the time server. In this paper, we will adopt the second approach because, regardless of the computing power of all involved entities, it can provide assured disclosure time under appropriate assumptions.

3   The Concept of Timed-Ephemerizer

Informally, a Timed-Ephemerizer protocol guarantees that data will only be available during a pre-defined lifecycle, beyond which no adversary can recover the data even if it has compromised all existing private keys in the system. Compared with Ephemerizer protocols [9,12,13], a Timed-Ephemerizer protocol explicitly provides the guarantee that data can only be available after the predefined initial disclosure time.

3.1   The Algorithm Definitions

Generally, a Timed-Ephemerizer protocol involves the following types of entities: time server, data generator, data consumer, and Ephemerizer.

- Time server, which will publish timestamps periodically. We assume that the time server acts properly in generating its parameters and publishing the timestamps. However, concerning the privacy of data, we take into account the fact that the time server may be curious, i.e. it may try to decrypt the ciphertext.
- Data generator, which will make its data available to a data consumer. The data generator defines the lifecycle of its data.
- Data consumer, which will access the data generator's data. A data consumer could be curious in the way that it may try to access data before the initial disclosure time.
- Ephemerizer, which is trusted to publish and revoke ephemeral public/private key pairs periodically. However, the Ephemerizer could be curious in the sense that it may try to decrypt the ciphertext.

Remark 1. Compared with an Ephemerizer protocol, a Timed-Ephemerizer protocol has one additional entity, namely the time server. One may have the observation that the Ephemerizer can be required to release timestamps so that the time server can be eliminated. However, we argue that the separation of functionalities provides a higher level of security in general. First of all, the time server only needs to publish timestamps without any additional interaction with other entities. In practice, the risk that time server is compromised is less than that for the Ephemerizer. Secondly, the risk that both the Ephemerizer and the time server are compromised is less than that any of them is compromised.

A Timed-Ephemerizer protocol consists of the following polynomial-time algorithms. Let ℓ be the security parameter.

- $\mathsf{Setup}_T(\ell)$: Run by the time server, this algorithm generates a public/private key pair (PK_T, SK_T).
- $\mathsf{TimeExt}(t, SK_T)$: Run by the time server, this algorithm generates a timestamp TS_t. It is assumed that the time server publishes TS_t at the point t. Throughout the paper, the notation $t < t'$ means t is earlier than t'.
- $\mathsf{Setup}_E(\ell)$: Run by the Ephemerizer, this algorithm generates a set of tuples $(PK_{t_{eph_j}}, SK_{t_{eph_j}}, t_{eph_j})$ for $j \geq 1$, where $(PK_{t_{eph_j}}, SK_{t_{eph_j}})$ is a public/private key pair and t_{eph_j} is the expiration time of the key pair. The Ephemerizer will securely delete $SK_{t_{eph_j}}$ at the point t_{eph_j}. We assume that there is only one ephemeral key pair for any expiration time t_{eph_j}. In addition, we assume $t_{eph_j} < t_{eph_k}$ if $j < k$.

- $\mathsf{Setup}_U(\ell)$: Run by a data consumer, this algorithm generates a public/private key pair (PK_U, SK_U).
- $\mathsf{Generate}(M, t_{int}, PK_U, PK_{t_{eph_j}}, PK_T)$: Run by the data generator, this algorithm outputs a ciphertext C. For the message M, t_{int} is the initial disclosure time and t_{eph_j} is the expiration time. We explicitly assume that both (t_{int}, t_{eph_j}) and C should be sent to the data consumer.
- $\mathsf{Retrieve}(C, TS_{t_{int}}, SK_U; SK_{t_{eph_j}})$: Interactively run between the data consumer and the Ephemerizer, this algorithm outputs a plaintext M or an error symbol $\perp$ to the data consumer. We explicitly make the following assumption. The data consumer has $(C, TS_{t_{int}}, SK_U)$ as the input and sends t_{eph_j} to the Ephemerizer in advance, so that the Ephemerizer uses $SK_{t_{eph_j}}$ as the input for the upcoming algorithm execution.

Remark 2. In the algorithm definitions, besides the explicitly specified parameters, other public parameters could also be specified and be implicitly part of the input. We omit those parameters for the simplicity of description.

With a Timed-Ephemerizer protocol, the workflow is similar to that of an Ephemerizer protocol.

1. The data generator runs the algorithm Generate to encrypt its data. The difference is that this algorithm involves the public key of the time server.
2. The data consumer runs the algorithm Retrieve to decrypt the ciphertext with the help from the Ephemerizer. The difference is that this algorithm needs a timestamp from the time server.

3.2 The Security Definitions

We first describe some conventions for writing probabilistic algorithms and experiments. The notation $u \in_R S$ means u is randomly chosen from the set S. If $\mathcal{A}$ is a probabilistic algorithm, then $v \xleftarrow{\$} \mathcal{A}^{(f_1, f_2, \cdots)}(x, y, \cdots)$ means that v is the result of running $\mathcal{A}$, which takes $x, y, \cdots$ as input and has any polynomial number of oracle queries to the functions $f_1, f_2, \cdots$. As a standard practice, the security of a protocol is evaluated by an experiment between an attacker and a challenger, where the challenger simulates the protocol executions and answers the attacker's oracle queries. Without specification, algorithms are always assumed to be polynomial-time.

A Timed-Ephemerizer protocol is aimed to guarantee that data will only be available during its lifecycle, while neither before the initial disclosure time nor after the expiration time. We assume that the validation of public keys in the protocol can be verified by all the participants. Nonetheless, we generally assume that an outside adversary is active, which means that the adversary may compromise the protocol participants and fully control the communication channels (i.e. capable of deleting, relaying, and replacing the messages exchanged between the participants). Considering the threats against confidentiality, we identify three categories of adversaries.

- Type-I adversary: This type of adversary wants to access data before its initial disclosure time. Type-I adversary represents a curious data consumer and also a malicious outside entity which has compromised the Ephemerizer and the data consumer before the initial disclosure time of the data.
- Type-II adversary: This type of adversary wants to access data after its expiration time. Type-II adversary represents a malicious outside entity which has compromised the time server, the Ephemerizer, and the data consumer after the expiration time of the data.
- Type-III adversary: This type of adversary represents a curious time server and a curious Ephemerizer, and also a malicious outside entity which has compromised the time server and the Ephemerizer.

The implications of a Type-I adversary and a Type-II adversary are clear for a Timed-Ephemerizer protocol. Nonetheless, the existence of a Type-III adversary still makes sense even in the presence of these two types of adversary. Compared with a Type-I adversary, a Type-III adversary has the advantage of accessing the private key (and all timestamps) of the time server; while compared with a Type-II adversary, a Type-III adversary has the advantage of accessing all the private keys of the Ephemerizer. However, a Type-III adversary does not have direct access to the data consumer's private key.

Remark 3. It is worth stressing that when the adversary compromises an entity (the time server, the Ephemerizer, or the data consumer) it will obtain the private keys possessed by that entity. For example, if the Ephemerizer is compromised at the point t, then it will obtain all the private keys $SK_{t_{eph_j}}$ for $t_{eph_j} > t$. However, we do not take into account the compromise of ephemeral session secrets during the executions of algorithms.

Definition 1. *A Timed-Ephemerizer protocol achieves Type-I semantic security if any polynomial-time adversary has only a negligible advantage in the following semantic security game (as shown in Figure 1), where the advantage is defined to be $|\Pr[b' = b] - \frac{1}{2}|$.*

1. $(PK_T, SK_T) \overset{\$}{\leftarrow} \mathsf{Setup}_T(\ell); (PK_{t_{eph_j}}, SK_{t_{eph_j}})$ for $j \geq 1 \overset{\$}{\leftarrow} \mathsf{Setup}_E(\ell); (PK_U, SK_U) \overset{\$}{\leftarrow} \mathsf{Setup}_U(\ell)$
2. $(M_0, M_1, t^*_{int}, PK_{t_{eph_i}}) \overset{\$}{\leftarrow} \mathcal{A}^{(\mathsf{TimeExt})}(SK_{t_{eph_j}} \text{ for } j \geq 1, SK_U)$
3. $b \overset{\$}{\leftarrow} \{0,1\}; C_b \overset{\$}{\leftarrow} \mathsf{Generate}(M_b, t^*_{int}, PK_U, PK_{t_{eph_i}}, PK_T)$
4. $b' \overset{\$}{\leftarrow} \mathcal{A}^{(\mathsf{TimeExt})}(C_b, SK_{t_{eph_j}} \text{ for } j \geq 1, SK_U)$

Fig. 1. Semantic Security against Type-I Adversary

In more detail, the attack game between the challenger and the adversary $\mathcal{A}$ performs as follows. In this game the challenger simulates the functionality of the time server.

1. The challenger runs Setup_T to generate (PK_T, SK_T), runs Setup_E to generate $(PK_{t_{eph_j}}, SK_{t_{eph_j}})$ for $j \geq 1$, and runs Setup_U to generate (PK_U, SK_U). Except for SK_T, all private keys and all public parameters are given to the adversary.
2. The adversary can adaptively query the TimeExt oracle, for which the adversary provides a time t and gets a timestamp TS_t from the challenger. At some point, the adversary sends the challenger two equal-length plaintext M_0, M_1 on which it wishes to be challenged, and two timestamps (t^*_{int}, t_{eph_i}). The only restriction is that the TimeExt oracle should not have been queried with $t \geq t^*_{int}$.
3. The challenger picks a random bit $b \in \{0, 1\}$ and gives the adversary $\mathcal{C}_b$ as the challenge, where

$$\mathcal{C}_b = \mathsf{Generate}(M_b, t^*_{int}, PK_U, PK_{t_{eph_i}}, PK_T).$$

4. The adversary can continue to query the TimeExt oracle with the same restriction as in Step 2.
5. Eventually, the adversary outputs b'.

In the above attack game, the adversary is Type-I because it has access to SK_U and $SK_{t_{eph_j}}$ for any $j \geq 1$

Remark 4. The restriction in steps 2 and 4 of the above game, namely "the TimeExt oracle should not have been queried with $t \geq t^*_{int}$.", implies that the adversary tries to recover a message before the initial disclosure time. This coincides with the definition of Type-I adversary.

Definition 2. *A Timed-Ephemerizer protocol achieves Type-II semantic security if any polynomial time adversary has only a negligible advantage in the following semantic security game (as shown in Figure 2), where the advantage is defined to be* $| \Pr[b' = b] - \frac{1}{2}|$.

---

1. $(PK_T, SK_T) \xleftarrow{\$} \mathsf{Setup}_T(\ell); (PK_{t_{eph_j}}, SK_{t_{eph_j}})$ for $j \geq 1 \xleftarrow{\$} \mathsf{Setup}_E(\ell); (PK_U, SK_U) \xleftarrow{\$} \mathsf{Setup}_U(\ell)$

2. $(M_0, M_1, t^*_{int}, PK_{t_{eph_i}}) \xleftarrow{\$} \mathcal{A}^{(\mathsf{Retrieve})}(SK_T, SK_{t_{eph_j}}$ for $j > i, SK_U)$

3. $b \xleftarrow{\$} \{0, 1\}; C_b \xleftarrow{\$} \mathsf{Generate}(M_b, t^*_{int}, PK_U, PK_{t_{eph_i}}, PK_T)$

4. $b' \xleftarrow{\$} \mathcal{A}^{(\mathsf{Retrieve})}(C_b, SK_T, SK_{t_{eph_j}}$ for $j > i, SK_U)$

Fig. 2. Semantic Security against Type-II Adversary

In more detail, the attack game between the challenger and the adversary $\mathcal{A}$ performs as follows. In this game the challenger simulates the functionalities of both the Ephemerizer and the data consumer.

1. The challenger runs Setup_T to generate (PK_T, SK_T), runs Setup_E to generate $(PK_{t_{eph_j}}, SK_{t_{eph_j}})$ for $j \geq 1$, and runs Setup_U to generate (PK_U, SK_U). The private key SK_T and all public parameters are given to the adversary.

2. The adversary can adaptively issue the following two types of Retrieve oracle queries.

   (a) D-type Retrieve oracle query: In each oracle query, the adversary impersonates the Ephemerizer and provides (t_{int}, t_{eph_j}) and C to the challenger, which then uses $(C, TS_{t_{int}}, SK_U)$ as input and runs the Retrieve algorithm with the adversary to decrypt C by assuming that the initial disclosure time is t_{int} and the expiration time is t_{eph_j}.

   (b) E-type Retrieve query: In each oracle query, the adversary impersonates the data consumer to the Ephemerizer and sends t_{eph_j} to the challenger, which uses $SK_{t_{eph_j}}$ as the input and runs the Retrieve algorithm with the adversary.

   At some point, the adversary sends the challenger two equal-length plaintext M_0, M_1 on which it wishes to be challenged, and two timestamps (t_{int}^*, t_{eph_i}). In this phase, the adversary can query for SK_U and $SK_{t_{eph_j}}$ for any $j > i$ with the following restriction: if SK_U has been queried, then any E-type Retrieve oracle query with the input t_{eph_j} for any $j \leq i$ is forbidden.

3. The challenger picks a random bit $b \in \{0, 1\}$ and gives the adversary C_b as the challenge, where

$$C_b = \mathsf{Generate}(M_b, t_{int}^*, PK_U, PK_{t_{eph_i}}, PK_T).$$

4. The adversary can continue to issue oracle queries as in Step 2 with the same restriction.

5. The adversary $\mathcal{A}$ outputs b'.

In the above attack game, the adversary is Type-II because it has access to the private keys SK_T, SK_U, and $SK_{t_{eph_j}}$ for any $j > i$.

Remark 5. In the above game, the privilege, that the adversary can issue the two types of Retrieve oracle queries, reflects the fact that the adversary has complete control over the communication link between the data consumer and the Ephemerizer. In practice, such an adversary can initiate the Retrieve algorithm with both the Ephemerizer and the data consumer. The first case is modeled by the E-type Retrieve query, while the second case is modeled by the D-type Retrieve query.

Remark 6. The restriction in the above game, namely "if SK_U has been queried, then E-type Retrieve oracle query with the input t_{eph_j} for any $j \leq i$ is forbidden.", reflects the fact that the adversary tries to recover a message after its expiration time t_{eph_i} (when the ephemeral keys $SK_{t_{eph_j}}$ for any $j \leq i$ should have been securely deleted by the Ephemerizer). This coincides with the definition of Type-II adversary.

Definition 3. *A Timed-Ephemerizer protocol achieves Type-III semantic security if any polynomial time adversary has only a negligible advantage in the following semantic security game (as shown in Figure 3), where the advantage is defined to be $|\Pr[b' = b] - \frac{1}{2}|$.*

---

1. $(PK_T, SK_T) \overset{\$}{\leftarrow} \mathsf{Setup}_T(\ell); (PK_{t_{eph_j}}, SK_{t_{eph_j}})$ for $j \geq 1 \overset{\$}{\leftarrow} \mathsf{Setup}_E(\ell); (PK_U, SK_U) \overset{\$}{\leftarrow} \mathsf{Setup}_U(\ell)$

2. $(M_0, M_1, t_{int}^*, PK_{t_{eph_i}}) \overset{\$}{\leftarrow} \mathcal{A}^{(\mathsf{Retrieve})}(SK_T, SK_{t_{eph_j}}$ for $j \geq 1)$

3. $b \overset{\$}{\leftarrow} \{0, 1\}; C_b \overset{\$}{\leftarrow} \mathsf{Generate}(M_b, t_{int}^*, PK_U, PK_{t_{eph_i}}, PK_T)$

4. $b' \overset{\$}{\leftarrow} \mathcal{A}^{(\mathsf{Retrieve})}(C_b, SK_T, SK_{t_{eph_j}}$ for $j \geq 1)$

Fig. 3. Semantic Security against Type-III Adversary

In more detail, the attack game between the challenger and the adversary $\mathcal{A}$ performs as the following. In this game the challenger simulates the functionality of the data consumer.

1. The challenger runs Setup_T to generate (PK_T, SK_T), runs Setup_E to generate $(PK_{t_{eph_j}}, SK_{t_{eph_j}})$ for $j \geq 1$, and runs Setup_U to generate (PK_U, SK_U). The private key SK_T, all ephemeral private keys $SK_{t_{eph_j}}$ for $j \geq 1$, and all public parameters are given to the adversary.
2. The adversary can adaptively issue the D-type Retrieve oracle query (defined as above). At some point, the adversary sends the challenger two equal-length plaintext M_0, M_1 on which it wishes to be challenged, and two timestamps (t_{int}^*, t_{eph_i}).
3. The challenger picks a random bit $b \in \{0, 1\}$ and gives the adversary C_b as the challenge, where

$$C_b = \mathsf{Generate}(M_b, t_{int}^*, PK_U, PK_{t_{eph_i}}, PK_T).$$

4. The adversary can continue to query the Retrieve oracle as in Step 2.
5. The adversary $\mathcal{A}$ outputs b'.

In the above attack game, the adversary is Type-III because it has access to the private keys SK_T and $SK_{t_{eph_j}}$ for any $j \geq 1$.

Remark 7. In the above game, expect for the data consumer's private key, the adversary is allowed to access all other secrets. In particular, this means that the adversary can compromise both the time server and the Ephemerizer at any time. This coincides with the definition of Type-III adversary.

4   A New Timed-Ephemerizer Protocol

4.1   Preliminary of Pairing

We review the necessary knowledge about pairing and the related assumptions. More detailed information can be found in the seminal paper [2]. A pairing (or, bilinear map) satisfies the following properties:

1. $\mathbb{G}$ and $\mathbb{G}_1$ are two multiplicative groups of prime order p;
2. g is a generator of $\mathbb{G}$;

3. $\hat{e} : \mathbb{G} \times \mathbb{G} \to \mathbb{G}_1$ is an efficiently-computable bilinear map with the following properties:
   - Bilinear: for all $u, v \in \mathbb{G}$ and $a, b \in \mathbb{Z}_p$, we have $\hat{e}(u^a, v^b) = \hat{e}(u, v)^{ab}$.
   - Non-degenerate: $\hat{e}(g, g) \neq 1$.

The Bilinear Diffie-Hellman (BDH) problem in $\mathbb{G}$ is as follows: given a tuple $g, g^a, g^b, g^c \in \mathbb{G}$ as input, output $\hat{e}(g, g)^{abc} \in \mathbb{G}_1$. An algorithm $\mathcal{A}$ has advantage ϵ in solving BDH in $\mathbb{G}$ if

$$\Pr[\mathcal{A}(g, g^a, g^b, g^c) = \hat{e}(g, g)^{abc}] \geq \epsilon.$$

Similarly, we say that an algorithm $\mathcal{A}$ has advantage ϵ in solving the decision BDH problem in $\mathbb{G}$ if

$$|\Pr[\mathcal{A}(g, g^a, g^b, g^c, \hat{e}(g, g)^{abc}) = 0] - \Pr[\mathcal{A}(g, g^a, g^b, g^c, T) = 0]| \geq \epsilon.$$

where the probability is over the random choice of $a, b, c \in \mathbb{Z}_p$, the random choice of $T \in \mathbb{G}_1$, and the random bits of $\mathcal{A}$.

Definition 4. *We say that the (decision) (t, ϵ)-BDH assumption holds in $\mathbb{G}$ if no t-time algorithm has advantage at least ϵ in solving the (decision) BDH problem in $\mathbb{G}$.*

Besides these computational/decisional assumptions, the Knowledge of Exponent (KE) assumption is also used in a number of papers (e.g. [1,4]). The KE assumption is defined as follows.

Definition 5. *For any adversary $\mathcal{A}$, which takes a KE challenge (g, g^a) as input and returns (C, Y) where $Y = C^a$, there exists an extractor $\mathcal{A}'$, which takes the same input as $\mathcal{A}$ returns c such that $g^c = C$.*

4.2   The Proposed Construction

The philosophy behind the proposed protocol is similar to the blind encryption technique [12,13]. The data generator encrypts the data jointly using the ephemeral public key of the Ephemerizer and the public key of the time server, then the ciphertext is encrypted using the public key of the data consumer. The main difference (and advantage) is that we avoid using the blind encryption technique while using an efficient re-randomization technique with the XOR ($\oplus$) operation.

Let ℓ be the security parameter and $\{0, 1\}^n$ be the message space of data consumer, where n is a polynomial in ℓ. The polynomial-time algorithms are defined as follows.

- $\mathsf{Setup}_T(\ell)$: This algorithm generates the following parameters: a multiplicative group $\mathbb{G}$ of prime order p, a generator g of $\mathbb{G}$, and a multiplicative group $\mathbb{G}_1$ of the same order as $\mathbb{G}$, a polynomial-time computable bilinear map $\hat{e} : \mathbb{G} \times \mathbb{G} \to \mathbb{G}_1$, a cryptographic hash function $H_1 : \{0, 1\}^* \to \mathbb{G}$, and a long-term public/private key pair (PK_T, SK_T) where $SK_T \in_R \mathbb{Z}_p$ and $PK_T = g^{SK_T}$. The time server also publishes $(\mathbb{G}, \mathbb{G}_1, p, g, \hat{e}, \mathsf{H}_1)$. Suppose the time server possesses the identity ID_T.

- TimeExt(t, SK_T): This algorithm returns $TS_t = \mathsf{H}_1(ID_T \| t)^{SK_T}$.

- Setup$_E(\ell)$: Suppose that the Ephemerizer possesses the identity ID_E. The Ephemerizer uses the same set of parameter $(\mathbb{G}, \mathbb{G}_1, p, g, \hat{e})$ as by the time server and selects the supported expiration times t_{eph_j} $(1 \le j \le N)$ where N is an integer. The Ephemerizer generates a master key pair $(PK_E^{(0)}, SK_E^{(0)})$, where $SK_E^{(0)} \in_R \mathbb{Z}_p$ and $PK_E^{(0)} = g^{SK_E^{(0)}}$, and two hash functions

$$\mathsf{H}_2 : \{0,1\}^* \to \mathbb{G}, \ \mathsf{H}_3 : \mathbb{G}_1 \to \{0,1\}^n,$$

and sets, for $1 \le j \le N$,

$$PK_{t_{eph_j}}^{(0)} = ID_E \| t_{eph_j}, \ SK_{t_{eph_j}}^{(0)} = \mathsf{H}_2(ID_E \| t_{eph_j})^{SK_E^{(0)}}.$$

The Ephemerizer generates another master key pair $(PK_E^{(1)}, SK_E^{(1)})$ for an identity-based public key encryption scheme $\mathcal{E}_1$ with the encryption/decryption algorithms $(\mathsf{Encrypt}_1, \mathsf{Decrypt}_1)$, and generates the ephemeral key pairs $(PK_{t_{eph_j}}^{(1)}, SK_{t_{eph_j}}^{(1)})$ for $1 \le j \le N$, where $PK_{t_{eph_j}}^{(1)} = ID_E \| t_{eph_j}$. Suppose the message space and ciphertext space of the encryption scheme $\mathcal{E}_1$ are $\mathcal{Y}$ and $\mathcal{W}$, respectively.
The Ephemerizer keeps a set of tuples $(PK_{t_{eph_j}}, SK_{t_{eph_j}}, t_{eph_j})$ for $j \ge 1$, where

$$PK_{t_{eph_j}} = (PK_{t_{eph_j}}^{(0)}, PK_{t_{eph_j}}^{(1)}), \ SK_{t_{eph_j}} = (SK_{t_{eph_j}}^{(0)}, SK_{t_{eph_j}}^{(1)})$$

The Ephemerizer publishes the long-term public keys $PK_E^{(0)}, PK_E^{(1)}$.

- Setup$_U(\ell)$: This algorithm generates a public/private key pair (PK_U, SK_U) for a public key encryption scheme $\mathcal{E}_2$ with the encryption/decryption algorithms $(\mathsf{Encrypt}_2, \mathsf{Decrypt}_2)$. Suppose the message space of $\mathcal{E}_2$ is $\mathcal{X}$ and the ciphertext space is $\mathcal{D}$. The data consumer publishes the following hash functions $\mathsf{H}_4, \mathsf{H}_5, \mathsf{H}_6, \mathsf{H}_7, \mathsf{H}_8, \mathsf{H}_9$.

$$\mathsf{H}_4 : \mathbb{G} \times \mathbb{G} \to \mathbb{G}, \ \mathsf{H}_5 : \mathcal{X} \to \mathbb{G} \times \mathbb{G} \times \mathbb{G} \times \{0,1\}^n,$$

$$\mathsf{H}_6 : \mathcal{X} \times \mathbb{G} \times \mathbb{G} \times \mathbb{G} \times \{0,1\}^n \times \mathcal{D} \times \mathbb{G} \times \mathbb{G} \times \mathbb{G} \times \{0,1\}^n \to \{0,1\}^n,$$

$$\mathsf{H}_7 : \mathcal{Y} \times \mathbb{G} \times \mathbb{G} \times \mathbb{G} \times \{0,1\}^n \times \mathcal{W} \times \mathbb{G} \times \mathbb{G} \times \mathbb{G} \times \{0,1\}^n \to \{0,1\}^n,$$

$$\mathsf{H}_8 : \mathcal{Y} \times \mathbb{G} \times \mathbb{G} \times \mathbb{G} \times \{0,1\}^n \to \{0,1\}^n, \ \mathsf{H}_9 : \mathcal{Y} \to \mathbb{G} \times \mathbb{G} \times \mathbb{G} \times \{0,1\}^n.$$

- Generate$(M, t_{int}, PK_U, PK_{t_{eph_j}}, PK_T)$: This algorithm outputs a ciphertext C, where

$$r_1, r_2 \in_R \mathbb{Z}_p, \ X \in_R \mathcal{X}, \ C_1 = g^{r_1}, \ C_2 = g^{r_2}, \ C_3 = \mathsf{H}_4(C_1 \| C_2)^{r_1},$$

$$C_4 = M \oplus H_3(\hat{e}(H_2(PK_{t_{eph_j}}^{(0)}), PK_E^{(0)})^{r_1} \cdot \hat{e}(H_1(ID_T||t_{int}), PK_T)^{r_2})$$

$$= M \oplus H_3(\hat{e}(H_2(ID_E||t_{eph_j}), C_1)^{SK_E^{(0)}} \cdot \hat{e}(H_1(ID_T||t_{int}), C_2)^{SK_T}),$$

$$C_5 = \mathsf{Encrypt}_2(X, PK_U), \; C_6 = H_5(X) \oplus (C_1||C_2||C_3||C_4),$$

$$C_7 = H_6(X||C_1||C_2||C_3||C_4||C_5||C_6), \; C = (C_5, C_6, C_7).$$

- $\mathsf{Retrieve}(C, TS_{t_{int}}, SK_U; SK_{t_{eph_j}})$:

  1. The data consumer decrypts C_5 to obtain X, and aborts if the following inequality is true.

  $$C_7 \neq H_6(X||(C_6 \oplus H_5(X))||C_5||C_6)$$

  Otherwise it computes $C_1||C_2||C_3||C_4 = H_5(X) \oplus C_6$. The data consumer then computes and sends $(C', TS_{t_{int}})$ to the Ephemerizer, where

  $$M' \in_R \{0,1\}^n, \; C_1' = C_1, \; C_2' = C_2, \; C_3' = C_3, \; C_4' = M' \oplus C_4,$$

  $$Y \in_R \mathcal{Y}, \; C_5' = \mathsf{Encrypt}_1(Y, PK_{t_{eph_j}}^{(1)}), \; C_6' = H_9(Y) \oplus (C_1'||C_2'||C_3'||C_4'),$$

  $$C_7' = H_7(Y||C_1'||C_2'||C_3'||C_4'||C_5'||C_6'), \; C' = (C_5', C_6', C_7').$$

  2. If the ephemeral key $SK_{t_{eph_j}} = (SK_{t_{eph_j}}^{(0)}, SK_{t_{eph_j}}^{(1)})$ has not expired, the Ephemerizer decrypts C_5' to obtain Y, and aborts if

  $$C_7' \neq H_7(Y||(C_6' \oplus H_9(Y))||C_5'||C_6').$$

  It then computes $C_1'||C_2'||C_3'||C_4' = H_9(Y) \oplus C_6'$, and aborts if

  $$\hat{e}(C_3', g) \neq \hat{e}(C_1', H_4(C_1'||C_2')).$$

  Finally, it sends C'' to the data consumer, where

  $$C'' = H_8(Y||C_1'||C_2'||C_3'||C_4') \oplus C_4' \oplus H_3(\hat{e}(C_1', SK_{t_{eph_j}}^{(0)}) \cdot \hat{e}(TS_{t_{int}}, C_2'))$$

  $$= H_8(Y||C_1'||C_2'||C_3'||C_4') \oplus M' \oplus M.$$

  3. The data consumer recovers $M = H_8(Y||C_1'||C_2'||C_3'||C_4') \oplus M' \oplus C''$.

As in the case of the hybrid PKI-IBC protocol [9], the proposed protocol also adopts the concept of identity-based encryption [2,15]. As a result, the Ephemerizer avoids publishing a large volume of ephemeral public keys, which is however the case in [12,13]. Compared with the protocol in [9], the concrete difference is that the master private key $SK_E = (SK_E^{(0)}, SK_E^{(1)})$ is only required to be ephemeral, i.e. after generating the ephemeral private keys, the Ephemerizer can delete SK_E.

Remark 8. In the execution of Retrieve, the timestamp $TS_{t_{int}}$ is a required input. Intuitively, before the time server publishes the timestamp, it is infeasible for the data consumer and the Ephemerizer to run Retrieve to recover the message. Lemma 1 in the next subsection formalizes this intuition.

Remark 9. For a Timed-Ephemerizer protocol, the semantic securities against Type-I and Type-III adversaries are relatively easy to achieve, given the existing timed-release encryption techniques. The difficulty lies in the semantic security against Type-II adversary, which fully controls the communication channel and is capable of adaptively compromising all parties in the system. In fact, this has resulted in the complexity of the above protocol.

4.3   The Security Analysis

The following three lemmas show that the proposed protocol is secure against all three types of adversaries. Their proofs are in the technical report [16].

Lemma 1. *The proposed scheme achieves semantic security against Type-I adversary based on the BDH assumption in the random oracle model.*

Lemma 2. *The proposed scheme achieves semantic security against Type-II adversary based on the BDH and the KE assumptions in the random oracle model given that the public key encryption schemes $\mathcal{E}_1$ and $\mathcal{E}_2$ are one-way permutation.*

Lemma 3. *The proposed scheme achieves semantic security against Type-III adversary in the random oracle model given that the public key encryption schemes $\mathcal{E}_1$ and $\mathcal{E}_2$ are one-way permutation.*

5   Conclusion

In this paper we revisited the concept of Ephemerizer proposed by Perlman, and formalized the notion of Timed-Ephemerizer, aimed to provide an assured lifecycle for sensitive data, and proposed a new Timed-Ephemerizer protocol and proved its security in the proposed security model. For this new concept of Timed-Ephemerizer, a number of interesting research questions remain open. We list two of them here. One is to investigate more efficient and secure protocols for Timed-Ephemerizer. Especially, note that the random oracle paradigm has been heavily used in the security analysis of the proposed protocol. It is interesting to design secure protocols without using random oracles. The other interesting research question is to use Timed-Ephemerizer as a tool to solve practical security problems. Note that, as an application of Ephemerizer, Perlman [11] proposes a file system that supports high availability of data with assured delete.

References

1. Bellare, M., Palacio, A.: The knowledge-of-exponent assumptions and 3-round zero-knowledge protocols. In: Franklin, M. (ed.) CRYPTO 2004. LNCS, vol. 3152, pp. 273–289. Springer, Heidelberg (2004)
2. Boneh, D., Franklin, M.K.: Identity-based encryption from the weil pairing. In: Kilian, J. (ed.) CRYPTO 2001. LNCS, vol. 2139, pp. 213–229. Springer, Heidelberg (2001)

3. Cathalo, J., Libert, B., Quisquater, J.-J.: Efficient and non-interactive timed-release encryption. In: Qing, S., Mao, W., López, J., Wang, G. (eds.) ICICS 2005. LNCS, vol. 3783, pp. 291–303. Springer, Heidelberg (2005)
4. Damgård, I.: Towards practical public key systems secure against chosen ciphertext attacks. In: Feigenbaum, J. (ed.) CRYPTO 1991. LNCS, vol. 576, pp. 445–456. Springer, Heidelberg (1992)
5. Dent, A.W., Tang, Q.: Revisiting the security model for timed-release encryption with pre-open capability. In: Garay, J.A., Lenstra, A.K., Mambo, M., Peralta, R. (eds.) ISC 2007. LNCS, vol. 4779, pp. 158–174. Springer, Heidelberg (2007)
6. Halderman, J.A., Schoen, S.D., Heninger, N., Clarkson, W., Paul, W., Calandrino, J.A., Feldman, A.J., Appelbaum, J., Felten, E.W.: Lest We Remember: Cold Boot Attacks on Encryption Keys. In: van Oorschot, P.C. (ed.) Proceedings of the 17th USENIX Security Symposium, pp. 45–60. USENIX Association (2008)
7. Hwang, Y., Yum, D., Lee, P.: Timed-release encryption with pre-open capability and its application to certified e-mail system. In: Zhou, J., López, J., Deng, R.H., Bao, F. (eds.) ISC 2005. LNCS, vol. 3650, pp. 344–358. Springer, Heidelberg (2005)
8. May, T.C.: Time-release crypto (1993)
9. Nair, S.K., Dashti, M.T., Crispo, B., Tanenbaum, A.S.: A Hybrid PKI-IBC Based Ephemerizer System. In: Venter, H.S., Eloff, M.M., Labuschagne, L., Eloff, J.H.P., von Solms, R. (eds.) New Approaches for Security, Privacy and Trust in Complex Environments, Proceedings of the IFIP TC-11 22nd International Information Security Conference (SEC 2007). IFIP, vol. 232, pp. 241–252. Springer, Heidelberg (2007)
10. Department of Defense of the United States. National Industrial Security Program Operating Manual (NISPOM), DoD 5220.22-M (2006)
11. Perlman, R.: File system design with assured delete. In: SISW 2005: Proceedings of the Third IEEE International Security in Storage Workshop, pp. 83–88. IEEE Computer Society, Los Alamitos (2005)
12. Perlman, R.: The Ephemerizer: Making Data Disappear. Journal of Information System Security 1(1), 51–68 (2005)
13. Perlman, R.: The Ephemerizer: Making Data Disappear. Technical Report TR-2005-140, Sun Microsystems, Inc. (2005)
14. Rivest, R.L., Shamir, A., Wagner, D.A.: Time-lock puzzles and timed-release crypto. Technical Report Tech. Report MIT/LCS/TR-684, MIT LCS (1996)
15. Shamir, A.: Identity-based cryptosystems and signature schemes. In: Blakely, G.R., Chaum, D. (eds.) CRYPTO 1984. LNCS, vol. 196, pp. 47–53. Springer, Heidelberg (1985)
16. Tang, Q.: Timed-ephemerizer: Make assured data appear and disappear. Technical report, Centre for Telematics and Information Technology, University of Twente (2009), http://eprints.eemcs.utwente.nl/15802/

Privacy and Liveliness for Reputation Systems*

Stefan Schiffner[1], Sebastian Clauß[2], and Sandra Steinbrecher[2]

[1] K. U. Leuven, ESAT/SCD/COSIC and IBBT
Kasteelpark Arenberg 10 Bus 2446
B-3001 Leuven-Heverlee, Belgium
Stefan.Schiffner@esat.kuleuven.be
[2] Technische Universität Dresden
Institute of Systems Architecture
D-01062 Dresden, Germany
{Sebastian.Clauss,Sandra.Steinbrecher}@tu-dresden.de

Abstract. Privacy-respecting reputation systems have been constructed based on anonymous payment systems in order to implement raters'
anonymity. To the best of our knowledge, all these systems suffer from
the problem of having a "final state", i. e., a system state in which users
have no incentive anymore to behave honestly because they reached a
maximum reputation or they can no longer be rated. Thus the reputation is in fact no longer lively. We propose a novel approach to address
the problem of liveliness by the employment of negative ratings. We tie
ratings to actual interactions to force users to also deposit their negative
ratings at the reputation server. Otherwise they would not be able to
interact any more. Additionally we enhance users' anonymity by limit-
ing timing attacks through the use of transferable-eCash-based payment
systems.

Keywords: Reputation, Trust, Privacy Enhancing Technology,
Anonymity.

1 Introduction

Internet users find various opportunities to interact with each other. They sell
and buy various objects in electronic marketplaces such as eBay[1], discuss topics
in numerous discussion fora, wikis and so on. When interacting with other users,
they want to know what to expect from these users and based on this expectation
they have a certain amount of trust in the fulfillment of their expectations.

---

* This work was supported by the Integrated Projects IST-015964 AEOLUS on Algorithmic Principles for Building Efficient Overlay Computers and ICT-2007-216483
PrimeLife on Privacy and Identity Management in Europe for Life. Further, it was
supported in part by the Concerted Research Action (GOA) Ambiorics 2005/11 of
the Flemish Government and by the IAP Programme P6/26 BCRYPT of the Belgian
State (Belgian Science Policy).
[1] http://www.ebay.com/

F. Martinelli and B. Preneel (Eds.): EuroPKI 2009, LNCS 6391, pp. 209–224, 2010.
© Springer-Verlag Berlin Heidelberg 2010

People usually build their trust on already existing relationships. On the Internet users often use pseudonyms; thus, already known interaction partners might appear as new. In order to support users in estimating what to expect from an (apparently) new interaction partner, reputation systems have been designed and established to collect the experiences of others, e. g. by Resnick et al. [1]. Before interacting with others, users may investigate the interaction partner's reputation profile. Thereby users and designers of reputation systems assume implicitly that the users' past behavior gives a strong indication about their future behavior.

Reputation systems can be seen as databases that collect information about who interacted with whom in which context. Thus, they are a promising target for numerous data collectors. However, according to Bygrave [2], opinions about a natural person can be seen as personal data, so that the respective person's right on informational self-determination should be applied. Therefore, explicit reputation should only be accumulated about users who agreed on accumulation. Furthermore, reputation information should be protected by means of technical data protection, as outlined by Mahler and Olsen [3].

Current reputation systems often do not protect the privacy of their participants, i. e., the reputation provider knows who interacted with whom, how interaction partners rated each other and who queried whose reputation. Moreover, the granularity of the reputation is often very fine so that the reputation itself becomes a quasi-identifier. Proposals for privacy-respecting reputation systems often fall prey to liveliness problems, that is, the systems reach a final state where users' reputation cannot change anymore. We propose a technical solution which overcomes this problem. Our proposal protects the privacy of both parties, while it retains liveliness of the reputation system. We focus on the protection of who rated whom and who queried whose reputation, while we assume that the system assigns a small number of different reputation values to users in order to protect their privacy.

An overview of common reputation systems can be found in [4][2]. From these, eBay implements a popular reputation system. This system poses certain risks for the privacy of users, as it allows gathering profiles of a user's behavior, e. g., time and frequency of participation in interactions, and user's interest in specific products. Even if users can act pseudonymously, they run the risk of re-identification, as it typically happens to eBay partners during shipping and payment.

Hence, reputation systems that respect privacy are needed; systems that still enable users to investigate reputation profiles, which allow an estimation what to expect from interaction partners. In Sect. 2 we present related work both on privacy-respecting reputation systems as well as on anonymous payment systems and one-show credentials. Abstracting from this related work, in Sect. 3 we present a general model on how to define and evaluate requirements focusing on privacy for reputation systems. By means of this model existing privacy-

---

[2] Although this article is 10 years old the changes to reputation systems currently in use are only marginal.

respecting systems based on anonymous payment systems are analyzed in Sect. 4. In Sect. 5.1 we describe our proposal for a new privacy-respecting reputation system and we demonstrate its advantages over existing approaches. Finally, in Sect. 5.2 we analyze our protocol and conclude in Sect. 6.

2   Related Work

We first outline approaches for privacy-respecting reputation systems which are related to the system we propose in Sect. 5. Some of these protocols, as well as the system we propose, make use of anonymous payment systems to reach anonymity of raters. We further outline related work on this area.

2.1   Privacy-Respecting Reputation Systems

A central problem for privacy-respecting reputation systems is that they must guarantee that users cannot abolish negative reputation. This can be reached by only allowing positive reputation, as proposed by Voss and Androulaki et al. [5,6], by making it difficult for the user to distinguish between positive and negative ratings, as proposed by Steinbrecher et al. [7], or by a trusted third party. Thereby, this trusted third party can either be an external reputation provider, as proposed by Pingel et al. and Anwar et al. [8,9] or a trusted platform module for the user, as proposed in [5,10] by Voss et al. and Kinateder et al.

Anonymity of the users involved is not as easy as just using anonymizing services on the network layer. This approach reaches only anonymity for the users inquiring others' reputation, as suggested in [11] by Pavlov et al., who utilize an anonymized RING-Network. In order to obtain anonymity of raters *and* ratees, it needs to be ensured that many users are indistinguishable by an attacker, so that they are in large anonymity sets.

For anonymity of ratees, others should not be able to link previous interactions to a current one. The possibility of recognizing users by reputation is limited if the set of possible reputations is limited as shown in [12] by Steinbrecher or the reputation is only published as an estimated reputation as proposed by Dellarocas [13]. The recognition of users by pseudonym can be avoided by using transaction pseudonyms [6,14].

In order to obtain anonymity of raters, interactions and ratings related to these interactions need to be unlinkable. Again, this can be reached by a reputation provider who might only calculate a new user reputation after he collected not only one but several ratings [15] or who might only publish an estimation of the actual reputation [13]. A rater can also be anonymous against the reputation provider by using convertible credentials [12] or anonymous payment systems [6].

2.2   Anonymous Payment Systems and One-Show Credentials

We base our system on Chaum's eCash [16], an electronic cash system, which aims at emulating regular cash. Users withdraw coins from a bank to pay merchants, which are special users who offer a service. eCash is called transferable if a merchant can use such a coin to pay another user without the help of the bank. eCash provides anonymity properties. For our purposes, we assume a system that provides *perfect anonymity* as presented by Gouget et al. [17], that is a system where an adversary cannot link a spending to a withdrawal: he cannot decide if two coins are spent by the same user, and he cannot decide whether he already owned a coin or not. However, a user can see how old a coin is, i.e., how many times it has been spent. This can be seen as a weakness, but we will utilize this property for our protocol.

Furthermore we use one-show credentials, as described, e.g., by Brands [18], which are a primitive similar to electronic coins: they can be spent only once. The main difference is that no account-keeping bank is needed. However, all one-show credentials already shown need to be published in such a way that every user can check their validity by executing the `Deposit` algorithm.

3   System Model

For our system environment shown in Fig. 1, we assume a community system allowing pseudonymous interactions among users. This might be, e.g., a marketplace such as eBay where every user might be a seller (provider) or buyer (client). Let M be such a user offering interactions under the pseudonym P_M to other users. The community deploys a reputation system provided by a reputation provider ReP. The reputation system collects positive and negative experiences of users' behavior during interactions. Thus we assume that only interaction-derived reputation is aggregated by our system. If a user U becomes interested in the interaction offered by P_M, U inquires P_M's reputation under pseudonym P_{U_1}. If U decides to take part in this interaction, U uses another pseudonym P_{U_2} to interact. Afterwards, U rates P_M using a new pseudonym P_{U_3}. M can now include the rating P_M got in the overall reputation account at ReP.

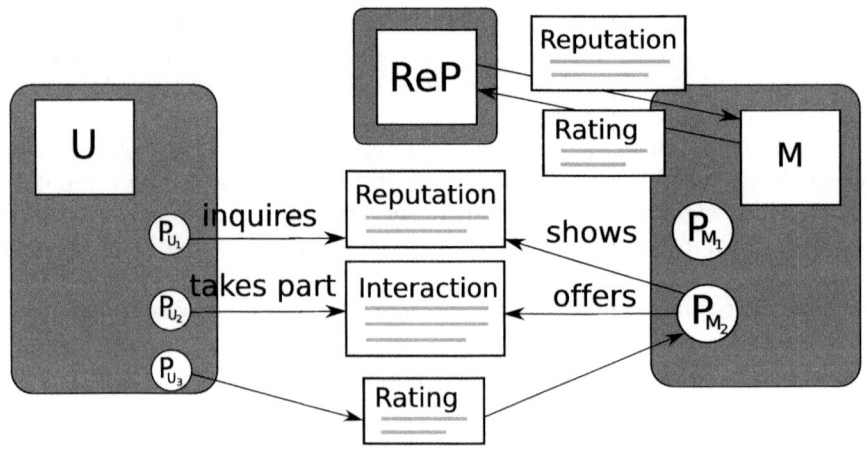

Fig. 1. Model of system environment

The aforementioned usage of pseudonyms is called transaction pseudonyms, as defined by Pfitzmann et al. [19], since for every transaction a new and unlinkable pseudonym is used. In the following we call transaction pseudonyms just pseudonyms, while long term pseudonyms are named by their role (e. g. user, seller, rater).

3.1 Requirements

The requirements we propose for a privacy-respecting reputation system have a significant overlap with the requirements for reputation systems derived in [12,20].

Rating. After an interaction between two pseudonyms P_M and P_{U_2}, the reputation system provides P_{U_2} with a rating function that allows him to rate P_M, now the so-called ratee. For the rating function the following requirements should be fulfilled:

1. *Integrity of ratings:* Users want ratings to be preserved from manipulations.
2. *Authorizability of ratings:* Only users who interacted with a ratee are allowed to rate him.
3. *Raters' anonymity:* Users want to rate anonymously in order to not allow attackers to link this rating to an interaction. This means the pseudonym P_{U_2} that interacted with P_M should not be linkable to the pseudonym P_{U_3} that rates P_M.

The reputation system updates M's global reputation aggregated from the received ratings. The rating of a user's behavior and the aggregation of his ratings to a reputation value have to follow specific rules fixed by the system designer. These rules typically depend on the application scenario and have to fulfill sociological and economic requirements. We abstract here from the concrete functions to allow a universal design interoperable with multiple application scenarios. An overview of possible functions is for example given by Mui [21]. For an economic introduction we refer to Dellarocas [22]. The following requirements should hold:

4. *Fairness of reputation:* Users want the aggregated reputation to consider all interactions which a user was involved in in a fair way. Note that this does not mean that a reputation function considers all ratings equally, but in a way that allows predicting future behavior of the ratee. This is difficult to define/decide, but the function must not be limited technically, hence it needs the full history of ratings. Especially, users should not be able to manipulate the aggregated reputation in a way that it neglects or emphasizes certain ratings.
5. *Liveliness of reputation:* Reputation should always consider all recent interactions or give users an indication that there are no more. Especially the reputation system should not offer users the possibility to reach a final state in which bad behavior no longer damages their reputation.

Showing Reputation. The aggregated reputation of the user M can be shown to other users on request. Therefore, the following requirements apply:

6. *Availability of reputation:* As a functional requirement, inquirers need to be able to access other users' reputation; however the query process might require the consent of the user whose reputation is queried.
7. *Inquirers' anonymity:* Users want to inquire reputation anonymously to prevent others from building personal behavior profiles of their interests.
8. *Ratees's anonymity:* Ratees do not want to be linked to their past interactions, except that these contributed to their reputation, to prevent others from building profiles about all their interactions and interaction partners. This means that M wants be anonymous by using different pseudonyms P_M for different interactions and possibly also reputation queries of inquirers.

Example. We consider an eBay-like marketplace where products are advertised. In such a marketplace, an interaction is a sale, in which a seller is offering a product or service. However, these sellers act pseudonymously, but clients want to inform themselves about the trustworthiness of the sellers. Therefore they can query a seller's reputation using the contact pseudonym indicated on the advertisement.

Registration. Every user registers under a pseudonym with a reputation provider. Because the user is able to terminate this registration, the following requirement should be fulfilled:

9. *Absolute linkability of a user's registration within a reputation system:* To prevent a user from leaving with a bad reputation and re-entering with a neutral reputation, registration actions of the same user have to be absolutely linkable. We want a user to register only once in the system and he should not be able to expunge his reputation once it has been developed and presented in the public domain.

3.2   Attacker Model

Availability of reputation (6) goes beyond the capabilities of cryptographic primitives since it depends on functioning communication lines and hardware. In this paper, we only consider it as far as protocols raise new problems, e. g., denial of service attacks that become possible because of protocol requirements.

As described in [12], *absolute linkability of a user's registration within a reputation system (9)* can be achieved by an infrastructure such as a privacy-enhancing identity management system [23].

For the remaining seven requirements we distinguish two types of attackers, namely, the privacy attacker and the security attacker.

Privacy attacker. As privacy attacks we subsume attacks on *raters' (3) inquirers' (7) and ratees' (8) anonymity.* We assume that reputation can be queried anonymously (e. g. by its publication on a website as it is the case for eBay) and therefore we concentrate on raters' and ratees' anonymity. We assume that the privacy attacker cannot observe who is communicating with whom, that is, all users are communicating via an anonymity service. Furthermore, the attacker might collude with the reputation provider, but cannot cheat on the reputation values, that is, he is an honest but curious attacker. In addition, the privacy attacker can only control a limited number of users so that a sufficiently large anonymity set (which contains the users not controlled by the attacker) is preserved.

Security attacker. We see the security attacker as an attacker on the *integrity (1) and authorizability of ratings (2)* and on the *fairness (4) and liveliness of reputation (5)*. We assume a global attacker who might observe all interactions between the users and between users and the reputation provider, but who cannot control the reputation provider. We show in our analysis that an attacker who controls all users in the system can only forge a reputation credential if he can break the underlying eCash system or forge the credential itself.

4   Analysis of Current Privacy-Respecting Reputation Protocols

In this section we present existing reputation systems that make use of anonymous payment systems in order to reach *raters' anonymity (3)*. We analyze the protocols with respect to the privacy and security attackers specified in Sect. 3.2.

For the protocols presented below, as well as for our approach presented in Sect. 5, the property of coins of an anonymous payment system that they can be spent anonymously but not twice is needed. This can be used to guarantee both *raters' anonymity (3) and authorizability of ratings (2)*. Please note that the usage of coins of an anonymous payment system does not imply that reputation becomes a currency. In order to guarantee anonymity on the network layer all communication is assumed to be anonymous by the usage of an underlying anonymizing network, e. g., AN.ON [24] or Tor [25].

The reputation systems presented are applicable to arbitrary anonymous interaction systems such as the communities in our model from Sect. 3. They require a trusted third party, the so-called reputation provider *ReP*.

4.1   Bounded above Reputation

In [26] Voss describes a protocol that requires an anonymous payment system that allows personalizing coins on generation. These coins cannot be transferred to another identity without sharing all secrets of this identity, but possession of a coin can be proven without authentication. Coins are used both as reputation and collateral coins. Collateral coins that a user received as guarantee are ineligible for other interactions, but can be marked as invalid to lower the spender's reputation in case of misbehavior.

Registration. When registering with the reputation provider *ReP*, a user M receives a pseudonym P_M and a secret to prove possession of this pseudonym. The reputation provider uses this pseudonym to personalize reputation and collateral coins for P_M. M withdraws a wallet with all his coins from *ReP*.

Showing Reputation and Interaction. Before an interaction, M gives some of his reputation coins to his interaction partner U as collateral. U together with ReP has to verify that the coins have not been used as collateral before. Thereby M does not show his whole reputation but only a part of it which is necessary as collateral and that might be damaged afterwards.

Rating. After an interaction, U hands over the collateral coins received beforehand to ReP. If U wants to give a bad rating, U asks ReP to invalidate a number of the collateral coins. If U wants to give a good rating, U asks ReP to create a number of extra coins for P_M and hand it over to P_M with the collateral coins. ReP does this only if U has not rated P_M before.

Privacy and Security Analysis

Privacy attacker. The reputation provider knows U and M at least pseudonymously and that they interact(ed) but does not know anything about the interaction they took part in except the collateral and reputation coins they use. *Raters' anonymity (3)* against the ratee is only given within the set of users the ratee interacted with in the same time frame. This set typically will be small because every interaction needs collateral coins that cannot be used as reputation coins anymore as long as the interaction has not been finished and the corresponding rating has not been given. *Inquirers' anonymity (7)* can easily be achieved by transaction pseudonyms for the interaction planned. *Ratees' anonymity (8)* is possible because the ratee shows in every interaction only the part of his reputation needed as collateral. After the interaction these coins are invalidated by the ReP and he possibly receives new coins as new reputation.

Security attacker. We assume the reputation provider to be trusted. Then, ratings can only be given if the ratee agreed beforehand to interact with the rater, because users will only hand over collateral coins to an interaction partner if they want to take part in an interaction with him. Thereby *authorizability of ratings (2)* is guaranteed. In this protocol it cannot be guaranteed whether the actual interaction really took place or not. The protocol could be extended in a way that both interaction partners hand over collateral coins to each other in a fair exchange. This allows both interacting users to rate the other one afterwards.

The *integrity of ratings (1)* is not addressed in this protocol but should be guaranteed by authentication systems between at least U and ReP. The *fairness of reputation (4)* needs all interaction partners who received coins to contact the reputation provider and initiate invalidation of the collateral coins. To prevent certain raters from giving too many ratings to interaction partners, every user is allowed to rate every pseudonym only once. This leads to the drawback that the reputation of a user cannot change any more after he was rated by all users. Thus, the *liveliness of reputation (5)* is breached.

4.2   Monotonic Reputation

Androulaki et al. [6] describe a protocol that requires a trusted third party, the reputation provider ReP, who keeps accounts of reputation coins for every user.

All coins have the same non-negative value. Why negative coins are impossible to model in this system is explained in the analysis part below. A user U can communicate using his publicly known identity, denoted as U, or he may use a randomly chosen pseudonym P_U. Fig. 2 shows a flowchart of the protocol, while the single phases are described in the paragraphs below.

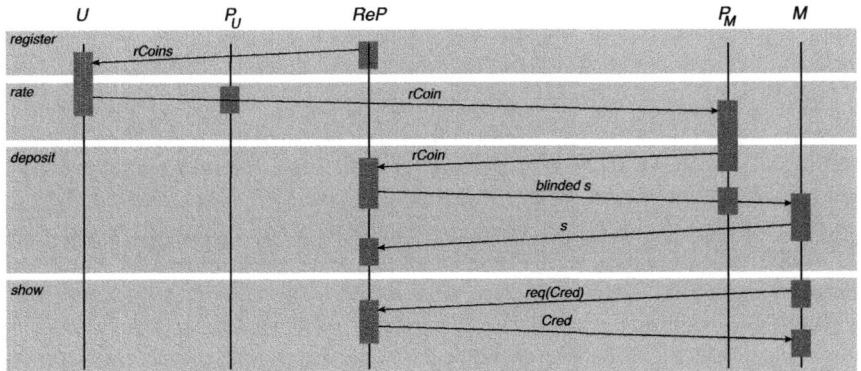

Fig. 2. The original protocol of Androulaki et al. as flowchart

Registration. Every user withdraws a wallet from ReP, which contains a number of reputation coins. Let (S, π) be one of these coins. Thereby S denotes the serial number, while π denotes the cryptographic payload of the corresponding payment system. In order to avoid inflation the number of coins a user can withdraw per time unit is limited.

Rating. The User U, acting as P_U, wants to rate user M, acting as P_M, after an interaction. In order to do this, P_U awards a reputation coin (S, π) to P_M. In order to dispose the received reputation coin, P_M deposits it at ReP. In exchange, P_M gets a blinded permission $blind(\sigma)$ from ReP. M unblinds this permission and sends it back to ReP so that ReP can credit this coin to M's reputation account and update M's reputation.

Showing Reputation. In order to demonstrate his reputation, M requests a credential from ReP. ReP aggregates the current reputation from the ratings[3] of M. Then ReP issues the requested reputation credential containing M's current reputation to M. Later on, M, as P_M, can show this credential to any other pseudonymously acting user P_U.

Privacy and Security Analysis

Privacy attacker. With regards to users' privacy, even the reputation provider ReP should not get information about who interacted with whom. However,

---

[3] As outlined above, the concrete design of a function for aggregation is out of scope of this work and needs to be chosen for a specific application.

ReP will always learn that a user was rated since it has to keep the reputation accounts.

The *rater's anonymity (3)* is based on the anonymity of coin spending and thus remains anonymous among all possible raters.

Furthermore, showing or querying a reputation might reveal personal information about both peers. However *inquirers' anonymity (7)* can be protected by transaction pseudonyms.

The *ratee's anonymity (8)* is less protected. The problem is the step "deposit" (shown in Fig. 2), which consists of communication between ReP and P_M as well as ReP and M, and there is a dependency between both communications. So, the step "M sends σ to ReP" can only be performed by a M that deposited a reputation coin at ReP as P_M beforehand. As these steps will usually be performed by M without a significant time delay, ReP can decrease the set of pseudonyms that deposited a coin significantly by a timing attack. So, the ratee is only anonymous among all ratees that dispose their coin at the same time. The number of ratees that dispose coins at the same time can be increased by batching, i.e., defining certain times where users can dispose their coins. The ratee also needs to be protected when showing his reputation. The reputation system needs to ensure that repeated queries are not linkable, i.e., an attacker cannot tell if two reputation values are from the same user. Therefore, the reputation function must map only to a few reputation categories in order to keep the anonymity sets as large as possible.

Security attacker. The *integrity of ratings (1)* should be guaranteed by an authentication system between at least M and ReP.

Since the rater cannot give negative feedback, the reputation of the users will never decrease. Furthermore, the number of reputation values is fixed and small. Even if we do not specify a concrete reputation function here, this requirement must be met in order to restrict identifiability of users by their reputation values, see requirement *(7)*. All users will finally have the best reputation value and will keep it, and thus the system reaches a final state and becomes useless, i.e., no user has an incentive to behave fairly anymore, which violates *fairness (5) and liveliness of reputation (4)*.

Also, a decay of the reputation would not resolve liveliness issues sufficiently, thereby inactive users are indistinguishable from misbehaving users and thus a highly active user could gather a good reputation and then misbehave for a while, but would appear as reputable as a user who was just inactive for a while.

Therefore negative feedback is needed. However, in the above protocol the ratee cannot be forced to deposit received reputation coins, i.e., the ratee can decide on his own whether he wants to deposit the received rating and of course the ratee would not deposit a negative coin. Blinding the coin value would not solve the problem either, since users usually know whether they misbehaved. Moreover, to the best of our knowledge there is no blindeable eCash protocol proposed. In the next section we present a protocol that solves these problems.

5 Non-monotonic Reputation

A drawback of the reputation systems presented in Sect. 4 is that the *liveliness of reputation (5)* cannot be guaranteed because both systems suffer from an explicit or de facto upper bound of reputation. If we allow negative ratings we will have to guarantee that these ratings cannot be suppressed by the ratee. Thereby a negative rating is a rating that lowers the ratee's reputation immediately or may lower it in the future. As outlined in Sect. 1 a trusted third party can help to implement this; however, this trusted third party might be implemented in a distributed way to guarantee availability. How this can be done is beyond the scope of this work, but our work supports distribution since the reputation provider keeps as little as possible user data. We propose an external reputation provider, which is described in the remainder of this section.

5.1 System Design

The reputation provider ReP keeps an interaction account and a reputation account for every user. ReP thereby guarantees that every interaction is actually rated, possibly also in a negative way, and considered for the user's reputation. We implement both accounts as accounts of an anonymous payment system and the ratings and interactions both as coins. Thereby, negative coins can be implemented by two instances of an anonymous payment protocol with a joint account, where coins of the first system are counted as +1 and coins of the second one as -1. For this, we use two instances of the protocol outlined in Sect. 4.2:

- *Interaction counter:* This instance is used to count the number of interactions a user U was involved in and should be rated for.
- *Reputation counter:* The other instance aggregates the ratings received, both positive and negative ones.

In the following paragraphs we outline the actual protocol. A flowchart of the protocol is given in Fig. 3.

Registration. In order to initialize the reputation system, every user withdraws a wallet from ReP, that contains n interaction coins (S_i, π_{it}) and reputation coins (S_i, π_{ir+}) for positive ratings and (S_i, π_{ir-}) for negative ratings. The coins are issued in triples with the same serial number S_i and π_{it}, π_{ir+} and π_{ir-} are the double-spending tacks and signatures with $i = 1 \ldots n$.

Interaction. If user U wants to interact with an interaction partner M (whom U knows as P_M) using a pseudonym P_U, U starts the interaction by awarding an interaction coin (S, π_t) to P_M. P_M spends this coin to its registered pseudonym M, which deposits this coin and requests a one-show credential from the reputation provider stating the fact that the number of coins in the interaction account has been increased. P_M shows this credential to P_U. Now the actual interaction can take place. Furthermore every party needs to check the age of the coin to prevent undetectable double spending, as outlined in the analysis.

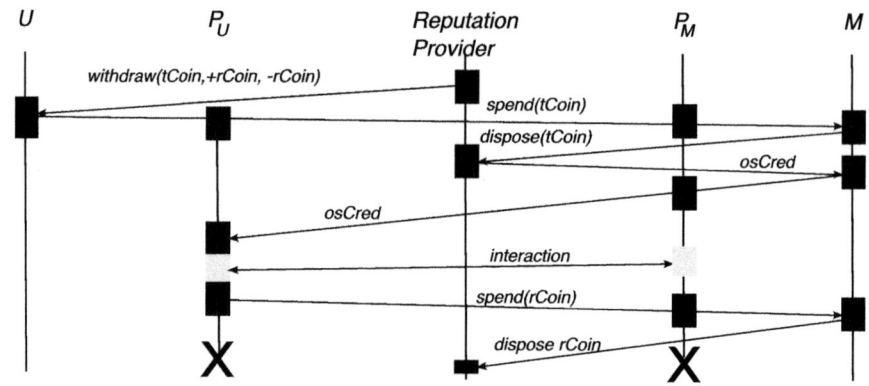

Fig. 3. The reputation granting is bound to interactions

Rating. After an interaction, P_U rates P_M by awarding a reputation coin (S, π_{r+}) or (S, π_{r-}). P_M deposits this coin. During the deposit the reputation provider checks whether the serial number of an earlier deposited interaction coin equals the serial number of the reputation coin to avoid that M uses one of his own coins to rate himself with a positive rating instead of the (possibly negative) one received from P_U. As for the interaction coins, the age of the rating coins needs to be consistent.

Showing Reputation. If users want to show their reputation to someone, they need to request a reputation credential from the reputation provider. The reputation provider issues a reputation credential only if the interaction account and the reputation account contain the same number of coins. The reputation credential contains a time stamp to avoid that users can use old reputation credentials to show them to possible interaction partners while they misbehaved in the meantime. The reputation provider can also play the role of a global *time provider* in a very natural way by using the number of total (by every user) deposited coins as global time. This also gives an estimate on how much users could cheat about their reputation, since the time difference between issuing the credential and now is the maximum number of possibly negative coins a user could have received in between.

However, highly active users might always have some open interactions and would never be able to show their reputation, hence the requirement of equal coin numbers in both accounts needs to be softer. That could be done by accepting a maximal number of missing coins or by filling up all missing coins by negative ratings; which solution is practical depends on the application.

Batching. The protocol presented above might still raise timing issues on users' anonymity. In order to minimize this problem, we propose to batch all user activities in rounds of three phases. In every round users get wallets with n coin triples and a sufficient amount of credentials about their reputation level, which they achieved in the round before. After that, users find their at most n interaction partners (using the credentials) and spend on them an interaction coin. In a second phase the interaction partners deposit their interaction coins and the actual interaction takes place. After the interaction the users spend on their interaction partner a reputation coin with the intended value. In the third phase all interaction partners deposit their reputation coins. In the following section we discuss the expected size of the anonymity sets of this protocol.

5.2   Privacy and Security Analysis

Availability. In the protocol presented in Sect. 5.1 the user might not give the reputation coin to the interaction partner. This blocks the ratee since the reputation provider does not issue new credentials if interaction counter and reputation counter do not contain the same number of coins. However simultaneous rating might solve the problem.

Security Attacker. The interaction registration phase depends on the security of the transferable eCash system: even if all users collude a double spending can be proven and traced back to its origin. The user U, who starts the interaction, cannot forge the interaction coin without revealing his registered user name U, since the dispose algorithm would recognize this double spending. The user M, however, might transfer the coin multiple times from P_M to M. In this case the deposit algorithm will return a proof that P_M double-spent the coin, where P_M is a non-registered pseudonym. However, since the number of hops for a coin is known, only a pseudonym controlled by M can double-spend. Since M needs to reveal its identity to the reputation provider it can get its deserved punishment in case of double-spending. The argumentation for the rating is similar. These properties ensure the security properties *integrity (1) and authorizability of ratings (2)* as well as *fairness of reputation (4)*.

Privacy Attacker. Anonymity of the inquirer (7) can be guaranteed by inquiring with a one-time pseudonym or publication of P_M's reputation. The *rater's anonymity (3)* against the reputation provider is perfectly preserved by the anonymous payment system: the rater is anonymous among all the users who withdrew interaction and reputation coins during this round. The *ratee's anonymity (8)* of M cannot be guaranteed because the disposal of the interaction coin before the interaction and the reputation coin after the interaction are in principle linkable to M. This is not a problem as long as it is assumed that ReP cannot observe any peer to peer traffic. Batching allows to relax this condition. Assume that ReP can observe which peers communicate, then ReP could link a P_U with its corresponding U if there is only one user who deposits a coin at this time. If it is assumed that many users deposit their coins at the same time, these users would be anonymous among each other. Batching allows to concentrate these steps. Furthermore, batching helps to protect naive users from outside attackers who re-query the reputation of their interaction partners, since the reputation of a user stays constant within the duration of a round.

However, batching is the more effective the longer the rounds are, but the longer a round is the longer a malicious node stays unpunished. The right trade-off between security and privacy depends on the application and is beyond the scope of this work.

6   Conclusion

We have analyzed reputation protocols based on anonymous payment systems to enable anonymity of raters. We pointed out weaknesses of these protocols in terms of liveliness and anonymity. We have proposed a lively system, which binds ratings to interactions and we deploy transferable-eCash-based payment systems to limit timing attacks. An analysis of the security and privacy requirements is given in comparison to the existing systems.

The aim was to protect the link between interaction pseudonym P_M and registered user name M. Since P_M never communicates with the reputation provider and the anonymous payment system is assumed to be anonymous the reputation provider cannot link M and P_M unless P_M double-spent a coin.

The more interactions take place in one round, the larger the anonymity set is. However, since the reputation of a user is fixed per round a user can misbehave within a round without being punished directly. Hence, the duration of a round is a trade-off between user anonymity and security. How to find this balance depends on the actual system and is beyond the scope of this paper.

Finally in Table 1 we compare our system with the existing systems presented in Sect. 4.

Although the results of the analysis of our system are already quite promising for actual deployment, future research is needed on denial of service prevention and on the privacy problems caused by traffic analysis. Furthermore, the problem of self rating needs to be solved.

Table 1. Comparison of reputation protocols

	Bounded above reputation [26]	Monotonic reputation [6]	Non-monotonic reputation (this work)
Integrity of ratings (1)	yes	yes	yes
Authorizability of ratings (2)	yes	no	yes
Anonymity of raters (3)	yes	yes	yes
Fairness of reputation (4)	no	no	yes
Liveliness of reputation (5)	no, upper bound	no, de facto upper bound by only-positive ratings	yes, negative ratings possible
Anonymity of ratees (8)	yes	yes, but timing issues	yes, less timing issues

References

1. Resnick, P., Kuwabara, K., Zeckhauser, R., Friedman, E.: Reputation systems. Communications of the ACM 43(12), 45–48 (2000)
2. Bygrave, L.: Data Protection Law, Approaching Its Rationale, Logic and Limits. Kluwer Law International, The Hague (2002)
3. Mahler, T., Olsen, T.: Reputation systems and data protection law. In: eAdoption and the Knowledge Economy: Issues, Applications, Case Studies, pp. 180–187. IOS Press, Amsterdam (2004)
4. Kollock, P.: The production of trust in online markets. Advances in Group Processes 16, 99–123 (1999)
5. Voss, M., Heinemann, A., Mühlhäuser, M.: A Privacy Preserving Reputation System for Mobile Information Dissemination Networks. In: First International Conference on Security and Privacy for Emerging Areas in Communications Networks (SECURECOMM 2005), pp. 171–181. IEEE, Los Alamitos (2005)
6. Androulaki, E., Choi, S.G., Bellovin, S.M., Malkin, T.: Reputation systems for anonymous networks. In: Borisov, N., Goldberg, I. (eds.) PETS 2008. LNCS, vol. 5134, pp. 202–218. Springer, Heidelberg (2008)
7. Steinbrecher, S., Groß, S., Meichau, M.: Jason: A scalable reputation system for the semantic web. In: Proceedings of IFIP Sec 2009, IFIP International Information Security Conference: Emerging Challenges for Security, Privacy and Trust. IFIP AICT, vol. 297, pp. 421–431. Springer, Heidelberg (2009)
8. Pingel, F., Steinbrecher, S.: Multilateral secure cross-community reputation systems. In: Furnell, S.M., Katsikas, S.K., Lioy, A. (eds.) TrustBus 2008. LNCS, vol. 5185, pp. 69–78. Springer, Heidelberg (2008)
9. Anwar, M., Greer, J.: Reputation management in privacy-enhanced e-learning. In: The proceedings of the 3rd Annual Scientific Conference of the LORNET Research Network (I2LOR 2006) (November 2006)
10. Kinateder, M., Pearson, S.: A Privacy-Enhanced Peer-to-Peer Reputation System. In: Bauknecht, K., Tjoa, A.M., Quirchmayr, G. (eds.) EC-Web 2003. LNCS, vol. 2738, pp. 206–215. Springer, Heidelberg (2003)
11. Pavlov, E., Rosenschein, J.S., Topol, Z.: Supporting privacy in decentralized additive reputation systems. In: The Second International Conference on Trust Management, Oxford, United Kingdom, March 2004, pp. 108–119 (2004)
12. Steinbrecher, S.: Enhancing multilateral security in and by reputation systems. In: Proceedings of the IFIP/FIDIS Internet Security and Privacy Summer School, Masaryk University Brno, September 1-7. IFIP AICT, vol. 298, pp. 135–150. Springer, Heidelberg (2009)
13. Dellarocas, C.: Immunizing online reputation reporting systems against unfair ratings and discriminatory behavior. In: EC 2000: Proceedings of the 2nd ACM conference on Electronic commerce, pp. 150–157. ACM Press, New York (2000)
14. Steinbrecher, S.: Design options for privacy-respecting reputation systems within centralised internet communities. In: Proceedings of IFIP Sec 2006, 21st IFIP International Information Security Conference: Security and Privacy in Dynamic Environments, May 2006. IFIP, vol. 201, pp. 123–134. Springer, Heidelberg (2006)
15. Dellarocas, C.: Research note – how often should reputation mechanisms update a trader's reputation profile? Information Systems Research 17(3), 271–285 (2006)
16. Chaum, D., Fiat, A., Naor, M.: Untraceable electronic cash. In: Goldwasser, S. (ed.) CRYPTO 1988. LNCS, vol. 403, pp. 319–327. Springer, Heidelberg (1990)

17. Canard, S., Gouget, A.: Anonymity in transferable E-cash. In: Bellovin, S.M., Gennaro, R., Keromytis, A.D., Yung, M. (eds.) ACNS 2008. LNCS, vol. 5037, pp. 207–223. Springer, Heidelberg (2008)
18. Brands, S.: A technical overview of digital credentials (1999)
19. Hansen, M., Pfitzmann, A.: Anonymity, unobservability, and pseudonymity - a proposal for terminology. In: Balzer, R., Köpsell, S., Lazarek, H. (Hg.): Fachterminologie Datenschutz und Datensicherheit Deutsch - Russisch - Englisch; FGI - Forschungsgesellschaft Informatik, Technische Universität Wien, Wien, pp. 111–144 (February 2008), Version 0.31 available from http://dud.inf.tu-dresden.de/literatur/Anon_Terminology_v0.31.pdf
20. ENISA: Position paper. reputation-based systems: a security analysis (2007), http://www.enisa.europa.eu/doc/pdf/deliverables/enisa_pp_reputation_based_system.pdf (last visit 16/06/09)
21. Mui, L.: Computational Models of Trust and Reputation: Agents, Evolutionary Games, and Social Networks. PhD Thesis, Massachusetts Institute of Technology (2003)
22. Dellarocas, C.: The digitization of word-of-mouth: Promise and challenges of online feedback mechanisms. Management Science, 1407–1424 (October 2003)
23. Clauß, S., Pfitzmann, A., Hansen, M., Herreweghen, E.V.: Privacy-enhancing identity management. The IPTS Report 67, 8–16 (2002)
24. Berthold, O., Federrath, H., Köpsell, S.: Web mIXes: A system for anonymous and unobservable internet access. In: Federrath, H. (ed.) Designing Privacy Enhancing Technologies. LNCS, vol. 2009, pp. 115–129. Springer, Heidelberg (2001)
25. Dingledine, R., Mathewson, N., Syverson, P.: Tor: The second-generation onion router. In: Proceedings of the 13th USENIX Security Symposium, August 2004, pp. 21–21 (2004)
26. Voss, M.: Privacy preserving online reputation systems. In: International Information Security Workshops, pp. 245–260. Kluwer, Dordrecht (2004)

A Multidimensional Reputation Scheme for Identity Federations*

Isaac Agudo, Carmen Fernandez-Gago, and Javier Lopez

Department of Computer Science, University of Malaga,
29071, Málaga, Spain
{isaac,mcgago,jlm}@lcc.uma.es

Abstract. Deciding who to trust in the internet of services paradigm is an important and open question. How to do it in an optimal way is not always easy to determine. Trust is usually referred to a particular context whereas a single user may interact in more than one given context. We are interested in investigating how a *Federated Reputation System* can help exporting trust perceptions from one context to another. We propose a model for deriving trust in online services. In this context, trust is defined as the level of confidence that the service provider holds on the subject interacting with it to behave in a proper way while using the service. Thus, we derive trust by using the reputation values that those users have gained for interacting with these services.

1 Introduction

Deciding who to trust in the current internet is an important task that sometimes needs of certain techniques in order to be determined. It is easier when the interactions among users and services occur in both a physical and a virtual way.

The concept of reputation is defined by the Concise Oxford Dictionary as 'what is generally said or believed about a person's or thing's character or standing'. This definition corresponds well to the view of social network researchers [33]. In fact, some efforts have been made in order to add some sociological meaning to the understanding of the reputation concept before providing a model of reputation ratings for [18].

The concept of reputation is closely linked to that of trustworthiness [16]. As mentioned in this work, the difference between trust and reputation can be easily understood by looking at these two statements:

- 'I trust you because of your good reputation.'
- 'I trust you despite your bad reputation.'

These two sentences illustrate how subjective the concept of trust is, compared to the concept of reputation.

Trust is based on various factors or evidences apart from reputation, although in the absence of any other previous experience reputation is a useful mechanism for establishing trust relationships. In some systems such as for example, online communities

---

* This work has been funded by MEC I+D and MICT of Spain under the research projects CRISIS (TIN2006-09242), ARES (CSP2007-00004) and by the European Commission through the research project SPIKE (FP7-ICT-2007-1-217098).

F. Martinelli and B. Preneel (Eds.): EuroPKI 2009, LNCS 6391, pp. 225–238, 2010.

[11,30] the problem is twofold. First, we have to make sure that the members are who they claim to be (authentication) and then that we can trust them. Using reputation of a user in order to build trust relationships can be an interesting approach, although limited by the accuracy of the reputation system.

The issue of authentication is solved most of the times by using an Identity Management system composed of a Service Provider (SP) and an Identity Provider (IDP). The SP requests the IDP information about certain user who is registered with the IDP and is interested in accessing some service provided by the SP. Our intention is to solve the other part of the problem, that is, once a user has been authenticated by the Identity Management system we are interested in establishing whether we can trust that user. In order to achieve this we propose that the IDP maintains a reputation engine that updates and provides reputation information about users in such a way that this information can be used by the SP. By using this reputation engine users in a system can also establish trust among users. This will guide them in order to establish better interactions.

The paper is organized as follows. Section 2 presents some related work. Section 3 provides a classification of what we consider are the aims for improving reputation. Section 4 describes our proposal for a federated reputation system and how the reputation values can be calculated. Section 5 shows how trust can be derived within a federation by using the federated reputation system. Section 6 concludes the paper and outlines the future work.

2   Related Work

There are several reputation systems running in actual systems. Many of them are listed on the Reputations Research Network site[1]. Some are used to aid people to decide whether a seller is reliable or not; others to judge whether a book is worth reading; others are used to order news according to their relevance. Even though they use different measures for reputation all of them follow the same target: to improve the user experience.

According to Resnick [27], a working reputation system must have at least the following three properties:

1. Entities must be long lived, so that with every interaction there is always an expectation of future interactions.
2. Feedback about current interactions is captured and distributed. Such information must be visible in the future.
3. Past feedback guides buyer decisions. People must pay attention to reputations.

The third principle is focused on an e-commerce scenario, although changing buyer by user of a service provider, makes it perfectly understandable . None of these properties is exempt of difficulties. One of the main risks is the use of pseudonyms, which allows one single user having multiple online identities, making thus difficult the computation of a unique reputation value for this user.

---

[1] http://databases.si.umich.edu/reputations/index.html

A reputation system is more effective when there are some incentives for maintaining a good reputation level and when it is difficult to get rid of bad ratings (e.g., by creating a new account). In [16] some systems are mentioned, such as Epinions, which offer a reward to members who try to maintain a good reputation; Ebay, where the reputation itself is the reward and influences future sells; or Advogato which is non profit oriented and there is no reward, it is only the ego of the members what leads them to improve their reputation.

Another important factor in a reputation system is time. Timeless reputation systems consider all reputation values as if they were gathered in the same instant, whereas time aware reputation systems will use the time instant when the reputation value was gathered in order to adjust it and modify the final reputation value. However, some authors have realised that time can influence trust. Thus, in [12] the authors mentioned that trust is a very dynamic phenomenon evolving in time and having a history. In [17] a dynamic trust model for mobile ad-hoc networks is introduced. Another trust model that takes into account past trust history of users is [3]. Herrmann [15] also considers the influence of time on trust and proposes to use cTLA (compositional Temporal Logic of Actions [14]) as a method for modelling and verifying trust mechanisms. One of the latest approaches to consider time as a parameter is that presented in [2]

As we mentioned above, there are many factors that define a reputation system. Among those factors are also the ones identified by Jeff Ubois [31]:

- **Participants.** Who is rating whom? Is the system customer-about-buyer, or peer-to-peer? Do the users that provide feedback have reputations themselves? Are they known or anonymous?
- **Incentives.** Are the participants explicitly taking part in a reputation system, or are they performing 'normal' tasks such as writing a newspaper article or offering advice in a Usenet group?
- **Criteria.** What issues matter to the users? Do they care about prompt shipping or about product quality? That is, what factors go into calculating a reputation: numeric feedback from counterparts to a transaction, observed behaviour, seals and credentials, press coverage, etc.?
- **Access and recourse.** Who can see the data, and who can change it? Who gets to know about that change? Who knows about who has rated whom? Can someone respond to a reputation he is assigned? Can an opinion be corroborated?
- **Presentation and tools.** Offline reputation is rich and nuanced: people can use all five senses to determine reputation. Online users can only see and interact with data points. With what tools can users interact with and filter data? To what extent is the data abstracted or aggregated?

Several research initiatives are working on the reputation field. Some of them are, for example, the Task Force on European Middleware Co-ordination and Collaboration (TF-EMC2) [29], under the auspices of the TERENA Technical Programme. Its main objective is to promote the development and deployment of open and interoperable middleware infrastructures among national and regional research and education networking organizations and academic and research institutions.

The European Network and Information Security Agency (ENISA) is also highly interested in reputation and how it could be handled in online communities. The First position paper [8] presents, as its tenth technical recommendation, the use of reputation techniques, quoting: "Encourage the Use of Reputation Techniques". The second position paper [9] aims to provide a useful introduction to security issues affecting reputation-based systems by identifying a number of possible threats and attacks. It also provides some links to Identity Management. It mentions as the eighth recommendation the following: "Encourage Research into a standardization of Portable Reputation Systems" and emphasize the need for a standardized Transport Mechanisms for Reputation Data. However, none of these proposals tackle the issue of aggregated or federated reputation systems. The work presented in [23] deals with the problem of reputation systems for federations of online communities while taking into account privacy preserving issues.

There is no a uniform way to build reputation, however the project Venyo [32], released recently, tries to build a unified reputation value of a user who is a member of different systems. Also the OASIS Open Reputation Management Systems (ORMS) TC [19] is leading towards this direction. The aim of this TC is to develop an ORMS that provides the ability to use common data formats for representing reputation data, and standard definitions of reputation scores. However, they do not intend to define algorithms for computing these scores, which is in our opinion an interesting open issue. This topic has also captured the attention of some identity federation solutions such as OpenID [21]. There is a proposal to extend OpenID in order to support exchange of reputation data [26].

3   Aims for Improving Reputation

Reputation helps to extrapolate the behaviour of a user in order to predict what these behaviours will be like in future actions carried out by such a user. Reputation is not a well defined concept as there is not a standard definition or way to measure it. In different scenarios the reputation of a user might have different meanings and can also be computed differently. Reputation is a rather global and subjective concept that depends on different factors such as the context where the user is performing the actions and the nature of these actions. Another important factor to take into account is the aim that leads users to improve their reputation, which might differ depending on their interests or the nature of the application and its context. It might be difficult to gather all the possible aims that lead a user to perform in order to improve his/her reputation. Below we provide a possible classification which we consider covers some of the most relevant aims for improving reputation. These classification has come out mainly as a result of matching the observation of the behaviour of the systems, more precisely, of the users of these systems.

Profit. A higher reputation will directly provide more profit to the user. This is the model followed by eBay [7]. eBay is a popular online auction site where practically anyone can sell almost anything at any time. In eBay, the feedback represents a person's permanent reputation as a buyer or seller on eBay. It is built based on comments and ratings left by other eBay members who have sold or bought items to or from the member who has to be rated. There are three types of feedback ratings: positive, neutral and negative. The sum of these feedback ratings are shown as a number in parentheses next to the User ID. This feedback system has been updated recently with the intention of increasing buyer and seller accountability. eBay has eliminated the ability to produce negative ratings on buyers. Instead, sellers may contact the Seller Reporting Hub of eBay in order to solve disputes. Also neutral ratings will not be taken into account. Thus, suspended buyers can no longer negatively impact on a seller's record.

Reward. A higher reputation will provide a reward to the user. This is the model followed by Epinions [10]. Epinions is a web site where members can write reviews, as well as other type of opinions. To post a review members must rate the product or service on a rating scale from 1 to 5 stars, one star being the worst rating, five stars being the best. For several years now, all opinions also come with a brief Pros and Cons section and a 'The Bottom Line'. In Social Science a rating scale is a set of categories designed to elicit information about a quantitative attribute. Epinions offers an 'Income Share' which ostensibly rewards reviewers for how much help they have given users on deciding to purchase products. All members can rate opinions by others as 'Off-Topic' (OT), 'Not Helpful' (NH), 'Somewhat Helpful' (SH), 'Helpful' (H), and 'Very Helpful' (VH). Opinions shorter than 200 words are called *Express Opinions* and rated 'Show' (S) or 'Don't Show' (NS). Members can also decide wether to 'trust' or to 'block' (formerly known as 'distrust') another member. All the trust and block relationships interact and form a hierarchy known as the Web of Trust. This Web of Trust (WOT) is combined with ratings in order to determine in what order opinions are shown. The order members see depends on their own ratings and their own trust and block choices. The order a visitor sees is determined by a default list of members a visitor supposedly trusts. The Web of Trust formula is secret.

Fear to retaliation. This could be considered as a negative version of the previous bullet. In these cases if users act in such a way that cause negative effects on the site, and therefore, their reputation values decreased to certain threshold, they might be punished by the site administrators by reducing their privileges or access rights, or sometimes even by expelling them from the site.

This happens for instance, in forums. If the contents of the comments submitted by a certain user are not appropriate this user might be banned from the forum. This means this user will not be able to post any more comments for a certain amount of time. In case he repeats his behaviour the user can be expelled from the site.

World of WarCraft [20] is an online gaming community where fear of retaliation is an issue to users. Users with a low reputation in a given faction will be attacked on sight. Thus, keeping a high reputation will keep the user safe.

Ego. A higher reputation might not rovide any profit to the user, but a higher status in the community and maybe some privileges not related to profit. This is the model followed by Advogato [1]. Advogato is an online community site dedicated to free software development, created by Ralph Levien. It describes itself as 'the free software developer's advocate.' Advogato was an early pioneer of 'online diaries', which later became known as blogs, and one of the earliest social networking web sites. Advogato combined the most recent entries from each user's diary together with a single continuous feed called the *recentlog*. Many high profile members of the free software and open source software movements are or have been users of this site.

The motivation behind Advogato was to try out in practice Levien's ideas about attack resistant trust metrics, having users to certify each other in a kind of peer review process and use this information to avoid the abuses that plague open community sites. Levien observed that his notion of attack resistant trust metric was fundamentally very similar to the PageRank [22] algorithm used by Google in order to rate articles interest. In the case of Advogato, the trust metric is designed to include all individuals who could reasonably be considered members of the Free Software and Open Source communities while excluding others.

It is worth to mention that we have identified these four factors as important factors that influence reputation, however, there could be others.

This distinction can help understanding the distinct existing mechanisms for building trust based upon reputation. The Reward model can be seen as an intermediate model between the Ego and the Profit models, and can be applied to any kind of community. One of the main difficulties when defining a reputation system is the definition of the mechanism for aggregating reputation values from different interactions. Some sites like Amazon [4] use the average. Other factors such as the value of the interaction and the reputation of the user providing the feedback could also be taken into account.

One way to classify reputation systems could be according to the aims that lead users to improve their reputation (as mentioned above). Another way could be according to the way reputation is computed, differentiating between centralized reputation systems where reputation is stored, updated and made available to other users in a central server; and distributed reputation systems where reputation is stored, distributed and usually computed on demand by collecting reputation values from the distributed system.

The importance of analyzing the aim for improving reputation resides in the relevance of the respective score. We are interested in aggregating reputation values from different sources and then investigating how to define the weights associated to them. A reputation value will be more valuable when the aim of the user for improving it becomes crucial for his interests.

We could represent these four factors in a two dimensional axis as depicted in Figure 1. The semi-axis correspond to the four factors we have proposed as an influence on reputation.

These are

$$(Ego, Reward, Fear, Profit)$$

Then, each system represented in the axis will have four vertices associated to it, which are $(e, 0)$, $(-f, 0)$, $(0, r)$ and $(0, -p)$, where e is the coordinate for Ego, f is the coordinate for Fear, r is the coordinate for Reward and p is the coordinate for Profit. Each of them represents the level of influence of the particular aim in the overall reputation of the system. If these vertices are connected we obtain a polygon that represents the reputation aims of the system. In order to make this representation homogeneous or normalized the addition of all the 'measurements' should be 1. These 'measurements' depend on the way reputation is computed in the system and they should be defined by the system itself. Note that the position of these factors in the axis does not mean they are conflicting concepts.

If we observe two different systems with clearly different aims such as Advogato and eBay we can provide an example of this graphical representation (see Figure 1). We can put in relevance that for the Advogato site the Ego factor is of a high influence whereas it is of a very little influence for the case of eBay (as we mentioned above). Thus, as eBay is a mainly Profit oriented site, this is reflected in the corresponding axis of the Figure.

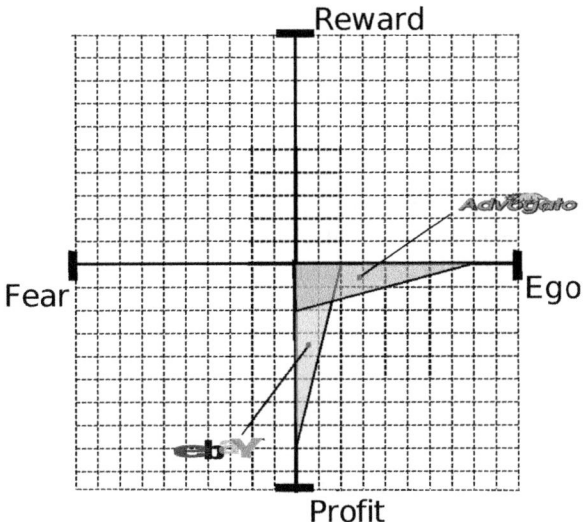

Fig. 1. Dimensions of Reputation

Each reputation value is associated to the above defined dimensions by means of the *Reputation Definition Vector*. Note that we used for our example as a base for the reputation definition vector $(Ego, Reward, Fear, Profit)$ but there might be others that can be used for this purpose.

Definition 1 (Reputation Definition Vector - RDV). *The vector that has as coordinates each of the relative weights for the given reputation base is called a Reputation Definition Vector. A reputation definition vector is a vector $\bar{v} = (v_1, \ldots, v_n) \in [0,1]^n$ such as*

$$\sum_{i=1}^{n} v_i = 1$$

4   Federated Reputation System

The reputation engines maintained by some networks depend very much on the context of the network such as social communities, eBay or some engine proper of a specific company that carried out a specific task (see [16] for a survey on reputation engines). Assuming there are different reputation evidences for a user but in different contexts, we might be interested in obtaining a unique value as an overall of the different reputation values. This can not be as simple as adding these evidences as they were obtained in different contexts. We should find a 'similarity' among these evidences in order to be able to compute a reputation value for a different context.

Federated reputation systems are raising some interest in the area of online communities and services, however, the development of federated reputation systems is still in its inphancy. There are already existing approaches that aim to build a unique reputation from different reputation sources. In [23] the authors set the preconditions for designing an interoperable reputation system for online communities. A similar approach is followed in [6] where the author tries to solve the problem of free-riding in BitTorrent by using reputation. He considers that any BitTorrent network behaves as a federation and calculates the reputation within the federation. Venyo is another attempt to create a kind of a federated reputation system. Venyo [32] is an organization that offers a universal online reputation service. The reputation is expressed in the form of a personal reliability index - the Vindex^{TM}- which is based on the evaluation by the community of the user's web contributions such as blog posts, pictures, videos, etc. Users registered at Venyo link their Venyo profile to the identities they use in the sites used as a source of reputation.

Our approach is slightly different. We propose an Identity Federation model where there exists an Identity Provider (IDP). Thus, a user is identified by his/her IDP in any context with a unique identity within the federation. This IDP will keep reputation

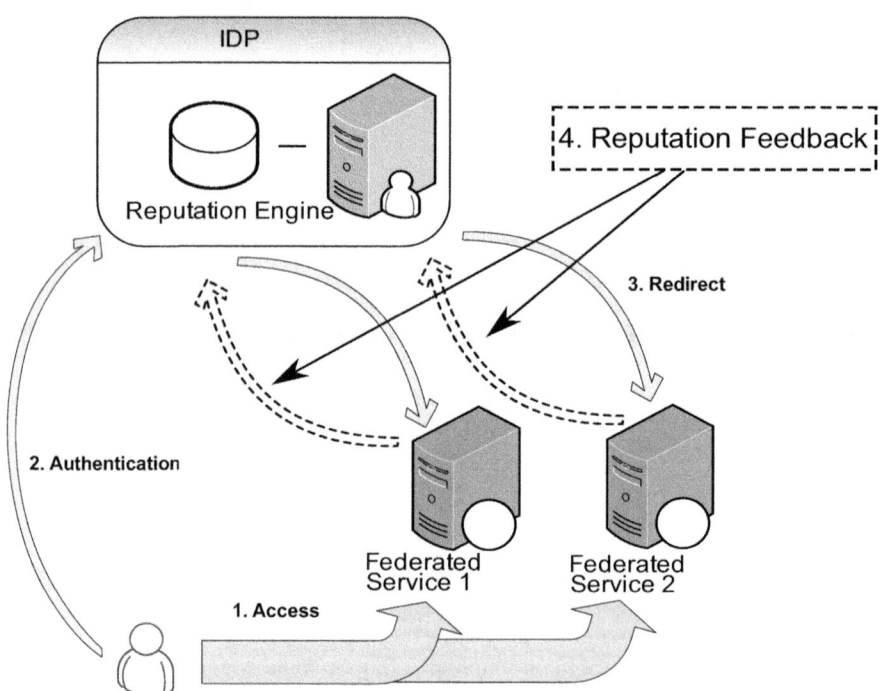

Fig. 2. Federated Reputation Model

of a user by maintaining a Reputation Manager engine. We call this model *Federated Reputation Model*.

Figure 2 shows the architecture of the proposed model. In this model a user will request a service from a Service Provider (SP), either *Federated Service* 1 or 2 in the Figure (step 1). After that, the user will be redirected to its IDP for authentication (step 2). Then, once the IDP has successfully authenticated the user, this will be again redirected to the SP, but with the proper credentials (step 3). This is the usual way Identity Federation systems work, which is represented as a continuous line. However, we propose an extra step, step 4, for our model where the IDP includes a *Reputation Engine* that stores and updates reputation values coming from different service providers. This reputation values can be provided back to the SP as user attributes when requested. This extra step is represented by dashed arrows.

Prior to be able to participate in the feedback system, the SP has to define a proper reputation definition vector that classifies somehow the expected behaviour of the user with respect to reputation within its services. This information is added to the actual metadata needed for setting the identity federation.

Apart from that, the IDP has to maintain a database of reputation values. This database stores, for each user, the reputation that such a user holds in each of the SPs that have provided reputation feedback about such a user.

4.1   Computation of the Federated Reputation

Let us assume a scenario where different service providers might hold some information about reputation of a user, u, in the identity federation that is managed by the IDP. In our approach the reputation engine is managed within the IDP. The purpose of this engine is to calculate a federated reputation value for users managed by this IDP. This federated reputation value takes into account the reputation history of the users.

Definition 2 (Federated Reputation Value). *The Federated Reputation Value is calculated as*

$$fr_B(u) = \sum_{i=1}^{n} \frac{r_{A_i}(u)w(A_i,B)}{\sum_{i=1}^{n} w(A_i,B)}$$

where

- *n represents the number of service providers that feed the IDP with reputation information about user u,*
- *$r_{A_i}(u)$ is the reputation value stored for user u regarding service provider A_i and*
- *$w(A_i,B)$ is the weight assigned to how 'similar' or 'close' the different service providers, A_i, are to B .*

The most important parameter of the previous formula is the weight that measures the similarity of two SP with regard to the aim of their users to improve reputation. This weight ranges from 0 to 1 where 0 is assigned when two service providers are not related at all and 1 when they share the same aim. Then, when computing the federated reputation, all the reputation values coming from irrelevant SPs (i.e. those which are not similar at all to the target service provider) will not be taken into account as their weight will be 0.

In Figure 1 we showed a two dimensional representation of the reputation definition vector (RDP), which is indeed a four dimensional vector. This representation helps us decide whether two services have a common aim for reputation by looking at the quadrilaterals that represent both services, but does not help us giving a precise measure for this similarity. For this purpose we can use the norm in $\mathbb{R}^4$. Let us assume that the reputation definition vector of the target SP, B, is represented by v_0 and that v_i represents the reputation definition vector of the SP A_i. Then, the similarity weight is calculated as follows:

$$w(A_i, B) = 1 - \|\bar{v}_i - \bar{v}_0\| \tag{1}$$

Thus, as expected, if a RDV of a service provider is close to the one of the target service then $\|v_i - v_0\|$ is close to 0 and, therefore the similarity weight i.e., $w(A_i, B)$ will be close to 1.

It is difficult to show how distances work in a four dimensional space, but if we focus on two of the coordinates of the reputation definition vector, the situation could be depicted in Figure 3.

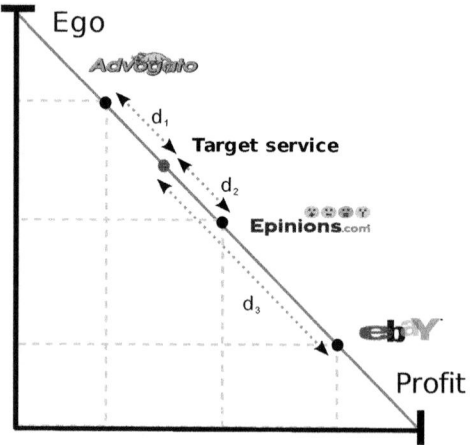

Fig. 3. Distances between Reputation Definition Vectors

In Figure 3 we have represented three reputation definition vectors for three services: Advogato $(0.2, 0.8)$, eBay $(0.8, 0.2)$ and Epinions $(0.5, 0.5)$. We have subjectively considered Advogato to be more Ego oriented, whereas eBay can be considered more profit oriented. Regarding Epinions we could say that it is neutral with regards to those two factors. The actual reputation definition vectors have to be provided by the service provider. Here we only provide an example. There is also a fourth service provider that is our target service provider with a reputation definition vector $(0.3, 0.7)$.

In order to compute the federated reputation value for the target service provider we need to compute first the similarity weights:

- $w_1 := w(Advogato, Target) = 1 - d_1 = 1 - \|(0.2, 0.8) - (0.3, 0.7)\| = 0.86$
- $w_2 := w(Epinions, Target) = 1 - d_2 = 1 - \|(0.5, 0.5) - (0.3, 0.7)\| = 0.72$
- $w_3 := w(eBay, Target) = 1 - d_3 = 1 - \|(0.8, 0.2) - (0.3, 0.7)\| = 0.30$

Let us assume that two users, u_0 and u_1, have the following reputation values 0.8 , 0.5 and 0.3 for u_0 and 0.3 , 0.5 and 0.8 for u_1 in Avogato, Epinions and eBay respectively.

Then, the federated reputation values of these two users in the target service provider are,

$$f_B(u_0) = \frac{0.8 \cdot 0.86 + 0.5 \cdot 0.72 + 0.3 \cdot 0.3}{1.88} = 0.6$$

and

$$f_B(u_1) = \frac{0.3 \cdot 0.86 + 0.5 \cdot 0.72 + 0.8 \cdot 0.3}{1.88} = 0.45$$

As expected, user u_0 whose reputation in the closer providers, i.e. Advogato and Epinions was better than the reputation of u_1, obtains a better federated reputation value for the target service B.

The reputation value computed in Definition 2 can be used as an initial reputation value when the user first accesses a new service or as a reputation value for services without a reputation engine. In any case, the federated reputation value is an estimation of the expected behaviour of the user. This estimation will be more accurate when all the available information for the computation corresponds to very close service providers. The accuracy of this estimation can be measured by the mean of the distances of all the observations. In the example above the accuracy of the estimation is as follows,

$$\frac{w_1 + w_2 + w_3}{3} = \frac{1.88}{3} = 0.62$$

There might be other alternatives in order to obtain the federated reputation value, however we believe the approach we follow has a good balance between expressiveness and complexity.

The reputation engine might incorporate mechanisms to filter out reputation values that come from service providers that are only marginally related. This will make the federated reputation function more robust. Thus, in the example above we could apply a filter that only considers as useful those values of w_i such as $w_i > 0.5$. Then, only w_1 and w_2 are the considered values and the value assigned to eBay is not considered as a relevant service provider.

Then the new federated reputation values of these two users in the target service provider are,

$$f_B(u_0) = \frac{0.8 \cdot 0.86 + 0.5 \cdot 0.72}{1.58} = 0.66$$

and

$$f_B(u_1) = \frac{0.3 \cdot 0.86 + 0.5 \cdot 0.72}{1.58} = 0.39$$

The value for user u_0 has been increased as the filter ruled out a low reputation value whereas the value for u_1 has been decreased as the one removed after applying the filter was a high reputation value.

The accuracy of the estimation is in this case

$$\frac{w_1 + w_2}{2} = \frac{1.58}{2} = 0.79$$

which has been increased.

Another parameter useful for estimating the robustness of the federated reputation value is the number of evidences taken into consideration. We have to find a balance between accuracy, defined as a mean of the weights, and the number of evidences used for the computation of the federated reputation value.

5   Building Trust from Federated Reputation Systems

The ultimate purpose of the introduction of the Federated Reputation system presented in Section 4 is to build trust of the members of the federations. We believe this way of building trust can be useful when users can interact among them.

5.1   Site to User Trust

Federation of identities has been an issue in the past few years. Some of the proposals that aim at achieving Identity Federations are Higgins project [13], Windows CardSpace [5], Shibboleth [28] or OpenID [21]. This way, a user does not necessarily need to perform a registration process in each site but the identity of the user can be transferred somehow from one member to the federation to another. This concept is also related to the single sing-on feature.

Unfortunately, none of the proposals mentioned above provide a link to the reputation systems that may be running on the user central registration site or even on the federated sites. It is true that the reputation on the central registration site might be transferred as a user attribute but the reputation obtained on the federated sites is not considered in any way.

5.2   User to User Trust

Sometimes it is difficult to decide who to trust. It is even more difficult when we use second hand information for the entity to be trusted. In those cases we can use information regarding to the reputation of users in order to decide whether to trust them or not. Moreover, we could, after that, trust their trustees (or users they trust) following recommendations. This procedure will help expanding our trust circle. This is specially useful when the SPs are social communities. In these cases users can interact among them and therefore the exchange of reputation values can take place without having to necessarily do it through the SP.

It is difficult to derive a trust value only based on reputation. Normally, reputation is linked to some kind of activity and we may wonder whether to trust a user regarding to a different and independent context. In case there is not a reputation value related to the context we are dealing with, we have to first consider the reputation of the user out of the context by combining values from different and heterogeneous contexts (see

Section 4.1). This way we detach the context from the reputation value. Moreover, if we apply the method introduced in the aforementioned section we can assign an appropriate weight to all the reputation values accordingly and therefore, we can derive a better trust value for this user.

6   Conclusions and Future Work

In this paper we have introduced a federated reputation model that can be used in order to derive trust. Besides the usual way Identity Federations work, we propose to add an additional step to them in such a way that once the identity of the users have been provided by the IDP to the SP, the last one could also provide the IDP with additional information about the reputation of a given user that will be maintained by the IDP. The reputation values are stored and managed by the IDP by using a reputation manager located in it.

In this scenario users registered with the federation can benefit from the already existing reputation values on their IDP in order to gain access to a given service offered by a SP member of the federation. We have based our approach on the way the factors that influence reputation can be represented. Thus, we allocate these factors into an n- dimensional axis representation, which also allows us to calculate the relationship between the different service providers by calculating the distances between them with respect to these axis.

Using these reputation values trust can be built from user to user and from a site to the user. This latter case might be easier to handle as the scope of reputation is wider. In the user to user interactions scenario we have to solve several issues regarding to the subjectivity of the computed reputation value.

Our model considers that the IDP is a trusted entity and thus, privacy is not a problem for it. However, we are aware that in an ideal solution the reputation manager might not be hosted in the IDP and therefore, some privacy issues may arise. Investigating this other approach could be a very interesting challenge worth to be investigated in the future.

There are several research initiatives in the field of social and online communities that focuses on trust establishment issues where we are interested in applying our model. One of such approaches is the PICOS project[24]. The ideas presented in this work may also help research on the topic of networked enterprisers or alliances, where reputation might help building those alliances in an optimal way, selecting the 'best' reputed companies for each task. One of such approaches is the SPIKE project[25].

References

1. Advogato, http://advogato.org/
2. Agudo, I., Fernandez-Gago, C., Lopez, J.: An Evolutionary Trust and Distrust Model. In: 4th Workshop on Security and Trust Management, Trondheim, Norway. Electronic Notes in Theoretical Computer Science (2008)
3. Almenarez, F., Marin, A., Dyaz, D., Sanchez, J.: Developing a Model for Trust Management in Pervasive Devices. In: PERCOMW 2006: Proceedings of the 4th annual IEEE international conference on Pervasive Computing and Communications Workshops, Washington, DC, USA, p. 267. IEEE Computer Society, Los Alamitos (2006)

4. Amazon, http://www.amazon.com/
5. Microsoft CardSpace,
   http://msdn.microsoft.com/en-us/library/aa480189.aspx
6. Crespo, J.P.: Aretusa: Sistema de reputacion para bittorrent. Master's thesis, Universidad Rey Juan Carlos (2008)
7. eBay, http://www.ebay.com
8. ENISA. Position paper no.1 Security Issues and Recommendations for Online Social Networks
9. ENISA. Position paper no.2 Reputation-based Systems: a Security Aanalysis
10. Epinions, http://www.epinions.com
11. Facebook, http://www.facebook.com
12. Falcone, R., Castelfranchi, C.: The Socio-Cognitive Dynamics of Trust. In: Falcone, R., Singh, M., Tan, Y.-H. (eds.) AA-WS 2000. LNCS (LNAI), vol. 2246, pp. 55–72. Springer, Heidelberg (2001)
13. Freehaven. Freehaven, http://www.eclipse.org/higgins/
14. Herrmann, P., Krumm, H.: A Framework for Modeling Transfer Protocols. Computer Networks 34(2), 317–337 (2000)
15. Herrmann, P.: Temporal logic-based specification and verification of trust models. In: Stølen, K., Winsborough, W.H., Martinelli, F., Massacci, F. (eds.) iTrust 2006. LNCS, vol. 3986, pp. 105–119. Springer, Heidelberg (2006)
16. Jøsang, A., Ismail, R., Boyd, C.: A Survey of Trust and Reputation Systems for Online Service Provision. Decision Support Systems 43(2), 618–644 (2007)
17. Liu, Z., Joy, A.W., Thompson, R.A.: A Dynamic Trust Model for Mobile Ad-Hoc Networks. In: FTDCS 2004: Proceedings of the 10th IEEE International Workshop on Future Trends of Distributed Computing Systems, Washington, DC, USA, pp. 80–85. IEEE Computer Society, Los Alamitos (2004)
18. Mui, L.: Computational Models for Trust and Reputation:Agents, Evolutionary Games, and Social Networks. PhD thesis, Massachusetts Institute of Technology (2003)
19. OASIS, http://www.oasis-open.org/committees/orms
20. World of Warcraft. WOW, http://www.worldofwarcraft.com/info/basics/reputation.html
21. OpenID, http://openid.net/
22. Google PageRank, http://www.mipagerank.com/
23. Pingel, F., Steinbrecher, S.: Multilateral secure cross-community reputation systems for internet communities. In: Furnell, S.M., Katsikas, S.K., Lioy, A. (eds.) TrustBus 2008. LNCS, vol. 5185, pp. 69–78. Springer, Heidelberg (2008)
24. PICOS Project, http://www.picos-project.eu/
25. SPIKE Project, http://www.spike-project.eu/
26. OpenID Reputation Service,
   http://myidproject.net/?openidreputationservice
27. Resnick, P., Zeckhauser, R., Friedman, E., Kuwabara, K.: Reputation Systems. Communications of ACM 43(12), 45–48 (2000)
28. Shibboleth, http://shibboleth.internet2.edu/ (visited on 11/6/2009)
29. TERENA,
   http://www.terena.org/activities/tf-emc2/docs/tf-emc2-tor08-10.pdf
30. Tuenti, http://www.tuenti.com/
31. Ubois, J.: Online Reputation Systems. In: Release 1.0, vol. 21 (2003), http://www.edventure.com
32. Venyo, http://www.venyo.org/
33. Wasserman, S., Faust, K., Iacobucci, D.: Social Network Analysis: Methods and Applications (Structural Analysis in the Social Sciences). Cambridge University Press, Cambridge (1994)

On the Usability of User Interfaces for Secure Website Authentication in Browsers

Massimiliano Pala and Yifei Wang

Computer Science Department
Dartmouth College
6211 Sudikoff Laboratory, Hanover, NH 03755, US
{Massimiliano.Pala,Yifei.Wang}@dartmouth.edu

Abstract. Public Key cryptography has become, in many environments, a fundamental building block for authentication purposes. Although many applications already support the usage of Public Key Certificates (PKCs), the usability of the many security features and their understanding by users is still not fully addressed. Moreover, with the increasing number of services offered via Internet and their impact on many aspects of everyday life of millions of users, the need to address usability of security is compelling. In our work we provide a usability study that highlights the status of the current User Interfaces (UIs) in browsers. In particular we focus our attention on the effectiveness of the messages related to website authentication. We also provide a set of guidelines aimed at improving the user experience and the incisiveness of security-related warnings. A prototype of a user interface is provided and analyzed.

Keywords: Usable Security, Website Authentication, User Interfaces, Anti-Phishing, PKI.

1   Introduction and Motivations

Today, the security of communication over the Internet is a fundamental aspect of online browsing that every user has to deal with. Users rely on Internet provided services for many everyday tasks. On-line banking, Internet shopping, and managing bills or credit-card payments are examples of the many services that people utilize every day. But what do users know about security, authenticated connections (SSL/TLS) or digital certificates ?

On the client side, user authentication is mostly performed by using passwords, personal identification numbers (PINs) or other technology aimed to help humans [13] in remembering secrets (eg., OpenID [2]).

No matter what the user authentication method is, a secure (encrypted and authenticated) connection is required to guarantee the protection of exchanged information between the client and the server. Our work focuses on the effectiveness of security messages in browsers related to the authentication of secure (SSL/TLS) connections to web servers.

F. Martinelli and B. Preneel (Eds.): EuroPKI 2009, LNCS 6391, pp. 239–254, 2010.

Motivations. Since the effectiveness of security depends on its ease of use and users' understanding of security information and features, it is important to comprehend how users perceive security. In particular, it is important to know if the current User Interfaces (UIs) are well understood by experienced and inexperienced users when it comes to trust decisions about the security of connections to web servers. It is also important to understand if users utilize the browsers' security features and if they comprehend the underlying technology (PKIs) and usage logic that stem from assumptions made by security professionals and application developers.

Paper Organization. In Section 2 we explore the related work and we provide a description of the basic concepts behind the word "Usability". In Section 3 we describe current interfaces of the most used browsers (relevant to our study). The performed experiments and methodology are reported in Sections 4 and 5. Section 6 describes the proposed solution to improve usability of the browsers' interfaces. Finally Section 7 summarizes our conclusions and describes the future work.

2   Related Work

One important aspect that is often neglected in security (and particularly in PKIs) is *Usability*. Our work is aimed at improving the effectiveness of authentication information from SSL/TLS connections to provide users with easier, more clear and usable UI design for Internet secure browsing. In this section we provide an overview of related work and the definition of the concepts behind Usability and User Interfaces.

Web Server Authentication

Current research focuses on the authentication of the identity of websites by integrating server-side multimedia aids [9, 4] to allow users to easily identify websites. Besides user-configured security questions and displayed images to fight phishing attacks [3, 12], authentication of websites on the Internet is performed by using Public Key Certificates (PKCs).

To improve online identity assurance and browser representation of online identities, several browser vendors added a special category of certificates to be included in their applications: Extended Validation (EV) certificates. To obtain an EV certificate, a company has to complete a thorough documentation process and verify current business licensing and incorporation paperwork. In addition, the usual verification process to check the authorization from the entity named in the certificate is performed. The CAB Forum [1] introduced EV certificates in order to protect users from "malicious and suspicious activity". Although EV certificates were introduced several years ago, no real benefit for users has been observed. Usability studies conducted at Stanford University and Microsoft Research [10] verified that EV certificates often do not help users identify phishing attacks. They also conclude that instead of moving toward better authentication of certificate holders, browser developers should create an interface that some-how resists picture-in-picture and homograph attacks [5]. Other usability studies have come to similar conclusions [7, 8] about the effectiveness of EV certificates in fighting phishing.

In [6] the authors provide a series of indications on why current phishing at-tacks work. One important point highlighted in this work is the lack of knowledge about SSL authentication and the use of security indicators in browsers.

Our work goes beyond these results by focusing on understanding how to improve the awareness of users when it comes to authentication over the Inter-net. Our research examines how users evaluate the information provided by a browser's UI and how this can be improved in order to optimize the user experi-ence. By leveraging the analysis provided in this work, the design of future UIs can be improved and rendered consistent across applications.

Usability

Usability is a general term that comprises everything related to "ease of use", such as how easily people can use product's controls or displays, for example a tool, a computer display, a mobile device, kitchen appliances, etc. In the com-puter industry, usability is often related to the ease of use in terms of the human-computer interaction.

One of the main ideas behind usability is to design applications and devices with the user in mind. Experts in the security area often argue that security has to be one of the building blocks when designing an application, a protocol or a whole system. This guarantees that the outcome of the development con-siders security as a whole, thus minimizing design flaws that are very common when adding security to existing designs. In the same way usability should be considered in the early stages of a system's design. In fact, putting the user first in the design process results in greater efficiency, reduced learning time, and in general, greater user satisfaction.

To achieve an optimized user experience requires a systematic approach to usability in the design process. This is accomplished through expert empirical usability testing where naive users can be observed to determine what works and what does not work. In this work, we use the results of our usability study to change the design parameters of current user interfaces and provide design guidelines that permit an "optimized" user interface.

3 Security Interfaces in Browsers

In this section we focus on the usability of basic features of connection-based (SSL/TLS) web server authentication in browsers. We focus our attention on the User Interfaces and, in particular, on the messages provided to users that should help them take trust decisions about the authenticity of a web server.

The design of interfaces for website authentication has not changed in a long time. Since the introduction of SSL capabilities in Netscape and Internet

Explorer, the only indicators provided to users when a secure connection was established with a website was a lock present in the browser's interface and, on error, a pop-up indicating that some sort of error was present. The problem with this approach is related to the inability of most users to comprehend the origin of the problem and its propensity to hit the "Continue" button without any understanding about the possible threats.

Some of the constrains that browser vendors claim to have driven the design of past (and current) interfaces are:

- The impossibility to provide reliable messages within the page rendering area. Each aspect of the page is, indeed, fully customizable by the page content (active or static) and messages can be faked by the website.
- The impossibility to provide big icons inside the browser's UI in order to avoid clogging

Only recently some browser vendors introduced changes in their interfaces. The reason for this choice was mainly related to liability of browsers vendors in case of damages caused to users. Therefore, to protect users from phishing websites and security-related issues, some vendors introduced more complex interfaces, adding options and displaying messages directly into the page display area (thus infringing the first constraint). If an authentication error occurs, the website page is prevented from being displayed until a decision is made by the user. Although this approach increased the visibility of security-related messages, some of the information displayed is either too technical or misleading. In the following paragraphs, we provide a summary of the current status of the UIs provided by different vendors and their characteristics related to the authentication of the identity of secure websites.

Internet Explorer. The first browser to adopt a more interactive messaging mechanism was Internet Explorer (IE). Unfortunately the introduction of such messages misled many users. For example, when the server's certificate did not chain back to one of the Trust Anchors present in the browser's certificate store, the displayed message had many users think that the contacted website was not working. The security message is displayed in the page rendering area, but no lock is presented anywhere in the user interface. Furthermore the use of counter-intuitive colors for the displayed icons confused the user about which option to use to continue. A red icon is used to display the "continue with the connection" option, while a green icon was used for the "close this website" option. Moreover the message presents terms like "Security Certificate" and "Trusted Certification Authority" which are mostly unknown to the average user. The same user interface is present in both IE7 and IE8.

Firefox. Recently, Firefox followed the same path that Internet Explorer pioneered by introducing an even more complex and misleading message in case some problems with a secure connection are present. Figure 1 depicts the message presented on Firefox 3.0+. The displayed message suffers from all the problems reported for the Internet Explorer browsers. To proceed on to the contents of

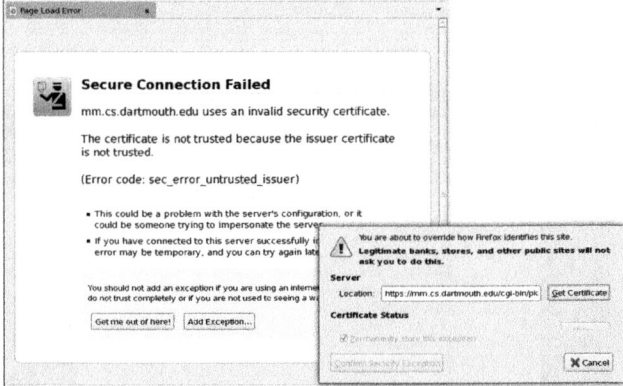

Fig. 1. Firefox UI—Understanding the required actions in order to proceed to view the requested web page is beyond the ability of the average user and of many advanced ones: the interface is misleading and too complex. More importantly, it does not provide any useful information to a naive user.

the website, the user has to go through the adding of a "security exception" which involves downloading the certificate, verify its contents and deciding if the exception should be temporary or permanent. Overall, to proceed to the website a total number of six clicks in different parts of the UI are needed to display the page.

Chrome. Chrome is the new browser offered by Google. Its interface presents clear warning messages on a red background. Although the displayed message is quite long, the presented information is clear. For example, if a problem with the domain name of the website is present (i.e., the URL does not match the one present in the website's certificate) a "This is probably not the site you are looking for!" warning message is displayed in the page display area. Another interesting feature uniquely present in this browser is the use of a red line going across the "https" part of the URL in the location bar on security-related errors.

Other Browsers. Other browsers like Safari, Opera, and Konqueror still provide an approach based on popup messages. Both Safari and Konqueror display one (or more in case of Konqueror) popup message(s) before displaying the page to the user. A problem with this approach is that past the popup message point, the browser interface does not display any permanent warnings that indicate the original problem (eg., certificate not trusted). The Opera browser, besides displaying clear and short messages to the user, also provides a small indicator in the location bar displaying a question mark that the user can click in order to get more information about the security problem. Although it is a first step in the right direction, the indicator remains barely noticeable.

Considerations. When it comes to authentication of a web server's identity by means of X.509 digital certificates, current User Interfaces in browsers do not

Fig. 2. Chrome UI—The provided interface is easier to understand, especially when compared to Firefox and Internet Explorer ones

excel in usability as reported in Section 5. As the authentication of web servers on the Internet is paramount to protect users' privacy and the confidentiality of information exchanged when accessing online services, the need to enable a more consistent UI for security–related interactions is compelling. Our work analyzes the weaknesses of current approaches and propose changes in the UI interface design to provide a more usable SSL/TLS status display approach.

4   Study Methodology

To understand user awareness about the security features related to secure connections to websites, we designed a survey-based usability study. The study required participants to complete simple browsing tasks such as logging into their webmail account or recognizing if a website was malicious or legitimate. Each of these activities was followed by a brief online questionnaire that asked participants about the performed actions.

The participants were seated in front of a computer in a University laboratory. Each participant was asked to come to the laboratory at a set time and perform the tasks during individually supervised sessions. We provided participants with the choice of different computers that offered a range of different Operating Systems (OS) and Browsers. In particular, participants were able to chose their preferred OS and Browser in order to maximize the proficiency of the user and to understand the participant's normal browsing behavior. The list of OSes and Browsers available during the study is reported in Table 1.

The study was divided into two different parts. The participants were asked to use their preferred web browser and follow the indications provided to them via the study website (which was preloaded as the initial page in the provided

Table 1. List of provided Browsers and Operating Systems for the study

| Browser | | Operating System | | |
Name	Version	Windows Vista	Linux	MacOS X
Firefox	3.0.3	✓	✓	✓
Internet Explorer	8.0	✓		
Opera	9.63	✓	✓	✓
Chrome	2.0	✓		
Safari	3.2.3			✓
Konqueror	4.2.3		✓	

browsers). The average completion time for both parts of the study was approximately 20 minutes.

In the first part of this study we asked the subjects to respond to a series of questions in the form of a web-based survey about their general knowledge on security, how they rated themselves in terms of computer usage, and their general understanding of Internet browsing security. In the second part we asked the participants to perform some simple tasks (e.g., logging into personal email accounts) and then respond to some questions related to the performed activities. Participation was voluntary and no money was offered.

4.1 Participants Demographic

23 people participated in the study. The participants were selected from the undergraduate and graduate student population of the computer science department.

The majority of participants (45.9%) were between 19 and 21 years old, another significant portion of participants were between 22 and 25 (34.8%), a small number of participants were less than 18 (8.7%) or between 26 and 35 (8.7%). Only one participant was more than 35 years old. More than half of the participants were undergraduate students (60.9%). The remaining participants were divided between masters students (17.4%) and Ph.D students (21.7%).

We asked our participants to report how often they use each of the available browsers by choosing one of *Always*, *Almost Always*, *Often*, *Almost Never*, and *Never* for each browser. Most of the participants reported to *Always* use Firefox (43.5%), Safari (13.0%), and Internet Explorer (4.3%). Participants reported to *Almost Always* use Firefox (34.8%), Safari (8.7%), Internet Explorer (13.0%), and Chrome (4.3%). Opera, Konqueror and Chrome were reported as being *Never* used by the vast majority of the participants (78.3%), followed by Safari (21.5%) and Internet Explorer (8.7%).

To understand users ability and confidence, we asked the participants to self-rate themselves (i.e., *Expert*, *Experienced*, *Capable*, and *Novice*) on different activities they perform with a computer. The majority of participants rated themselves competent, especially for General computer use (34.8% Expert, 39.1% Experienced, 26.1% Capable) and Internet Browsing (34.8% Expert, 52.2% Experienced, 13.0% Capable). Although no participants rated themselves as *Expert* in *Online Banking*, more than half of the participants rated themselves as proficient in *Online Banking* (47.8% *Experienced* and 26.1% *Capable*). Moreover, most of the participants showed confidence both in *Email Managing* (34.8% Expert, 56.5% Experienced, 8.7% capable) and in *Social Web* (21.7% Expert, 30.4% Experienced, 34.8% capable).

The activities participants felt most confident in were *Internet browsing* and *Email Managing* followed by *Social Web*, *Online Banking* and *Online Shopping* respectively.

5   Experiments

Before starting the actual experiments, we presented the users with information about the aims of the study. In particular, we informed participants that the goal of the project was to understand how users perceive the security features of current browsers in order to fix many of the current problems.

The results of this study are quite interesting in that, differently from previous work, they highlight **the difference between how users perceive the security features related to web authentication and their real browsing habits**. Although all of our participants were well educated and familiar with the usage of computers and the Internet, the results of our study show that the correct utilization of browser's security features by users is quite poor.

In this section we present a more detailed discussion of the different parts of the study, the related experiments, and the collected results.

5.1   Part One: Self Awareness of Security Features

In the first part of the study we asked the participants to answer some simple questions about their general knowledge of the security features present in browsers and their level of confidence in using on-line applications such as Online Banking, OnLine Shopping, and services offered by their own institution (eg., the university). In particular, we focused our attention on the knowledge and usage habits of the security indicators present in browsers.

Results Discussion

The collected answers suggest that user perception about one's action related to the usage of security indicators is, in many cases, different from the real habits of users as evidenced in the analysis of the experiments carried out in the second part of the study.

Security Indicators. In the initial survey participants claimed to look for security indicators in the web-browser interface (82.6% Yes, 17.4% No) more than other indicators present in the page, that is "Secured by ..." logo (34.8% Yes, 65.2% No) or the merchant's logo (26.1% Yes, 73.9% No).

Surprisingly, several participants reported that they "Don't Know where to look" (27.3%) and they "Don't Mind" (27.3%). When asked to report which

Security Indicators they look for to establish if a website is secure, participants reported that they to look for—as their primary choice—the "Lock" in the browser interfaces, the "https" in the location bar followed by "Security Indicators" in the browser interface. As shown in the following section, this self-reported behavior is in contrast with the actual browsing habits we observed in the second part of our usability study. This is due to the fact that embedding security information in several places (and not in the browsing area where the user's attention is drawn) confuses many users.

5.2   Part Two: Browsing Websites

In the second part of the study we asked the users to complete some Internet browsing tasks. We warned them that some of the websites they were going to use might not be the original ones and that they should not complete a task if they did not feel confident to do so.

In order to maximize their confidence in the interfaces provided by the websites we used in our study, we limited the tasks to ones very familiar to our participants. In particular we asked users to perform the following:

(a.) Login into their University Account
(b.) Login into their Webmail Account from the University
(c.) Recognize if a well known online store website[1] was original or not
(d.) Recognize if the provided University Homepage was original or not

For activities related to (a) and (d) we used copies of the original services/website hosted on a phishing server controlled by us, while for (b) and (c) we provided the original URLs.

Results Discussion

This part of the study provided us with valuable information about the real browsing behaviors of participants. In the next paragraphs, we describe each of the performed tasks and the lessons we learned from each one. It is important to notice that we found that the issues related to the browsing behavior of users was not related to a specific browser. In fact, we could not find any statistical correlation between the user's lack of awareness about the security of a website and the used browser.

DND Login. When asked to login into the University account (actually a phishing site we set up) only a small percentage of participants decided not to login (30.4%) thus indicating that most of the checks were not performed by them and that they trusted the look which was similar to the original authentication service from the University. Surprisingly, our copy of the College Authentication System (CAS) was able to successfully fool almost 70% of our participants. This experiment shows that the information about the security of the connection

---
[1] Best Buy.

and the address bar itself is often ignored because the attention of the user is drawn to the page itself. The lack of active messaging about the security of the website (or the lack thereof) allowed us to successfully fool most of our population nevertheless the used service was well known by the participants.

Webmail Login. When asked to login into the Webmail service (original website), almost a fifth of the participants decided not to login because they thought it was a fake website. Besides checking the lock and the URL, many relied on the content of the Webmail page in order to verify its authenticity. One participant recognized the website only after logging in into his account and reading a previously read email. Interestingly enough, two participants reported to verify the authenticity of the website by Googling the Webmail service name and checking to see if the suggested URL[2] matched the one in the location bar. We think that the presence of more noticeable notifications about the successful validation of the identity of the website would provide the users with more confidence when using authenticated services. Moreover, this could lead users to notice the complete lack of authentication, for example when using HTTP, thus increasing the user awareness about the security status of browsing sessions.

Online Store Website. We asked the users to try to verify the identity of the secure server from a well known online store[3]. Because of an error in the configuration of the load balancing service (this is our best estimate based on our network traffic analysis), the server presents a certificate with an error in the server's domain name. We wanted to verify if the users were willing and capable to retrieve more information to understand what the problem was[4]. Less than half of the participants were able to identify that "The security of the website was compromised" (47.5%). The other half of participants had problems in understanding the browser messages, in particular less than a fifth of them (17.4%) thought that the website was not working, a small percentage reported that there was some problem with the Internet connection (8.7%) or they had no idea about what was happening (8.7%). Among the ones that closed the page when the browser's error message appeared, more than half thought that the security was compromised (52.1%) while a noticeable percentage was convinced something was wrong with the connection to the website (30.4%), and others reported that they read the information provided by the browsers but that they were still confused (13.0%). One person reported not to have read all the information while no one reported that reading the information caused more confusion in their decision making process.

6   Proposed Changes: New UI Design Principles

From the results of our study, it is clear that although some users look for website authentication indicators, many do not actively check for the authenticity of the

---

[2] https://webmail.dartmouth.edu

[3] https://www.bestbuy.com

[4] During our search for anomalies we found this to be a quite common error for many websites that use external load balancing services, eg. https://www.irs.gov

website. Some non-invasive but still visually effective mechanism to communicate authentication information about the website is needed.

We believe that a broken SSL connection should not be considered more dangerous than a normal HTTP one and that browsers should not treat them differently. The presence of a security certificate on the server should provide the user with more options when it comes to trust decisions, not less. Exactly as the user is prompted only when sending information over an unprotected HTTP channel, the user should be actively prompted only when harmful interactions with the website are about to take place.

In order to provide the user with a better and more useful notification system, we propose the following changes:

  i. Provide the information where the user attention is actually focused, that is inside the page
 ii. Provide active messages both when the connection is securely established and when there are security-related problems
iii. Provide simple, non-technical and short messages to the users
 iv. Provide easy access to additional information
  v. Provide the information securely

We designed and implemented a prototype of an interface for browser applications that keep these requirements in mind. In the following section, we provide a detailed description of the interface design and the benefits introduced by its usage.

6.1   A Simple, Secure and Usable Interface

We developed an extension for Firefox that complies with the aforementioned requirements. We kept the interface design as simple as possible and we believe that the same interface can be implemented easily on Internet Explorer and other browsers.

When designing the proposed changes to the Firefox interface, we leveraged the possibilities offered by the Geko framework to directly interact with the UI and the ability (largely used by Firefox and Internet Explorer) of the browser to display slide-in messages from the top of the page. This type of message is familiar to users as it is used extensively by Firefox and Internet Explorer to provide information about software download or popup blocking.

By overriding the current error messages from Firefox (3.0+ versions) each time a new SSL connection is established with a website, an active notification is showed to the user.

An important feature of our extension is portability. In fact, by using only javascript functionality, our extension works on any OS because it does not require OS/CPU specific code.

More Usable Messages

Our extension provides a clean interface that appears exactly where and when the information is needed. An example of the designed UI is depicted in Figure 3. In

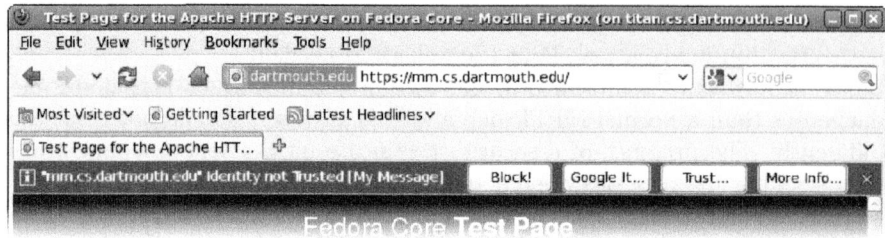

Fig. 3. Prototype UI—Our interface provides (from left to right): a customized logo, the status message, a personalized phrase ("My Message"), and the available options for the reported status. In this case, the security status is "Identity not Trusted", meaning that the certificate used by the web server does not chain back to a Trust Anchor already present in the browser's certificate store.

particular, the extension's message is displayed only when a new secure connection is established with a web-server. The displayed connection status are:

- *"example.domain.org" is Secure, Verified and Trusted.* This message is displayed when the certificate presented by the website is correctly verified (i.e., the validation process is successful and the certificate chains back to a Trust Anchor inside the browser's certificate store) *and* the user has trusted the server by hitting the "Trust.." button in our prototype interface during a previous session to the same site. Moreover the "Block!" button allows the user to block future access to the website.

- *Secure and Verified as "example.domain.org" (Do you trust it?).* This message is displayed when the connection is "secure" as intended by the browsers. This happens when the chain of certificates has been successfully verified and traced back to one of the Trust Anchors present in the browser's certificate store. The user has the possibility to actively setting the Trust level of the connection to the website to "Secure" by selecting the "Trust" button.

- *"example.domain.org" Identity Not Trusted.* This message is displayed when the validation of the certificate presented by the web server is correctly performed but the Trust Anchor the certificate's chain points to is not present in the certificate store. The user is given the possibility to display the additional properties about the connection by hitting the "More Info..." button. The "Trust..." button allows the user to trust the server's certificate while the "Block" button is provided to block future access to the website.

- *Insecure.* This message is displayed when the path validation for the server's certificate fails (e.g., the certificate is revoked or expired, a domain mismatch is detected, etc.). In this case an additional "(WARNING: ...)" message is appended to inform the user about the issue with the server's certificate. The user has the possibility to continue with the navigation in the website, but the message will remain active in the browser window until the user clicks on the "close" button (a cross present in the top-right corner of the slide-in panel).

The new interface addresses the need for displaying the information where the user's attention is actually focused (i.) and it actively informs the user about the status of the connection both on secure and insecure status (ii.). This provides a consistent interface to the user, thus "optimizing" the user experience.

The displayed information is simple and use clear messages about the status of the connection (iii.). This addresses the learnability aspect of usability. The messages are short and the possibility to retrieve more detailed information about the available options is provided in a contextually-aware style (iv.).

Moreover, this new interface is non-invasive in the sense that the user is able to continue to examine other elements of the page contents (as the page is displayed as normal) together with the security information provided in the slide-in message.

6.2   Implementation Details

Our implementation makes use of a `notificationBox` object provided by the Mozilla's Geko UI rendering engine. This type of object can display an image, a text message, and a row of configurable buttons. Moreover the `notificationBox` provides also a configurable priority level setting for the message which determines some of the visual (background) and procedural aspect of the message displaying. To convey more critical messages (i.e., the *Insecure* status) that demand prompt user interaction we use the `PRIORITY_CRITICAL_BLOCK` priority level. By using this setting, although the page is fully displayed, no interaction with its contents is enabled until the user interacts with our notification box. For less critical messages (i.e., *Not Verified*, *Verified* and *Secure*) we use the lower priority `PRIORITY_WARNING_HIGH` level that allows users to continue interacting with the web page.

In order to address the (v.) requirement, we provided a simple anti-phishing mechanism built in into the interface that uses well established authentication mechanisms (personalization) to ensure the authenticity of the origin of the information (the browser itself).

The Anti-phishing Mechanism

Upon installation, the extension requires the user to choose a picture and a phrase that will be displayed in the browser authentication message together with the information about the security status of the connection.

By adopting user-interface customization, we overcome the problem related to the impossibility of providing secure messages within the page rendering area. By providing a simple method to personalize the look of the slide-in message, we efficiently address this concern (v.). Malicious websites will not be able to provide the same interface to users because of its personalization.

Limitations of the Current Prototype

Our implementation, although it offers a good starting point for improving the user experience, suffers from several limitations imposed by the Geko framework and the properties of the `notificationBox` object:

- *Image Size.* The image size is quite small and it can be hard for the user to correctly identify it. It would be desirable to be able to accommodate bigger size images. Because of this limitation, we decided to limit the choice of the customized image to the ones provided in the extension.
- *Customized Text.* Unfortunately it is not possible to customize the look of the notification message in the `notificationBox` object. Allowing the configuration of the text style and its position would provide us to separate more clearly the notification message from the anti-phishing configuration text.

6.3   Preliminary Results

After developing the Firefox extension that implements the prototype, we ran additional experiments to validate our work. Although the results are encouraging, the limited number of participants (10) does not allow us to provide conclusive data at this time. In this section we describe the early results from two experiments aimed at understanding if the new UI is really effective in helping the users to be more aware of implications related to PKI and and network security.

In particular, we asked the participants to install a prototype of our extension[5] and perform two browsing tasks:

- *Verifying the identity of a university's website.* The participants have been asked to recognize if a website was the original homepage from their associated university or a phishing site. The majority of the participants correctly identified the website as a fake (66.7% reported to be sure it was a fake and 16.7% reported they were "convinced" the website was fake). Interestingly, the participants that reported to be sure about their decisions also reported that they read the new UI messages (83.3%) and that they found the provided information to be "really useful" (83.3%). Moreover, the majority of the participants declared to have understood the new UI's messages (83.3% "completely" and 16.7% "pretty much"), while the information provided through the traditional interface (eg., the Lock in the browser interface) were far less understood (25% "completely", 25% "not very well", and 50% did not noticed it).
- *Logging in to the university account.* The participants were asked to login to their university account by following a provided link that actually pointed to a phishing website. This experiment showed that the use of the new UI reduced the percentage of participants willing to login to only 25% (from 70% in our previous experiment). Among the people willing to login, only one person reported himself as "confident" while logging in. The results of this experiment also revealed that the information provided by the new UI was read by the majority of the participants (66.7%). Furthermore, it was reported that even though the new UI was too invasive for some users (12.5%), in each case they still acknowledged that the provided information was useful.

---

[5] An early version of the prototype is available at http://ftp.openca.org/easywarnings

7   Conclusions and Future Work

In this paper we present the results of our usability study on the effectiveness of SSL/TLS security messages in current browsers' UIs. We also introduced several general design principles that address the problems revealed in our usability study. More specifically, our work suggests that security indicators in applications should (a) provide consistent and active messages, (b) provide simple, clear and short information, (c) minimize the impact of the browsing experience to the user and (d) appear where the user's attention is focused.

We implemented a prototype interface that satisfies all of the usability requirements by introducing the concept of personalization to user interfaces in browsers. This novel approach allows vendors to securely provide sensitive information within the page rendering area. Moreover this approach opens up the possibility to remove many of the current indicators present in browsers and to design more clean and simpler interfaces.

Future work will be focused on integrating additional configuration options (e.g., the possibility to select different background colors for different notification messages) into our prototype interface and study its impact on the ability of users to take more effective trust decisions.

We will also investigate how to extend our work to estimate the extent to which user-browser interactions can be securely reduced in both frequency and disruption when it comes to authentication issues via X.509 certificates. We will also focus our attention on how to leverage the integration of new protocols (e.g., PKI Resource Query Protocol [11]) that allow for an increased level of automation in digital certificates management in order to improve the usability of browsers.

Acknowledgments

This work was supported in part by the NSF (under grant CNS-0448499), the U.S. Department of Homeland Security (under Grant Award Number 2006-CS-001-000001), and Sun. The views and conclusions contained in this document are those of the authors and should not be interpreted as necessarily representing the official policies, either expressed or implied, of any of the sponsors.

We also thank Scott A. Rea for providing support in setting up the experiments and the OpenCA community for currently participating in our open internet survey.

References

1. Cab forum homepage, http://www.cabforum.org
2. OpenID Specifications, http://openid.net/developers/specs/
3. Wikipedia. phishing, http://en.wikipedia.org/wiki/Phishing

4. Abdullah, M.D.H., Abdullah, A.H., Ithnin, N., Mammi, H.K.: Towards identifying usability and security features of graphical password in knowledge based authentication technique. In: AMS 2008: Proceedings of the 2008 Second Asia International Conference on Modelling & Simulation (AMS), pp. 396–403. IEEE Computer Society Press, Washington (2008)

5. Cova, M., Kruegel, C., Vigna, G.: There is no free phish: an analysis of "free" and live phishing kits. In: WOOT 2008: Proceedings of the 2nd conference on USENIX Workshop on offensive technologies, pp. 1–8. USENIX Association, Berkeley (2008)

6. Dhamija, R., Tygar, J.D., Hearst, M.: Why phishing works. In: CHI 2006: Proceedings of the SIGCHI conference on Human Factors in computing systems, pp. 581–590. ACM Press, New York (2006)

7. Egelman, S., Cranor, L.F., Hong, J.: You've been warned: an empirical study of the effectiveness of web browser phishing warnings. In: CHI 2008: Proceeding of the twenty-sixth annual SIGCHI conference on Human factors in computing systems,, Italy, pp. 1065–1074. ACM, New York (2008)

8. Herzberg, A., Jbara, A.: Security and identification indicators for browsers against spoofing and phishing attacks. ACM Trans. Internet Technol. 8(4), 1–36 (2008)

9. Hinds, C., Ekwueme, C.: Increasing security and usability of computer systems with graphical passwords. In: ACM-SE 45: Proceedings of the 45th annual southeast regional conference, pp. 529–530. ACM, New York (2007)

10. Jackson, C., Simon, D.R., Tan, D.S., Barth, A.: An evaluation of extended validation and picture-in-picture phishing attacks. In: Dietrich, S., Dhamija, R. (eds.) FC 2007 and USEC 2007. LNCS, vol. 4886, pp. 281–293. Springer, Heidelberg (2007)

11. Pala, M.: The PKI Resource Query Protocol (PRQP). Internet Draft (May 2009), http://www.ietf.org/internet-drafts/draft-ietf-pkix-prqp-03.txt

12. Rabkin, A.: Personal knowledge questions for fallback authentication: security questions in the era of facebook. In: SOUPS 2008: Proceedings of the 4th symposium on Usable privacy and security, pp. 13–23. ACM, New York (2008)

13. Yan, J., Blackwell, A., Anderson, R., Grant, A.: Password memorability and security: Empirical results. IEEE Security and Privacy 2(5), 25–31 (2004)

Validity Models of Electronic Signatures and Their Enforcement in Practice

Harald Baier[1] and Vangelis Karatsiolis[2]

[1] Darmstadt University of Applied Sciences and
Center for Advanced Security Research Darmstadt,
Mornewegstraße 32, D-64293 Darmstadt, Germany
baier@cased.de
[2] Technische Universität Darmstadt,
Department of Computer Science,
Hochschulstraße 10, D-64289 Darmstadt, Germany
karatsio@cdc.informatik.tu-darmstadt.de

Abstract. An electronic signature is considered to be valid, if the signature is mathematically correct and if the signer's public key is classified as authentic. While the first property is easy to decide, the authenticity of the signer's public key depends on the underlying validity model. To our knowledge there are three different validity models described in various public documents or standards. However, up to now a formal description of these models is missing. It is therefore a first aim of the paper at hand to give a formal definition of the common three validity models. In addition, we describe which application in practice requires which validity model, that is we give a mapping of use cases to validity models. We also analyse which standard implements which model and show how to enforce each model in practice.

Keywords: X.509 certificate, signature validity, certification path validation, validity models, certificate revocation.

1 Introduction

Electronic communication disseminates more and more in our private and commercial life. In order to achieve classical security goals like authenticity, integrity, and non-repudiation, asymmetric electronic signatures are used in practice. However, the question if an electronic signature is valid is not as trivial to answer as one may believe at a first glance.

It is a common approach to postulate two properties for an electronic signature to be valid: First, a signature has to be mathematically correct. This means that the mathematical algorithm (e.g. RSA [RSA78], DSA [NT94], ECDSA [ANS05]) verifies the signature successfully using the signer's public key. Second, the signer's public key classifies as authentic and the corresponding private key is under exclusive control of its owner.

In this paper we concentrate on the second aspect of validity of digital signatures, that is we exclude the algorithmic level and concentrate on the semantical

F. Martinelli and B. Preneel (Eds.): EuroPKI 2009, LNCS 6391, pp. 255–270, 2010.

level. The topic we are addressing is therefore whether a mathematically correct digital signature is also valid.

There are different reasons why a mathematically correct signature may be considered to be invalid. For instance, let PubKey_S be the signer's public key which is certified in a public key certificate that has expired regularly at a certain point of time (say e.g. T_e). Does the validation procedure of a signature at time T_v with $T_v > T_e$ using PubKey_S yield the value `valid` or `invalid`? Alternatively, let the certificate of PubKey_S be marked as revoked at T_r. Is a digital signature which is verified at $T_v > T_r$ `valid` or `invalid`? And if there may be different validation answers, which answer is the best with regard to the use case?

In general, the validity of a digital signature depends on the underlying model. If the verifier switches the validity model, a valid signature may become invalid and vice-versa. In different PKI standards, books, and publications three different validity models are mentioned: The shell model (e.g. PKIX working group, [CSF+08]), the modified shell model ([PPR08]), and the chain model ([BNe]). However, to our knowledge, a formal definition is missing. It is therefore a first aim of this paper to formalize the three known validity models.

Our next aim is to provide the technical details for implementing these models and enforcing therefore validity of electronic signatures. We see that the necessary steps require different techniques, like time-stamping, building of certification paths, and collecting revocation information as well as archiving services. We also briefly discuss the effect of the use of the different models on the revocation methods of a PKI.

Additionally, although the validity property of an electronic signature is of fundamental importance for use in practice, there is no discussion, which practical application requires which validity model. Our next contribution is therefore the classification: *Use Case ⟷ Security Goal ⟷ Validity Model*. For instance, in several contexts it is desired to create a digital signature which can be verified in the long term. The current PKI standard that is used in the internet ([CSF+08]) does not allow this. According to [CSF+08], digital signatures can only be validated successfully as long as the certificates in the certificate chain are valid.

This paper is organised as follows: In order to discuss the validity models, we define a sample public key infrastructure and our notation in Section 2. Then, in Section 3 we formalize the three validity models, discuss their details, and give a comparison of them. Section 4 discusses the details of the technical realisation of the three models, that is how to implement them. The effect of revocation on these models is examined in Section 5. The applicability of the models in different contexts is discussed in Section 6. We conclude our paper in Section 7.

2   A Sample Public Key Infrastructure and Notation

In order to discuss each validity model, we consider a sample public key infrastructure (PKI) as follows: Our sample PKI has one root certification authority (CA). This CA is the trust anchor and has issued a self-signed certificate. The root CA has issued two certificates to two other subordinate CAs. The subordinate CAs issue certificates only to end-entities. This setup is depicted in Figure 1.

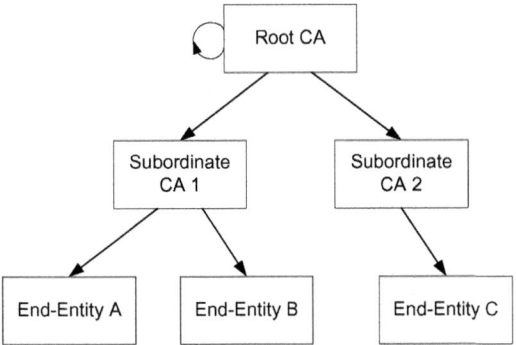

Fig. 1. A sample PKI structure

In Figure 2 sample validity periods of three certificates are given. In what follows, we make use of the following notation: The common PKI standard X.509 ([IT05]) makes use of the two certificate fields `NotBefore` and `NotAfter` to define the validity period of the certificate. By T_i we denote the date as given by `NotBefore` (time of issuance) and by T_e we denote the date as given by `NotAfter` (date of regular expiry). For example, we consider the certificate of the root CA. From Figure 2 we conclude T_i = 2009-01-01 and T_e = 2011-01-01 (for presentation reasons, we neglect the time within a day). We make use of this hierarchy and validity periods for the rest of this work in all our examples.

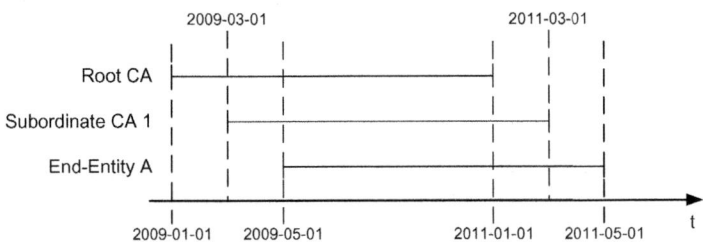

Fig. 2. Certificate of entities and their validity

The validity of a digital signature is of interest for the entity who verifies the signature. We call this entity the *verifier* or *relying party*. The point in time when the relying party verifies the signature is called the *verification time*. We denote the verification time by T_v. On the other hand, the time when a signature is calculated is called *signing time*. If a signature is generated by an end-entity, we denote the signing time by T_s. However, if the signature is calculated by a CA over a certificate, we assume that the signing time is the issuance time and we denote it as above by T_i. We assume that the verification time is always later than the signature time, that is $T_v > T_s$ holds.

We assume that every certificate in the chain has a mathematical correct digital signature. Moreover, the signer is always end-entity A while the verifier is always end-entity C. In addition, signatures calculated by the end-entity over data structures are also mathematically correct. Finally, the certification path starts with the self-signed certificate of the root CA which is the trust anchor for both the signer and the verifier. Note that the validation algorithm specified in [CSF+08, Sec. 6] does not contain the certificate of the trust anchor in the certification path. We further discuss this behaviour in Section 4.

To formalize our presentation we subscript each certificate holder with respect to his location within the certification path. Let N be the length of the certification chain (in our sample PKI, we have $N = 3$). Then we assign the index $k = 1$ to the root CA and the index $k = N$ to an end-entity. We write $\mathsf{Cer}(k)$ for the k-th certificate in the chain. By $T_i(k)$ and $T_e(k)$ we denote the issuance date and expiry date of $\mathsf{Cer}(k)$, respectively. We assume $T_i(k) \leq T_i(k+1)$ for all $1 \leq k \leq N - 1$ (typically this means that a CA certificate is valid when this CA issues a certificate).

Finally, we define two validity periods: First, by Val_S we denote the time period, when an end-entity may generate a valid signature for a document (that is the signature is valid for $T_v = T_s$). Second, by $\mathsf{Val}_V(T_s)$ we denote the time period, when a signature generated at $T_s \in \mathsf{Val}_S$ is verified successfully by the relying party.

3   The Three Common Validity Models in Literature

In this section we introduce formally the three validity models which may be found informally in literature.

3.1   The Shell Model

This model is the one commonly met in most PKI applications. It is used, for instance, in [IT05] or [CSF+08] to verify digital signatures. In this model the *verification time* T_v of a digital signature is the basis for the validation decision.

Definition 1 (Shell Model). *A digital signature is valid at verification time T_v if:*

1. *All certificates in the certification chain are valid at T_v: $T_i(k) \leq T_v \leq T_e(k)$ for all $1 \leq k \leq N$ and no certificate is revoked at T_v.*
2. *The end-entity certificate $\mathsf{Cer}(N)$ is valid at signing time T_s: $T_i(N) \leq T_s \leq T_e(N)$ and it is not revoked at T_s.*

The German Federal Network Agency (GFNA) has published a presentation (see [BNe]) for illustrating the shell model. The GFNA explicitly requires that *all* certificates in the certificate chain are valid at signing time, too. We show, that this is equivalent to our definition. First, let the agency's definition hold. Then all certificates in the chain are valid at signing time T_s, that is our definition holds. Now let property 2 of our definition be true and assume a signature is valid at verification time T_v. Then the property $T_i(k) \leq T_i(k+1)$ for all $1 \leq k \leq N-1$ in the certificate chain and property 2 of Definition 1 imply that *all* certificates in the certificate chain are valid at signing time.

We consider the example of Figure 2 and suppose that the end-entity has signed a document at T_s = 2010-01-01. If the relying party verifies this signature at T_v = 2010-05-05 this signature is classified as valid within the shell model. However, if the same signature is verified at T_v = 2011-02-01, it is considered to be invalid, because $T_v > T_e(1)$, that is the certificate of the root CA is expired.

Note that the validity periods Val_S and Val_V of the shell model are

$$\mathsf{Val}_S = \bigcap_{k=1}^{N} [T_i(k), T_e(k)] = [T_i(N), \min\{T_e(k) : 1 \leq k \leq N\}] \quad \text{and} \quad (1)$$

$$\mathsf{Val}_V(T_s) = [T_s, \min\{T_e(k) : 1 \leq k \leq N\}] \quad \text{for all } T_s \in \mathsf{Val}_S , \quad (2)$$

if no certificate in the chain is revoked. Our sample PKI yields

$$\mathsf{Val}_S = [2009 - 05 - 01, 2011 - 01 - 01] \quad (3)$$

$$\mathsf{Val}_V(T_s) = [T_s, 2011 - 01 - 01] \quad \text{for all } T_s \in \mathsf{Val}_S . \quad (4)$$

We point out that the most prominent standard which uses the shell model (the PKIX standard, [CSF+08]) does *not* require the second property of Definition 1. We assume that this is due to the fact that the typical application of [CSF+08] is verifying the authenticity of a claimed identity during the handshake of an internet protocol. Then one may assume $T_s \approx T_v$, and property 1 of Definition 1 implies property 2. We call this variant of the shell model the *internet shell model*. However, if we abandon this demand, an invalid created signature may become valid. An example of such a signature in our sample PKI is one created by end-entity A at 2009-04-01 and verified at 2010-05-05.

The internet shell model is mostly used by applications that do not store or do not evaluate the signature time. Such an application is the PKIX validation algorithm [CSF+08, Sec. 6]. The signing time T_s is not provided as an input and therefore it is never evaluated. A detailed overview of this validation algorithm is given in Section 4.

3.2   The Modified Shell Model

This model is sometimes called *hybrid model*, too. Although not explicitly stated, it is found e.g. in [PPR08]. In the modified shell model the *signing time* T_s is the basis for the validation decision.

Definition 2 (Modified Shell Model). *A digital signature is valid at verification time T_v if all certificates in the certification chain are valid at T_s: $T_i(k) \leq T_s \leq T_e(k)$ for all $1 \leq k \leq N$ and no certificate is revoked at T_s.*

We consider our sample PKI of Figure 2 and suppose that the end-entity has signed a document at $T_s = 2010\text{-}09\text{-}01$. If the relying party verifies this signature at $T_v \geq T_s$ this signature is always classified as valid within the modified shell model.

In general, the modified shell model has, in contrast to the shell model, the fundamental property that a signature, which is valid at T_s remains valid for all the time. Therefore, the validity period $\mathsf{Val}_V(T_s)$ is always $\mathsf{Val}_V(T_s) = [T_s, \infty[$ for all $T_s \in \mathsf{Val}_S$. It is easy to see that

$$\mathsf{Val}_S = \bigcap_{k=1}^{N} [T_i(k), T_e(k)] = [T_i(N), \min\{T_e(k) : 1 \leq k \leq N\}], \tag{5}$$

if no certificate in the chain is revoked. Our sample PKI yields $\mathsf{Val}_S = [2009\text{-}05\text{-}01, 2011\text{-}01\text{-}01]$.

3.3   Chain Model

The chain model is e.g. illustrated in [BNe]. Unlike the other two models, the dates when signatures are created by each party (end-entity and certification authorities) are affecting the validity of a signature.

Definition 3 (Chain Model). *A digital signature is valid at verification time T_v if:*

1. *The end-entity certificate $\mathsf{Cer}(N)$ is valid at the signing time T_s: $T_i(N) \leq T_s \leq T_e(N)$ and $\mathsf{Cer}(N)$ is not revoked at T_s.*
2. *Every CA certificate in the chain is valid at the issuance time of the subordinate certificate in this chain: $T_i(k-1) \leq T_i(k) \leq T_e(k-1)$ and the certificate $\mathsf{Cer}(k-1)$ is not revoked at $T_i(k)$ for all $2 \leq k \leq N$.*

Again, we have a look at our sample PKI. If the end-entity signs documents at 2010-09-01, 2011-02-01, or 2011-04-01, all signatures are verified successfully within the chain model.

The chain model has the same fundamental property as the modified shell model: Once a signature is valid at signing time T_s it remains valid for all the time. Thus, again the validity period $\mathsf{Val}_V(T_s)$ of the chain model is $\mathsf{Val}_V(T_s) = [T_s, \infty[$ for all $T_s \in \mathsf{Val}_S$. Additionally, the signing period Val_S is

$$\mathsf{Val}_S = [T_i(N), T_e(N)], \tag{6}$$

if the end-entity certificate $\mathsf{Cer}(N)$ is not revoked. Our sample PKI yields $\mathsf{Val}_S = [2009\text{-}05\text{-}01, 2011\text{-}05\text{-}01]$.

We point to an interesting property of the chain model: If the end-entity certificate $\mathsf{Cer}(N)$ is issued and $\mathsf{Cer}(N-1)$ is valid at issuing time $T_i(N)$, a revocation of a certificate $\mathsf{Cer}(k)$ $(1 \leq k \leq N-1)$ does not affect the validity of a signature generated by the end-entity.

3.4   Additional Constraints

Certificate policies of various public key infrastructures do not allow the issuance of certificates with validity longer than their issuer's certificate, that is the policies require $T_e(k+1) \leq T_e(k)$ for all $1 \leq k \leq N-1$ (see for example [Tha06, Sec. 6.3.2]). Also some applications, like Certificate Services [Tec05], prohibit this behaviour.

In this case Val_S is determined for all models exclusively by the validity period of the end-entity certificate $\mathsf{Cer}(N)$. More precisely, we have $\mathsf{Val}_S = [T_i(N), T_e(N)]$. This is because the certificate $\mathsf{Cer}(N)$ is then the first certificate to expire and in all models the end-entity is not able to produce any valid signatures after the expiration of its certificate. For the shell model the $\mathsf{Val}_V(T_s)$ is limited by the expiration date of the end-entity certificate, that is $\mathsf{Val}_V(T_s) = [T_s, T_e(N)]$.

3.5   Comparison of the Models

We end this section with an overview of the periods Val_S and Val_V for each model (see Table 1). From this table the differences among the three models regarding these periods can be seen. The shell model and the modified shell model have a shorter period for producing a valid signature than the chain model. The modified shell model and the chain model have a longer period for verifying a signature. For this reason these two models are important for the long-term verification of digital signatures.

Table 1. Overview of the periods Val_S and Val_V for all validity models

	Shell Model	Modified Shell Model	Chain Model
Val_S (from)	2009-05-01	2009-05-01	2009-05-01
Val_S (until)	2011-01-01	2011-01-01	2011-05-01
$\mathsf{Val}_V(T_s)$ (until)	2011-01-01	∞	∞

Note that the necessity to verify signatures for a long period by using the shell model exists. To address this topic the *private key usage period* extension was specified in the previous PKIX specification [HPFS02, Sec. 4.2.1.4]. This extension is not specified at all in the newer PKIX specification [CSF+08]. With this extension it is possible to limit the signing period for the private key that corresponds to the public key in the certificate. Therefore certificates could be issued with a long validity period (for example 50 years) but a short private key usage period (for example 2 years). Therefore it is possible to validate a signature using the shell model for 50 years but it is possible to sign only for two years. However, this approach is alone not sufficient for implementing the other two models. As we see in the next section, various techniques are necessary for realising the verification of electronic signatures in the long-term.

4 Technical Implementation of the Models

In this section we show how to put each of the three validity models into practice. We focus on the modified shell model and the chain model as implementations of the shell model are well-known. At the end of this section we discuss alternative implementation algorithms.

4.1 Shell Model

The shell model is implemented by most applications. Its implementation is based on the basic path validation algorithm described in Section 6 of the PKIX standard [CSF⁺08]. Most implementations ignore the signing time T_s. They only consider the special case of the shell model for which the signing time and the verification time are the same, i.e. $T_s \approx T_v$. The implementation details of the PKIX validation procedure are well-known and we do not discuss this further.

4.2 Modified Shell Model

We propose to implement the modified shell model using the CAdES (CMS Advanced Electronic Signatures) specification. CAdES is an ETSI technical specification [ETS08] and a request for comments [PPR08]. It specifies the mechanisms and the format for electronic signatures that can remain valid for a long period of time. These signatures are called advanced electronic signatures and their format conforms to the Cryptographic Message Syntax specification (CMS, [Hou04]).

There are different types of CAdES signatures defined in [PPR08]. We next introduce the signature types which are relevant for our purposes. First, CAdES assumes that a document is signed with the signer's private key. This is the *basic electronic signature* (CAdES-BES). It is possible to include some attributes which are also signed. For instance the policy according to which this signature should be validated can be included as a signed attribute. This is the *explicit policy-based electronic signature* (CAdES-EPES).

Afterwards this signature is time-stamped (or time marked, but we consider only time-stamping for the rest of this paper). This time-stamp proves that the signature existed before a certain point in time. This is an *electronic signature with time* (CAdES-T).

In order to provide the complete certification path and revocation information, which are necessary to validate the signature, references to this data can be appended to this signature. This is an *electronic signature with complete validation data references* (CAdES-C). It is also possible to include the referenced data itself, which however leads to increasing the size of the signature. This is an *extended long electronic signature* (CAdES-X Long).

Time-stamps are used to protect the references to the required verification data against future compromise (e.g. of a cryptographic key): Either the whole CAdES-C is time-stamped (CAdES-X-Type 1) or only the references (CAdES-X-Type 2). These two types can be combined with the CAdES-X Long signature, which stores all necessary data, producing two new signature types, namely the CAdES-X Long Type 1 and Type 2.

These last two types or the plain CAdES-X Long are finally time-stamped to provide proof of existence before a certain point in time. This is an *archival electronic signature* (CAdES-A). This signature is regularly time-stamped in order to address weaknesses in cryptographic algorithms or keys.

The CAdES specification allows to record the time when a signature is calculated. This is achieved by the first time-stamp. This signature is the CAdES-T. Second, it records all certificates and revocation information, that are necessary for validating a signature, exactly at the point certified by the first time-stamp. This is the CAdES-X Long Type 1 or Type 2 signature which contains a time-stamp over this data. Third, this signature is protected for a long period in time by time-stamping it appropriately before the underlying cryptography becomes weak or broken. Therefore, a CAdES-A signature supports verification according to the modified shell model. Our proposed verification procedure is described in Algorithm 1.

Algorithm 1. Verification for the Modified Shell Model

1: $T_s \leftarrow$ time when a document is claimed to be signed
2: Verify the document signature
3: Verify that the CAdES-T time-stamp matches T_s
4: Verify that the CAdES-X Long Type 1 or Type 2 time-stamp matches T_s
5: Verify the certification path with revocation checking using the data from the CAdES-X Long Type 1 or Type 2 signature
6: Verify the CAdES-A time-stamp is recent enough
7: Output **true** if all verifications are correct, **false** otherwise

---

4.3 Chain Model

We propose to implement the chain model by using CAdES, too. This is due to the fact that CAdES seems to become a broadly accepted standard. However, our algorithm (see Algorithm 2) is more complicated as for the modified shell model. Nevertheless we are not aware of any alternative implementation proposal of the chain model.

We explain our algorithm using our sample PKI from Section 2. In this example three CAdES-A signatures need to be calculated. The first is at 2009-03-01 when the certificate of the subordinate CA 1 is issued. The second is at 2009-05-01 when the certificate of end-entity A is issued. Finally, the third CAdES-A signature is generated at the signing time T_s. The signer (i.e. end-entity A) should include the other two CAdES-A signatures. Therefore, the issuing CA (i.e. the subordinate CA 1) should also deliver to end-entity A (along with her certificate) a CAdES-A for this certificate as well as all other CAdES-A signatures that are necessary for verifying the certification path.

As a general rule CAdES-A signatures should be managed by the certificate holder. In our example, the first CAdES-A signature from 2009-03-01 is managed by the subordinate CA 1. This is because it can be re-used by all subordinate end-entities that need to create a signature which can be verified according to the chain model. The CAdES-A about end-entity A's certificate and the one about the document signature are managed by the signer himself. This eliminates the need that a CA administrates CAdES signatures for each certificate that it issues.

In addition, the first two CAdES-A signatures can be stored along with each signature that end-entity A creates. For example they can be stored as a signed attribute in the CAdES-BES signature. The advantage of this approach is that these signatures are archived within end-entity A's CAdES-A signature and do not need to be independently archived. Our proposed verification procedure for the chain model is given in Algorithm 2.

Algorithm 2. Verification for the Chain Model

1: $T_s \leftarrow$ time when a document is claimed to be signed
2: Verify the document signature
3: Verify that the CAdES-T time-stamp matches T_s
4: **for** $k = N$ to 1 **do**
5:     Extract the CAdES-A signature of $\mathrm{Cer}(k)$
6:     Verify that the CAdES-A time-stamp is near T_s
7:     $T_s \leftarrow T_i(k)$
8:     Verify that the CAdES-T time-stamp of the current CAdES-A matches T_s
9:     Verify that the CAdES-X Long Type 1 or Type 2 time-stamp matches T_s
10:     Verify the certification path of length 1 with revocation checking using the data from the CAdES-X Long Type 1 or Type 2 signature
11: **end for**
12: Verify the CAdES-A time-stamp is recent enough
13: Output `true` if all verifications are correct, `false` otherwise

---

For a CA this means practically that every time it issues a certificate it also needs to create a CAdES-A signature for this certificate. Special PKI protocols that support the issuance of CAdES-A signatures when a certificate is issued, as well as their delivery to the end-entity need to be designed. This creates an extreme workload to certification service providers and time-stamping servers. For this reason performance issues need to be addressed and efficient methods that perform these tasks to be developed.

4.4 Alternative Implementations

The current wide-spread implementation of the shell model is specified in the PKIX standard [CSF+08, Sec. 6]. This algorithm has as input a certification path, the current time which is the time of the validation, information about policies and finally information about the trust anchor.

There are two important and substantial differences of the PKIX verification algorithm to our Definition 1 of the shell model. First, the validity of the certificate of the trust anchor is not considered at all. This is because the PKIX verification algorithm excludes the certificate of the trust anchor from the certification path. The trusted public key and associated key parameters, the algorithm of the key, the name of the issuer, and the signing algorithm (see also [CSF$^+$08, Sec. 6.1.2]) are given as input to the algorithm. These are considered valid and trusted by the verifier and they may be extracted from the trust anchor's certificate.

A second important difference between the PKIX verification routine and our definition is that the PKIX algorithm does not consider the signing time T_s (or it assumes that signing and verification time are identical). Therefore it is possible for users to sign a document, when they do not possess a valid certificate. However, if $T_i(k) \leq T_v \leq T_e(k)$ for all $1 \leq k \leq N$, then the signature may be considered to be valid at T_v according to the PKIX verification algorithm (if no certificate in the chain is revoked).

The PKIX algorithm is implemented by many applications and therefore we modify the PKIX algorithm to verify according to the modified shell model and the chain model. Note that these modifications are on the level of the algorithm. We assume that the certificates and revocation information have been obtained from a reliable source. This source can provide guarantees that this data can be used for the purpose of verifying signatures calculated long before the current date. Moreover, the signing-time of the document is also provided and is trustworthy. The complete and secure technical implementation of those models (without the above mentioned assumptions) has already been given in Sections 4.2 and 4.3.

Modified Shell Model. It is sufficient to set the signing time T_s as input to the PKIX algorithm (instead of the verification time T_v). The rest of the PKIX algorithm remains unchanged. We point out that this modification does not check whether the trust anchor certificate is valid at T_s.

For changing this behaviour the validity period of the trust anchor's certificate needs to be supplied as an additional input in the "Initialization" step of the PKIX algorithm and a check needs to be added. This checks whether T_s is inside the validity period which was supplied as an additional input.

Chain Model. In order to implement the chain model using the PKIX algorithm, four steps need to be taken:

1. The current date/time input of the algorithm is deleted as well as those steps of the algorithm that make use of this variable. A new variable is defined. This is the *validity period*. This variable is initialised with the period between the notBefore and notAfter field values of the trust anchor certificate.
2. In step "Basic Certificate Processing" ([CSF$^+$08, Sec. 6.1.3]) a check is added whether the value of the *validity period* variable contains the date located in the notBefore field of certificate i.

3. In step "Prepare for Certificate i+1" ([CSF$^+$08, Sec. 6.1.4]) the *validity period* variable is set to the period between the notBefore and notAfter field values of certificate i.
4. In Step "Wrap-Up Procedure" ([CSF$^+$08, Sec. 6.1.5]) the *validity period* variable is set to the period between the notBefore and notAfter field values of certificate i. Finally, it is checked whether the *validity period* contains the date of the signature creation (supplied as an additional input).

5   Revocation and Validity Models

In this section we discuss how revocation using a Certificate Revocation List (CRL) affects the validity of electronic signatures within the different validity models. Also two interesting questions in the context of CRLs arise: First, how do we handle certificates in the CRL, which are expired and removed from the CRL? Second, do we need indirect CRLs within the chain model when used for qualified signatures?

For the revocation of a certificate there are two important points in time. The first one is the time when a certificate is publicly known to be revoked. We denote this time by T_r. In a CRL T_r is equal to the CRL field thisUpdate. The second one is the time when a revocation is initiated. We denote this point in time by T_{rd}. This is the revocationDate field of a CRLEntry in the CRL. If this field is not set by the CRL issuer then $T_{rd} = T_r$.

In the Online Certificate Status Protocol (OCSP), these points in time are expressed by the producedAt and thisUpdate fields of an OCSP response, respectively. The time period $[T_{rd}, T_r]$ is sometimes referred to as *revocation latency*. This period should be kept as short as possible. We do not discuss how to keep this time period small or how the point in time T_{rd} is determined by each CA, but rather how this affects the validity of digital signatures.

We examine how revocation of a certificate in a certification path invalidates a signature. We assume that the k-th certificate in the chain is revoked in what follows (remember that T_v denotes the validation time of the signature and $T_r(k)$ the time when the revocation of the certificate becomes publicly known):

- **Shell Model:** If $T_v \geq T_r(k)$ the signature is invalidated, otherwise not.
- **Modified Shell Model:**

$$\begin{cases} T_v \leq T_{rd}(k) & \text{is not invalidated} \\ T_{rd}(k) < T_v < T_r(k) & \text{is not invalidated} \\ T_v \geq T_r(k) & \text{is not invalidated if } T_s < T_{rd}(k) \\ T_v \geq T_r(k) & \text{is invalidated if } T_s \geq T_{rd}(k) \end{cases}$$

- **Chain Model:** For all $1 \leq k \leq N - 1$, the signature is not invalidated if $T_r(k) > T_i(k + 1)$, otherwise it is. For $k = N$:

$$\begin{cases} T_v \leq T_{rd}(N) & \text{is not invalidated} \\ T_{rd}(N) < T_v < T_r(N) & \text{is not invalidated} \\ T_v \geq T_r(N) & \text{is not invalidated if } T_s < T_{rd}(N) \\ T_v \geq T_r(N) & \text{is invalidated if } T_s \geq T_{rd}(N) \end{cases}$$

To simplify the presentation we have assumed that there is no revocation latency when CA certificates are revoked, that is $T_{rd}(k) \approx T_r(k)$ for all $1 \leq k \leq N - 1$.

In all models revocation latency has an impact on the validity of a signature. If $T_{rd} \leq T_v < T_r$, that is the validation time of a digital signature lies inside this period, a signature is not affected at all by the revocation. In the modified shell and chain model a revocation invalidates signatures calculated after the revocation of a certificate, that is $T_s \geq T_{rd}(N)$ and $T_v \geq T_r(N)$. In some applications revocation invalidates signatures only with $T_s \geq T_r(N)$, that is they ignore the time of the revocation. However, we propose to validate a signature taking the revocation date into account when this information is available.

In the shell model all signatures are invalidated after a revocation. This also demonstrates why it is not possible to use the shell model for qualified signatures. Users could just revoke their qualified certificates and invalidate with this action previously calculated qualified signatures.

Let us turn to the first question presented at the beginning of this section. The PKIX specification of revocation lists allows to remove expired certificates from a CRL. Applications that implement the modified shell model without using the CAdES specification or a mechanism with similar functionality may face problems. As we have discussed in Section 4.2 CAdES stores at T_s within its CAdES-X Long signature data needed for validation, like the CRL. However, if the modified shell model is implemented using the PKIX algorithm, the CRL issued near T_s, that lists a certificate in the chain, may not be available. Then, for example, the application uses the CRL issued near the verification time T_v which may not list this certificate if it has already expired.

For illustrating this, consider that end-entity A (or someone else) calculates a signature at 2010-01-01, which may be verified using end-entity A's public key. But assume that the underlying certificate has already been revoked at 2009-12-01. If a client verifies this signature using the modified PKIX algorithm at T_v =2012-01-01 using a CRL issued near T_v the verifier accepts this signature. This is due to the fact that the revoked certificate has been removed from the CRL since it has expired on 2011-05-01. The same effect appears when the chain model is used. However, if these models are implemented using CAdES as proposed in this paper it is safe to remove expired certificates from CRLs.

The second question is to consider indirect CRLs within the chain model for qualified signatures. An indirect CRL is a revocation list with the property that the CRL issuer and the issuer of at least one revoked certificate in the CRL are different entities. Although they are not very common and few clients support their use, they are mandatory when the chain model is used for verifying qualified signatures. The key observation with regard to revocation is that qualified certificates belong by law only to natural persons.

To explain this assertion, we have again a look at our sample PKI. End-entity A can create a valid signature after 2011-03-01 within the chain model, although the certificate of the subordinate CA 1 has expired on 2011-03-01. However, it may be necessary to revoke end-entity A's certificate after this date. For this, a valid subordinate CA certificate is needed. But it may not be possible to renew this certificate since it belongs to a natural person who herself or whose private key is no more available. Therefore, in general revocation within the chain model in the qualified context is delegated to another entity leading to indirect CRLs.

6   Validity Model versus Use Case

In this section we discuss which practical application (use case) of digital signatures requires which validity model. Electronic signatures always ensure the security goals authenticity and integrity: By *authenticity* we mean that a claimed (electronic) identity or the originator of an information is confirmed. *Integrity* denotes that an information is not altered. Both symmetric signatures (Message Authentication Code, MAC) and asymmetric signatures (electronic signatures) guarantee authenticity and integrity. A third security goal in the context of signatures is *non-repudiation*, which means that a third party may be convinced of authenticity and integrity of an information. Non-repudiation may only be achieved by asymmetric electronic signatures, as a MAC grants access to two or more parties to the signature generation key.

It is obvious that non-repudiation implies authenticity and integrity. In order to come up with a relation of use cases and validity models, we distinguish short-term security goals and long-term security goals. Short-term security means that the security goal must be achieved for some seconds, minutes, or at most hours. On the other hand, long-term security is characterised by the fact that the security goal holds for years.

For us, authenticity and integrity (in the absence of non-repudiation) are short-term security goals as only the communication parties have to verify authenticity and integrity. A convenient example is the authentication of browser and web server during the handshake of the TLS protocol [DR08]. Thus both a MAC and an (asymmetric) electronic signature may be used to achieve these goals, that is the shell model as introduced in [CSF$^+$08] is adequate.

However, if non-repudiation (that is long-term security) by each entity in a certification hierarchy is needed, the chain model is appropriate. The reason is that (as described in Section 3.3) once a signature is valid at signing time T_s it remains valid for all the time. A practical example is a contract (e.g. concerning a bargain), which must be verified for years to guarantee legal issues like warranty.

An application of the modified shell model is described in [Res07] for the management of clinical trials. It states: "... *Signed documents can be viewed and validated for long periods into the future as the validation uses the time when the signature was made (and not the current time) when computing the validity of the signer's certificates...*" This is actually an application of the modified shell model in which the signature time is important for the validation of a digital signature. However, requirements deriving from the context of qualified signatures like non-repudiation for each signer, do not apply here. As the modified shell model is easier to implement in practice, it is employed in this case.

Our mapping of use cases, security goals, and validity models is summarized in Table 2.

Table 2. Mapping of use cases, security goals, and validity models

Use Case	Security Goals	Validity Model
Short-term security	Authenticity, integrity	Shell Model
Long-term security	Non-repudiation (full)	Chain Model
Long-term security	Non-repudiation (partial)	Modified Shell Model

7 Conclusions

We addressed the problem of semantical validity of an electronic signature. We formally defined three validity models and discussed their implementation. We analysed various issues that derive from their use in a PKI. Finally we examined which model is appropriate in various scenarios.

Realising the modified shell and the chain model is complex since various issues need to be addressed. Therefore, efficient implementations and PKI protocols that support verification of signatures according to these two models are needed.

References

[ANS05] American National Standards Institute ANSI. X9.62: Public Key Cryptography for the Financial Services Industry: The Elliptic Curve Digital Signature Algorithm (ECDSA) (November 2005)

[BNe] German federal network agency: A presentation on validity models, http://www.bundesnetzagentur.de/media/archive/1343.pps

[CSF+08] Cooper, D., Santesson, S., Farrell, S., Boeyen, S., Housley, R., Polk, W.: Internet X.509 Public Key Infrastructure Certificate and Certificate Revocation List (CRL) Profile. IETF Request For Comments, 5280 (May 2008)

[DR08] Dierks, T., Rescorla, E.: The Transport Layer Security (TLS) Protocol Version 1.2. IETF Request For Comments, 5246 (August 2008)

[ETS08] ETSI. Electronic Signatures and Infrastructures (ESI): Electronic Signature Formats. TS 101 733 V1.7.4 (July 2008)

[Hou04] Housley, R.: Cryptographic Message Syntax (CMS). IETF Request For Comments 3852 (2004)

[HPFS02]   Housley, R., Polk, W., Ford, W., Solo, D.: Internet X.509 Public Key Infrastructure Certificate and Certificate Revocation List (CRL) Profile. IETF Request For Comments, 3280 (April 2002)

[IT05]   Recommendation, X.: 509 ITU-T. Information technology – Open Systems Interconnection – The Directory: Public-key and attribute certificate frameworks (August 2005)

[NT94]   National Institute of Standards NIST and Technology. FIPS 186 – Digital Signature Standard (DSS) (May 1994), http://www.itl.nist.gov/fipspubs/fip186.htm

[PPR08]   Pinkas, D., Pope, N., Ross, J.: CMS Advanced Electronic Signatures (CAdES). IETF Request For Comments, 5126 (February 2008)

[Res07]   Resnitzky, U.: The Directory-Enabled PKI Appliance: Digital Signatures Made Simple, Approach and Real World Experience. In: 6th Annual PKI R&D Workshop (April 2007), http://middleware.internet2.edu/pki07/proceedings/

[RSA78]   Rivest, R., Shamir, A., Adleman, L.: Ax Method for Obtaining Digital Signatures and Public-Key Cryptosystems 21(2), 120–126 (February 1978)

[Tec05]   Microsoft TechNet. Renewing a certification authority (January 2005), http://technet.microsoft.com/en-us/library/cc740209WS.10.aspx

[Tha06]   Thawte. Certification Practice Statement – Version 3.3 (November 2006), https://www.thawte.com/ssl-digital-certificates/free-guides-whitepapers/pdf/Thawte_CPS_3_3.pdf

Biometric Identity Based Signature Revisited

Neyire Deniz Sarier

Bonn-Aachen International Center for Information Technology
Computer Security Group
Dahlmannstr. 2, D-53113 Bonn Germany
denizsarier@yahoo.com

Abstract. In this paper, we describe a new biometric Identity Based
Signature (IBS) scheme based on the Sakai Kasahara Key Construction and prove its security in the framework of a stronger security model
compared to exisiting adversarial models. Besides, we present a new type
of a denial of service (DoS) attack and evaluate existing biometric IBS
schemes in this context. Based on the recently defined privacy notions,
we show that our scheme achieves weak signer-attribute privacy and the
security is reduced to the k-DHI computational problem in the ROM
with an efficient reduction. Finally, our scheme is compared to other error tolerant signature schemes and shown to be much more efficient in
terms of its each phase.

Keywords: Biometrics, fuzzy IBS, t-ABS, Unforgeability.

1 Introduction

In Eurocrypt'05, Sahai and Waters proposed a new Identity Based Encryption
(IBE) system called fuzzy IBE that uses biometric attributes as the identity
instead of an arbitrary string like an email address. This new system combines
the advantages of IBE with those of biometric identities, where IBE avoids the
need for an online Public Key Infrastructure (PKI), which is the most inefficient
and costly part of Public Key Encryption (PKE). Fuzzy IBE could be used in
an ad-hoc setting where the users are unprepared, namely without having any
public key or even predefined e-mail addresses. Instead, the signer could present
his biometrics to the verifier, who can check the signature for validity using the
biometric identity of the signer. Besides, the use of biometric identities in the
framework of IBE simplifies the process of key generation at the Private Key
Generator (PKG). Since biometric information is unique, unforgettable and non-
transferable, the user only needs to provide his biometrics at the PKG under the
supervision of a well-trained operator to avoid biometric forgery and to obtain
his private key instead of presenting special documents and credentials to convince the PKG about his identity. It should be noted that biometrics is assumed
as public information, hence the compromise of the biometrics does not affect
the security of the system. This point of view is also accepted in the biometrics
community, where the raw biometric data is assumed as public data whereas

F. Martinelli and B. Preneel (Eds.): EuroPKI 2009, LNCS 6391, pp. 271–285, 2010.
© Springer-Verlag Berlin Heidelberg 2010

the revocable biometric template that is stored in a central database or on a smartcard for biometric authentication is considered as private data. The signature analogue of fuzzy IBE is introduced in [21], where a provably secure fuzzy Identity Based Signature (IBS) scheme is described. Since the error tolerance property is satisfied, fuzzy IBS of [21] is applicable for biometric identities and it shares the same advantages of fuzzy IBE.

The private key components of a fuzzy system are generated by combining the values of a unique polynomial on each feature of the biometrics with the master secret key ms of PKG. However, due to the noisy nature of biometrics, a fuzzy system allows for error tolerance in the decryption stage for fuzzy IBE (or in the verification stage for fuzzy IBS). Particularly, a signature constructed using the biometrics ID could be verified by the receiver using a set of publicly computable values corresponding to the identity ID', provided that ID and ID' are within a certain distance of each other. Moreover, fuzzy IBS could be considered in the context of Attribute Based Signature (ABS), which allows the signer to generate a signature using the attributes she possess.

Another approach for incorporating biometrics into IBS is presented in [5], where the error tolerance is provided by a different identity structure compared to fuzzy IBS, namely by integrating a fuzzy extractor into the IBS scheme. This way, both the signer and verifier operate with the same public key, which is required for standard cryptographic schemes.

1.1   Related Work

The first fuzzy IBE scheme is described by Sahai and Waters in [13] and the security is reduced to the MBDH problem in the standard model, where the size of the public parameters is linear in the number of the attributes of the system or the number of attributes (or features) of a user. More efficient fuzzy IBE and biometric IBE schemes are achieved with short public parameter size by employing the random oracle model (ROM) [12,1,9,15].

Burnett et al [5] described the first biometric IBS scheme called BIO-IBS, where they used the biometric information as the identity and construct the public key (namely the identity) of the signer using a fuzzy extractor [8], which is then used in the modified SOK-IBS scheme [3]. Despite the fuzzy extraction process, the scheme is very efficient compared to fuzzy IBS of [21], which is the signature analogue of fuzzy IBE. However BIO-IBS is not secure against a new type of Denial of Service (DoS) attack that we are going to present in the next section.

Besides, the fuzzy IBS scheme of [21] is provably secure in the standard model, where the scheme is based on the Sahai-Waters construction [13] and the two level hierarchical signature of Boyen and Waters [20] and its security is reduced to the computational DH problem. However, the scheme is very inefficient due to the $d(n+4)$ exponentiations and the $d+2$ bilinear pairing computations during the verification process, where d is the error tolerance parameter of the scheme and n is the size of the feature (i.e. attribute) set of each user. Recently, a threshold ABS (t-ABS) scheme [16] with the same key generation phase as of fuzzy IBS and with threshold attribute based verification is designed, which suffers from the same disadvantages described for the fuzzy IBS. Due to the threshold verification, t-ABS can also be implemented as a biometric IBS scheme as opposed to other ABS schemes [11,10,18], which are proven secure in the ROM or generic group model. Thus, there is a need to devise an efficient and provably secure signature scheme with error-tolerance property in order to integrate biometric data.

1.2   Our Contribution

In this paper, we present a new biometric IBS scheme that is more efficient compared to the fuzzy IBS of [21] and the t-ABS scheme of [16] when implemented for biometric identities. Moreover, our scheme could function as a fuzzy IBS or threshold ABS (t-ABS) scheme and it is immune against a new type of a DoS attack that we are going to introduce. The new scheme is based on the Sakai Kasahara Key Construction [14] and the security is reduced to the k-DHI computational problem in the ROM with a different proof compared to [7,6,2]. The verification phase of the new scheme requires d exponentiations in group $\mathbb{G}$ and d pairing computations instead of $d(n + 4)$ exponentiations and $d + 2$ pairings as in [21,16] and achieves much shorter public parameter size, private key and signature sizes compared to [21,16]. Also, we have a structurally simpler key generation algorithm compared to [21,16], where the number of exponentiations in the group $\mathbb{G}$ is reduced from $n(n + 4)$ as in [21,16] to n and the cost of signing is half of the existing schemes. Finally, we do not require a MapToPoint hash function as opposed to the modified t-ABS scheme, which is obtained by replacing the computationally expensive T function in t-ABS of [16] with a MapToPoint hash function as described in [12]. The details of the modified t-ABS scheme and the security reduction of our new scheme in the framework of a stronger adversarial model is presented in the Appendix.

1.3   Outline of the Paper

In Sect. 2, we will state the necessary definitions and security model for fuzzy IBS. In Sect. 3, we present a new type of DoS attack and evaluate existing biometric IBS schemes with respect to this attack. Next, we describe our scheme and prove its security. Finally, we compare our scheme to related schemes that are provably secure and conclude our proposals in Sect. 5.

2   Definitions and Building Blocks

In order to introduce the new biometric IBS scheme, at first, we review the definitions and required computational primitives. Given a set S, $x \xleftarrow{\text{R}} S$ defines the assignment of a uniformly distributed random element from the set S to the variable x. Biometric identities will be element subsets of some universe, U, of size $|U|$, where each element is associated with a unique integer in $\mathbb{Z}_p^*$ as in [1,13]. The function $\epsilon(k)$ is defined as negligible if for any constant c, there exists $k_0 \in \mathbb{N}$ with $k > k_0$ such that $\epsilon < (1/k)^c$. Finally, we define the Lagrange coefficient $\Delta_{\mu_i, S}$ for $\mu_i \in \mathbb{Z}_p$ and a set S of elements in $\mathbb{Z}_p$ as

$$\Delta_{\mu_i, S}(x) = \prod_{\mu_j \in S, \mu_j \neq \mu_i} \frac{x - \mu_j}{\mu_i - \mu_j}$$

Bilinear Pairing: Let $\mathbb{G}_1, \mathbb{G}_2$ and $\mathbb{F}$ be multiplicative groups of prime order p and let g_1, g_2 be generator of $\mathbb{G}_1$ and $\mathbb{G}_2$, respectively. ψ is an isomorphism from $\mathbb{G}_2$ to $\mathbb{G}_1$ with $\psi(g_2) = g_1$ and $1_{\mathbb{G}_1}, 1_{\mathbb{F}}$ denote the identity elements of $\mathbb{G}_1$ and $\mathbb{F}$, respectively. A bilinear pairing is denoted by $\hat{e} : \mathbb{G}_1 \times \mathbb{G}_2 \to \mathbb{F}$ if the following two conditions hold.

1. $\forall (u, v) \in \mathbb{G}_1 \times \mathbb{G}_2$ and $\forall (a, b) \in \mathbb{Z}$ we have $\hat{e}(u^a, v^b) = \hat{e}(u, v)^{ab}$
2. If $\hat{e}(u, v) = 1_{\mathbb{F}} \ \forall v \in \mathbb{G}_2$, then $u = 1_{\mathbb{G}_1}$, namely the pairing is non-degenerate.

The security of our scheme is reduced to the well-exploited complexity assumption (k-DHI), which is stated as follows.

DH Inversion ((k-DHI) [7]: For $k \in \mathbb{N}$, and $x \xleftarrow{\text{R}} \mathbb{Z}_p^*$, $\hat{e} : \mathbb{G}_1 \times \mathbb{G}_2 \to \mathbb{F}$, given $(g_1, g_2, g_2^x, g_2^{x^2}, ..., g_2^{x^k})$, computing $g_1^{(1/x)}$ is hard.

2.1 Fuzzy Identity Based Signature

In [21], the generic fuzzy IBS scheme is defined as follows. The same definition applies for t-ABS [16], if the identity consists of a set of attributes.

- **Setup(1^{k_0}):** Given a security parameter k_0, the PKG generates the master secret key ms and the public parameters of the system.
- **Key Generation:** Given a user's identity $ID = \{\mu_1, ..., \mu_n\}$ and the master secret key ms, the PKG returns the corresponding private key D^{ID}. Here, n denotes the size of the set ID.
- **Sign:** A probabilistic algorithm that takes as input the private key D^{ID} associated to the identity ID, public parameters and a message $m \in M$ and outputs the signature σ.
- **Verify:** A deterministic algorithm that given an identity ID' such that $|ID \cap ID'| \geq d$, the signature σ together with the corresponding message m and the public parameters, returns a bit b. Here $b = 1$ means that σ is valid and d denotes the error tolerance parameter of the scheme.

Correctness: A fuzzy IBS scheme has to satisfy the correctness property, i.e., a signature generated by a signer with identity ID must pass the verification test for any ID' if $|ID \cap ID'| \geq d$.

2.2 Signer-Attribute Privacy

In [16], privacy of the signer is guaranteed with an additional algorithm for converting the t-ABS scheme to another signature scheme that is verifiable against the set of signer attributes that are known to the verifier, namely ID' in our setting. This way, the converted signature reveals only the d attributes of ID that are common with ID' chosen by the signer at the time of conversion. This property is defined as weak signer-attribute privacy and it is achieved by the following algorithms for our setting.

- **Convert:** Given the public parameters of the fuzzy IBS, a message signature pair (m, σ), and an identity ID', the signer generates a converted signature $\tilde{\sigma}$ on the message.
- **CvtVerify:** An algorithm that given an identity ID', a message converted-signature pair $(m, \tilde{\sigma})$ and the public parameters, returns a bit b. Here $b = 1$ means that $\tilde{\sigma}$ is a valid converted signature by a signer who has at least d of the attributes in ID', namely $|ID \cap ID'| \geq d$.

In addition, the authors of [16] define the full signer-attribute privacy, which guarantees that the verifier learns nothing more than the fact that $|ID \cap ID'| \geq d$ by combining the converted signature with an interactive verification protocol, which is a zero knowledge proof of knowledge of a valid converted signature with respect to the public inputs. For our scheme, we only consider the weak privacy level.

2.3 Security Model

A fuzzy IBS scheme is selectively unforgable under adaptive chosen message and given identity attacks (SUF-FIBS-CMA) if no probabilistic polynomial time (PPT) adversary has a non-negligable advantage in the game between a challenger and the adversary as follows [21,16].

- **Phase 1**: The adversary A declares the challenge identity $ID^* = \{\mu_1^*, ..., \mu_n^*\}$.
- **Phase 2**: The challenger runs the Setup algorithm and returns the system parameters to A.
- **Phase 3**: A issues private key queries for any identity ID' such that $|ID' \cap ID^*| < d$. The adversary issues signature queries for any identity.
- **Phase 4**: A outputs a forgery (ID^*, m^*, σ^*), where A does not make a signature query on (m^*, σ^*) for ID^*.

The success of the adversary A is defined as

$$\text{Succ}_A^{SUF-FIBS-CMA} = Pr[Verify(ID^*, m^*, \sigma^*)] = 1$$

For our scheme, we can consider a stronger notion of security, namely existential unforgability against chosen message and identity attacks (EUF-FIBS-CMA), since given a selectively unforgable scheme, one can construct an existentially unforgable scheme by hashing each component of the identity ID with the hash function H, where H is assumed to be a random oracle. By the employment of the ROM, this stronger notion is achieved with a better reduction cost compared to proofs in the standard model.

Collusion Resistance: It is important to note that the above definition of unforgeability guarantees collusion resistance since users with common biometric features cannot collude to generate a signature that is not generable by one of the colluders.

Remark 1. The security reduction of our scheme allows the adversary A to have as much power as possible by providing A with private key components of any identity ID' including the case of $|ID' \cap ID^*| > d$ except for the component $\mu^* \in ID^*$. Thus, our security model is stronger than the (SUF-FIBS-CMA) model of [21,16] and the details of this model is presented in Appendix B.

3   A New Attack on BIO-IBS

The first biometric IBS scheme is introduced in [5], where a fuzzy extractor is used to obtain a unique string ID via error correction codes from the biometrics b of the user in such a way that an error tolerance t is allowed. In other words, the same string ID is obtained even if the fuzzy extractor is applied on a different b' such that $dis(b, b') < t$. Here, $dis()$ is the distance metric used to measure the variation in the biometric reading and t is the error tolerance parameter. In particular, the authors of [5] describe a concrete fuzzy extractor using a $[n, k, 2t+1]$ BCH error correction code, Hamming Distance metric and a one-way hash function $H : \{0, 1\}^n \rightarrow \{0, 1\}^l$. Specifically,

- The **Gen** function takes the biometrics b as input and returns $ID = H(b)$ and public parameter $PAR = b \oplus C_e(ID)$, where C_e is a one-to-one encoding function. This function is called during the key generation phase of BIO-IBS.
- The **Rep** function takes a biometric b' and PAR as input and computes $ID' = C_d(b' \oplus PAR) = C_d(b \oplus b' \oplus C_e(ID))$. $ID = ID'$ if and only if $dis(b, b') \leq t$. Here C_d is the decoding function that corrects the errors upto the threshold t. This function is called during the verification phase of BIO-IBS.

BIO-IBS scheme of [5] requires the public storage of the value PAR, which is the information needed for error-tolerant reconstruction of the biometric identity string ID and subsequent fuzzy extraction. Since the verification is performed by combining the biometrics b' with the public value PAR of the signer, the presence of an active adversary who maliciously alters the public string PAR leads the verifier to use a wrong public key for the verification due to a different identity string computed by the fuzzy extractor. By the malicious modification of the public value PAR, an adversary cannot gain any secret information but the signature cannot be verified despite being valid. We define this type of DoS attack as Denial of Verification (DoV) attack. Since BIO-IBS is essentially an IBS scheme, no PKI is employed to publish certificates that binds the public value PAR to the signer as in PKE.

The first idea to prevent a DoV attack is using a robust fuzzy extractor, which is resilient to modification of the public value PAR [4], which is also proposed in [5] to prevent a legitimate signer from tampering with PAR in order to later disavow the signature. However, the robust fuzzy sketches/fuzzy extractors described in [4] assumes the biometrics as secret data and replaces the value PAR with $PAR^* = \langle PAR, H(b, PAR) \rangle$, where H is a hash function [4]. Since the adversary knows the biometric data b, he can easily modify the value PAR^* by computing a valid hash value, hence, the verifier cannot detect the modification of the public value.

Another solution is for the verifier to store PAR himself rather than obtain it from the server or the public store, but this defeats the purpose of biometric IBS, where the user does not need to store any additional cryptographic information [4].

However, since the identity ID of our scheme and fuzzy IBS of [21,16] consists of only the biometric features of the signer, i.e. the schemes do not integrate a fuzzy extractor in order to generate a unique identity string of the signer to be used in a signature scheme, there is no usage of the value PAR necessary for the reconstruction of the unique signer identity. Instead, we allow for a certain amount of error-tolerance in the signer identities ID and ID' that are measured at different times and use the set overlap as the distance metric, where the threshold t represents the error tolerance in terms of minimal set overlap of ID and ID'. Hence, fuzzy IBS of [21,16] and our scheme are immune against the Denial of Verification attack. It should be noted that DoV attack is a generic attack applicable to any biometric IBE/IBS scheme, where the authenticity of PAR is not provided.

4   A New Efficient Biometric IBS Scheme

The first idea for an efficient biometric IBS Scheme is to modify the t-ABS scheme of [16] by replacing T with a hash function used as a random oracle, which will reduce computational overhead in the key generation and verification algorithms dramatically. The same approach was used in [12] to obtain an efficient Attribute Based Encryption (ABE) scheme.

Since a new random polynomial is chosen for each private key, the modified t-ABS is secure against collusion attacks. The $n + 1$ exponentiations needed to solve T in [16,21] have been replaced with a single MapToPoint hash and signatures can contain a variable number of attributes, rather than be required to contain n as in [16,21]. Verification can be optimized to reduce the number of bilinear map operations by bringing the Lagrange coefficients in [12]. This optimization reduces the number of bilinear map operations from $3d$ to $d + 2$ at the expense of increasing the number of exponentiations from d to $3d$, thus the overall speed of verification is improved. The details of this scheme is presented in Appendix A.

However, as it is noted in [2,19], it is difficult to find groups $\mathbb{G}_2$ as the range of the MapToPoint hash function and to define an efficient isomorphism $\psi :$ $\mathbb{G}_2 \rightarrow \mathbb{G}_1$ at the same time. Thus, our new biometric IBS scheme uses the Sakai Kasahara Key Construction [14] for the generation of the private keys. This way, the problems stated above for the modified t-ABS are prevented and better performance is obtained due to the use of an ordinary hash function instead of MapToPoint hash function, which is called n times for the key generation and verification algorithms respectively. Besides, the total number of exponentiations and bilinear pairings required for the remaining phases are also reduced. Finally, the size of the public parameters and the signature is also much shorter compared to the fuzzy IBS scheme of [21,16]. The details of the new scheme is presented as follows.

- **Setup(1^{k_0}):** Given a security parameter k_0, the parameters of the scheme are generated as below.
  1. Generate three cyclic groups $\mathbb{G}_1, \mathbb{G}_2$ and $\mathbb{F}$ of prime order $p > 2^{k_0}$ and a bilinear pairing $\hat{e} : \mathbb{G}_1 \times \mathbb{G}_2 \to \mathbb{F}$. Pick a random generator $g_1 \in \mathbb{G}_1$ and $g_2 \in \mathbb{G}_2$ such that $\psi(g_2) = g_1$.
  2. Pick random $x, y \in \mathbb{Z}_p^*$, compute $P_{pub} = g_2^x \in \mathbb{G}_2$ and $\kappa = \hat{e}(g_1, g_2)^y$.
  3. Pick two cryptographic hash functions $H_1 : \mathbb{Z}_p^* \to \mathbb{Z}_p^*$ and $H_2 : \{0,1\}^{k_1} \times \mathbb{F} \to \mathbb{Z}_p^*$.

  The message space is $M = \{0,1\}^{k_1}$. The master public key is $(p, \mathbb{G}_1, \mathbb{G}_2, \mathbb{F}, \psi, \hat{e}, g_1, g_2, P_{pub}, \kappa, H_1, H_2)$ and the master secret key is $ms = x, y$.

- **Key Generation:** First, the set of biometric attributes $ID = \{\mu_1, ..., \mu_n\}$ of the signer are obtained from the raw biometric information as in [1,13,15]. Next, the PKG picks a random polynomial $q(\cdot)$ of degree $d - 1$ over $\mathbb{Z}_p$ such that $q(0) = y$ and returns $D_i^{ID} = g_1^{\frac{q(\mu_i)}{t_i}}$ for each $\mu_i \in ID$. Here $t_i = x + H_1(\mu_i)$.

- **Sign:** Given a message $m \in M$ and D^{ID}, the following steps are performed.
  1. Pick a random $z \in \mathbb{Z}_p^*$ and compute $h = H_2(m, \kappa^z) = H_2(m, r)$
  2. $\sigma_i = (D_i^{ID})^{z+h}$ for each $\mu_i \in ID$.

  The signature on the message m for identity ID is $\sigma = (\Sigma, h)$, where $\Sigma = \{\sigma_i : \mu_i \in ID\}$.

- **Verify:** Given σ, m and ID', choose an arbitrary set $S \subseteq ID \cap ID'$ such that $|S| = d$ and check $h = H_2(m, r')$ by computing

$$r' = \Big[\prod_{\mu_i \in S} \hat{e}(\sigma_i, P_{pub} \cdot g_2^{H_1(\mu_i)})^{\Delta_{\mu_i,S}(0)} \Big] \kappa^{-h}$$

$$= \Big[\prod_{\mu_i \in S} \hat{e}((D_i^{ID})^{z+h}, g_2^{t_i})^{\Delta_{\mu_i,S}(0)} \Big] \kappa^{-h}$$

$$= \Big[\prod_{\mu_i \in S} \hat{e}(g_1^{q(\mu_i)(z+h)}, g_2)^{\Delta_{\mu_i,S}(0)} \Big] \kappa^{-h}$$

$$= \hat{e}(g_1^{y(z+h)}, g_2) \kappa^{-h}$$

$$= \kappa^z$$

Here, the polynomial $q(\cdot)$ of degree $d - 1$ is interpolated using d points by polynomial interpolation in the exponents using Shamir's secret sharing method [17].

Theorem 1. *Suppose the hash functions H_1, H_2 are random oracles and there exists an adaptively chosen message and given identity attacker A that produces a forgery by making q_1, q_2 random oracle queries, and q_s signature queries. Then there exists an algorithm B that solves the k-DHI problem.*

Proof. See appendix B.

4.1 Weak Signer-Attribute Privacy

In [16], the verifier is able to identify which d common attributes are used in the generation of the converted signature, since $ID' \setminus S$ components of the converted signature are publicly simulatable. If only weak signer-attribute privacy is considered, more efficient **Convert** and **CvtVerify** algorithms could be designed by removing the bilinear pairings and exponentiations computed for the *dummy* components, namely $ID' \setminus S$. For applications that require full signer-attribute privacy, the modified t-ABS scheme could be a suitable choice as it is much more efficient compared to t-ABS of [16].

- **Convert:** On input the public parameters of the fuzzy IBS, the message signature pair (m, σ), and the identity ID', the signer selects $S \subseteq ID \cap ID'$ such that $|S| = d$ and sets $\forall \mu_i \in S$, $\tilde{\sigma}_i = \sigma_i$. Next, $\forall \mu_i \in ID' \setminus S$, the signer sets $\tilde{\sigma}_i = \bot$ and returns the verifier $(m, \tilde{\sigma})$.
- **CvtVerify:** Given an identity ID', a message converted-signature pair $(m, \tilde{\sigma})$ and the public parameters, the verifier can easily identify the d common attributes and verifies the signature as before.

5 Efficiency Discussions and Comparison

In this section, we compare different fuzzy IBS and ABS schemes applicable for biometric identities. For simplicity of the comparison, ψ is taken as the identity map (i.e. $\mathbb{G}_1 = \mathbb{G}_2 = \mathbb{G}$) and the computational cost for multiplication in $\mathbb{G}$ is omitted. All the computations are performed according to the optimization introduced in [12], where the dominant operations are considered as bilinear pairings followed by exponentiations. The abbreviations used in Table 1 denote the following: $|B|$ is the bit-length of an element in set (or group) B; n is the number of features in ID; T_e is the computation time for a single exponentiation in $\mathbb{G}$; T'_e is the computation time for a single exponentiation in $\mathbb{F}$; T_H is the computation time for a MapToPoint hash function; T_i is the computation time for a single inverse operation in $\mathbb{Z}_p$; T_p is the computation time for a single pairing operation; T'_i the computation time for a single inverse operation in $\mathbb{F}$; d is the error tolerance parameter; k_1 the size of the message; k_2 output size of the H_2 hash function.

Table 1. Comparison of error tolerant IBS schemes

	fuzzy IBS [21]	t-ABS [16]	Modified t-ABS	Our Scheme
Size of public parameters	$(n+k_1+4)|\mathbb{G}|+|\mathbb{F}|$	$(n+5)|\mathbb{G}|$	$4|\mathbb{G}|$	$2|\mathbb{G}|+|\mathbb{F}|$
Size of D^{ID}	$2n|\mathbb{G}|$	$2n|\mathbb{G}|$	$2n|\mathbb{G}|$	$n|\mathbb{G}|$
Size of σ	$3n|\mathbb{G}|$	$3n|\mathbb{G}|$	$3n|\mathbb{G}|$	$n|\mathbb{G}|+k_2$
Cost of Key Generation	$n(n+4)T_e$	$n(n+4)T_e$	$n(3T_e+T_H)$	$n(T_i+T_e)$
Cost of Sign	$(k_1+2n)T_e$	$2nT_e$	$2nT_e$	nT_e+T_e'
Cost of Verify	$d((n+4)T_e+T_p)$ $k_1T_e+2T_p$	$d((n+4)T_e+T_p)$ $2T_p+2T_i'$	$d(3T_e+T_p+T_H)$ $2T_p+2T_i'$	$d(T_p+T_e)$ $+T_e'$
Security Model	Standard Model	Standard Model	ROM	ROM

6   Conclusion

In this paper, we review the existing signature schemes applicable for biometric identities and propose a more efficient biometric IBS scheme by employing the Sakai Kasahara Key Construction. In addition, our scheme could function as a practical threshold ABS scheme with the claim that the new scheme is faster than all known pairing-based IBS methods for fuzzy identities similar to the claim in [2]. Considering the security of our scheme in the ROM, we achieve a better reduction cost compared to the reviewed signature schemes since the security penalty can be reduced to the maximum number of oracle queries the adversary can make. Besides, examining the full signer-attribute privacy for fuzzy IBS and our scheme could be an interesting future work since the user may use his biometrics in other applications such as biometric encryption or authentication systems, where the latter assumes the privacy of the identity-biometrics relationship rather than the secrecy of the biometrics of the user. Finally, an open problem is to prove the security of our scheme in the standard model.

Acknowledgement. The author is grateful to her supervisor Prof. Dr. Joachim von zur Gathen for his valuable support, encouragement and guidance.

References

1. Baek, J., Susilo, W., Zhou, J.: New Constructions of Fuzzy Identity Based Encryption. In: ACM Symposium on Information, Computer and Communications Security - ASIACCS 2007, pp. 368–370. ACM, New York (2007)
2. Barreto, P.S.L.M., Libert, B., McCullagh, N., Quisquater, J.-J.: Efficient and Provably-Secure Identity-Based Signatures and Signcryption from Bilinear Maps. In: Roy, B. (ed.) ASIACRYPT 2005. LNCS, vol. 3788, pp. 515–532. Springer, Heidelberg (2005)

3. Bellare, M., Namprempre, C., Neven, G.: Security Proofs for Identity Based Identification and Signature Schemes. In: Cachin, C., Camenisch, J.L. (eds.) EUROCRYPT 2004. LNCS, vol. 3027, pp. 268–286. Springer, Heidelberg (2004)
4. Boyen, X., Dodis, Y., Katz, J., Ostrovsky, R., Smith, A.: Secure remote authentication using biometric data. In: Cramer, R. (ed.) EUROCRYPT 2005. LNCS, vol. 3494, pp. 147–163. Springer, Heidelberg (2005)
5. Burnett, A., Byrne, F., Dowling, T., Duffy, A.: A Biometric Identity Based Signature Scheme. International Journal of Network Security 5(3), 317–326 (2007)
6. Chen, L., Cheng, Z., Malone-Lee, J., Smart, N.: Efficient ID-KEM based on the Sakai Kasahara Key Construction. IEE Proceedings Information Security 153(1), 19–26 (2006)
7. Chen, L., Cheng, Z.: Security proof of sakai-kasahara's identity-based encryption scheme. In: Smart, N.P. (ed.) Cryptography and Coding 2005. LNCS, vol. 3796, pp. 442–459. Springer, Heidelberg (2005)
8. Dodis, Y., Reyzin, L., Smith, A.: Fuzzy Extractors: How to Generate Strong Keys from Biometrics and Other Noisy Data. In: Cachin, C., Camenisch, J.L. (eds.) EUROCRYPT 2004. LNCS, vol. 3027, pp. 523–540. Springer, Heidelberg (2004)
9. Furukawa, J., Attrapadung, N., Sakai, R., Hanaoka, G.: A Fuzzy ID-Based Encryption Efficient When Error Rate Is Low. In: Chowdhury, D.R., Rijmen, V., Das, A. (eds.) INDOCRYPT 2008. LNCS, vol. 5365, pp. 116–129. Springer, Heidelberg (2008)
10. Khader, D.: Attribute Based Group Signatures. Cryptology ePrint Archive, Report 2007/159 (2007), http://eprint.iacr.org/
11. Maji, H., Prabhakaran, M., Rosulek, M.: Attribute-Based Signatures: Achieving Attribute-Privacy and Collusion-Resistance. Cryptology ePrint Archive, Report 2008/328 (2008), http://eprint.iacr.org/
12. Pirretti, M., Traynor, P., McDaniel, P., Waters, B.: Secure Attribute Based Systems. In: ACM Conference on Computer and Communications Security, pp. 99–112. ACM, New York (2006)
13. Sahai, A., Waters, B.: Fuzzy Identity Based Encryption. In: Cramer, R. (ed.) EUROCRYPT 2005. LNCS, vol. 3494, pp. 457–473. Springer, Heidelberg (2005)
14. Sakai, R., Kasahara, M.: Id based cryptosystems with pairing on elliptic curve. Cryptology ePrint Archive, Report 2003/054 (2003), http://eprint.iacr.org/
15. Sarier, N.D.: A New Biometric Identity Based Encryption Scheme. In: The 2008 International Symposium on Trusted Computing - TrustCom 2008, pp. 2061–2066. IEEE Computer Society, Los Alamitos (2008)
16. Shahandashti, S.F., Safavi-Naini, R.: Threshold Attribute-Based Signatures and Their Application to Anonymous Credential Systems. In: Preneel, B. (ed.) AFRICACRYPT 2009. LNCS, vol. 5580, pp. 198–216. Springer, Heidelberg (2009)
17. Shamir, A.: How to Share a Secret. ACM Commun. 22(11), 612–613 (1979)
18. Shanqing, G., Yingpei, Z.: Attribute-based Signature Scheme. In: International Conference on Information Security and Assurance - ISA 2008, IEEE Computer Society, Los Alamitos (2008)
19. Smart, N.P., Vercauteren, F.: On computable isomorphisms in efficient asymmetric pairing-based systems. Discrete Appl. Math. 155(4), 538–547 (2007)
20. Waters, B.: Efficient Identity-Based Encryption Without Random Oracles. In: Cramer, R. (ed.) EUROCRYPT 2005. LNCS, vol. 3494, pp. 114–127. Springer, Heidelberg (2005)
21. Yang, P., Cao, Z., Dong, X.: Fuzzy Identity Based Signature. Cryptology ePrint Archive, Report 2008/002 (2008), http://eprint.iacr.org/

Appendix A

The modified t-ABS scheme consists of the following phases.

- **Setup**(1^{k_0}): Given a security parameter k_0, the parameters of the scheme are generated as follows.
  1. Generate two cyclic groups $\mathbb{G}$ and $\mathbb{F}$ of prime order $p > 2^{k_0}$ and a bilinear pairing $\hat{e} : \mathbb{G} \times \mathbb{G} \to \mathbb{F}$. Pick a random generator $g \in \mathbb{G}$.
  2. Pick randomly $y \in \mathbb{Z}_p^*$ and $h, g_2 \in \mathbb{G}$ and compute $g_1 = g^y$.

  The public parameters are (g, g_1, g_2, h) and the master secret key is y.

- **Key Generation**: Let $H : \{0,1\}^* \to \mathbb{Z}_p$ be a collision resistant hash function and let $T : \mathbb{Z}_p \to \mathbb{G}$ be a MapToPoint hash function modeled as a random oracle. Let Γ be the set defined as $\Gamma = \bigcup_{\mu \in ID} H(\mu)$. A new random degree $d - 1$ polynomial $q(\cdot)$ over $\mathbb{Z}_p$ is selected such that $q(0) = y$ and $\forall i \in \Gamma$, a random r_i is chosen and $D_i^{ID} = (g^{q(\mu_i)} T(\mu_i)^{r_i}, g^{r_i})$ for each $\mu_i \in ID$

- **Sign**: Given a message $m \in M$ and D^{ID}, the following steps are performed.
  1. Pick a random $s_i \in \mathbb{Z}_p$ for $i \in [1, n]$
  2. Compute $\sigma_{1i} = g^{q(\mu_i)} T(\mu_i)^{r_i} (g_1^m \cdot h)^{s_i}$, $\sigma_{2i} = g^{r_i}$, $\sigma_{3i} = g^{s_i}$ for each $i \in [1, n]$.

  The signature on the message m for identity ID is $\sigma = (\sigma_{1i}, \sigma_{2i}, \sigma_{3i})$ for $i \in [1, n]$.

- **Verify**: Given σ, m and ID', choose an arbitrary set $S \subseteq ID \cap ID'$ such that $|S| = d$ and check

$$\hat{e}(g_2, g_1) = \prod_{\mu_i \in S} \left(\frac{\hat{e}(\sigma_{1i}, g)}{\hat{e}(T(\mu_i), \sigma_{2i}) \hat{e}(g_1^m \cdot h, \sigma_{3i})} \right)^{\Delta_{\mu_i, S}(0)}$$

The modifed t-ABS scheme satisfies both weak signer-attribute and full signer-attribute privacy if the additional protocols for signature conversion and interactive verification are applied. The reader is referred to [16] for the details of this application.

Appendix B: Proof of Theorem 1

Proof. Assume that a polynomial time attacker A produces a forgery, then using A, we show that one can construct an attacker B solving the k-DHI problem.

Suppose that B is given the k-DHI problem $(g_1, g_2, g_2^x, g_2^{x^2}, ..., g_2^{x^k})$, B will compute $g_1^{1/x}$ using A as follows.

- **Phase 1**: A declares the challenge identity $ID^* = \{\mu_1, ...\mu_n\}$.
- **Phase 2**: B picks a random feature $\mu^* \in ID^*$ and simulates the public parameters for A as follows.

1. B selects $h_0, ..., h_{k-1} \in \mathbb{Z}_p^*$ and sets $f(z) = \prod_{j=1}^{k-1}(z+h_j)$, which could be written as $f(z) = \sum_{j=0}^{k-1} c_j z^j$. The constant term c_0 is non-zero because $h_j \neq 0$ and c_j are computable from h_j. Here, h_0 denotes the hash value of the challenge attribute $\mu^* \in ID^*$, where μ^* is picked at random by B.

2. B computes $p_2 = \prod_{j=0}^{k-1}(g_2^{x^j})^{c_j} = g_2^{f(x)} \in \mathbb{G}_2$ and $p_1 = \psi(p_2) = g_1^{f(x)} \in \mathbb{G}_1$. Next, $p_2^x = g_2^{xf(x)} = \prod_{j=0}^{k-1}(g_2^{x^{j+1}})^{c_j}$ and $p_1^x = \psi(p_2^x)$. The public key is fixed as $P_{pub} \in \mathbb{G}_2 = p_2^{x-h_0}$. If $p_2 = 1$, then $x = -h_j$ for some j, then k-DHI problem could be solved directly [6].

3. B computes $f_j(z) = \frac{f(z)}{z+h_j} = \sum_{v=0}^{k-2} d_{j,v} z^v$ for $1 \leq j < k$ and $p_1^{1/(x+h_j)} = g_1^{f_j(x)} = \prod_{v=0}^{k-2} \psi((g_2^{x^v}))^{d_{j,v}}$.

4. Besides, we compute the following entity, which leads to a different proof compared to [6,7,2]. Namely, $p_1^{x/(x+h_j)} = g_1^{xf_j(x)} = \prod_{v=0}^{k-2} \psi((g_2^{x^{v+1}}))^{d_{j,v}}$. This way, the signature queries can be simulated for any identity chosen by A.

B picks a random $y \in \mathbb{Z}_p^*$ to compute $\kappa = \hat{e}(p_1, p_2)^y$ and returns A the public parameters $(p_1, p_2, \hat{e}, \psi, \mathbb{G}_1, \mathbb{G}_2, \mathbb{F}, \psi, P_{pub}, \kappa, H_1, H_2, d)$, where $d \in \mathbb{Z}^+$ and H_1, H_2 are random oracles controlled by B as follows.

H_1-**queries:** For a query on μ_i,
1. If $\mu_i \in ID^*$ and $\mu_i = \mu^*$,return h_0 and add $\langle \mu^*, h_0, \bot \rangle$ to H_1List.
2. Else return $h_i + h_0$, add the tuple $\langle \mu_i, h_i + h_0, p_1^{1/(x+h_i)} \rangle$ to H_1List.

Key extraction queries: Upon receiving a query for $|ID \cap ID^*| < d$, for every $\mu_i \neq \mu^* \in ID$, run the H_1-oracle simulator and obtain $\langle \mu_i, h_i + h_0, p_1^{1/(x+h_i)} \rangle$ from H_1List. Pick a random $d-1$ degree polynomial $q(\cdot)$ such that $q(0) = y$ and return $D_{\mu_i} = p_1^{q(\mu_i)/(x+h_i)}$ for each $\mu_i \in ID$.

Remark 2. The security model is stronger than the model of fuzzy IBS since the adversary has access to private key components of any ID including the case of $|ID \cap ID^*| \geq d$, as opposed to the security model of [21,16]. In particular, a random $d-1$ degree polynomial $q(\cdot)$ such that $q(0) = y$ is picked for the first query on ID such that $|ID \cap ID^*| \geq d$, and A is given the private key components $D_{\mu_i} = p_1^{q(\mu_i)/(x+h_i)}$ except for the case when $\mu_i = \mu^*$. Further queries on any identity ID' such that $|ID' \cap ID^*| \geq d$ are answered using the same polynomial $q(\cdot)$ without affecting the previously computed shares by computing $D_{\mu'_i} = p_1^{q(\mu'_i)/(x+H_1(\mu'_i))}$ for each $\mu'_i \in ID'$ due to the extensibility property of the Shamir's threshold secret sharing scheme. The only exception is for the component μ^*, since the simulator B does not know the corresponding private key $p_1^{q(\mu^*)/x}$.

Signature queries: For a query on a message-identity pair (m, ID),

1. If $|ID \cap ID^*| \geq d$ and $\mu^* \in ID$, B picks randomly $a, h \in \mathbb{Z}_p^*$, computes $r = \hat{e}(p_1^{ax} \cdot p_1^{-h}, p_2)^y = \hat{e}(p_1^{ax-h}, p_2)^y$ and backpatches to define the value $H_2(m, r)$ as h. Next, B obtains the corresponding private key components by simulating the key extraction oracle on ID and computes $\sigma_i = p_1^{axq(\mu_i)/(x+h_i)}$ for each $\mu_i \neq \mu^*$. For the feature $\mu_i = \mu^*$, he computes $\sigma_{\mu^*} = p_1^{aq(\mu^*)}$. Lastly, B returns $\sigma = (\Sigma, h)$ to A, where $\Sigma = (\sigma_i : \mu_i \in ID)$.
2. Else if $|ID \cap ID^*| < d$ and $\mu^* \in ID$, step 1 is repeated.
3. Else, B picks randomly $z, h \in \mathbb{Z}_p^*$, computes $r = \hat{e}(p_1^z, p_2)^y$ and backpatches to define $H_2(m, r)$ as h. Finally, B obtains the corresponding private key components by simulating the key extraction oracle and returns $(D_{\mu_i}^{ID})^{z+h}$ for each $\mu_i \in ID$.

B aborts in the unlikely event that $H_2(m, r)$ is already defined.

Remark 3. The simulation of the signature queries on any ID with $\mu^* \in ID$ is correct since given (σ, m), A chooses an arbitrary set $\mu^* \in S \subseteq ID$ such that $|S| = d$ and checks $h = H_2(m, r)$ by computing

$$r = \left[\prod_{\mu_i \in S} \hat{e}(\sigma_i, P_{pub} \cdot p_2^{H_1(\mu_i)})^{\Delta_{\mu_i, S}(0)} \right] \kappa^{-h}$$

$$= \left[\left(\prod_{\mu^* \neq \mu_i \in S} \hat{e}(p_1^{axq(\mu_i)/(x+h_i)}, p_2^{x-h_0} \cdot p_2^{H_1(\mu_i)}) \cdot \hat{e}(\sigma_{\mu^*}, p_2^{x-h_0} \cdot p_2^{H_1(\mu^*)}) \right)^{\Delta_{\mu_i, S}(0)} \right] \kappa^{-h}$$

$$= \left[\left(\prod_{\mu^* \neq \mu_i \in S} \hat{e}(p_1^{axq(\mu_i)/(x+h_i)}, p_2^{x-h_0} \cdot p_2^{h_i+h_0}) \cdot \hat{e}(\sigma_{\mu^*}, p_2^{x-h_0} \cdot p_2^{h_0}) \right)^{\Delta_{\mu_i, S}(0)} \right] \kappa^{-h}$$

$$= \left[\left(\prod_{\mu^* \neq \mu_i \in S} \hat{e}(p_1^{axq(\mu_i)/(x+h_i)}, p_2^{x+h_i}) \cdot \hat{e}(p_1^{aq(\mu^*)}, p_2^x) \right)^{\Delta_{\mu_i, S}(0)} \right] \kappa^{-h}$$

$$= \left[\left(\prod_{\mu^* \neq \mu_i \in S} \hat{e}(p_1^{axq(\mu_i)}, p_2) \cdot \hat{e}(p_1^{aq(\mu^*)}, p_2^x) \right)^{\Delta_{\mu_i, S}(0)} \right] \kappa^{-h}$$

$$= \left[\left(\prod_{\mu_i \in S} \hat{e}(p_1^{axq(\mu_i)}, p_2) \right)^{\Delta_{\mu_i, S}(0)} \right] \kappa^{-h}$$

$$= \hat{e}(p_1^{axy}, p_2) \hat{e}(p_1, p_2)^{-hy}$$

$$= \hat{e}(p_1^{ax-h}, p_2)^y$$

After the queries to the random oracles, the adversary has to forge a signature (m, r, σ) on the exact challenge identity $ID^* = (\mu_1, .., \mu^*, ..\mu_n)$. Next, the forking lemma is applied on (m, r, h, Σ). If the triples (r, h, Σ) can be simulated without knowing the private key components of ID^*, then there exists a Turing machine B' that replays a sufficient number of times on the input (P_{pub}, ID^*) to obtain two valid signatures (m^*, r, h', Σ') and (m^*, r, h'', Σ'') such that $h' \neq h''$ for the same message m^* and commitment r. If both forgeries satisfy the verification equation for all the sets $S \subseteq ID^*$ such that $|S| = d$ and $\mu^* \in S$, namely,

$$r = \Big[\prod_{\mu_i \in S} (\hat{e}(\sigma_i', P_{pub} \cdot p_2^{H_1(\mu_i)})^{\Delta_{\mu_i, S}(0)}) \Big] \kappa^{-h'}$$

$$= \Big[\prod_{\mu_i \in S} (\hat{e}(\sigma_i'', P_{pub} \cdot p_2^{H_1(\mu_i)})^{\Delta_{\mu_i, S}(0)}) \Big] \kappa^{-h''}$$

By verifying all the possible combinations for the set S, B is assured that each partial signature σ_i' and σ_i'' is valid. Since each private key component of $\mu_i \neq \mu^* \in ID^*$ is known by B (also by A), the solution to the k-DHI problem could only be obtained from the forgeries associated to $\mu^* \in ID^*$, namely $\sigma_{\mu^*}', \sigma_{\mu^*}''$.

Then, the computations are performed as in [2],

$$\hat{e}(\sigma_{\mu^*}', P_{pub} \cdot p_2^{H_1(\mu^*)})\hat{e}(p_1, p_2)^{-h'} = \hat{e}(\sigma_{\mu^*}'', P_{pub} \cdot p_2^{H_1(\mu^*)})\hat{e}(p_1, p_2)^{-h''}$$

$$\Rightarrow \hat{e}(\sigma_{\mu^*}', p_2^x)\hat{e}(p_1, p_2)^{-h'} = \hat{e}(\sigma_{\mu^*}'', p_2^x)\hat{e}(p_1, p_2)^{-h''}$$

$$\Rightarrow \hat{e}(\sigma_{\mu^*}'/\sigma_{\mu^*}'', p_2^x)^{(h'-h'')^{-1}} = \hat{e}(p_1, p_2)$$

Similar to the proof in [2], we set $T = p_1^{q(\mu^*)/x} = (\sigma_{\mu^*}'/\sigma_{\mu^*}'')^{(h'-h'')^{-1}}$.

The solution to the k-DHI problem, $g_1^{1/x}$ is obtained by outputting $(T^{1/q(\mu^*)}/\prod_{j=1}^{k-1} \psi(g_2^{x^{j-1}})^{c_j})^{1/c_0}$ since

$$T^{1/q(\mu^*)} = p_1^{1/x} = \psi(p_2)^{1/x} = \prod_{j=0}^{k-1}(\psi(g_2^{x^{j-1}}))^{c_j} = \psi(g_2)^{c_0/x} \cdot \prod_{j=1}^{k-1} \psi(g_2^{x^{j-1}})^{c_j}.$$

Remark 4. Since A already knows the private keys for each feature of the challenge identity ID^* except for the feature $\mu^* \in ID^*$, A only has to forge the partial signature σ_{μ^*} corresponding to μ^* of ID^*.

How to Construct Identity-Based Signatures without the Key Escrow Problem

Tsz Hon Yuen, Willy Susilo, and Yi Mu

University of Wollongong, Australia
{thy738,wsusilo,ymu}@uow.edu.au

Abstract. The inherent key escrow problem is one of the main reasons for the slow adoption of identity-based cryptography. The existing solution for mitigating the key escrow problem is by adopting multiple Private Key Generators (PKGs). Recently, there was a proposal that attempted to reduce the trust of the PKG by allowing a malicious PKG to be caught if he reveals the user's identity-based secret key illegally. Nonetheless, the proposal does not consider that the PKG can simply decrypt the ciphertext instead of revealing the secret key itself (in the case of identity-based encryption schemes).

The aim of this paper is to present an escrow-free identity-based signature (IBS) scheme, in which the malicious PKG will be caught if it releases a signature on behalf of the user but signed by itself. We present a formal model to capture such a scheme and provide a concrete construction.

1 Introduction

The notion of identity-based cryptography was put forth by Shamir [17]. This notion was proposed to simplify the authentication of a public key by merely using an identity string as the public key. From the verifier's or the encryptor's point of view, only the identity of the other party is required. Hence, there is no necessity to ensure the validity of the public key. Due to this nice property, a series of identity-based schemes have been proposed, including identity-based signatures [17], identity-based encryption [6], hierarchical identity-based cryptography [12] and so forth. For identity-based signatures (IBS), there exists a comprehensive discussion conducted by Bellare *et al.* [4]. Galindo *et al.* [10] further extended the discussion to IBS with various additional properties, which has more practical applications.

In these identity-based cryptosystems, there is a trusted party called the private key generator (PKG) who generates the secret key for each user identity. As the PKG generates and holds the secret key for all users, a complete trust must be placed on the PKG. Nonetheless, this may not be desirable in a real world scenario, where a malicious PKG can sell users' keys, sign messages or decrypt ciphertexts on behalf of users without being confronted in a court of law. This is known as the *key escrow problem*. This problem seems to be inherent in identity-based cryptosystems. Boneh and Franklin [6] proposed that employing

F. Martinelli and B. Preneel (Eds.): EuroPKI 2009, LNCS 6391, pp. 286–301, 2010.

multiple PKGs is a possible solution to the key escrow problem. The master secret key is jointly computed by a number of PKGs, such that no single PKG has the knowledge of it. However, this approach requires an extra infrastructure and communication cost between users and different PKGs. A user needs to run the key extraction protocol with different PKGs by proving his identity to them. Furthermore, maintaining multiple independent PKGs for a commercially used infrastructure is a daunting task.

Some cryptosystems have been proposed to solve the the key escrow problem. They use a "combination" of identity-based cryptography and the traditional public key cryptography, such as the certificateless cryptosystems [1], the certificate-based cryptosystems [11] and the self-certificated cryptosystems [13], in a non-trivial way. In these systems, a user possesses a user public key and a user secret key, together with his identity-based secret key computed by the PKG. The user secret key protects the user from the key escrow problem. The PKG acts like a certificate authority (CA) who authenticates the user public key using his master secret key. Unfortunately, these cryptosystems are *no longer* identity-based – the encryptor or the verifier has to know the user public key in addition to the user identity. Therefore these schemes lost the original advantages of identity-based cryptography.

Girault [13] defined three level of trust to the PKG:

- Level 1: The PKG can compute users' secret keys and, therefore, can impersonate any user without being detected. Identity-based signature schemes are the examples.
- Level 2: The PKG cannot compute users' secret keys. However, the PKG can still impersonate any user without being detected. Certificateless signature schemes are the examples.
- Level 3: The PKG cannot compute users' secret keys, and the PKG cannot impersonate any user without being detected. Certificate-based signature schemes and self-certificated signature schemes are the examples.

The current schemes achieving level 2 or level 3 of trust are no longer identity-based. It is an open problem to construct an identity-based signatures with level 2 or level 3 of trust, without publishing the user public key.

Recently, Goyal [14] proposed the concept of accountable authority identity-based encryption (A-IBE) to reduce the trust in the PKG and it was further

Table 1. Comparison of the public information known by the verifier and the level of trust to the PKG. ID is the identity, upk is the user public key, and W is the commitment of the user secret key using the public key of the PKG.

Schemes	Public Information	Level of Trust
Identity-based Signatures [17]	ID	Level 1
Certificateless Signatures [1]	ID, upk, W	Level 2
Certificate-based Signatures [16]	ID, upk	Level 3
Self-certificated Signatures [13]	ID, upk	Level 3
Our Scheme in §6	ID	Level 3

strengthened by [2,15]. In [14], the PKG helps the user to compute his identity-based secret key without knowing it. If the PKG computes another set of secret key by himself and reveals it to other parties, this key will be different from the user's original secret key with a high probability. Therefore the PKG can be caught when revealing the secret key and the user's original secret key is the evidence. However, the malicious PKG is still able to sell a signed message or decrypted ciphertext instead, without being detected. This is clearly an issue that is not yet addressed in Goyal's model [14]. Goyal *et al.* [15] further proposed the concept of black-box A-IBE. In black-box A-IBE, if a PKG sells a decoder box which can decrypt ciphertexts with non-negligible probability, he will be caught in a trace algorithm. It is an open problem to construct a similar blaming mechanism in the IBS setting.

Our Contributions. In this paper, we introduce the concept of *escrow-free identity-based signatures* to reduce the trust in the PKG. In this model, each signer has his own public key and secret key. The PKG generates the identity-based secret key for the signer with respect to the user public key (*à la* Goyal's approach [14]). Then, the signer uses both secret keys to sign a message. Therefore, the signer is protected against a malicious PKG. To verify the signature, it only requires the signer's identity and the message. This is the main difference between certificate-based signatures (CBS), certificateless signatures (CLS), self-certificated signatures (SCS) and our model. Their verification protocols require the signer's public key to verify. Hence, our model mimics closely the original IBS in this regard, and solves the key escrow problem at the same time.

Our scheme achieves level 3 of trust to the PKG, which is the best in the model proposed by Girault [13]. Theoretically, the escrow-free IBS is more efficient than CBS, CLS and SCS since the user public key is not involved and is not sent to the verifier. In this paper, we give the *first* construction of the escrow-free IBS. When comparing with the multiple PKGs solution by Boneh and Franklin [6], our scheme interacts with at most two authorities. While Boneh and Franklin's scheme interacts with a large number of authorities, the communication complexity of the their scheme is higher.

We then extend the escrow-free IBS to have an extra property called *user public key anonymity*. In CBS, CLS and SCS, user public keys are needed to verify a signature. Since the escrow-free IBS only use the identity to verify a signature, it is possible for the signature to be anonymous with respect to the user public key. We provide an additional security model to capture the user public key anonymity property and present a secure construction with anonymity.

2   Backgrounds

We briefly review the pairings and some candidate hard problems that will be used later. Let $\mathbb{G}, \mathbb{G}_T$ be cyclic groups of prime order p, writing the group action multiplicatively. Let g be a generator of $\mathbb{G}$. A map $\hat{e} : \mathbb{G} \times \mathbb{G} \to \mathbb{G}_T$ is called a pairings if, for all $g \in \mathbb{G}$ and $a, b \in \mathbb{Z}_p$, we have $\hat{e}(g^a, g^b) = \hat{e}(g, g)^{ab}$, and if g is a generator of $\mathbb{G}$, then $\hat{e}(g, g)$ generates $\mathbb{G}_T$.

DL Problem. The Discrete Logarithm problem is that, given g, $y \in \mathbb{G}$, to output $x = \log_g y$. We say that the (ϵ, t)-DL assumption holds in $\mathbb{G}$ if no t-time algorithm has the non-negligible probability ϵ in solving the DL problem.

DBDH Problem [6]. The decisional Bilinear Diffie-Hellman problem is that, given $g, g^a, g^b, g^c \in \mathbb{G}$ and $T \in \mathbb{G}_T$ for unknown $a, b, c \in \mathbb{Z}_p^*$, to decide if $T = \hat{e}(g, g)^{abc}$. We say that the (ϵ, t)-DBDH assumption holds in $\mathbb{G}$ if no t-time algorithm has the non-negligible probability ϵ over half in solving the DBDH problem.

q-SDH Problem [5]. The q-Strong Diffie-Hellman problem is that, given g, g^{α}, $\ldots, g^{\alpha^q} \in \mathbb{G}$ for unknown $\alpha \in \mathbb{Z}_p^*$, to output a pair $(g^{\frac{1}{\alpha+c}}, c)$ where $c \in \mathbb{Z}_p^*$. We say that the (ϵ, t, q)-SDH assumption holds in $\mathbb{G}$ if no t-time algorithm has the non-negligible probability ϵ in solving the q-SDH problem.

3 Security Model for Escrow-Free Identity-Based Signatures

3.1 Syntax

An escrow-free identity-based signature scheme has six polynomial-time algorithms, namely Setup, UserKeyGen, Extract, Sign, Verify, Blame.

1. Setup: On input a security parameter 1^k, it generates the system parameter param, the master secret key msk and the master public key mpk.
2. UserKeyGen: On input the system parameter param, the user generates the user secret key usk and the user public key upk.
3. Extract: This is an interactive algorithm between the PKG and the user. The common input are param, upk and an identity ID. The PKG's algorithm Extract$_p$ private input is msk. The user's algorithm Extract$_u$ private input is usk. The interaction includes the user giving the PKG a joining proof Pf which shows the user's participation with respect to upk[1]. Finally the user obtains the identity-based secret key sk_{ID}.
4. Sign: On input param, usk, sk_{ID} and a message m, the user with identity ID generates a signature σ.
5. Verify: On input param, mpk, ID, m and σ, it returns 1 or 0 for accept or reject, respectively.
6. Blame: This is an interactive algorithm between the PKG, the user and the judge. The common input are param, mpk, ID, upk, m and σ. The user's algorithm Blame$_u$ with private input usk sends a blame request φ to a judge. The judge's algorithm Blame$_j$ outputs "PKG" if:
   - φ shows that σ is related to upk, and
   - the PKG's algorithm Blame$_p$, with private input msk, fails to provide a public key upk', a joining proof Pf and a transcript ρ, such that:
     - upk' is related to σ,
     - Pf shows the user's participation with respect to upk', and
     - ρ is the transcript of the extract algorithm with upk'.
   Otherwise, the judge outputs "upk".

---

[1] The joining proof will be defined in Sect. 3.2.

3.2   Joining Proof

The joining proof Pf can be either an online proof or a proof in the real world. For the online proof, it can consist of a certificate issued by some authority with respect to upk, and a proof of knowledge with respect to upk. For the real world proof, it can be the user's signature on an application form, or the photocopy of the user's documentation.

The joining proof Pf is needed to protect both the PKG and the user in the Blame protocol. If there is no such proof:

- a malicious PKG can generate sk_{ID} using any upk generated by himself and an honest user cannot show that upk is not his public key;
- a malicious user can claim that the upk used in sk_{ID} is not his public key and frame an honest PKG.

The joining proof can be viewed as an authentication of user public key, which is separated from the identity-based secret key issuing. Similar concepts can be found in "anonymous identity-based key issuing" [18], where the duties of authentication and key issuing are separated to local registration authorities (LRA) and the PKG. Recently, Chow [9] proposed a new system architecture to realize "anonymous key issuing", by employing non-colluding identity-certifying authority (ICA) and PKG. However, these two systems only authenticate the user identity. If we modify the LRA or ICA to authenticate user public key as well, it can be used as a joining proof.

3.3   Correctness

Let $sk_{ID} \leftarrow$ Extract(param, upk, ID) and $(usk, upk) \leftarrow$ UserKeyGen(param). Then We define the *verification correctness* as follows:

$$\text{Verify}(\text{param}, mpk, \text{ID}, m, \text{Sign}(\text{param}, usk, sk_{ID}, m)) = 1.$$

We also define the *blaming correctness* as follows:

$$\text{Blame}(\text{param}, mpk, \text{ID}, upk, m, \text{Sign}(\text{param}, usk, sk_{ID}, m)) = upk.$$

3.4   Unforgeability

The security model for unforgeability captures the attack from the outsider to forge a signature when the PKG is honest. The adversary can obtain signatures of an honest user and can get the identity-based secret key of any identity except the challenge identity. We have the following game for unforgeability:

1. The simulator $\mathcal{S}$ gives param, mpk and upk' to the adversary $\mathcal{A}$.
2. $\mathcal{A}$ is allowed to query the following oracles adaptively:
   - Key Extraction Oracle $\mathcal{KEO}(upk, \text{ID})$: $\mathcal{A}$ runs the Extract$_u$ protocol to query the oracle. Finally the oracle returns an identity-based secret key sk_{ID} with respect to ID and upk.

- Signing Oracle $\mathcal{SO}(m, \mathsf{ID})$: it returns a valid signature σ for the message m and the identity ID with respect to upk'.
3. $\mathcal{A}$ returns a signature σ^* for a message m^* and an identity ID^*.

$\mathcal{A}$ wins the game if $\mathsf{Verify}(\mathsf{param}, mpk, \mathsf{ID}^*, m^*, \sigma^*) = 1$, such that there was no query that $\mathcal{SO}(m^*, \mathsf{ID}^*)$ and there was no query that $\mathcal{KEO}(\cdot, \mathsf{ID}^*)$.

Definition 1. *An escrow-free IBS scheme is (ϵ, t, q_e, q_s)-secure against unforgeability if there is no t time adversary winning the above game with probability at least ϵ with q_e and q_s queries to $\mathcal{KEO}$ and $\mathcal{SO}$ respectively.*

3.5   PKG Non-frameability

The security model for PKG non-frameability captures the attack from a malicious user having an identity-based secret key that wants to frame an honest PKG. If the attacker without any identity-based secret key wants to frame an honest PKG, he must firstly forge a valid signature. Since this scenario has been captured in the model of unforgeability, we only consider the case that a malicious user, who already obtains an identity-based secret key, wants to frame an honest PKG. We have the following game for PKG non-frameability:

1. The simulator $\mathcal{S}$ gives param and mpk to the adversary $\mathcal{A}$.
2. $\mathcal{A}$ is allowed to adaptively query the Key Extraction Oracle $\mathcal{KEO}(upk, \mathsf{ID})$: $\mathcal{A}$ runs the $\mathsf{Extract}_u$ protocol to query the oracle. Finally the oracle returns an identity-based secret key sk_{ID} with respect to ID and upk. $\mathcal{S}$ saves the transcript ρ in this query and also the user's joining proof Pf.
3. $\mathcal{A}$ returns a signature σ^* for a message m^* and an identity ID^*, such that he can blame the PKG by the Blame_u protocol with a public key upk^* and a blame request φ^*.

$\mathcal{A}$ wins the game if $\mathsf{Verify}(\mathsf{param}, mpk, \mathsf{ID}^*, m^*, \sigma^*) = 1$, $\mathsf{Blame}_j(\mathsf{param}, mpk, \mathsf{ID}^*, upk^*, m^*, \sigma^*, \varphi^*) = \mathrm{PKG}$, and there was a query in the form of $\mathcal{KEO}(\cdot, \mathsf{ID}^*)$.

Definition 2. *An escrow-free IBS scheme is (ϵ, t, q_e)-secure against PKG nonframeability if there is no t time adversary winning the above game with probability at least ϵ with q_e queries to $\mathcal{KEO}$.*

3.6   User Non-frameability

The security model for user non-frameability captures the attack from a malicious PKG that wants to frame an honest user. We have the following game for user non-frameability:

1. The simulator $\mathcal{S}$ gives param to the adversary $\mathcal{A}$. $\mathcal{A}$ gives a master public key mpk to $\mathcal{S}$. $\mathcal{S}$ gives a user public key upk^* and a joining proof Pf^* to $\mathcal{A}$.
2. $\mathcal{A}$ is allowed to query the following oracles adaptively:

- User Join Oracle $\mathcal{JO}(\mathsf{ID})$: it acts as the $\mathsf{Extract}_u$ protocol with input (upk^*, Pf^*) and interacts with $\mathcal{A}$ (running $\mathsf{Extract}_p$) for the identity ID. Finally the oracle obtains a identity-based secret key sk_{ID} and $\mathcal{A}$ obtains a transcript ρ.
- Signing Oracle $\mathcal{SO}(m, \mathsf{ID})$: it returns a valid signature σ for the message m with respect to the identity ID and the user public key upk^*.

3. $\mathcal{A}$ returns a signature σ^* for a message m^* and an identity ID^*.

$\mathcal{A}$ wins the game if $\mathsf{Verify}(\text{param}, mpk, \mathsf{ID}^*, m^*, \sigma^*) = 1$ and $\mathsf{Blame}(\text{param}, mpk,$ $\mathsf{ID}^*, upk, m^*, \sigma^*) = upk$ for all upk. The latter equation is always satisfied by $\mathcal{A}$ running Blame_p and giving (upk^*, Pf^*, ρ^*) to the judge (where ρ^* is the output of $\mathcal{JO}(\mathsf{ID}^*)$). We require that there was no query that $\mathcal{SO}(m^*, \mathsf{ID}^*)$.

Definition 3. *An escrow-free IBS scheme is (ϵ, t, q_j, q_s)-secure against user non-frameability if there is no t time adversary winning the above game with probability at least ϵ with q_j and q_s queries to $\mathcal{JO}$ and $\mathcal{SO}$ respectively.*

4 Generic Construction

We present a generic construction of escrow-free IBS from standard signatures. This is similar to the construction of certificate-based IBS in [4].

4.1 Our Scheme

Suppose there is a standard digital signature scheme $\mathcal{SS} = (\mathsf{SKg}, \mathsf{Sign}, \mathsf{Vf})$ which is unforgeable against chosen message attack (UF-CMA), we construct our escrow-free IBS scheme as follows:

Setup: On input the security parameter 1^k, it outputs $(mpk, msk) \leftarrow \mathsf{SKg}(1^k)$. The system parameter param is just the security parameter 1^k.

UserKeyGen: On input param, the user obtains $(upk, usk) \leftarrow \mathsf{SKg}(1^k)$.

Extract: The PKG algorithm $\mathsf{Extract}_p$ has input $(\text{param}, upk, \mathsf{ID}, msk)$. The user algorithm $\mathsf{Extract}_u$ has input $(\text{param}, upk, \mathsf{ID}, usk)$. The user computes $s \leftarrow \mathsf{Sign}_{usk}(\mathsf{ID})$ and sends $(s, \mathsf{ID}, upk, Pf)$ to the PKG. The PKG checks if $1 \leftarrow \mathsf{Vf}_{upk}(\mathsf{ID}, s)$ and Pf is a joining proof. If they are correct, then the PKG computes the identity-based secret key $sk_{\mathsf{ID}} \leftarrow \mathsf{Sign}_{msk}(\mathsf{ID}||upk)$. The PKG saves the join transcript $\rho = (s, \mathsf{ID}, upk, Pf)$ and then sends sk_{ID} to the user.

Sign: On input param, usk, sk_{ID} and a message m, the user computes $\sigma_1 \leftarrow \mathsf{Sign}_{usk}(m||\mathsf{ID})$. The user outputs the signature $\sigma = (\sigma_1, upk, sk_{\mathsf{ID}})$.

Verify: On input param, mpk, ID, m and $\sigma = (\sigma_1, upk, sk_{\mathsf{ID}})$, it returns 1 if $1 \leftarrow \mathsf{Vf}_{upk}(m||\mathsf{ID}, \sigma_1)$ and $1 \leftarrow \mathsf{Vf}_{mpk}(\mathsf{ID}||upk, sk_{\mathsf{ID}})$.

Blame: On common input param, mpk, ID, upk, m and $\sigma = (\sigma_1, upk, sk_{\text{ID}})$, the user asks the judge to blame the PKG. The judge asks the PKG to provide a transcript $\rho = (s, \text{ID}, upk, Pf)$. If $1 \leftarrow \text{Vf}_{upk}(\text{ID}, s)$ and Pf is a valid joining proof, the judge outputs upk. Otherwise, the judge outputs PKG.

Remarks. Although the user public key is part of the signature, the scheme is still considered as IBS. Similar approach is proposed by Shamir [17] and discussed in [4,10].

4.2   Security Proofs

The correctness of the scheme is straightforward. We state the security of the above construction in the following theorems.

Theorem 1. *The scheme is unforgeable if SS is a UF-CMA secure signature scheme.*

Proof. Assume there is a (ϵ, t, q_e, q_s)-adversary $\mathcal{A}$. We will construct another PPT $\mathcal{B}$ that uses $\mathcal{A}$ to forge a signature of SS with probability at least ϵ and in time at most t.

Setup. $\mathcal{B}$ runs the SS simulator twice and obtains two public keys pk_1 and pk_2. $\mathcal{B}$ gives $\mathcal{A}$ the master public key $mpk = pk_1$ and the honest user public key $upk' = pk_2$.

Oracles Simulation. $\mathcal{B}$ simulates the oracles as follow:

(*Key Extraction oracle.*) On input (upk, ID, s, Pf) from the Extract$_u$ protocol, $\mathcal{B}$ first check if Pf is a valid joining proof for upk and $1 \leftarrow \text{Vf}_{upk}(\text{ID}, s)$. If they are correct, $\mathcal{B}$ queries the signing oracle of SS for pk_1 with input $(\text{ID}\|upk)$. $\mathcal{B}$ forwards the result to $\mathcal{A}$.

(*Signing oracle.*) On input (m, ID), $\mathcal{B}$ queries the signing oracle of SS for pk_1 with input $(\text{ID}\|pk_2)$ and obtains sk. $\mathcal{B}$ queries the signing oracle of SS for pk_2 with input $m\|\text{ID}$ and obtains σ_1. $\mathcal{B}$ returns (σ_1, pk_2, sk).

Output. Finally $\mathcal{A}$ outputs a signature $\sigma^* = (\sigma_1^*, upk^*, sk^*)$ for a message m^* and an identity ID^*.

- If $upk^* \neq pk_2$, then $\mathcal{B}$ returns sk^* to the SS simulator. It is the forgery for the message $\text{ID}^*\|upk^*$ with respect to the public key pk_1.
- If $upk^* = pk_2$, then $\mathcal{B}$ returns σ_1^* to the SS simulator. It is the forgery for the message $m^*\|\text{ID}^*$ with respect to the public key pk_2.   □

Theorem 2. *The scheme is PKG non-frameable if SS is a UF-CMA secure signature scheme.*

Proof. Assume there is a (ϵ, t, q_s)-adversary $\mathcal{A}$. We will construct another PPT $\mathcal{B}$ that uses $\mathcal{A}$ to forge a signature of SS with probability at least ϵ and in time at most t.

Setup. $\mathcal{B}$ runs the SS simulator and obtains a public key pk. $\mathcal{B}$ gives $\mathcal{A}$ the master public key $mpk = pk$.

Oracles Simulation. The simulation of the *key extraction oracle* is the same as that of theorem 1.

Output. Finally $\mathcal{A}$ outputs a signature $\sigma^* = (\sigma_1^*, upk^*, sk^*)$ for a message m^* and an identity ID^*. $\mathcal{A}$ blames the PKG with a public key upk^*.

- If $(upk, ID, \cdot, \cdot)$ was not successfully queried in the key extraction oracle, $\mathcal{B}$ returns sk^* as the forgery for the message $ID^*||upk^*$ with respect to the public key mpk.
- Otherwise, $\mathcal{B}$ tries to reply to the judge with the transcript $\rho = (s', ID^*, upk^*, Pf)$ with respect to the blame from $\mathcal{A}$. $\mathcal{A}$ wins the game if either Pf is not a valid joining proof or s' is not a valid signature. However it is not possible since the transcript is checked during the oracle query. $\qquad\square$

Theorem 3. *The scheme is user non-frameable if SS is a UF-CMA secure signature scheme.*

Proof. Assume there is a (ϵ, t, q_j, q_s)-adversary $\mathcal{A}$. We will construct another PPT $\mathcal{B}$ that uses $\mathcal{A}$ to forge a signature of SS with probability at least ϵ and in time at most t.

Setup. $\mathcal{B}$ gives param $= 1^k$ to $\mathcal{A}$. $\mathcal{A}$ gives the master public key mpk and the target identity ID^* to $\mathcal{B}$. $\mathcal{B}$ runs the SS simulator with 1^k and obtains a public key pk. $\mathcal{B}$ obtains a joining proof Pf^* for pk from an honest CA. $\mathcal{B}$ gives $\mathcal{A}$ the user public key $upk^* = pk$ and Pf^*.

Oracles Simulation. $\mathcal{B}$ simulates the oracles as follow:

(*Join oracle.*) On input ID, $\mathcal{B}$ queries the signing oracle of SS with input (ID) to obtain s. $\mathcal{B}$ sends $\rho = (s, ID, upk^*, Pf^*)$ to $\mathcal{A}$. $\mathcal{A}$ stores the transcript ρ. $\mathcal{A}$ finally replies $\mathcal{B}$ with sk_{ID}.

(*Signing oracle.*) On input (m, ID), $\mathcal{B}$ first runs as the join oracle with input ID. Finally $\mathcal{B}$ obtains sk_{ID}. Then $\mathcal{B}$ queries the signing oracle of SS with input $m||ID$ and obtains σ_1. $\mathcal{B}$ returns $(\sigma_1, upk^*, sk_{ID})$.

Output. Finally $\mathcal{A}$ outputs a signature $\sigma^* = (\sigma_1^*, upk^*, sk^*)$ for a message m^* and an identity ID^*. $\mathcal{A}$ blames the user with a public key upk^* and a transcript ρ^*. $\mathcal{B}$ returns σ_1^* as the forgery of the SS signature for the message $(m^*||ID^*)$. $\qquad\square$

5   User Public Key Anonymity

In the previous section, we propose a generic construction of escrow-free IBS. However, the user public key is included in the ciphertext. Therefore it is similar to the certificate-based signatures to some extent. In some applications, it may not be desirable to let the verifier knowing the user public key (not the identity only). For example, assume a student has a long-term user public key. He may apply for an identity-based secret key for his student ID from the university. He may also apply for an identity-based secret key for his email address from the internet service provider. When a user uses the escrow-free IBS, he may not want the signatures for two different identities to be linked to the same user public key.

In order to construct an escrow-free IBS scheme which is *fully identity-based*, we require that the ciphertext contains no information about the user public key. We call this additional property as "user public key anonymity" [2]. In this section, we define the additional security model for the user public key anonymity.

5.1   Security Model for Anonymity

The security model for user public key anonymity captures the attack that wants to distinguish if a signature is signed by an honest user with a user public key *upk*. The attacker is given the master secret key, but cannot query any join oracle. In order words, the attacker can retrieve the master secret key from the real PKG, but not the join transcript from the real PKG. The users joining the real PKG will have anonymity even if the master secret key is stolen. We have the following game for anonymity:

1. The simulator $\mathcal{S}$ gives param, a master public key mpk, a master secret key msk, two user public keys upk_0, upk_1 and two corresponding certificates $cert_0$, $cert_1$ to the adversary $\mathcal{A}$.
2. $\mathcal{A}$ is allowed to query the oracle adaptively: Signing Oracle $\mathcal{SO}(m, \mathsf{ID}, b)$: it returns a valid signature σ for the message m and the identity ID with respect to upk_b.
3. $\mathcal{A}$ sends a message m^* and an identity ID^* to $\mathcal{B}$. $\mathcal{B}$ picks a random bit b' and computes $\sigma^* \leftarrow \mathsf{Sign}(\mathsf{param}, usk_{b'}, sk_{\mathsf{ID}^*}, m)$, where sk_{ID^*} is the identity-based secret key computed using $(msk, upk_{b'}, I^*)$ and $usk_{b'}$ is the user secret key for $upk_{b'}$. $\mathcal{B}$ sends σ^* to $\mathcal{A}$.
4. $\mathcal{A}$ is allowed to query the above oracles adaptively.
5. $\mathcal{A}$ returns a bit b^*.

$\mathcal{A}$ wins the game if $b' = b^*$. We require that there was no query that $\mathcal{SO}(m^*, \mathsf{ID}^*, \cdot)$. The advantage of $\mathcal{A}$ is the probability of $\mathcal{A}$ winning the above game over $1/2$.

Definition 4. *An identity-based signature scheme is (ϵ, t, q_s)-secure against anonymity if there is no t time adversary winning the above game with probability at least ϵ with q_s queries to $\mathcal{SO}$.*

---

[2] An escrow-free IBS scheme can either has the "user public key anonymity" property or not.

Remark. The security model for *key-privacy* or *anonymity* in traditional public key encryption was proposed by Bellare *et al.* [3]. In this section, we follow their notion of "indistinguishability of keys under chosen-ciphertext attacks" and adopt the indistinguishability game into our IBS setting.

The main difference between Bellare *et al.*'s model and our model is that the challenge user secret keys and the user public keys are not chosen by the adversary in our model. It is because our Blame algorithm requires that the PKG is able to show that "the *upk* is related to the signature σ" if σ is signed by the corresponding *usk*. If both the *msk*, usk_0 and usk_1 are known to the adversary, he can generate the join transcript by himself and checks if upk_0 or upk_1 is related to the challenge signature σ^*. It will break the anonymity. Therefore in our anonymity model, the adversary is not given usk_0 and usk_1. The adversary is given the signing oracle for usk_0 and usk_1 instead.

6   Construction with User Public Key Anonymity

In this section, we provide a concrete construction with the property of user public key anonymity. Our construction for escrow-free IBS is based on the signature schemes from Boneh and Boyen [5] and Boneh *et al.* [7]. We also use the "signatures of knowledge" (SoK) notion from Chase and Lysyanskaya [8].

6.1   Intuition

We use the signature scheme from Boneh and Boyen [5] as the identity-based secret key. Suppose the master secret key is α and the master public key is g^α. For a user with secret key x and public key $y = g^x$, his identity-based secret key is A where

$$A^{\alpha+\mathsf{ID}}v^x = u,$$

and g, u, v are a generator of $\mathbb{G}$.

For the signing protocol, the part of the signature useful for the blame protocol is derived from Boneh *et al.* [7]. Denote this part as S and we have

$$S = \hat{e}(v, H_2(m))^x,$$

where m is the message. The the signing protocol becomes:

$$SoK\{(A, x) : A^{\alpha+\mathsf{ID}}v^x = u \ \wedge \ S = \hat{e}(v, H_2(m))^x\}(m).$$

6.2   Our Scheme

We give the detailed construction of the escrow-free IBS with anonymity.

Setup: The algorithm first chooses a random prime p of bit size $\Theta(k)$. Let $\mathbb{G}, \mathbb{G}_T$ be a bilinear group of order p and a pairing $\hat{e} : \mathbb{G} \times \mathbb{G} \rightarrow \mathbb{G}_T$. It also chooses generators $g, u, v \in \mathbb{G}$. It picks collision resistant hash functions $H_1 : \{0,1\}^* \rightarrow \mathbb{Z}_p^*$

for hashing the identity string, and $H_2 : \{0,1\}^* \to \mathbb{G}$ for hashing the message. It also chooses generators $g_0, g_1, g_2 \in \mathbb{G}$ used for the signature of knowledge. The system parameter param is $(\hat{e}, \mathbb{G}, \mathbb{G}_T, p, g, u, v, g_0, g_1, g_2, H_1, H_2)$.

The PKG randomly selects his master secret key $\alpha \in \mathbb{Z}_p^*$. He computes the master public key $g_a = g^\alpha$.

UserKeyGen: The user randomly selects his user secret key $x \in \mathbb{Z}_p^*$. He computes $y = g^x$ as his user public key.

Extract: The user calculates $v' = v^x$. He also computes a non-interactive zero-knowledge (NIZK) proof [3] Σ of x with respect to v' and v (We omit the details of the NIZK proof for discrete logarithm for simplicity). He sends v', ID, y, a joining proof Pf and the NIZK proof Σ to the PKG. The PKG checks the validity of Pf, Σ. If so, the PKG computes:

$$A = (uv'^{-1})^{\frac{1}{\alpha + i}},$$

where $i = H_1(\text{ID})$ and returns A to the user. The PKG stores the transcript $\rho = (v', \Sigma, \text{ID}, y, Pf)$.

Sign: The user signs a message m with the user secret key x and the identity-based secret key A. He computes the signature of knowledge (SoK):

$$SoK\{(A, x) : A^{\alpha + i}v^x = u \ \wedge \ S = \hat{e}(v, H_2(m))^x\}(m)$$

The SoK is specified as follows. The user randomly chooses $s, r, r_2 \in \mathbb{Z}_p^*$, $R_1 \in \mathbb{G}$ and computes:

$$t_0 = g_0^s, \quad t_1 = Ag_1^s, \quad t_2 = v^x g_2^s, \quad \tau_0 = g_0^r, \quad \tau_1 = R_1 g_1^r,$$
$$\tau_2 = v^{r_2} g_2^r, \quad \tau_3 = [\hat{e}(g_1, g_a g^i) \cdot \hat{e}(g_2, g)]^r, \quad \tau_4 = \hat{e}(g_2, H_2(m))^r.$$

The user computes $c = H_3(t_0, t_1, t_2, \tau_0, \ldots, \tau_4, m, mpk, \text{ID})$ and:

$$z_0 = r - cs, \quad Z_1 = R_1 A^{-c}, \quad z_2 = r_2 - cx.$$

The signature is $\sigma = (t_0, t_1, t_2, c, z_0, Z_1, z_2, S)$.

Verify: Upon input a signature σ for a message m and an identity ID, it computes:

$$i = H_1(\text{ID}), \quad t_3 = \hat{e}(t_1, g_a g^i) \cdot \hat{e}(t_2, g) \cdot \hat{e}(u, g)^{-1}, \quad t_4 = \hat{e}(t_2, H_2(m)) \cdot S^{-1},$$
$$\tau_0 = g_0^{z_0} t_0^c, \quad \tau_1 = Z_1 g_1^{z_0} t_1^c, \quad \tau_2 = v^{z_2} g_2^{z_0} t_2^c,$$
$$\tau_3 = [\hat{e}(g_1, g_a g^i) \cdot \hat{e}(g_2, g)]^{z_0} \cdot t_3^c, \quad \tau_4 = \hat{e}(g_2, H_2(m))^{z_0} \cdot t_4^c.$$

It outputs 1 if $c = H_3(t_0, t_1, t_2, \tau_0, \ldots, \tau_4, m, mpk, \text{ID})$. Otherwise, it outputs 0.

---

[3] Although v' can be used to prove the knowledge of x via pairing, we need the extractor of the NIZK proof to obtain x in the security proof.

Blame: On common input the master public key mpk, an identity ID, a message m, a signature σ, a user public key y, the user with user secret key x first computes $\varphi = v^x$. The user sends φ to the judge as the blame request.

The judge checks if $\sigma = (t_0, t_1, t_2, c, z_0, Z_1, z_2, S)$ is a valid signature and:

$$\hat{e}(v, y) = \hat{e}(\varphi, g) \qquad \wedge \qquad \hat{e}(\varphi, H_2(m)) \neq S.$$

If they are not equal, the judge returns "upk".

Otherwise, the judge requests the PKG to provide a transcript $\rho = (v', \Sigma,$ ID, y', Pf'). If Pf' is a valid joining proof for y' and

$$\hat{e}(v, y') = \hat{e}(v', g) \qquad \wedge \qquad \hat{e}(v', H_2(m)) = S.$$

If they are equal, the judge returns "upk". Otherwise, the judge returns "PKG".

6.3   Security Proofs

The correctness of the signature scheme is straightforward.

We first prove that the SoK protocol above is a secure signature of knowledge. We use the game-based definition (SimExt-secure) in [8]. Chase and Lysyanskaya [8] proved the equivalence of the game-based definition and the UC framework definition.

Lemma 1. *The SoK protocol above is a SimExt-secure signature of knowledge of a witness (A, x).*

Theorem 4. *The scheme is (ϵ, t, q_e, q_s)-unforgeable if the (ϵ', t', q)-SDH assumption holds in $\mathbb{G}$ in the random oracle model, with:*

$$t \leq t' + \Theta((q_e + q_s)\delta + q_s\tau), \qquad q = q_e + 1, \qquad \epsilon' \geq (\frac{\epsilon}{C_{q_e}^{q_h}} - \frac{1}{p})^2$$

where q_h is the number of query to the H_1 oracle, δ and τ are the time for computing exponentiation in $\mathbb{G}$ and pairing respectively.

Theorem 5. *The scheme is (ϵ, t, q_e)-PKG non-frameable if the (ϵ', t', q)-SDH assumption holds in $\mathbb{G}$ in the random oracle model, with:*

$$t \leq t' + \Theta(q_e\delta), \qquad q = q_e + 1, \qquad \epsilon' \geq (\frac{\epsilon}{C_{q_e}^{q_h}} - \frac{1}{p})^2$$

where q_h is the number of query to the H_1 oracle, δ is the time for computing exponentiation in $\mathbb{G}$, respectively.

Theorem 6. *The scheme is (ϵ, t, q_j, q_s)-user non-frameable if the (ϵ', t')-DL assumption holds in $\mathbb{G}$ in the random oracle model, where:*

$$t \leq t' + \Theta((q_j + q_s)\nu + q_s\tau), \qquad \epsilon' \geq (\epsilon - \frac{1}{p})^2$$

where ν and τ are the time for computing exponentiation in $\mathbb{G}$ and pairing respectively.

Theorem 7. *The scheme is (ϵ, t, q_s)-anonymous if the (ϵ', t')-DBDH assumption holds in the random oracle model, with:*

$$t \leq t' + \Theta(q_s(\delta + \tau)), \qquad \epsilon' \geq (\frac{\epsilon}{q_h} - \frac{1}{p})^2$$

where q_h is the number of query to the H_2 oracle, δ and τ are the time for computing exponentiation in $\mathbb{G}$ and pairing respectively.

The proofs are given in the full version of the paper [19] due to the space limit.

7   Comparison

In this section, we provide a comparison of our scheme against the existing schemes. Denote (s, P) as a pair of secret key and public key computed by the user. Denote (d, I) as a pair of identity-based secret key and identity computed by the PKG. Let (α, β) be a pair of secret key and public key of the PKG. Let c be the secret key of a certificate authority. Let $Sig_a(b)$ be a signature of message b using the secret key a. Let $Com_a(b)$ be a commitment of the value a using the public parameter b. We compare the public information that a verifier needs to know (except β), the secret keys used by the signer and the witness to link the identity with the public key. We use W to represent a witness which is different from the above parameters.

Notice that the certificateless signatures, the certificate-based signatures and the self-certificated signatures aim to resolve the key escrow problem. Nonetheless, these schemes are no longer identity-based since the user public key P has been introduced into the public information. On the contrary, our scheme in Sect. 6 is *the only scheme* that solves this problem while staying at the framework of identity-based cryptography in a strict sense. However the price we have to pay is to include a joining proof involved in the extraction protocol.

On the other hand, our generic construction in Sect. 4 provides a more efficient solution than our scheme in Sect. 6. The signature of the escrow-free IBS in Sect. 4 only consists of two standard signatures and a user public key. The computational cost of signing is the same as signing one standard signature; the computational cost of verifying is the same as verifying two standard signatures. It is as efficient as the generic IBS scheme in [4].

Table 2. Comparison of our scheme against the existing schemes

Schemes	Public Information	Secret Key	Witness
IBS [17]	I	d	-
IBS + Cert	I, P, W	s, d	$W = Sig_c(I, P)$
Certificateless Sig [1]	I, P, W	s, d	$W = Com_s(\beta)$
Certificate-based Sig [16]	I, P	s, d	$d = Sig_\alpha(I, P)$
Self-Certificated Sig [13]	I, P	s	$P = d = Sig_\alpha(I)$
Our Scheme in §4	I, P, d	s	$d = Sig_\alpha(I, P)$
Our Scheme in §6	I	s, d	$d = Sig_\alpha(I, P)$

8   Conclusion

In this paper, we introduced the concept of escrow-free identity-based signatures to solve the key escrow problem in identity-based signature. We proposed an extra *user public key anonymity* property to escrow-free identity-based signatures and proposed a concrete construction. Our construction solves the open problem of key escrow in identity-based signatures, without requiring multiple PKGs. Our scheme is the *first* to achieve level 3 of trust of the PKG in Girault's model [13], in the identity-based setting.

Acknowledgements

We thank David Galindo and the anonymous reviewers of EuroPKI 2009 for helpful comments and suggestions.

References

1. Al-Riyami, S.S., Paterson, K.G.: Certificateless public key cryptography. In: Laih, C.-S. (ed.) ASIACRYPT 2003. LNCS, vol. 2894, pp. 452–473. Springer, Heidelberg (2003)
2. Au, M.H., Huang, Q., Liu, J.K., Susilo, W., Wong, D.S., Yang, G.: Traceable and retrievable identity-based encryption. In: Bellovin, S.M., Gennaro, R., Keromytis, A.D., Yung, M. (eds.) ACNS 2008. LNCS, vol. 5037, pp. 94–110. Springer, Heidelberg (2008)
3. Bellare, M., Boldyreva, A., Desai, A., Pointcheval, D.: Key-privacy in public-key encryption. In: Boyd, C. (ed.) ASIACRYPT 2001. LNCS, vol. 2248, pp. 566–582. Springer, Heidelberg (2001)
4. Bellare, M., Namprempre, C., Neven, G.: Security proofs for identity-based identification and signature schemes. In: Cachin, C., Camenisch, J.L. (eds.) EUROCRYPT 2004. LNCS, vol. 3027, pp. 268–286. Springer, Heidelberg (2004)
5. Boneh, D., Boyen, X.: Short signatures without random oracles. In: Cachin, C., Camenisch, J.L. (eds.) EUROCRYPT 2004. LNCS, vol. 3027, pp. 56–73. Springer, Heidelberg (2004)
6. Boneh, D., Franklin, M.K.: Identity-based encryption from the weil pairing. In: Kilian, J. (ed.) CRYPTO 2001. LNCS, vol. 2139, pp. 213–229. Springer, Heidelberg (2001)
7. Boneh, D., Lynn, B., Shacham, H.: Short signatures from the weil pairing. In: Boyd, C. (ed.) ASIACRYPT 2001. LNCS, vol. 2248, pp. 514–532. Springer, Heidelberg (2001)
8. Chase, M., Lysyanskaya, A.: On signatures of knowledge. In: Dwork, C. (ed.) CRYPTO 2006. LNCS, vol. 4117, pp. 78–96. Springer, Heidelberg (2006)
9. Chow, S.S.M.: Removing escrow from identity-based encryption. In: Jarecki, S., Tsudik, G. (eds.) Public Key Cryptography – PKC 2009. LNCS, vol. 5443, pp. 256–276. Springer, Heidelberg (2009)
10. Galindo, D., Herranz, J., Kiltz, E.: On the generic construction of identity-based signatures with additional properties. In: Lai, X., Chen, K. (eds.) ASIACRYPT 2006. LNCS, vol. 4284, pp. 178–193. Springer, Heidelberg (2006)

11. Gentry, C.: Certificate-based encryption and the certificate revocation problem. In: Biham, E. (ed.) EUROCRYPT 2003. LNCS, vol. 2656, pp. 272–293. Springer, Heidelberg (2003)

12. Gentry, C., Silverberg, A.: Hierarchical ID-based cryptography. In: Zheng, Y. (ed.) ASIACRYPT 2002. LNCS, vol. 2501, pp. 548–566. Springer, Heidelberg (2002)

13. Girault, M.: Self-certified public keys. In: Davies, D.W. (ed.) EUROCRYPT 1991. LNCS, vol. 547, pp. 490–497. Springer, Heidelberg (1991)

14. Goyal, V.: Reducing trust in the PKG in Identity Based Cryptosystems. In: Menezes, A. (ed.) CRYPTO 2007. LNCS, vol. 4622, pp. 430–447. Springer, Heidelberg (2007)

15. Goyal, V., Lu, S., Sahai, A., Waters, B.: Black-box accountable authority identity-based encryption. In: Ning, P., Syverson, P.F., Jha, S. (eds.) CCS 2008, pp. 427–436. ACM, New York (2008)

16. Kang, B.G., Park, J.H., Hahn, S.G.: A certificate-based signature scheme. In: Okamoto, T. (ed.) CT-RSA 2004. LNCS, vol. 2964, pp. 99–111. Springer, Heidelberg (2004)

17. Shamir, A.: Identity-based cryptosystems and signature schemes. In: Blakely, G.R., Chaum, D. (eds.) CRYPTO 1984. LNCS, vol. 196, pp. 47–53. Springer, Heidelberg (1985)

18. Sui, A.F., Chow, S.S.M., Hui, L.C.K., Yiu, S.M., Chow, K.P., Tsang, W.W., Chong, C.F., Pun, K.K.H., Chan, H.W.: Separable and anonymous identity-based key issuing. In: ICPADS 2005, pp. 275–279. IEEE Computer Society, Los Alamitos (2005)

19. Yuen, T.H., Susilo, W., Mu, Y.: How to construct identity-based signatures without the key escrow problem. Cryptology ePrint Archive, Report 2009/421 (2009), http://eprint.iacr.org/

Author Index

GPSR Compliance

The European Union's (EU) General Product Safety Regulation (GPSR) is a set of rules that requires consumer products to be safe and our obligations to ensure this.

If you have any concerns about our products, you can contact us on ProductSafety@springernature.com

In case Publisher is established outside the EU, the EU authorized representative is:

Springer Nature Customer Service Center GmbH
Europaplatz 3
69115 Heidelberg, Germany

Batch number: 09490872

Printed by Printforce, the Netherlands